John Parry is Professor of Oceanic History and Affairs at Harvard University. His historical interests have been concentrated principally upon the establishment and government of colonial empires, and upon maritime history. His previous publications include *Europe and the Wide World, The Sale of Public Office in the Spanish Indies, A Short History of the West Indies* and *The Age of Reconnaissance.*

Also in this series and available in Cardinal

HISTORY OF CIVILISATION

TRADE AND DOMINION

The European Oversea Empires
in the Eighteenth Century

J. H. Parry

CARDINAL edition published in 1974
by Sphere Books Ltd
30/32 Gray's Inn Road, London WC1X 8JL

First published in Great Britain by
Weidenfeld & Nicolson Ltd 1971
© 1971 J. H. Parry

Set in Intertype Baskerville

Printed in England by Cox & Wyman Ltd,
London, Reading and Fakenham

ISBN 0 351 17742 6

CONTENTS

LIST OF ILLUSTRATIONS

ACKNOWLEDGMENTS

The author and publishers would like to thank the following for supplying photographs for use in this volume: The Trustees of the British Museum, Plates 6, 10, 11, 13, 16, 17; The President and Fellows of Harvard College, Plates 5, 23; Draper Hill, Esq., Plate 31; The Trustees of the John Carter Brown Library, Plates 24. 25, 26, 27, 28, 29, 30; The Trustees of the National Maritime Museum, Plates 1, 2, 3, 4, 7, 9; The Trustees of the National Portrait Gallery, Plates 18, 19, 21; The Secretary of State for Foreign and Commonwealth Affairs, Plates 14, 15, 20, 21, 22, 23.

LIST OF MAPS

PREFACE

The purpose of this book is to trace in outline the development of the European maritime empires in the eighteenth century; to define the factors which stimulated the expansion of European commercial and political influence outside Europe; and to describe briefly the consequences, both for Europeans themselves and for the peoples of the areas where they operated.

The author of a book on so wide a topic must accumulate debts of gratitude, too numerous to be acknowledged separately in a brief preface. My thanks are due principally to three groups of people: first, to colleagues at Harvard and elsewhere who helped me, in many conversations, with information and advice. Then, to students: to members of seminars in which the ideas summarised in this book were discussed, and to undergraduates who listened courteously, but by no means uncritically, to lectures on the subject. Third, to those people – learned, patient and kind – who run the great libraries and museum collections in which work of this sort must be done. Here it is possible to be more specific, and I should like particularly to thank Mr T. R. Adams, Miss Jeanette Black, Mr Ernest Dodge, Mr G. P. B. Naish, Mr F. E. Trout and Miss Helen Wallis.

Special thanks are due to my wife, who read bravely through the entire manuscript, and who discovered more slips and obscurities than I care to remember. The errors which remain, of course, are mine.

Harvard University   J.H.P.

INTRODUCTION

Men have been building empires since before history began. Wherever an organised group of people, or their rulers, have reduced other, alien groups, or *their* rulers, to the status of subjects, tributaries or subordinate allies; or have sent some of their number to settle in distant places and subsequently retained control of the settlements: there were the makings of an empire. The use of the word in this sense, it is true, is relatively modern. When Henry VIII proclaimed his realm of England to be an empire, he was not thinking of English dominion in, say, Wales; he meant simply that he considered himself an uncommanded commander. Since the later eighteenth century, however, in normal English usage the word has described a particular kind of political organisation, a super-state, comprising a metropolis and dependencies.[1] In this sense the word 'empire' is to be understood in this book.

In all empires – in this sense – of more than fleeting duration, the essential feature is the metropolis–dependency relation; and in this relation three main elements can be discerned. The first and most obvious is dominion, command. This is what *imperium* originally meant. In major matters the metropolis, or rather the metropolitan government – with whatever consultations, modifications or circumlocutions policy, custom or circumstance may dictate – makes the final decisions, gives the orders. Its orders may or may not be effective; people in the dependencies may protest, may exert pressure; they may evade, procrastinate or defy; but if their defiance becomes open, habitual and successful, the empire comes to an end. The second element is profit, the benefits drawn by the metropolis from its relation with the dependencies. These may accrue either to the metropolitan government, to its metropolitan subjects, or both. They may take the form of actual tribute, public or private; or of a privileged position in trade within the empire; or of strategic advantages over enemies outside it. They may amount to no more than the emotional satisfaction derived from a feeling of power, however illusory, or from consciousness of a civilising or proselytising mission; for the bonds of empire are emotional as well as economic and political. The third element is service, the services rendered by the metropolis to the dependencies. These may amount merely to a degree of protection against the attentions of other predators; but often they include much more – defence, the maintenance of order and stability, the whole machinery of administration. The metropolitan government may confer upon the dependencies the benefits, or supposed benefits, of metropolitan religion, ideological revelation, technical skill, political ingenuity, general culture. It may grant financial subsidies to its poorer and weaker dependencies, as most European imperial governments did in the middle decades of the twentieth century. These services may be welcome or unwelcome; but all imperial governments have found it necessary, in some measure, to justify their position of command by rendering some of them.

The middle decades of the twentieth century were remarkable for the break-up or abandonment of a number of major empires administered from centres in Western Europe. The process gave occasion for much rhetoric and consequent semantic confusion. The derivatives 'imperialism', 'imperialist' ceased to have, for many people, any precise connection with empires and became indiscriminate terms of abuse. The word 'empire' itself, except for historical purposes, lost favour. Both in the empires which broke up and in others which survived and expanded, a range of ingenious euphemisms came into use. The terms 'commonwealth' and 'union' served to cover, for Great Britain and France respectively, a retreat from the responsibilities of empire. In the Asiatic dominions of Russia, on the other hand, the same word 'union' was and is used to describe an organisation imperial in all essentials, in which major decisions emanate from Moscow. The Portuguese provided a further variant; while clinging to the fact of empire, they affect to regard their colonies as integral provinces of Port-

14

ugal. Further confusion has arisen from a widespread but ill-defined illusion that an empire in which the metropolis is separated from the dependencies by a wide expanse of sea is more 'imperial' than one which covers a continuous expanse of land. Obviously maritime empires differ significantly in many respects from land empires, but the differences are in organisation and circumstance, not in the essentials of command, the drawing of benefits, the rendering of services. Siberia is as much a colony of settlement (including penal settlement) as Australia was. Portuguese administrators in Central Africa are not necessarily more alien (except, indeed, in skin colour) than Russians in Kamtchatka or Kazakhstan, and they have been there much longer. They are simply more vulnerable to attack. Even the British in India were not much more alien, and probably never more unwelcome or oppressive, than the Chinese at present in Tibet; though the Chinese have merely re-asserted, brutally and effectively, a loose suzerainty which had existed for centuries and was recognised by the British themselves.[2] The fact that some empires have recently broken up should not deceive us. The political species 'empire' survives under a screen of verbal subterfuge and seems unlikely to become extinct.

This book is concerned with a particular stage in the growth of a particular group of empires, most of which have since broken up, or seem likely to break up. Most European governments have accepted the loss of colonial empire, in an overt political form, with relatively little resistance. They have disbanded their colonial ministries and pensioned, or persuaded the successor states to pension, their colonial civil servants. The break-up of these empires – most particularly that of the largest, the British – was the outcome more of abdication than of revolution. The decisions to abdicate were made in haste. It is true that there had been, between the two world wars, cautious preliminary moves in many colonies, towards greater consultation and towards some degree of internal self-government; but the implications of these moves had never been faced. In the British empire, where the moves had gone furthest, 'dominion status' provided a familiar formula; but government had not proposed to apply it immediately, even to India, much less to dependencies such as Jamaica or the Gold Coast. At the end of the Second World War, indeed, most administrators thought optimistically of development rather than of devolution, as a panacea for the troubles of the territories for which they were responsible.[3] There were, of course, many pressures in the other direction. There were local nationalisms, more or less of European type and in considerable measure the product of European education; education has often proved a Trojan horse in imperial situations. There was agitation by articulate and politically ambitious colonial subjects, who wanted power of a kind they could not hope for under European rule. Since the agitators also wanted money for development, however, and were not sure that they could get both, the agitation was sometimes ambiguous. Finally, in some places there were actual armed rebellions. On the imperial side, there were undercurrents of misgiving about the righteousness of imperial rule, strengthened in England by uncomfortable recollections of the Boer War. The principal factor influencing the decisions to abdicate, however, was a shift in the balance between benefits and services; between the advantages which a metropolis derived from the possession of colonies and the services it was expected to render to them. European states, weakened and impoverished by war, could not afford the immense expenditure on development which their colonies required, in order to hold their own in the economic conditions of the twentieth century. Still less could they afford the enormous military effort – out of all proportion to the apparent value of the territories concerned – which would be called for, should it become necessary to suppress widespread colonial rebellion by force. The cost and effort of maintaining even normal good government, by twentieth-century standards, had come to outweigh the advantages of empire. These conclusions were unwelcome. They were accepted reluctantly, but realistically. *Populus Romanus repente factus est alius*: intelligent Europeans suddenly became willing, sometimes eager, to transfer power to almost any plausible claimants, and to transfer it as quickly as was consistent with maintaining an appearance of stability. Great Britain enjoyed an important advantage in this respect, in the experience derived from many earlier experiments with local self-government. In most British territories the actual transfer of power was orderly and smooth, ceremonious even. The fighting, where there was any, began later.

16

The imperial abdications were political in character. Economically and culturally they made little immediate difference. Colonial production of raw materials, colonial markets for manufactured goods, remained available when the colonies ceased to be colonies; though in some instances they had already become so marginal to the metropolitan economies that they could have been written off without serious loss. Some former colonies began to develop local empires of their own; but many more either remained dependent, for the supply of capital and expertise needed for their economic development, upon the former metropolitan states; or else escaped from being dependencies of one metropolis, only to become clients of another. Some major western states, notably the United States of America, whose political traditions included a profound suspicion of imperialism, found themselves drawn, with much misgiving, into widespread ventures and responsibilities of a quasi-imperial kind. Culturally, the process of 'westernisation' which the European empires had fostered, and the spread of European languages assisted by mechanised communications, continued.

Politically, the imperial abdications represented a major change. For many years a large part of the world's inhabited surface had been included in one or another of a group of empires administered from centres in Europe. Small bodies of Europeans had been responsible for the government, the economic welfare and development, the political good behaviour, of hundreds of millions of people in dependent territories all round the world, mainly in the Tropics. Then in a few years, the European governments withdrew from nearly all these responsibilities, leaving their former subjects to defend and govern themselves, with varying degrees of success. Yet major political structures do not disappear without trace; revolutions are never total. The contemporary world society may or may not be better off without the European colonial empires; but it is inescapably a society which they helped in large measure to create. The story of their establishment and growth, no less than that of their decay and fall, deserves attention, both for its intrinsic interest, and as a key to the understanding of the world of today.

Colonial acquisitiveness was characteristic of all Europe. At one time or another, between the middle of the fifteenth century and the middle of the twentieth, every European state which possessed an Atlantic seaboard (and some which did not) acquired oversea territory, if no more than a minor West Indian island, an African barracoon, or a trading station somewhere in the East. Among the many European national groups involved, however, five stood out from the rest: Portuguese, Spanish, Dutch, English, French. These five groups were all active throughout the greater part of the five-century period; all operated in several continents and in all the major oceans; all acquired possessions of great territorial extent and great diversity; all maintained control over some, at least, of their possessions through long periods of time. Naturally these scattered, sprawling empires differed one from another, not only geographically, but in social and economic structure, in administrative style. The similarities between them, however, were more significant than the differences. They formed, so to speak, a family group. None was the creation of a dynastic conqueror or of a great folk migration. All originated in the activities of small groups of individuals seeking land, trade or plunder; European governments authorised, encouraged, and subsequently sought to control, but they rarely initiated. Each empire comprised within itself a great variety of types of enterprise and settlement, and many inherent divergencies of interest. In this very heterogeneity, they resembled one another. They were all maritime empires, by force of circumstance rather than by policy or choice. The major states of Western Europe often fought fiercely among themselves by land; they undertook great wars and repeatedly impoverished their peoples, to move their frontiers a few score miles in this or that direction; but they were too evenly matched in strength to create empires by conquering one another, and none was ever strong enough to advance effectively into the Eurasian hinterland. Only by sea could any of them expand on a satisfyingly imperial scale. Maritime skill and pugnacity enabled Europeans to operate in areas far distant from their own homelands. The empires which they created depended for their existence on the regular and reliable movement of shipping; in all of them, the number, capacity and speed of available ships imposed limits on communication, and so upon the effectiveness of central control. In all, naval strength was the essential defence against plunder or dismemberment. It was not, perhaps, entirely accidental that the eclipse of the European empires coincided with a decline in the effectiveness of power exerted on the surface of the sea. All the empires were strongly influenced by commercial considerations. In some, dominion was acquired for the sake of trade; in others, trade developed in consequence of dominion; but in all, the orderly regulation of trade, in accordance with fixed economic principles or assumptions, was a major object of policy. Each metropolitan government tried – with varying degrees of determination and success – to develop an imperial economy serving the exclusive interest of its own subjects, and contributing exclusively to its own power and revenue. None of the empires, however, was ever effectively isolated from the others. They interacted constantly one upon another, by direct imitation, by clandestine migration and trade, by commercial competition, sometimes by grudging co-operation, often by open war. They grew up with similar objectives, operated in similar ways, and disintegrated for similar reasons.

It may be objected that the European empire-builders, though they followed roughly similar paths, followed them at widely different times. Certainly Spaniards had established an extensive empire in the Americas, and created elaborate machinery for governing it, long before the first French or English settlements took root. The Portuguese had been running regular trading fleets to the East, and guarding them with garrisons and formidable naval forces, for nearly a century before the first English or Dutch traders passed the Cape. Certainly, also, the Europe of Richelieu was not the Europe of Charles v. Nevertheless, in the story of European expansion as a whole, a general chronological pattern can be seen. There were three principal stages: first, reconnaissance, the time of tentative beginnings, covering perhaps the first two centuries of the story. During this period Europeans first learned to think of the world as a whole, of all seas as one, and drew the rough outlines of the world which we know. They visited most of the habitable regions of the globe – nearly all those which were accessible by sea – and established themselves permanently in places where settlement was relatively easy and obviously rewarding, and where resistance was weak.

The world proved too small for the number of quarrelsome adventurers who roamed its seas. Growing territorial empires, and still more rapidly growing commercial systems, fought repeatedly for exclusive control of the most productive plantations and the most promising centres of trade. A country like England, already in the late seventeenth century aggressively pushing the products of handcraft industry, and a colonial system like that of Spain, obstinately conserving a stagnant commercial monopoly, could hardly co-exist without conflict; while English and French commercial designs in Spanish America were mutually incompatible. Similarly, in their plans for expansion in the East, both governments and trading companies expressed from time to time a preference for peaceful and profitable trade rather than armed and expensive dominion; but frequently they discovered – or their agents persuaded them – that without dominion, satisfactory trade was not to be had. The second stage in the story of the maritime empires, then, was the stage of collisions; but it was also a stage of expanded operations, of mutinies and alterations of course. Commercially, both governments and business men became more interested in volume and less in unit value. Even the most conservative imperial governments, by the early eighteenth century, were beginning to understand that light charges on a big volume of colonial trade could produce more revenue than heavy charges on a small volume – much more than crude attempts to levy direct tribute from their colonies. Commercial corporations discovered that it was more profitable to sell large quantities of exotic products, at low prices for mass consumption, than to purvey restricted quantities in a luxury market, at prices maintained artificially, and with increasing difficulty, by monopoly. Politically, as the century progressed, governments became more interested in efficient and rational administration, both as a means of increasing revenue, and as an end in itself. Colonial offices came to be regarded more as posts of duty, less as places of profit for their holders. Public opinion and policy alike, in the later eighteenth century, reflected a heightened feeling of responsibility for subject races, even for slaves; and a new movement of religious proselytising, chiefly Protestant, began. In many colonies of settlement, increased administrative efficiency and intensified metropolitan solicitude for native races were the last things the settlers wanted, and resentment against tightened control in some places contributed to rebellion. The first successful colonial rebellion, that against British government in North America, was at first sight a disaster, a major set-back for empire. Subsequent developments in the United States, it is true, emphasised what *avant-garde* economists were already teaching: that assertions of colonial independence, however damaging to power and prestige, did not necessarily damage the economic interests of a metropolitan country; that trade in distant places did not always depend upon dominion. A vigorous newly independent state, if prosperous and politically stable, could provide an industrialising metropolis with a great and growing market, without the trouble and expense of imperial supervision. European statesmen were slow to grasp this point, however; and not all rebellious colonies met the requirements. There was a brief pause in the process of European imperial expansion, but no general revulsion against empire as such.

The third stage was that of industrial dominance. The nineteenth and early twentieth centuries were a period of rapid growth in the population of Western Europe, and of rapid development in industrial technology. Entrepreneurs now sent overseas, and increasingly to the Tropics, to find not only exotic goods for the consumer market, but also raw materials for their industries. They marketed the cheap products of mechanised industry in places which formerly had produced, by handcraft industry, all the manufactures they needed. As factory organisation spread, they sought also new settlement colonies to receive people uprooted by economic change at home. These were not new ideas, of course, but they were applied on a quite unprecedented scale. The immense economic and military strength conferred by machinery enabled Europeans to reach many parts of the world where formerly they had been unable to penetrate, or had not thought penetration worth while. In many places, business activities of the kind which Europeans considered normal could only be pursued – or so it was asserted – under European political protection. Governments were induced, sometimes very reluctantly, to acquire colonies and assume protectorates, whether by treaty or by force. As colonial dependencies grew once more in number, in area and in variety, the drive for administrative efficiency gained momentum, and professional colonial civil services were developed to provide it. Missionary societies made their contribution, not only in proselytising, but in providing, in so far as their means allowed, European education and medical care. Gradually, many North Europeans in the nineteenth century came to assume, as many Spaniards had assumed in the sixteenth, that the Europeanising of non-European peoples was a public duty as well as a way to profit. Naturally, there was a fresh bout of quarrelling over colonial territory; but quarrelling kept, as a rule, within diplomatic bounds. Jointly the European nations established an economic and political predominance over the less industrialised parts of the world, which lasted until recent years.

Of these three stages in the story of European empires, the first was discussed in an earlier volume in this series.[4] The second stage, roughly from the late seventeenth century to the beginning of the nineteenth century, is the subject of the present work. By the late seventeenth century, the first tentative charting of the size, shape and disposition of the continents, the exploration of those areas which clearly had something to offer economically, had long been accepted as complete; complete enough, at least, for immediate practical purposes. Seaborne skill and strength had enabled Europeans to exploit their geographical knowledge, and by the later seventeenth century they had settled here and there in all the known continents except Australia. The nature of their settlements varied greatly, but all alike depended, economically and administratively, on metropolitan countries in Europe. The hold of the European nations upon many of their outposts was still weak. Only a relatively few small areas could be said to be Europeanised, and the most potent factor in determining the nature of a European colony was the character of the native race among whom it was planted. In some places Europeans had settled as a permanent resident aristocracy among more primitive, but settled peoples, living by their labour and to some extent inter-breeding with them. This had long been the situation in Spanish America; though the areas under effective European government still covered only a small part of the immense regions claimed by Spain, and no province was without its Indian frontier. In the

West Indies, also, and on the coast of Brazil, Europeans formed a resident aristocracy; though the labour force which produced the sugar and tobacco exports of those areas consisted chiefly of imported African slaves. In other regions, where the native population was too sparse or too intractable to furnish an adequate labour force, and where settlers did not want, or could not afford to buy, imported slaves, Europeans had cleared land and formed purely European communities, living largely by their own labour as farmers, fishermen or traders. A thin fringe of settlements of this type stretched along the Atlantic seaboard of North America; settlements with small harbour towns looking towards Europe, with a dangerous forest frontier not far inland. English and French Americas still lagged far behind Spanish America in population, wealth and cultural attainments. In the eighteenth century, however, they were to grow rapidly in assertiveness and strength.

In the Old World, Europeans had concentrated their efforts upon regions long known to produce articles of value. Trade, with a view to purchasing exotic goods for sale in Europe, had been their principal object. Territorial empire on any considerable scale would have been beyond their power, even had they seriously attempted it. In West Africa, source of gold, ivory and slaves, the climate and the forest had discouraged European settlement on the coast; and the coastal rulers, eager for trade and determined to monopolise it, were strong enough to prevent penetration inland. In the East, the Europeans had encountered numerous and civilised peoples, organised and well-armed states. Here there could be no question of invading, of settling as a resident aristocracy. They came as armed traders, sometimes as pirates, constantly quarrelling among themselves. Their impact upon the great empires of Asia had been very slight; and so, as yet, was the impact of Asia upon them. They were kept at arm's length. The government of China, with its cultivated, highly organised official hierarchy, barely condescended to notice the uncouth foreign hucksters in the Canton river. In the territories subject to the Mughal empire, various European groups had secured footholds, as merchants residing on sufferance, as vassals, as allies and somewhat unreliable mercenaries, in a few places as minor territorial rulers, nowhere as

23

overlords. With Persia they had little direct contact, save through the Dutch factory at Bandar Abbas. Among the smaller principalities on the southern fringe of Asia, European invaders had asserted themselves more effectively; but even here, except for a few small areas in South India and in the East Indian islands, actual European possessions were still confined, at the end of the seventeenth century, to isolated forts and trading factories. In the eighteenth century, these toe-holds were to prove inadequate to support a rapidly growing trade; a wave of orientalising fashion was to sweep over Europe; the agents of the great trading corporations were, some of them, to turn *conquistador*; and, whether to support or restrain them, the governments of Europe were to be drawn into direct intervention.

Seventeenth-century activity in distant trade and planting was accompanied by a fierce competitive pugnacity. It was carried on by the subjects of half-a-dozen mutually suspicious and jealous national kingdoms, in an age when foreign trade was generally regarded as a mild form of war. In the seventeenth century, however, none of these kingdoms possessed navies or dockyard organisations adequate for protracted fighting in distant waters. In raiding one another's shipping and harbours, or, a little later, endeavouring to capture one another's plantations or factories, they had usually employed auxiliaries – privateers, buccaneers, native mercenaries, pirates. In both the East and the West Indies, any gang of cut-throats whose predatory activities could be made to serve an immediate national advantage, could secure letters of marque and could be sure of the support and countenance of one or another colonial governor or factory president. The result was the creation, by the middle of the century, of great areas of savage, unorganised conflict, through which only the very well-armed or the very inconspicuous could move with any confidence. In this chaos, the merchant shipping and the plantations of all nations suffered alike; and in the last two decades of the century there emerged a common determination to formalise the procedures of colonial conflict. The possession, or the cession, of colonial territories began to be embodied in formal treaties, just as territorial changes in Europe were recognised. French, English and Dutch colonial governors were gradually induced by their home governments to co-operate with naval forces in the suppression of buccaneers. Naval officers themselves, it is true, were not above occasional piracy; but gradually the practice of egging on pirates to attack other nations' harbours and shipping ceased to be regarded as a respectable expedient of international conduct, even in the West Indies. This did not mean, of course, an end of inter-European fighting overseas. It merely meant that major hostilities were entrusted to formal naval forces and confined to periods of formal war. In the eighteenth century, the navies of the principal Western European powers were to increase greatly in size and strength, and wars were to be frequent. Throughout the century, colonial possessions were to be among the principal bones of contention in every major war, and among the principal prizes in every major treaty. It is a sign of the growing importance of distant colonies and oceanic trades in the estimation of all Europe, that the age of the buccaneers should be followed by the age of the admirals.

NOTES

1. 'The aggregate of many states under one common head.' Burke, speech on conciliation with America, 22 March 1775, *Works*, 1808–13, III, p. 69. For a detailed semantic history of the word see Richard Koebner, *Empire*, Cambridge, 1961.
2. Dorothy Woodman, *Himalayan Frontiers*, London, 1970.
3. J. Lee, *Colonial Government and Good Government, a study of the ideas expressed by the British official classes in planning decolonisation, 1939–1964*, Oxford, 1967.
4. J. H. Parry, *The Age of Reconnaissance*, London, 1963.

PART I

The Areas of Operation at the End of the Seventeenth Century

1

Spanish America

Has Heaven reserved in pity to the poor
No pathless waste or undiscover'd shore?
No secret island in the boundless Main?
No peaceful desart, yet unclaim'd by Spain?

Johnson's sonorous lines reflected a long tradition of envy and resentment. At the beginning of Johnson's century, the Spanish empire in the Americas was already a hundred years old; the most solidly established of the European oversea empires, the biggest, both in population and territorial extent, by common consent the most productive (at least potentially) in terms of profit to those in a position to exploit its wealth. Its territorial boundaries were, for the most part, undefined. Officially, in its formal external dealings, the Spanish Crown claimed a general sovereignty over the whole of the Americas, and an exclusive right of navigation in the Pacific and the Caribbean, except where it had itself admitted exceptions. This claim – though unenforceable in its extreme form, and though only brought into the open when major Spanish interests seemed to be threatened – was still, and was long to remain, a basic principle of Spanish foreign policy. By the end of the seventeenth century, however, the exceptions explicitly or tacitly admitted were fairly numerous.

Of the explicit exceptions, the biggest was also the oldest, having been made, unwittingly, at the very beginning of New World settlement. An immense area of land in South America undoubtedly lay to the east of the demarcation line established by the Treaty of Tordesillas in 1494, and so was reserved, so far as Spain was concerned, to Portugal. The line had never been fixed on the ground, and could not be, with the navigational techniques then available. It was generally supposed to cross the coast somewhere in the muddy no-man's-land west of the Amazon delta, and again to the south somewhere near the mouth of the Río de la Plata. Disputed territory on the lower Amazon was no great matter in the seventeenth century: for although the great river had first been navigated by a boatload of Spaniards in 1542, Spain had shown little interest in it since Orellana's day. Disputed territory on the Río de la Plata was more serious. The territory itself was not of much importance; indeed it was almost unoccupied, except for a few ranchers running free-range cattle. There were two small townships, Spanish Buenos Aires on the right bank, Portuguese Sacramento on the left. South of Buenos Aires lay a thousand miles of wild Indian country, unexplored by Europeans. The river, however, was of great importance, in a negative sense: it was a back door to Upper Peru, a door which the Spanish government wished to keep firmly closed and guarded. Some Brazilians, as smuggling middlemen, wished to keep the door open; and the Portuguese authorities wished to maintain their claim to a large area of good cattle country. For these reasons, the left bank of the Río was the scene of repeated clashes between Spanish and Portuguese local forces in the later seventeenth century and through much of the eighteenth. Montevideo, the first formal Spanish settlement on the Banda Oriental, was founded in 1729. Eventually, after much bickering and some actual fighting, a boundary treaty was to be agreed in 1751, based partly on actual possession, partly on geographical convenience; in the outcome, the territory now known as Uruguay was to be colonised by Spaniards, not by Portuguese. Inland, the boundary at the beginning of the eighteenth century was even more uncertain. Wherever it was, it ran through unmapped bush, and the Spanish government rightly suspected that slave-hunting *bandeiras* from São Paulo were ranging the forest, raiding Jesuit mission villages and kidnapping Indians, far to the west of the Tordesillas line. These encroachments upon the Spanish Jesuit 'reductions' were eventually to be recognised by the 1751 treaty, which was to give Portuguese America approximately the boundaries which Brazil has today.

In the Caribbean area, explicit exceptions to the general rule of Spanish sovereignty had been made more recently, more grudgingly, and usually as the result of war. The Treaty of Münster in 1648 had confirmed the Dutch in their possession of Saba, St Martin, St Eustatius and Curaçao. These tiny crumbs of land had little or no value except as trading stations and bases for smuggling; and though the first three had been uninhabited when the Dutch arrived, Curaçao had actually been occupied by Spaniards, and was taken from them by force in 1634. English settlers had, in the first half of the seventeenth century, planted a number of islands, never occupied by Spain, in the Lesser Antilles. In 1655 the English government itself, grown bolder, had mounted a combined naval and military assault on the Spanish West Indies, which was defeated at Santo Domingo, but succeeded in capturing Jamaica. Militarily this was no great feat, since the Spanish population there was small, poor, and lacking in formal defences; but its consequences were serious. The island provided an excellent base, not only for smugglers, but for buccaneers, who soon graduated from the primitive business of hunting feral cattle and selling the meat and hides, to the more lucrative sack and plunder of Spanish settlements elsewhere in the Caribbean. Spain was in no condition to contemplate reconquest, and was constrained to recognise the English occupation, by the Treaty of Madrid in 1670, in return for an English undertaking to suppress the Port Royal buccaneers. Enforcement was another matter – it was easier to disown buccaneers than to suppress them – but in 1680 the Treaty of Windsor reaffirmed and strengthened the agreement. The Dutch – their power in America much reduced by their wars with England and with France – made a similar agreement at the Treaty of the Hague in 1673. As France, rather than Spain, more and more appeared as the principal enemy in the Caribbean, so the buccaneers became, for the English and the Dutch, more of a liability than an asset. French admirals and colonial governors continued for a time to encourage and employ the large bands which frequented Tortuga and the forests of northwest Hispaniola, but eventually they too agreed, at a price, to suppress their buccaneers. The steady killing-out of wild cattle and the spread of planting in the original buccaneer retreats, assisted the process. The Treaty of Ryswyck of 1697 marked the end of buccaneering as a serious political and military force in the area; and by it, Spain ceded St Domingue (western Hispaniola) to France. In general, then, by the end of the seventeenth century, the Caribbean area had been brought within the normal conventions of peace, war, and diplomacy in Europe. In peacetime, at least, the inhabitants of dozens of small harbours round the Caribbean could sleep securely in their beds. For this relief, Spain had to pay a price: the cession of a few islands, the recognition of foreign settlement in many others, and the public admission that Caribbean navigation and trade was no longer an Iberian monopoly.

In the Pacific, no such admission had been made, and no political price exacted for security. There were no European settlements, other than those of Spain, anywhere on the shores of the Pacific. The Dutch East India Company, by far the strongest European force in the East Indian archipelago, minded its own business and discouraged its captains from fruitless ocean voyages. No European ships regularly sailed Pacific waters, except Spanish ships engaged in the coasting trade between Panama and the harbours of the viceroyalty of Peru, and the famous Manila galleons which plied annually between Acapulco and the Spanish settlements in the Philippines. These ships, on the eastbound passage, made their landfall off California, and ran down the coast; but they never went close in, and no attempt had been made to survey the coast, much less to settle. European cartographers disputed, even, whether Lower California was a peninsula or an island. Apart from the regular Spanish routes, the Pacific was not only almost unvisited by Europeans; it was still unexplored. There had been English incursions from the Atlantic side from time to time in the seventeenth century. In 1669 Sir John Narborough had commanded an expedition into the Pacific, but, meeting Spanish resistance, had got no farther north than Valdivia. Parties of buccaneers occasionally crossed the Isthmus, seized Spanish vessels, raided minor Pacific harbours, and returned the way they had come. One such marauder, Bartholomew Sharp, in 1680 took from a Spanish ship a confidential *derrotero*, a collection of charts and sailing directions for the Pacific coast, with which he made an extended cruise, and eventually returned to the West Indies by sea. He was the first Englishman to round Cape Horn. His exploit, so soon after the Treaty of Windsor, caused a considerable stir; some of his men were later apprehended in Jamaica; one was hanged as a scapegoat, the rest acquitted, pardoned or allowed to escape. Sharp himself took passage for England. He was well aware of the value of his prize: 'The Spaniards,' he wrote, 'cryed out when I gott the book (farewell South Sea now).' The precious charts were copied by William Hack of Wapping – former buccaneer or hanger-on of buccaneers, and a good cartographical draughtsman – and bound in a handsome manuscript atlas, the *Wagoner of the Great South Sea*, which Sharp, with brazen effrontery, presented to Charles II.[1] He was rewarded with a captain's commission in the Navy, but soon went back to piracy. Sharp's success encouraged other ambitious voyages by self-styled 'privateers': notably Cowley's circumnavigation of 1683–6, and the wanderings of Dampier between 1679 and 1691.[2]

These expeditions, however, though alarming and exasperating to the Spanish authorities, were still no more than isolated forays. They did not amount to a concerted drive for trade and settlement in the South Pacific. No incursion or threat of incursion, before the end of the century, materially impaired the Spanish position there. The sea passage from the Atlantic, whether by Magellan's Strait, or round Cape Horn, was difficult and dangerous. Southern Chile, like Patagonia, was unfortified, and indeed unoccupied except by its 'wild' Indians, the redoubtable Araucanians; but its cold, wet forests would have been no more hospitable to invading interlopers than they were to Spaniards. The Spanish claim to exclude foreigners from South America and foreign ships from the South Sea was still plausible; and the Spanish government, relying for defence on the facts of geography rather than on military or naval strength, showed no disposition to retreat or compromise.

Eastern North America formed the largest tacit exception to Spanish monopoly. Since the end of the sixteenth century no serious attempt had been made, either by force or by diplomatic protest, to prevent other European settlements on the Atlantic coast. The extensive areas planted by English settlers had never been the subject of negotiation with Spain; though they were naturally presumed to be included in the terms of the 1670 treaty, which recognised the right of free navigation between England and English colonies. Spaniards were not interested in the region. There had even been talk, in the early seventeenth century, of abandoning Florida.[3] Unattractive and unprofitable, it had been retained because of the strategic necessity of commanding the Florida Channel, through which the east-bound convoys had to pass. The fortress of St Augustine on the Atlantic coast had been founded in the sixteenth century. At the end of the seventeenth, the place was an impoverished military outpost, maintained by subsidies from the royal treasury in New Spain.[4] Apart from the garrison, the Spanish population was very small. There were a few cattle ranches inland,[5] but little agriculture and no towns. Between St Augustine and the most southerly English settlements in Carolina lay the great area of what is now Georgia, then unoccupied, and destined to be an object of dispute in the eighteenth century. West Florida, the north coast of the Gulf of Mexico, was almost unoccupied; though moves were being made to settle Spaniards there, as a counter to incipient French attempts to control the Mississippi valley and to establish settlements near the river mouth. The fortification of Pensacola, by an expedition sent from Vera Cruz in 1697, was a direct retort to a projected French settlement (actually planted in 1718 at New Orleans).[6] Similar motives prompted attempts to settle south Texas. San Antonio was contemporaneous with New Orleans. Further west, New Mexico had been a Spanish province with a Spanish governor for a hundred years. Though well out of the way of European intruders, it was thinly held, and in 1680 a widespread revolt among the Pueblo Indians had driven the Spanish ranchers and settlers down the Río Grande to El Paso.[7] In the 1690s the military reconquest began, and at the end of the century the systematic, wary process of establishing missions and *presidios* (frontier blockhouses manned by soldiers) was still going on. Further west still, between 1687 and 1702 the Jesuit missionary Eusebio Francisco Kino was engaged in his remarkable career of exploring and proselytising in Arizona and Lower California.[8] There was talk from time to time of sending missionaries to Upper California; but at the end of the seventeenth century there were still no European settlements north or west of the *presidios* of New Mexico.

The pre-emption of a whole continent by Spain, then, was a mere formal pretence, and was so regarded even by Spaniards in their more realistic moments. Even in provinces unquestionably recognised as Spanish, great tracts of mountain and forest, great stretches of coastline, had never been occupied or even explored. Unsubdued and often hostile Indian tribes lived upon the Isthmus of Panama itself, within striking distance of the main treasure route from Peru to Spain, and of Puerto Belo, where the greatest trade fair in the Americas was held. The 'Moskito' Indians on the coast of Nicaragua maintained an intermittent alliance with the English against Spain. Small bands of English settlers lived in scattered camps at Belize in Honduras and at Black River, making a hard living by cutting and selling logwood for the dyeing industry. In the eighteenth century these Baymen were to cause trouble out of all proportion to their numbers and to the value of their trade. They received intermittent support from the government of Jamaica, and although well within Spanish territory they could not be dislodged.

The list of territorial exceptions, losses and defaults is a long one, and covers an immense area; but too much should not be made of it. Foreign settlement in distant, heavily forested coastal areas, foreign planting in unoccupied islands – even foreign seizure of a few occupied ones – were galling to Spanish pride, and potentially dangerous, but not disastrous. Actual territorial losses during the seventeenth century were, in themselves, relatively trifling. The first Spanish conquerors and settlers had concentrated their efforts on areas which promised immediate gain: fertile land, already cleared and needing no pioneer toil; abundant supplies of basic necessities – food, building materials, textiles for clothing; precious metals, in evidence as artefacts and in prospect in the ground; a numerous, sedentary and docile native population to provide the necessary labour. The regions which had originally offered these advantages were still, at the end of the seventeenth century, the chief centres of colonial population and wealth. They were mostly either inland, protected by mountain ranges, or far down the Pacific coast. Vast, scattered, difficult of access, they

35

offered a daunting prospect to foreign invaders. From the point of view of peninsular Spain, the problem which they presented was one less of defence, than of administrative control.

Central and southern Mexico (New Spain), Yucatán, Guatemala, Antioquia in what is now Colombia, the highland plateaux and coastal river valleys of Peru, the coastal plain of central Chile, were all old areas of Spanish settlement. The Spaniards, always urban dwellers by preference, congregated in the towns, especially in the viceregal and provincial capitals, some of which were big cities by European standards, with considerable handcraft industries and craft guild organisations, with heterogeneous populations of Europeans, *mestizos*, more or less Hispanicised Indians, and Negro slaves. The insistent demands of these urban centres had affected patterns of land-holding throughout the areas of old settlement. Much of the best land had become incorporated in large self-contained estates, owned usually by Creole Spaniards and worked by Indian labour.[9] These *haciendas* produced most of the food consumed in the Spanish towns, and also, where climate and transport facilities allowed, considerable quantities of cash crops for export: sugar, cocoa, indigo, cochineal, tobacco. Cattle and sheep ranching, preferred occupations among the early Spanish settlers, had moved out from the more populous districts in the course of the seventeenth century.[10] Immense areas of open range were grazed in northern New Spain, in the Orinoco plains and, increasingly towards the end of the century, in the neighbourhood of the Río de la Plata. In this vast, slovenly, heavily romanticised operation, meat and tallow were relatively unimportant by-products. The beasts were valued chiefly for their hides. No commodity had then a wider range of uses in the western world than leather, for boots and shoes, protective clothing, bags and boxes, saddlery and harness. The mining industry in the Indies absorbed a great deal of it, for pumps, bellows, buckets, and belts for driving primitive machines; and large quantities were exported to Europe. Hides and tropical cash crops were enough in themselves to ensure a modest prosperity for Spaniards in the Indies. The industry in which fortunes were made (and lost), however, the industry which gave the Indies their peculiar character and importance, which attracted the envy of all Europe, was mining. Silver was mined in large quantities – large by the standards of the time – both in New Spain and Peru. New Granada, modern Colombia, produced small quantities of gold, but this was comparatively unimportant; it was silver which made the Spanish Indies, in appearance at least, the crutch of crippled Spain and the envy of Europe.

Silver-mining, unlike surface prospecting for gold, involved digging, and for that reason was narrowly localised. With primitive techniques, lacking effective pumps, miners could operate deep shafts only in places where the danger of flooding was small. On the other hand, since mining required a large and concentrated labour force, it could not be carried on in absolute desert; for though food, at a price, could be transported over big distances, water could not. In New Spain the exploitable mines were confined to a relatively narrow belt of territory in the north and north-west, in New Galicia. The area was remote from settled land, inhabited by primitive and warlike nomads to whom the Spaniards gave the general name of *Chichimecas*, the wild people. In the seventeenth century these Chichimecas acquired horses and firearms. Their hostility made life at the mines precarious, and travel impossible except for well-armed parties. The only important exception to these generalisations was the *real* of Guanajuato, which lay nearer to Mexico City than the older mines of Zacatecas and which had near by a fertile and productive area, the Bajío; but the Guanajuato mines were liable to heavy flooding, and it was only in the later eighteenth century that improved techniques enabled their rich veins to be fully exploited. In Peru, the corresponding critical balance between habitability and adequate drainage in silver-producing areas was found not in semi-arid hills but in high mountains. Potosí, the prodigious mountain of silver in what is now Bolivia, lies at an extreme limit of habitability, at a height of over 12,000 feet, where heavy manual labour, whether above ground or below it, is difficult and dangerous; but at the height of its productivity Potosí was probably the biggest single concentration of population in the Spanish Indies.

Some Spaniards and more Indians worked small claims by hand; but the typical silver-miner was a capitalist on a fairly large scale. Extensive plant – extensive for those days – was needed for

37

crushing the ore and extracting the silver, usually by the *patio* or mercury amalgamation process. Peru had its own source of mercury, the ancient Inca mine of Huancavélica; a circumstance which greatly assisted the prosperity of Potosí.[11] New Spain sometimes imported Huancavélica mercury by sea, but more usually drew its supplies from Spain. The supply of mercury, carried awkwardly in leather bags, was in itself a vital and lucrative trade, and naturally the subject of constant official regulation and concern. Besides mercury, the miners needed steady supplies of beef, on the hoof the most portable form of food, leather and tallow candles. They needed also great numbers of mules to carry supplies to the mines and to take the silver back to civilisation. Mining and ranching were therefore complementary. Above all, mining required labour, both pick-and-shovel labour and the labour of skilled craftsmen in the *ingenios*. High wages could attract craftsmen; Indians could acquire the necessary skills, and most of the skilled work was done by them. The demand for unskilled labour was met partly by the import of Negro slaves, but most of this work also was done by Indians who, though paid, had to be recruited largely by coercion; either through the system of public forced labour known in New Spain as *repartimiento*, in Peru as *mita*; or else by the wholly illegal operations of private press-gangs.

Much of the silver which came from the mines was sent to Spain, but much also remained in the Indies and was coined and spent there. Both in New Spain and in Peru a steady stream of new wealth flowed to the capital cities, where it served both to pay for European and Chinese imports, and to stimulate local handcraft industry. The mining towns, though busy and populous, never quite lost their makeshift character, never became major administrative or social centres. They were too remote from the sea and from contact with Spain, too disorderly, too uncomfortable. The production of Potosí was controlled from Lima, to a lesser extent from Arequipa; that of Zacatecas from Mexico, to a lesser extent from Guadalajara. The main sources of wealth in the Indies – *haciendas*, ranches, mines – were often owned by the same people, and nearly always by the same kind of people. These rich men, many of them descendants of old conquerors and settlers, ran their

38

enterprises through managers. They themselves lived for most of the year in the capital cities which their ancestors had founded.

In the early and middle seventeenth century, the interlocking economy of mines, ranches and plantations had passed through a long period of depression, due largely to depletion of the Indian population and acute shortage of labour.[12] Productivity, and to a limited extent population, had recovered in the later seventeenth century. Silver production, at its lowest between 1650 and 1660, had regained by the 1690s approximately the level of the 1580s, and continued to grow.[13] The growth was uneven; most of it came from new mines in northern New Spain, while the decline of Potosí continued. On the whole, however, Spanish economists were right in believing that the economies of the Indies, despite the wretched conditions in which many of the inhabitants lived, were more buoyant and lively than that of Spain. Less and less of the silver produced in America actually reached Spain. The problem for Spanish statesmen was to ensure that Spain, itself depressed, hungry, ravaged by repeated epidemics, and impoverished by recurrent unsuccessful war, should share in, and profit by, the growing productivity of the Indies.

Spanish official policy on the fiscal relations between crown and colonies was primitive and direct. It owed little or nothing to the intricacies of current mercantilist theory; it did not insist on the value of colonies as sources of tropical 'staples' for re-export in Europe, or as markets for the 'vent' of Spanish manufacturers. It simply assumed that, since the kingdoms of the Indies were subject directly to the king of Castile, their duty was to render him tribute. The Spanish Crown deliberately and avowedly taxed its colonial subjects in order to defray its expenses in Europe. Revenue was chiefly raised not by duties on transatlantic commerce – though there were duties, and stiff ones – but by taxes levied directly in the Indies: the *alcabala* or sales tax, a percentage charged on most buying and selling transactions; the *quinto* or silver tax, charged at a flat rate of (usually) one-fifth of gross production and collected in bar form at the mines; the Indian *tributo*, an ancient and obviously discriminatory poll-tax, originally levied in kind for the support of the Spanish community, but long commuted to silver. The proceeds of these and other taxes, after deductions, authorised in some detail beforehand, to meet the cost of colonial government, were supposed to be remitted in silver to Spain. In the regulation of transatlantic shipping, the safe carriage of bullion was the first official preoccupation. To this, all other considerations, nautical, social, industrial or commercial, were always subordinate.

For many years the policy of Spanish governments had been to restrict all trade between Europe and the Indies to officially organised and escorted fleets. Two such convoys were supposed to leave Cadiz in the late spring or early summer each year, the 'galleons' for Puerto Belo on the Isthmus, where their cargoes would be sold and trans-shipped for Peru, the *flota* for New Spain. Both were escorted by warships, to defend the merchant packets against pirates in peace or enemy warships in war, and to carry the royal bullion on the return passage. The cost of convoy was defrayed by a special duty on the goods carried. Both fleets wintered in the Indies, the *flota* at San Juan de Ulúa, the galleons at Cartagena, both fortified harbours. Early in the following year they made their way to Havana, another heavily fortified place, whence they sailed in company, if possible in June, before the hurricane season, through the Florida Channel for Spain.

The fleets of the *Carrera de Indias* had a long and famous history. In the early seventeenth century they had been big fleets, sometimes more than a hundred sail, but by the end of the century the lawful trade had dwindled, and so had the fleets: ten or a dozen ships in a good year. In some years there were no sailings at all. The privilege of freighting ships for the Indies was restricted to a small group of conservative, extremely respectable Andalusian merchant houses, associated together in the *consulado*, the merchant guild, of Seville. Their supercargoes dealt, at the Jalapa and Puerto Belo fairs, with the representatives of similar firms, sometimes relatives or associates, organised in corresponding *consulados* in Mexico and Lima.[14] They had no particular interest in expanding the trade; like most such monopolists, they preferred to sell a limited and predictable quantity of manufactured goods, in a protected market, at artificially maintained prices. In the later seventeenth century, because of the uncompetitive nature of Spanish industry, and the difficulty of communication between Cadiz and the Spanish manufacturing centres, such as they were, most of the goods shipped were of foreign origin, chiefly French, the Spanish shippers often acting merely as agents. The shippers took some colonial products; but since one shipload of manufactured goods would buy several shiploads of hides or sugar, the quantity taken was narrowly limited by the capacity of the fleets, as well as by the low level of Spanish industrial demand. Most of the returns were in silver, much of which (like much of the royal silver) on arrival in Spain was promptly remitted abroad.

The fleets never, in practice, monopolised the market. Much silver leaked away through the smaller harbours of the Indies in payment for goods smuggled in by foreign ships, some French, some Dutch, but mostly English. These illicit traders, in normal times, had usually to keep clear of the major harbours, and even in the minor ones had sometimes to trade at the pike's point, using a show of force, whether real or feigned, in addition to the customary bribes, to persuade the local officials to connive at their proceedings. In straight commercial competition with the officially licensed traders they had all the advantages: they paid no duties, and so could sell cheaper; and they were willing to take a larger part of their returns in sugar, hides and the like, which they could sell at a profit in northern Europe. As the official fleets dwindled, so the trade of the smugglers increased. At the same time, the cost of colonial administration and defence mounted steadily, so that a smaller and smaller proportion of the yield of colonial taxes was available for remittance to Spain.

Spaniards have always been among Spain's severest critics. Spanish colonial policy had often been attacked by Spanish writers in the past, but usually on the ground that it lacked justice. Late seventeenth- and early eighteenth-century critics were more apt to complain that it lacked economic sophistication. It was easy enough to denounce, on mercantilist principles, the excessive and self-defeating restrictions on trade and the failure to encourage metropolitan industry. Many writers such as Martínez de Mata,[15] Uztáriz,[16] Ulloa[17] and Campillo,[18] to name only the most distinguished examples, did so with force and cogency. To secure effective action was another matter. The kingdoms of the Indies did not, at the best of times, lend themselves to tidy administration. Their physical inaccessibility and the patrician individualism of their leading subjects combined to give them remarkable powers of passive resistance, not only to the pressures of intruding foreigners, but to the wishes of their own sovereign. The Council of the Indies, responsible under the king for central government, was a cautious, slow-moving, deliberative and judicial body, incapable of major innovation unless stiffened by royal decision, by royal ruthlessness in handling vested interests. Carlos II, for his part, was incapable of effective command, or even of understanding the issues involved. Nor could it be said that his Bourbon successor, despite all the good advice showered upon him by Frenchmen and Frenchified Spaniards, provided much more intelligent or inspiring leadership. Indeed in some ways matters grew worse in Philip V's reign, as a consequence of the destruction of the Succession War and the break-down of communications which it caused. The provisions of the bravely worded *Proyecto para galeones y flotas* of 1720, designed to restore the annual convoys after the interruption of the war, proved unworkable. All the time the smugglers seemed to be gaining ground. In the early 1740s Campillo could still write:

> With such high duties and such restrictive freights and other notable hindrances, it may be said that we have shut the door of the Indies upon the manufacturers of Spain, and invited all other nations to supply those goods to the Spanish dominions, since every port in fourteen thousand leagues of coast is open to them, and those provinces must be supplied from somewhere.[19]

Some patriotic Spaniards analysed the whole situation of the empire, not only its economic circumstances, with feelings near despair. Macanaz[20] went so far as to question, in the Las Casas tradition, the right of Spain to rule the Indies. In his bitter *Testament of Spain* he denounced injustice and tyranny as well as administrative incompetence and economic sloth. So, with less rhetoric, did Juan and Ulloa,[21] the two clever but impressionable young naval officers who were sent to South America on a scientific mission in 1735, and who wrote a confidential report on the administration of the provinces they visited. Foreign writers, though they noted the imperial difficulties of Spain, often with avaricious glee, were usually somewhat more objective in their comment. 'An English merchant' (John Campbell), an acute though certainly not a disinterested observer (he was urging an aggressive anti-Spanish policy upon his government) was probably not wide of the mark when he wrote: 'The weakness of the Spaniards is, properly speaking, the weakness of their government. There wants not people, there wants not a capacity of defence, if the governors and other royal officers were not so wanting in their duty. ...' The author gives a list of foreign attacks on Spanish colonial possessions, of which some succeeded, but others were beaten off by spirited local resistance; and concludes: 'So it seems to be a thing out of dispute, that it is not so much the weakness of the Spaniards, as the weakness of their councils, which have occasioned their losses in those parts.'[22]

Spaniards, in short, though they could not occupy all the Americas, had occupied, and still endeavoured to monopolise, the most desirable parts. The burden of foreign complaint was that they occupied far more than they could effectively use and develop. Some envious and sanguine foreigners added the corollary, that Spaniards occupied more than their metropolitan government could administer or defend.

NOTES

1. Christopher Lloyd, 'Bartholomew Sharp, Buccaneer', *The Mariner's Mirror*, XLII, 1957, pp. 291–301. On Hack and his work see Edward Lynam, *The Mapmaker's Art*, London, 1953, pp. 101 ff.
2. William Hack, *Collection of Original Voyages*, London, 1699. Hack included a mutilated version of Cowley's journal. William Dampier, *A New Voyage round the World*, 3 vols, London, 1697. John Masefield, ed., *Dampier's Voyages*, 2 vols, London, 1906.
3. D. B. Quinn, *The Roanoke Voyages*, 2 vols, London, 1952–5, II, p. 777.
4. John Jay Te Paske, *The Governorship of Spanish Florida, 1700–1763*, Durham, N.C., 1964, p. 6.
5. The ranches did not, apparently, survive the Spanish Succession War. Charles W. Arnade, 'Cattle raising in Spanish Florida 1513–1763', *Agricultural History*, XXXV, 1961, pp. 116–24. See also, by the same author, 'The Failure of Spanish Florida', *The Americas*, XVI, 1959–60, pp. 271–81.
6. William Edward Dunn, *Spanish and French Rivalry in the Gulf Region of the United States, 1678–1702*, Austin, Texas, 1917.

7. Charles W. Hackett and Charmion C. Shelby, *Revolt of the Pueblo Indians of New Mexico and Otermín's attempted Reconquest 1680–1682*, 2 vols, Albuquerque, 1942.

8. Herbert Eugene Bolton, *Rim of Christendom: A Biography of Eusebio Francisco Kino, Pacific Coast Pioneer*, New York, 1936.

9. François Chevalier, *La formation des grands domaines au Mexique: terre et société aux XVIᵉ–XVIIᵉ siècles*, Paris, 1952, pp. 195 ff.

10. For an account of this shift in Mexico see William H. Dusenberry, *The Mexican Mesta: The Administration of Ranching in Colonial Mexico*, Urbana, Ill., 1963, pp. 24 ff.

11. H. Lohmann Villena, *Las minas de Huancavélica en los siglos XVI y XVII*, Seville, 1952.

12. Woodrow W. Borah, *New Spain's Century of Depression*, Berkeley, 1951.

13. *Ibid.*, p. 43.

14. See Robert Sidney Smith, *The Spanish Guild Merchant, a History of the Consulado, 1250–1700*, Durham, N.C., 1940; and by the same author, 'The Institution of the *Consulado* in New Spain', *Hispanic American Historical Review*, XXIV, 1944, pp. 61–83.

15. Francisco Martínez de Mata, a conventional but able mercantile economist, who published between 1650 and 1660 a series of *Discursos*, analysing the causes of depopulation and poverty, urging the freeing of internal trade, and outlining programmes of industrial development. An *Epítome de los discursos* is printed in P. Rodríguez, Conde de Campomanes, *Apéndice a la educación popular*, 4 vols, Madrid, 1775–7.

16. Gerónimo de Uztáriz, *Teoría y práctica del comercio y de la marina*, Madrid, 1724; trans. J. Kippax, *The Theory and Practice of Commerce and Maritime Affairs*, 2 vols, London, 1751. Uztáriz was probably the most influential of the Spanish Francophil economists of the first half of the eighteenth century. His book contains (I, pp. 209–13, in Kippax' translation) a discussion of smuggling to the Indies, and its causes.

17. Bernardo de Ulloa, *Restablecimiento de las fábricas y comercio español*, Madrid, 1740. There is a long discussion (pp. 98–168) of the failure of Spanish industry to supply the American market.

18. José Campillo y Cosío, *Nuevo sistema de gobierno económico para la América*, Madrid, 1789. The attribution of this book to Campillo is not beyond doubt. Campillo was a finance minister as well as an intelligent economist, but he died early, in 1743, before he had time to put into effect the proposals made in this book.

19. *Ibid.*, p. 20.

20. M. de Macanaz, *Testamento de España*, Mexico, 1821.

21. Jorge Juan and Antonio de Ulloa, *Noticias secretas de América*, Madrid, 1749. The purpose of their voyage was to participate in a French expedition to measure the length of a degree of meridian arc at the equator. Antonio de Ulloa was the son of Bernardo de Ulloa, the economist.

22. *The Spanish Empire in America*, by an English merchant (John Campbell), London, 1747.

2

The South Atlantic and the West Indies

The Spanish empire in America was a maritime empire only in the sense that communication between colonies and metropolis was necessarily by sea. Spain itself was a maritime power, though in the later seventeenth century a somewhat decayed one; but the kingdoms of the Indies were territorial kingdoms, whose chief centres of population lay mostly inland. Their people showed little interest in the sea. Ships for the *Carrera de Indias* were sometimes built in the Indies, particularly at Havana, but much less often than they had been fifty or sixty years earlier, and they were rarely owned or manned there. The long-standing royal prohibition of inter-colonial trade was unnecessary; there was very little to prohibit. Coastal trade between Mexico and Peru had flourished in the sixteenth century and died in the seventeenth. There was no considerable seafaring population, European or native. Most of the dangers which threatened the Spanish inhabitants of the Indies came from the sea. They feared it, and so far as they could, they turned their backs on it. To their territorial inaccessibility, they owed their comparatively uneventful history over two hundred years.

The Portuguese empire, by contrast, was an empire of coastlines and harbours. All its important settlements were in sight of the sea. They all depended for their safety and prosperity on seaborne communication, not only with Portugal but with one another. It was a true empire of the sea. This is not to say, of course, that the men who settled, defended and subsequently administered Portuguese establishments overseas were necessarily sailors by trade.

Professional sailors, in Portugal as in Spain, were usually men of humble social rank; soldiering was the traditional trade for a gentleman who was not content to live on his estates. In Portugal, as in Spain, the successful admirals throughout the sixteenth and seventeenth centuries were trained soldiers who learned, in addition, to navigate and to fight by sea. Geographical circumstance, however, had made the Portuguese overseas much more dependent than the Spaniards on seafaring skill and experience. Most of their initial settlements had been in places where the hinterland was either physically inhospitable and menacing, or else dominated by rulers hostile to European intrusion and powerful enough to repel it. The most dangerous threats to their forts and factories had come from the landward side, their reinforcements from the sea. At sea, apart, of course, from the perils of the sea itself, they could feel secure; no Asian or African principality had ships or ship-borne armament equal to theirs.

In the seventeenth century this security had largely disappeared. During the period of political union with Spain, from 1580 to 1640, Portuguese possessions had been fair game for Spain's many enemies, without the protection of effective Spanish support. Well-armed European marine predators and competitors had appeared in formidable force, off the coasts and harbours whose trade with Europe had long been a Portuguese monopoly. Portugal suffered major territorial and maritime losses, and a serious diminution of overseas trade. There were compensations; the Lisbon slaving firms, in particular, profited from access, under *asiento* arrangements, to slave markets in the Spanish Indies. In general, however, union with Spain became associated in the Portuguese mind with humiliation and loss, national independence with commercial profit and imperial success. When an independent monarchy was re-established under the Braganza house in 1640, it was natural that the crown and its leading subjects, at home and overseas, should embark on a determined effort to recover, as far as possible, the possessions and connections which had been lost, and to develop and strengthen those which had been retained. They achieved notable naval and commercial successes; but these successes, like the losses which preceded them, indicated a radical shift of economic emphasis within the Portu-

46

guese imperial structure. They were not in the original areas of Portuguese aggressiveness, on the Guinea Coast or in the East. They were all in the south Atlantic.

In Guinea, the principal Portuguese trading factories – Elmina with its massive fort, Axim, Gorée, near modern Dakar on the southern curve of Cape Verde – had all been taken by the Dutch in the 1630s, and the Portuguese never recovered them. The only toeholds which they retained in the Upper Guinea area were Bissau and Cacheu, two remote unhealthy harbours in what is still called Portuguese Guinea, difficult of access from the sea, screened by the scattered and dangerous barrier of the Bissagos Islands. In Angola; on the other hand, the Portuguese quickly regained all they had lost. The principal slaving harbours, Luanda and Benguela, which had been taken by the Dutch in 1641, were recovered in 1648 by a fleet under the formidable sea-fighter and colonial entrepreneur, Salvador Correia de Sá,[1] who had been governor of Rio de Janeiro. Almost simultaneously, in Pernambuco in northern Brazil, an energetic revolt among the Portuguese inhabitants had broken out in 1645, supported from Bahia; all this at a time when the Dutch were also moving towards a naval and commercial war with England. Despite the great disparity between Portugal and the Netherlands in wealth and seaborne strength, therefore, the Dutch West India Company was unable to support its Brazilian government adequately. The Dutch were finally expelled in 1654. In 1674 their company went bankrupt. In so far as Europeans were concerned, therefore, from the Amazon to the Río de la Plata and from São Thomé and Príncipe islands to the Cape of Good Hope (except for the small Dutch settlement on the Cape itself), the shores of the south Atlantic were left to the Portuguese.

Independent Portugal was still, in the late seventeenth century as it had been in the late fifteenth, a small country, sparsely inhabited and with scanty natural resources. Its wealth lay chiefly in its marine salt pans, the product of which was sold all over western Europe; to a lesser extent in the Douro valley vineyards, though it was not until near the end of the seventeenth century that 'port' found an extensive and profitable market in England. The country was deficient in cereals, and in most years had to import Baltic grain, brought in Dutch ships; for since the Dutch needed salt for their herring fishery as urgently as the Portuguese needed grain, the two countries traded regularly even in the height of war. Portugal was deficient also in meat. The protein in the Portuguese diet came chiefly from fish; a precarious dependence, and one demanding courage and enterprise, since the Portuguese coast is abrupt, with no extensive continental shelf to provide an abundant home fishery. The need to supplement the sardines of Portuguese waters was prominent among the causes which had initially drawn Portuguese sailors away on distant voyages, down the Mauretanian coast after tunny, or over to Iceland and Newfoundland for cod. In the seventeenth century the need was still as acute as ever. Except for their rivals the Dutch, no Europeans were more dependent on the sea for their livelihood than the Portuguese; no people more persistently drawn to oversea adventure, for which the fisheries provided a steady stream of trained and hardy seamen. In the seventeenth century, no European crown – not even that of Spain – depended more heavily on revenue drawn, directly or indirectly, from colonial sources; in no country was there greater disparity between home resources on the one hand, overseas commercial commitments and imperial responsibilities on the other.

In the pursuit of exotic trade and dominion during two centuries and more, the Portuguese had developed to an unusual degree the quality which an eminent Brazilian sociologist calls 'Ulyssism';[2] not simply a propensity to wander, a willingness to search, emigrate and settle, but a capacity to adapt to unfamiliar surroundings. More than any other Europeans, Portuguese oversea traders, emigrants and officials displayed an ability to come to terms with the Tropics. It showed itself not only in an easy-going attitude towards inter-racial marriage and the rapid production of mixed populations (the Portuguese were not alone in that) but in a ready acceptance of tropical crops, both for daily food and as cash crops for purposes of long-distance trade; in ingenious adaptations of European architecture to tropical conditions; and in the adoption of local conventions and loose, comfortable native clothing. One can speak plausibly, with Gilberto Freyre, of a Luso-tropical culture; hardly of a Hispano- or Anglo-tropical culture.

Spaniards, it is true, emigrated to the Tropics in considerable numbers; but they settled, as far as possible, in highland or in temperate areas, and in some at least of these areas, central Mexico, for example, they found a country which bore some physical resemblance to the *meseta* they had left behind. They remained notoriously conservative in matters of food and dress. As for North Europeans, they were willing to live permanently only in places where climate, vegetation and agricultural possibilities resembled those of Europe; and most of them regarded 'native' dress as compromising to European dignity. Portuguese emigrants, on the other hand – partly, perhaps, because they had fewer avenues open to ambition – took to life in the Tropics, even the humid and lowland Tropics, with the determination and the enthusiasm of pioneers proud of a new home.

Their adaptability and versatility enabled the Portuguese to conduct successfully a number of distinct and very diverse oversea enterprises (though nearly all in the Tropics) and to move the emphasis of their endeavour from one to another to suit changing economic and political circumstances. In the later seventeenth century, with the Guinea trade gone, Ceylon and Malacca lost and Goa in decline, the attention of crown, merchants and emigrants was heavily concentrated in Brazil, especially in the north-east coastal captaincies of Bahia and Pernambuco; a harsh country, but profitable, not indeed flowing with milk and honey, but certainly with rum and sugar. When João IV, the first Braganza king, described Brazil as his *vacca de leite,* he was alluding in homely metaphor to the revenue derived from the sugar trade. In the fifteenth century sugar had been for Europeans a scarce 'drug' or spice; in the sixteenth, a sweetening for wine or an ingredient in confectionery, familiar at least at the tables of the rich. In the seventeenth century it became widespread as a minor luxury, not indeed cheap, but easily purchasable in hard dark loaves in the retail shops of most European towns. This was largely a Portuguese achievement; Portuguese Madeira, Portuguese São Tomé, Portuguese Brazil, were in succession the principal sources of Europe's sugar. Madeira was too small to supply a rapidly expanding market; São Tomé fell out of the running in the early seventeenth century because of a series of violent servile mutinies; but

49

Brazil was vast, with fertile coast lands and abundant water for irrigation, seemingly capable of furnishing unlimited sugar for sale all over Europe.

The sugar trade between Brazil and Portugal in the late seventeenth century was probably the largest in volume of all the European trans-oceanic trades. It employed far more ships than the trade between Spain and the Spanish Indies, and probably rivalled that trade in the value of its total cargoes. The quantity of sugar carried varied greatly; in a very good year it might exceed 2,000,000 *arrobas* of about 25 lb;[3] in a year of drought it might be down to a few hundred thousand. Precise figures are scarce. Antonil,[4] an accurate and detailed observer, gives 1,600,000 *arrobas* for the whole of Brazil in 1710. Most of this was white sugar, refined in Brazil; there was no refining industry in Portugal.

There were two distinct systems of export. In all the main centres there were merchant houses which bought sugar from the producers, warehoused it, and shipped it as convenient; but many of the larger planter–manufacturers owned or rented their own jetties and storage facilities, and shipped their sugar in their own name and at their own risk, for sale in Europe. Sugar was packed for export in wooden boxes or chests, each holding from thirty to forty *arrobas*, each with the name of the owner, whether planter or merchant, burned into the wood. Ships engaged in the trade were commonly described in terms of the number of chests they could carry. The relation of chests to tonnage is difficult to fix precisely. In the second half of the seventeenth century the crown imposed a lower limit of 350 tons on ships in the Brazil trade, in the interests of defence.[5] It is unlikely that such a rule could have been strictly enforced; smaller ships probably remained in the trade, as they did in that of the Spanish Indies; but the few ships whose cargoes are still recorded carried, as a very rough average, between 500 and 700 chests,[6] and this seems a possible load for a ship between 350 and 400 tons.

Brazilian sugar, like Mexican and Peruvian silver, was carried in organised convoys under armed escort; a system originally designed for defence against Dutchmen and Spaniards, but retained, after peace with both nations, against those systematic predators, the Barbary corsairs. From 1649 to 1720 the convoys were organised and the escorts provided by the Brazil Company (*Companhia geral do estado do Brasil*), a semi-naval, semi-commercial concern royally chartered for the purpose. In return for its services, the company levied its own charges on all merchandise carried, and in its early years also operated sundry commercial monopolies: the import into Brazil of wine, olive oil, flour and salt cod, and the export from Brazil of the red dye-wood from which the country originally took its name. The company's fleets, from the principal ports of Rio, Olinda and Bahia, assembled at Bahia and sailed for Portugal annually in the spring. The passage to Portugal, *via* the Azores, usually took from eight to twelve weeks, and in a good year the total strength of the fleets might exceed a hundred sail. Not all the ships were Portuguese. Portugal had neither the materials nor the men to build and man enough ships. Many Dutch and English ships participated in the trade under Portuguese licence. Many more, without licence, smuggled sugar to Amsterdam direct. Nevertheless, despite the obstacles, inefficiencies and leaks inseparable from oceanic monopoly, the volume of the lawful trade was great, by seventeenth-century standards. To the end of the century it remained the principal channel through which Europe got its sugar.

The wealth derived from sugar left monuments in the cities of Brazil which survive to this day. The capital city, Salvador (Bahia), at the end of the seventeenth century was acknowledged to be the second city of the Portuguese empire, bigger and richer than Goa, surpassed only by Lisbon. Its population can only be guessed. An archiepiscopal estimate of 1706 gave 4,296 hearths, with 21,601 communicants, for the city, without the neighbouring townships in its *reconcavo*;[7] considerably smaller than Mexico or Lima. It was medieval in layout, with narrow winding streets, lacking the rectilinear formality of Spanish-American cities; but its buildings were splendid. All visitors admired them. Dampier, who visited the place in 1699, wrote an enthusiastic account.[8] The 'Mannerist' churches – often loosely described as Baroque – do not compare with the best in Mexico, but are overwhelming nevertheless in their number and in their profusion of ornament. All this, with the elegance of Olinda in Pernambuco, the rising vigour of its neighbour and rival Recife, the pushing prosperity of Rio de

Janeiro, was supported by sugar; and Portugal, too, naturally got its share of the profits of the trade. Brazilian sugar buoyed up the Portuguese economy, otherwise poor and weak, during the frequent periods of general depression in the later seventeenth century, notably in the 1670s. The merchants of Lisbon retailed and re-exported sugar, mainly in Dutch bottoms, to Amsterdam, whence it was distributed through northern Europe. The crown, naturally, taxed it. Sugar entering and leaving Portugal was liable to a number of different duties, most of which had originated in specific occasions of royal financial need, but had become permanent. The total burden of these duties amounted to at least thirty per cent of the value of the sugar in Portugal. Brazilian sugar passing through the Azores also paid ten per cent on entering harbour, and ten per cent on leaving. In addition, the Portuguese crown, like the Spanish but unlike the metropolitan governments of northern Europe, taxed its colonial subjects directly, to defray European as well as colonial expenses. Throughout the seventeenth century the most important tax was the *dizimos*, the tenths, levied on gross production. *Dizimos* were due in theory to the Order of Christ for the upkeep of the Church in Brazil, but in practice the crown, as administrator of the order's revenues, applied the proceeds where it thought fit. The tax was always farmed. The farmer collected it in kind at the source – in the case of sugar, at the mill – and sold the produce as best he could. He usually made his contracted payments to the treasury part in money, part in kind; with the result that the royal garrisons in Brazil sometimes, to their intense indignation, received their pay in the form of unsaleable sugar.

According to Antonil,[9] there were in his day 528 sugar mills in Brazil, 246 in Pernambuco, 146 in Bahia, 136 in Rio de Janeiro. Many of these were *trapiches*, small mills turned by cattle; but many, especially in Bahia, were *engenhos* properly so-called, with larger, heavier, triple vertical rollers, turned by water power at a much higher speed than oxen could achieve. Speed, timing, continuity are essential factors in successful sugar production. Expensive and elaborate machinery – and a big *engenho* was very elaborate by seventeenth-century standards – must not be allowed to stand idle, once the harvest has begun, waiting for irregular supplies of raw material. On the other hand, the raw material cannot be 'stock-piled'. Sugar cane is perishable; it must be cut as soon as ripe, carted and milled as soon as cut. As the juice flows from the rollers, it must be channelled immediately to the first of the series of great boilers which reduce it to syrup; it must be transferred from boiler to boiler (laboriously, in the seventeenth century, with huge iron ladles), and 'tempered', usually with wood ash then, to clarify it. When, in the last boiler of the series, it reaches the required consistency, it must be cooled and crystallised at once. In the seventeenth century the resulting wet, dark sugar could simply be drained of its surplus molasses and sold as 'muscavado'; but in Brazil, sugar intended for shipment to Europe was usually refined. The full refining process, to produce white sugar, was an elaborate business. The muscavado had to be washed, drained, dissolved again into syrup, and once more boiled, clarified and crystallised. There was a compromise: the process known as 'claying'. Here the muscavado was run into moulds of baked, unglazed pottery, and covered with a crust of dried and pulverised clay, to absorb some of its impurities and lighten its colour.[10] This produced the loaf sugar commonly sold for domestic use in northern Europe. Both processes had the obvious advantage of reducing bulk, and so freight charges, in relation to the price.

To ensure the necessary timing and continuity, the whole complicated range of processes had to be under a unified control. The *senhor de engenho* was both manufacturer and planter; the sugar estate both factory and farm. The bigger, the faster the mill, the more land would be needed to keep it supplied with canes; and not only canes, but vast quantities of firewood for the boilers, pasturage for the work cattle, provisions for the work people. Cane land might be quite a small proportion of the area of an estate; and usually the proprietor of a big estate would not plant all his cane land himself. Some of it, on some plantations most, was let to *lavradores* – share-cropping farmers, who brought their canes in by river barge, by sea, or by ox-waggon to the owner's mill. By thus leasing his outlying lands, a planter could effect an important economy in his transport, while ensuring his supply of canes. Grants of land in Brazil, originally made by captains-donatory under the late medieval system known as *sesmaria,* had been very large. When sugar land became worn out, fresh virgin ground was usually available within the estate to be cleared and broken by share-croppers; and in this way place could be found for the considerable numbers of peasants, men without capital, who emigrated from Portugal to Brazil in the course of the seventeenth century.

Besides *lavradores*, estate and mill required a small staff of Europeans as overseers, foremen and craftsmen. Some of the final processes of manufacture called for skill and judgment, and had to be carefully supervised. In general, however, the work about a sugar estate was heavy unskilled labour. The owner needed a large, disciplined, permanent labour force, which could be concentrated at will and driven relentlessly during the busy time of crop, the six months or so from August to February when the canes were cut and the sugar made. In seventeenth-century colonial terms this meant slave labour. Sugar, from its European colonial beginnings until fairly recent times, was everywhere closely identified with slavery; and everywhere sugar was grown, it set the style for other activities. In Brazil, not only sugar planters, but small farmers, miners, artisans, shopkeepers, all employed slaves, and household slaves formed a recognised part of all but the poorest families. In their early settlements the Portuguese in Brazil had enslaved Amerindians. Missionaries, the Jesuits especially, often protested against the practice;[11] but the Portuguese crown took no effective measures to stop it. The Brazilian forest dwellers, however – shy, primitive, given to wandering – were neither physically nor mentally suited to regular heavy work; they made indifferent slaves. Hence the crucial importance of Angola in the seventeenth century as a source of slaves for the sugar plantations; apart from a relatively modest trade in ivory, this was indeed in European eyes its only importance.

In this respect Angola differed from the Guinea coast, which the Portuguese had discovered long before, and from which the Dutch had expelled them. Guinea had had many trades – gold, ivory, gums and resins, *malagueta* pepper – besides slaves. There were other differences. Physically, Angola with its coast of sand and red rock, its hinterland of scrub savannah, contrasted sharply with the coastal mangrove swamps and lagoons, the inland tall forest, of Guinea. The Bantu peoples of Angola were considered to be more tractable in slavery than the Sudanic peoples of Guinea. They appear to have been less effectively organised, politically and militarily; certainly they were less successful in resisting European penetration. In Guinea, the European establishments were simply fortified factories on the coast, occupied by treaty. Slaves, though they might come from far inland, were bought from the coastal rulers, who acted as middlemen. Neither Europeans nor their agents went inland. In Angola, slaves were collected by dealers, *pombeiros*, often Portuguese half-castes, who travelled to the inland slave markets with loads of wine and cloth from Portugal, of Brazilian tobacco, and of cowries, also shipped from Brazil for the purpose. The *pombeiros* bought slaves on behalf of Portuguese slave merchants resident at Luanda, which was a Portuguese town, not a mere barracoon. During the second half of the seventeenth century the governors of Luanda made persistent efforts to reduce the inland rulers of Angola to vassalage, to make them pay taxes and furnish porters and labourers. They achieved considerable, though costly success; the period has justly been named 'the fall of the black monarchies'.[12] The process of military conquest was roughly complete by 1700; eighteenth-century governors of Angola were rarely called upon to engage in full-scale local wars or even to dispatch punitive expeditions. From the Portuguese point of view, however, the results were disappointing. Statistics of the export of slaves from Luanda survive from 1710. In that year the figure was 3,549.[13] It rose fairly steadily over the next twenty years, but never approached the figures (admittedly only estimates) of 10,000 to 12,000 annually in the middle years of the seventeenth century. The decline was due partly to depopulation and disturbance, caused by half a century of war, in which military commanders often by-passed the *pombeiros* and took to kidnapping on their own account; and to disastrous epidemics of smallpox – that sinister gift of Europe to the Tropics – in the 1680s. Luanda also suffered from the competition of other European buyers, who disregarded Portuguese claims to monopolise the whole Angola coast, and bought slaves in the minor harbours. The Portuguese, for their part, never accepted their exclusion from the Gulf of Guinea. In 1721, despite the hostility of the Dutch at Elmina, they established, on land ceded to them by a local ruler, the little factory of São João Baptista d'Ajuda, near Whydah. This inconspicuous territory, a few acres only, remained Portuguese until 1962. Its Government House still stands, plaster dropping from its walls, a sagging sentry box at the gate, beside the modern road from Cotonou to Lomé. In the eighteenth century São João was a slaving centre of some importance. Luanda, however, remained the one sure, reliable source of slaves for the Portuguese, the essential complement of Brazil, without which the sugar plantations were unworkable. From Luanda to Bahia was a comfortable trade-wind run, with no serious navigational hazards, except for the coral archipelago of the Abrolhos, which, though dangerous, was well known. From Portugal to Angola, from Angola to Brazil, from Brazil to the Azores and so to Portugal; or from Portugal to Brazil and back; or from Brazil to Angola and back to Brazil; so the ships moved in great figures of eight, their routes dictated not only by the possibilities of trade, but also by the pattern – which the Portuguese were the first Europeans to discover – of trade winds, of equatorial calms and variables, of equatorial current and gulf stream, and of the westerlies of their own home latitudes. Throughout the seventeenth century this incessant coming and going of ships across the south Atlantic was kept in motion by Europe's insatiable appetite for sugar.

Sugar, of course, was not the only commercially important product of Brazil. Tobacco of good quality was grown in Bahia and sent to Portugal; much more tobacco, of much poorer quality, went to Angola to pay for slaves, in a direct out-and-back trade. Curiously, this characteristic tropical crop, since it was packed in leather satchels, helped to encourage the raising of cattle. In the southern captaincies, between Rio de Janeiro and the Río de la Plata, cattle-ranching had long been established, though on a relatively small scale. In the last decades of the seventeenth century, ranchers began pushing up the São Francisco and into the uplands of São Paulo, gradually occupying the immense areas of the central plateau. Antonil in 1710 gives 800,000 head for the *sertão* in Pernambuco, 500,000 for Bahia, 80,000 for Rio.[14] Before 1640, central Brazil had regularly imported salt beef and leather. By the end of the century hides had become a considerable item of export. Timber has already been mentioned. Portugal imported from Brazil not only dye-wood, much of it for re-export, but jacaranda and other hardwoods for furniture and the beams of houses. Ship-building timber also was a constant problem in Portugal, as in Spain. Brazil had an abundance of suitable timber, and though the shipment to Portugal of quantities adequate for this purpose was impracticable, ships could be built in Brazil. Such ships were little, if any, cheaper than those built in Portugal,[15] presumably because the high cost of skilled labour offset the low cost of timber; but at times in the seventeenth century Portugal was cut off from Baltic supplies, and ships for the Atlantic trades had to be built in Brazil or not built at all. Brazilian yards built most of the small ships needed for local purposes, coastal trades, fishing and whaling. The Brazilian whale fishery was a rich one, subject throughout the seventeenth century to a royal monopolistic concession. The whales were towed ashore at Bahia or Rio for rendering, and considerable quantities of the oil were used locally, especially for illuminating the sugar mills, which worked night and day in crop time. The meat was often salted and sold as food for slaves.

One major activity remains to be considered: mining. The highland plateau of São Paulo de Piratininga, only about thirty miles from the sea, but cut off from it by the rugged Serra do Mar, was the home of a population of independent small settlers, mostly of mixed Portuguese and Guaraní blood. Alone among the settler groups of Brazil, these *Paulistas* resolutely turned their backs on the sea. They had nothing to export, they could not grow sugar in São Paulo, they could not afford to import Negroes. They did, however, employ Amerindian slaves, and regularly varied their farming by armed expeditions far into the interior, in search of captives and of anything else they could find, including gold or silver. Like all Europeans exploring and settling in the Tropics, the Portuguese hoped – expected – to find precious metals. No one knew how far it was to Potosí, or how many other Potosís existed. Eventually, in the 1680s and 1690s, Paulista *bandeiras* found, in what are now the highlands of Minas Gerais, stream beds containing paying quantities of alluvial gold. The length of time taken for this news to penetrate to the coastal towns is evidence, not only of Paulista secretiveness, but also of the almost total lack of inland communications; but in the late 1690s the rush began. It was the beginning of a revolution in the economy of Brazil, as significant as that which had followed the discovery of Zacatecas and Potosí a century and a half before; unlike Spanish-American silver, however, Brazilian gold was relatively easy to get; it was a matter, not of deep mining, a technique virtually unknown in the Portuguese empire, but of surface washing. Any slave could do it, if his owner could reach the area, and support himself there. Little initial capital was needed – it was a question of numbers, and the numbers were available. People streamed inland, taking their slaves if they had any; routes were opened, up rivers and through the bush; the smelters began their assault on the forests, which eventually made Minas Gerais the rocky semi-desert it is today; the gold poured down to the coast at Rio, Bahia and Santos. Here, indeed, was a commodity for the crown to tax. It attempted to do so, by requiring all gold mined to be smelted at royal smelting houses in the São Paulo region, and by collecting 'fifths' of the gold smelted. What proportion of gold escaped this leaky net can only be guessed; two-thirds was Antonil's guess. Even so, the quantities reaching the Lisbon mint by lawful channels, in the company's fleets, having paid *quinto*, were impressive, and increased very rapidly in the early years of the eighteenth century; 725 kg in 1699, 1,785 in 1701, 4,350 in 1703, 14,500 in 1712.[16] By then a vast amount of Brazilian gold must have been in circulation, lawfully or otherwise, on both sides of the Atlantic. According to Magalhães Godinho, by 1703 the amount of gold imported into Portugal from Brazil already exceeded the total amount received from Guinea during the whole period of Portuguese trade there.

These dramatic developments enabled Portugal to maintain in the eighteenth century a gold currency renowned for its purity, and to pay for imports and public works which it could not otherwise have afforded. The imports, textiles in particular, came chiefly from England. Close and favourable commercial relations with Portugal enabled England also to establish and maintain a gold currency. The defence of Portugal and the maintenance of British influence there became fixed objects of British policy. The situations of Portugal and of Spain in the early eighteenth century were thus roughly analogous. Reliance on New World silver made Spain, to a dangerous extent, financially dependent on Spanish America and politically dependent on France. To an even greater extent, reliance on New World gold made Portugal politically dependent on England and financially dependent on Brazil.

In Brazil itself, many people moved from the coastal strip to the interior, to the *sertão*; vast areas inland were opened – more or less – for settlement; the cattle industry expanded enormously, the ranchers following the miners, as they had done earlier in New Spain. Political and economic power slowly moved south, from Bahia and Pernambuco to São Paulo, Minas Gerais and Rio de Janeiro. Sugar ceased to be the overwhelmingly predominant product. It was still important, especially in Bahia, where quality and productivity were well maintained; but over the coastal areas as a whole there was a slow, but perceptible, decline, if not in the quantity produced year by year (on that, estimates are contradictory) then certainly in the profits. To a considerable extent, the reasons were internal. Costs rose steadily. Gold mining employed slave labour, drew slaves away from the plantations, and raised their price to the sugar growers. Land prices rose also; even in Brazil, the area of good cane land was not unlimited; frequent complaints of drought and flood in the later seventeenth century suggest land exhaustion and erosion. External competition, probably, was even more significant. One answer to labour shortages in the western hemisphere was to import labour-intensive products from the East. In the first two decades of the eighteenth century the Dutch East India Company built a number of ships expressly designed to carry Javanese sugar to Europe;[17] and the French and English companies even found it worth while to import appreciable quantities from China.[18] This helped to reduce sugar prices. It was one phase, relatively short-lived, of the continuous economic dialogue between East and West in European markets. Above all, the rise in the price of slaves and the fall, subject to wartime fluctuations, in the price of sugar[19] at this time were due to the competition of planters buying the one, producing and selling the other, in the West Indian islands.

The first founders of the sugar industry in the French and British West Indies were Dutchmen, who during their company's occupation of Pernambuco, took to the Caribbean both cane cuttings and knowledge and experience of sugar production. As the universal dealers and carriers of the West Indies, it was to their advantage to encourage the production of any West Indian crop which could be sold in Europe.[20] They could supply the equipment and were prepared to lend the initial capital, on credit against the first crop. All the early French and English colonies in the West Indies had been founded during a tobacco boom; but during the seventeenth century the price of tobacco dropped steadily, to a level far below that at which the crop could be produced profitably by small farmers on small islands. In Barbados and St Kitts, in Guadeloupe and Martinique, planters gladly turned from tobacco to sugar, from indented white labourers to black slaves. The slaves came mostly from the old Portuguese factories on the Guinea coast. These had been seized by the Dutch in the 1630s, but the Dutch in turn, in the later seventeenth century, lost some of them: Cape Coast to the English in 1664, Gorée (Senegal) to the French in 1677. Supplies of slave labour were thus available from several competing sources. By the middle of the seventeenth century, both English and French sugar planters had overcome their initial technical difficulties. By the end of the century, they were producing sugar in formidable quantity, and were selling it very profitably in Europe. Their sugar may not have been more cheaply produced than Brazilian, and certainly was not of better quality; but it was more cheaply transported. Dutch, English and French had better access to ship-building timber than had the Portuguese; their shipyards were more up-to-date; they built more ships, more cheaply, and operated them with fewer men. Their ships sailed without escort, and so (although some were lost to pirates and corsairs in most years) they escaped the cost of convoy. They paid lower duties and fewer taxes. In France and England, respectively, the West Indians enjoyed protected markets for their sugars; markets formerly supplied, directly or indirectly, from Brazil. They could not, from half-a-dozen islands, supply all Europe; but even in the great open market of Amsterdam, Brazilian sugar had by 1700 – perhaps by 1680 – lost its easy pre-eminence and was feeling the wind of competition. In the Antilles, two little Brazils had grown up side by side: two sets of mercantile monopolists, two rival groups of settlers, each with its uneasy, quarrelsome planting oligarchy and its mass of recently imported mutinous Negro slaves.

NOTES

1. C. R. Boxer, *Salvador de Sà and the Struggle for Brazil and Angola*, London, 1952, pp. 261 ff.
2. Gilberto Freyre, *The Portuguese and the Tropics*, Lisbon, 1961, p. 50.
3. Frédéric Mauro, *Le Portugal et l'Atlantique au XVIIe siècle*, Paris, 1960, pp. 238–9.
4. Antonil (João Antonio Andreoni, SJ), *Cultura e opulencia de Brasil por suas drogas e minas* (1711), Bahia, 1950.
5. Mauro, *Le Portugal*, p. 48.
6. *Ibid.*, pp. 238–9.
7. C. R. Boxer, *The Golden Age of Brazil*, Berkeley, 1962, p. 395.
8. William Dampier (J. A. Williamson, ed.), *A Voyage to New Holland in the Year 1699*, London, 1939, pp. 33–43.
9. Antonil, *Cultura e opulencia*, p. 169.
10. *Ibid.*, pp. 133–4.
11. The great missionary writer Antonio Vieira asserted in 1657 that over 2,000,000 Indians had died in Brazil as the result of enslavement. Antonio Vieira, SJ, João Lucio d'Azevedo, ed., *Cartas*, 3 vols, Coimbra, 1925–8, I, p. 468.
12. Ralph Delgado, *História de Angola*, 4 vols, Lobito, 1948–55.
13. David Birmingham, *Trade and Conflict in Angola: The Mbundu and their Neighbours Under the Influence of the Portuguese 1483–1790*, Oxford, 1966, p. 137.
14. Antonil, *Cultura e opulencia*, p. 295.
15. Mauro, *Le Portugal*, p. 49.
16. V. Magalhaes Godinho, 'Le Portugal, les flottes du sucre et les flottes de l'or, 1670–1770', *Annales: Économies, sociétés, civilisations*, 1951, pp. 192–3.
17. K. Glamann, *Dutch Asiatic Trade 1620–1740*, Copenhagen, 1958, pp. 24–5, 161–4.
18. L. Dermigny, *La Chine et l'Occident, 1719–1833*, 3 vols, Paris, 1964, I, pp. 428–30.
19. The wholesale price of muscavado sugar in Amsterdam fell from forty-five gulden in 1640 to fourteen gulden in 1677. N. Deerr, *The History of Sugar*, 2 vols, London, 1950, II, p. 530.
20. The predominance of the Dutch in Caribbean trade in the middle decades of the seventeenth century is best described in Jean Baptiste du Tertre, *Histoire générale des Antilles habitées par les François . . .*, 4 vols, Paris, 1667–71, I, p. 9. See also Melvin H. Jackson, *Salt, Sugar and Slaves: The Dutch in the Caribbean*. James Ford Bell Lectures, no. 2, 1965. For the beginnings of sugar planting in the British islands see R. Ligon, *A True and Exact History of the Islands of Barbados*, London, 1657.

3

The West Indies and North America

The West Indian islands together represented, in miniature, a world of competing maritime empires. Most European states with maritime pretensions were concerned, at one time or another, with the West Indies: with territorial possessions there, or claims to them; with trade in the area, or predatory designs on other peoples' trade. At the end of the seventeenth century, however, the field was somewhat narrowed. Portuguese and Genoese had dropped out from the business of supplying African slaves to Spanish settlements. The Courland Company and its settlements had failed. Neither Danes nor Swedes had yet entered the field. The Dutch retained their Guiana settlements, restored to them by the Treaty of Breda in 1667, and their island possessions, Curaçao and St Eustatius, valued not for what they produced (which was very little) but for their use as commercial entrepôts. The long attrition of war with France, however, had damaged the naval and commercial strength of the Netherlands. Dutch business in the Caribbean had suffered also from the determined endeavours of both English and French governments to exclude foreign carriers from the trades of their respective colonies. The Dutch share both of the carrying trade and of the slave trade was still substantial, but relatively less important than it had been; and since, by the laws of other nations in the area, it was largely clandestine, the Dutch walked warily and tried to avoid giving open offence. The state of affairs in the West Indies, political and commercial, then, depended chiefly upon the relations between the three remaining groups of contenders, Spanish, English and French.

The role of Spain in Caribbean trade and politics at the end of the seventeenth century was, perforce, almost wholly defensive. There could be no question of an initiative; if a decayed, though still valuable, inheritance could be preserved intact, that was the best that could be hoped for. The presence of thriving French and English settlements in some of the islands made preservation much more difficult than it had been at the beginning of the century. Foreign observers were apt to observe smugly that this was the Spaniards' own fault. First in the field, and for several decades alone in it, they had ignored the Lesser Antilles, the long chain of lovely and fertile islands, stretching from the Virgin Islands in the north to Trinidad in the south, forming an arching breakwater between Caribbean and Atlantic. These islands, or at least the more northerly of them, possessed not only beauty and fertility, but also the advantage of a windward position, from which their possessors could at will threaten the inhabitants of the Greater Antilles, their plantations, their harbours and their trade. The Spaniards had settled the Greater Antilles; but then, drawn away by the superior attractions of the mainland, had neglected them. The Spanish populations of Cuba, Hispaniola, Jamaica and Puerto Rico had remained sparse and poor, their production small – a few hides, a little sugar. The powerful fortifications of Havana and San Juan had been sited and designed to ensure the safe passage of the Seville fleets through the islands, not primarily to protect or develop the islands themselves. The pattern of Spanish settlement had left a vacuum which other Europeans, in the course of the seventeenth century, had proceeded to fill.

At the end of the century British settlements included Barbados, Antigua, Nevis, Montserrat and part of St Kitts, all in the Lesser Antilles; and Jamaica, captured from the Spaniards in 1655. The French held, in the Lesser Antilles, Martinique, Guadeloupe, Grenada and the other half of St Kitts. In the greater islands they held St Domingue, modern Haiti, the western portion of the island of Hispaniola. St Domingue had become formally French in 1697, by cession from Spain; but for forty or fifty years before that date it had been gradually colonised by Frenchmen, first as cattle-hunters varying their butchers' business by raiding at sea, latterly as settlers and planters. In 1698 the French planters in Ste Croix were transferred *en masse* to St Domingue, on the ground that ships – whether for fear of pirates or for lack of cargoes – would not go to Ste Croix. The process of clearing the forest and shooting out the cattle in St Domingue was a long one, and for many years the colony retained, in its social and political habits, traces of its buccaneer origin.[1] Spain retained Cuba, Puerto Rico and the rest of Hispaniola: poor pensioners of New Spain, whence came the subsidies by which their fortifications were maintained. There were still a few major islands without European masters. Trinidad was officially Spanish, by default, since British attempts at settlement in the middle of the seventeenth century had failed;[2] but there were very few Spaniards there, and for practical purposes the island was still no-man's-land. Dominica, St Lucia and St Vincent, all mountainous, forested, beautiful and forbidding, were by tacit agreement left to their Carib inhabitants, whose reputation for ferocity was still credible enough, in 1700, to keep settlers away. There were many hundreds of small islands, unclaimed, unsettled, even unvisited; but most of these were too insignificant or remote to attract attention, except as temporary refuges for pirates. In general, the territorial division of the West Indies had reached, by 1700, a rough equilibrium. The time was past when an island could change hands ten times in a decade, as had been the lot, between 1664 and 1674, of St Eustatius – that scrub-covered rock which Dutch commercial genius made the richest free port in the Americas.

The territorial pattern which emerged at the end of the seventeenth century looked precarious; but it was comprehensive, recognised by treaty, guarded by naval force; in the event it proved surprisingly stable. It left little room for the operations of buccaneers, or *flibustiers*, as the French more accurately called them. *Flibustiers* were unreliable auxiliaries. They were individualists, expert with the musket, as might be expected from their cattle-hunting antecedents, but unfamiliar with heavy guns.[3] They usually baulked at attacking warships or formal fortifications. Moreover, the French and English stakes in the West Indies were, by 1700, too valuable economically, too delicate diplomatically, too uncertain strategically, to be exposed to the risk of incidents caused by unpredictable mercenaries. In the English possessions, measures against the buccaneers had begun to take effect in the 1680s. Pressure upon them by colonial governors and naval commanders drove them to other occupations. Some, who could afford to acquire land and slaves, settled down as planters; some took themselves off to the Honduras creeks, to a rough but not unprofitable life, cutting and shipping wild logwood in territory technically Spanish; a few, like Dampier, became explorers or naval officers. Many turned simple pirate – an easy transition. The *flibustiers* of Tortuga lasted longer, as a more or less organised community, than the buccaneers of Port Royal. Du Casse, commanding in St Domingue from 1691, employed them against both English and Spanish settlements during the war of the Grand Alliance: unsuccessfully against Jamaica in 1694, successfully, in conjunction with formal naval forces, against Cartagena in 1697. This was their last appearance in a major operation. Thereafter their bands broke up. Some turned to planting in St Domingue, others, like their English counterparts, to piracy. Piracy itself, however, was becoming a risky occupation. The sharp increase in the number of pirates in the 1680s had produced naval reactions; governors and planter assemblies clamoured for warships permanently 'on the station', and their clamour was increasingly attended to.[4] In the first two decades of the eighteenth century many pirates were hunted down and hanged, or left the Caribbean for waters less frequented by men-of-war: the Bahamas, the South Atlantic or the Indian Ocean.

The disappearance of buccaneering and the gradual reduction of piracy in the eighteenth century did not, of course, mean an end of violence in the Caribbean; only that violence was to be formalised, confined to periods of declared war and conducted by regular forces or at least by properly accredited privateers. By 1700 the West Indies had been fitted into the general pattern of European international relations. It became part of the standard strategy of France and England, often of Spain also, on the outbreak of any European war, to send great armaments to the Caribbean. There were many particular reasons for this. Disputes originating in the West Indies were nearly always among the irritants which led to declarations of war; inevitably, when the colonies of several mutually suspicious powers were scattered in the same limited area, and when winds, ocean currents and the disposition of islands compelled them all to use the same confined sea channels for their communications and trade. There was, in addition, a general financial reason. West Indian possessions contributed directly to the incomes of influential individuals, indirectly to the revenues of the metropolitan states. The contribution was of considerable importance and was generally believed, throughout the eighteenth century, to be more important still.[5] Each contender, therefore, had a strong motive to strike first; to devastate the enemy's plantations, dislocate his colonial trade, and so reduce his revenue and his capacity for making war. So, as Bryan Edwards later put it, the warring nations of Europe regularly betook themselves to the West Indies 'as to a cockpit'.

The income for which French and English expended so much naval effort was mostly derived from sugar. Many other cash crops were grown, or had been, but none ever approached sugar in quantity or profit.[6] By 1700, tobacco had almost run its course in the French and British islands. So had cotton, also a small man's crop at that time.[7] Tree crops were attractive, requiring relatively little effort; Labat praised cocoa, in particular, as a small man's crop;[8] but many cocoa trees in Jamaica and St Domingue were destroyed in the late seventeenth century by blight, and coffee was not introduced on a commercial scale until the 1730s. Ginger was never more than a sideline. Indigo was a valuable crop, a half-way house to large-scale plantership, but its cultivation and manufacture both presented technical difficulties, and no West Indian island produced indigo comparable with that of Guatemala.[9] No West Indian product rivalled sugar. The demand for it could be expanded indefinitely. Confectionery, the preservation of fruit, brewing, distilling, all required sugar. Cocoa and coffee might rival one another, and both, later in the eighteenth century, compete with tea; but all three, in most people's opinion, needed sugar to make them drinkable. Every West Indian planter on a big scale turned to sugar sooner or later, and having turned to it, he hardly ever turned back to anything else.

Sugar, like tobacco, declined in price as it became more plentiful; but because of the elasticity of the demand for it, production was not discouraged; it was merely concentrated in larger and more economical units. The small sugar islands – Barbados, St Kitts and their neighbours – were past the height of their early prosperity by 1700. Martinique and Guadeloupe somewhat larger, were still expanding their operations; but the great eighteenth-century centres of production were Jamaica and St Domingue. Both these islands had big areas of virgin land, and in both, as in Brazil, land was parcelled out from the beginning in large properties.[10] Sugar planters there did not have to go through the uncomfortable process (as in Barbados) of buying up small properties and evicting the occupier, in order to make room for their own operations. Nor had they to incur the trouble and expense of constantly grubbing up cane roots, manuring exhausted land, and replanting. They could 'ratoon' their canes – that is, harvest repeatedly from the old roots for several years, until the roots wore out, and then plant on fresh land. They had also, in the big islands, as in Brazil, the advantage of abundant water, to irrigate the fields and turn the mills.

Sugar was a tyrant and set its own terms. The processes of production in the West Indies resembled, in general, those in Brazil. There were some differences, however. Refining was much less general. French and English governments were more ambitious and more up-to-date in their application of current mercantile theory, than the Portuguese; towards the end of the seventeenth century they both legislated against colonial refining and sought, by discriminatory taxation, to protect home refiners.[11] There was a difference between the French and English colonial reactions to this discrimination. The law could be evaded to some extent by the process of claying, which was not expressly forbidden. In the eighteenth century the French plantations produced great quantities of clayed sugar. English planters shipped mostly muscavado; only in Barbados was claying at all common. Since France in the eighteenth century was usually weaker than England at sea, French planters had a stronger interest in producing sugars which took up less shipping space than muscavado; or perhaps they were simply more enterprising.[12] Another difference between the West Indies and Brazil was that West Indian planters grew their own canes on their own land. The practice of leasing out land to tenant cane-farmers was almost unknown. The Portuguese peasants who emigrated in such numbers to Brazil had been willing to settle as tenants under the *sesmaria* system. In the West Indies there was no comparable feudal arrangement. English and French emigrants who had secured land in the islands in the early days, had settled as freeholders, most of them on a small scale, farming grants which they could work themselves with one or two servants. By 1700, however, small farmers were fast disappearing from the West Indian scene. With the introduction of sugar, a somewhat barbarous, relatively egalitarian society of pioneers had given way to the rigidly stratified society of large planters employing either indented servants or slaves in large numbers. Colonial societies, characteristically, are highly mobile. In the English islands, most of the small men had pulled up and left, many for the mainland colonies. Only in Barbados did any appreciable number remain. In the French islands, St Domingue never had many small farmers; only Martinique and Guadeloupe retained into the eighteenth century a considerable population of *petits blancs*.[13]

The supply of indented servants, also, had gradually ceased.[14] The prospect of a piece of land had been the main inducement offered by the indenture system; but in the smaller islands there was no empty land left. There was land in Jamaica and St Domingue; but what was the use of thirty or forty acres of uncleared bush, in a country dominated by sugar barons? Conversely, what was the use of indented servants as unskilled field and factory hands, to planters who could get African slaves? Slaves cost more initially; but in the long run they were more economical. They and their children served for life (though admittedly their lives were often short) instead of a brief term of years; and they could be fed and housed at a lower level than that which law and custom prescribed for Europeans. The Royal African Company from 1672, the Compagnie du Sénégal from 1673, and countless private traders, poured Guinea slaves into the West Indies.[15] Specialists – craftsmen, coachmen, refiners, private tutors – were still recruited in Europe; and the English islands still received a trickle of transported felons. MacHeath's gibe at his wives – 'ship yourselves off for the West Indies' – had still a grim topicality. Otherwise, there was little demand for European labour. Shipmasters, crimps, promoters in the indenture business took their emigrants to the mainland colonies instead. Of a total population of, perhaps, 150,000 in all the English islands in the early eighteenth century, probably not more than 30,000 were Europeans. The narrow community of planters with their overseers, a few merchants and professional men, a few privileged craftsmen and shopkeepers, had become, in most islands, virtually a garrison among the slaves.

The structure of West Indian society governed the nature of West Indian trade. Slaves had no purchasing power. Usually they consumed only the bare minimum of food and clothing, which their owners supplied. In the English islands, the sugar shipped to England greatly exceeded, both in value and in bulk, the goods arriving from England. After 1700, British ships hardly ever had full outward freight to the West Indies.[16] This fact, together with the long-term tendency of sugar prices to decline, was connected with the virtual elimination of merchants, both English merchants and those resident in the islands, from the transatlantic sugar trade. There were merchants in the islands, of course, and those in Bridgetown and Kingston were in a large way of business; but Bridgetown merchants dealt chiefly with the receipt and onward shipment of incoming slaves; Kingston merchants were interested in the import and distribution of North American cargoes, and in trade to Spanish America. They did not, for the most part, handle sugar. Planters shipped their sugars on their own account to correspondents in England who acted as factors and sold the sugars on commission. From the same factors, the planters ordered such goods as they required from England. The system had its conveniences; it enabled planters to buy slaves on credit and pay for them with bills on London;[17] on the other hand it saddled the planters with all the risks of the trade. In the French islands (where slaves and credit were equally in demand) the system was different. Planters sold their sugars to merchants in the islands, who shipped them to France.[18] Goods shipped to the islands came as the investment of merchants in France. St Domingue was a partial exception: there both systems existed in 1700, as they did in Brazil, and the planters had a choice; but in Martinique and its neighbours the system was uniform. A partial explanation of the difference between French and English practice may lie in the larger European populations of Martinique and Guadeloupe; but this argument should also apply to Barbados. Absenteeism, which was commoner, or at least developed earlier, among English planters, may have had something to do with it. The main reason for the difference, however, was probably that the French islands at the end of the seventeenth century still drew nearly all their imports, including bulky imports of food and wine, from France; whereas the English islands imported only manufactured goods and luxuries, necessarily in limited quantity, from England. Their wine came from Madeira, and already they were getting their bulky provisions largely from North America. Whatever the mercantile theorists might say, North America rather than England was becoming the economic complement of the British West Indies.

From the point of view of most responsible people in England, the merchants, manufacturers, economic theorists, politicians and officials, all the colonies of English North America, taken together, were still of less value and interest than a dozen or so small West Indian islands. At the end of the seventeenth century the West Indies supplied nine per cent (by value) of English imports, as against eight per cent from the mainland colonies; they took more of English exports than the mainland (four per cent, as against a little less than four per cent) and they accounted for seven per cent of the total of English trade (including the slave trade) as against six per cent by the mainland.[19] Not only was West Indian trade more valuable; the whole nature of West Indian economic activity conformed more nearly to the theories of imperial organisation then current. The seventeenth century had been, on the whole, a period of demographic stagnation, or at least of very slow growth, for England as for most of Europe.[20] In the last two or three decades, population began to grow more rapidly; but so did industrial and commercial activity. The agrarian unemployment of the early years of the century had been absorbed; men were in demand; the old desire to get rid of surplus people had given way to the opposite, to a fear of depopulation. For mercantile theorists, the ideal colony was one where a small number of English planters supervised a large non-English labour force in producing tropical commodities, for sale in England and re-sale in continental

Europe. All the better, if the labour force itself was an article of trade in English hands. The West Indies fitted this pattern; the mainland colonies, generally speaking, did not. On the contrary: they produced nothing as valuable as sugar; they clamoured for people to fill their empty spaces; and the indenture system made emigration to the colonies, for ambitious or discontented peasants and artisans, all too easy.

In 1700 eleven separate English colonies occupied a continuous strip of coastal territory from Maine to South Carolina. It was a narrow strip. Most settlements were on the coast or the lower reaches of navigable rivers; nearly everywhere, a day or two's travel from sea or stream brought the pioneer into untouched Indian country. The population, probably not more than 300,000 in all, was predominantly agricultural. The largest town, Boston, had only seven or eight thousand people.[21] Most economic activity, necessarily, was on a small scale. Virginia, however, and to a smaller degree Maryland and the Carolinas, produced cash crops for export, tobacco in Virginia and Maryland, rice in the Carolinas, by a plantation organisation somewhat similar to that in the West Indies. The tobacco planters of Virginia would, no doubt, have turned to sugar like the Barbadians had they been able to; but their winter climate prevented it. They stuck to tobacco, employing mostly indented labour, and made a success of it despite the steady fall in prices. Tobacco is a notorious 'land-killer', and probably the main reason why the Virginians succeeded where the Barbadians had failed was that they had access to all the land they wanted and much more than they could use. Since they needed little in the way of fixed equipment, they could shift their cultivation whenever the symptoms of land exhaustion appeared. The first Robert Carter (a much quoted example) owned some 300,000 acres;[22] but most of it was 'thicket'; the cultivated area consisted of a dozen or so separate plantations, each with ten or twenty workers under an overseer. Plantations of this size were characteristic of Virginia in the seventeenth century. Towards the end of the century, however, a marked tendency towards larger units began to appear; the larger planters, also, increasingly changed the nature of their labour force from European indented servants to imported African slaves. Virginia, in this respect,

71

slowly followed the example of the West Indies. In 1700 there were about 18,000 slaves, in all the mainland colonies together, and most of them were working on tobacco plantations.[23] In another respect, also, Virginian planters – at least the big ones – followed the West Indian example. In the late seventeenth and early eighteenth centuries they usually shipped their tobacco to London or Glasgow on their own account, and so acquired credit in England, rather than selling it to merchants in the colony.[24] Tobacco was a valuable crop and an important factor in imperial trade. It remained, nevertheless, sugar's poor relation. As income-producing units, the estates of, say, the Carter family never approached in value the Beckford holdings in Jamaica or the Codrington properties in Barbados and the Leeward Islands.

From the point of view of the mercantile theorist Virginia was, economically, a comparatively satisfactory colony (not necessarily politically – its assembly could be cantankerous like all the others). The same could not be said of the northern colonies, which either could not or would not conform to the theoretical pattern. Pennsylvania and Delaware, not separated until 1702, formed a modest farming area whose inhabitants, many of whom were Scandinavians or Germans, minded their own business and gave no trouble, but produced nothing much for export. Philadelphia, founded in 1683, was still little more than a village. New York, formerly New Amsterdam, seized from the Dutch in 1664, was in 1700 a small metropolis of perhaps 5,000 people, an important entrepôt in intercolonial as well as transatlantic trade, a favourite market with privateers and pirates for the disposal of loot, and one of the leakiest joints in the official mercantile system. Its hinterland, which had been New Netherland, was still very sparsely populated and produced little; but the Hudson and Mohawk valleys provided a back door, through the territory of the formidable Iroquois middlemen, to the immense fur-producing region about the Great Lakes, and valuable quantities of furs came down through Albany, to be shipped from New York harbour.

The New England colonies presented special problems to imperial administrators. They bought few slaves; not because their people had any feeling against slavery – they sometimes enslaved Indians – but because, except to a limited extent in Rhode

Island,[25] they had no agricultural estates big enough to need slave labour. They produced little that was wanted in England, except timber. Their virgin forests were the only source in British territory of trees big enough for the masts of large warships. The imperial government made repeated attempts to reserve the best mast trees for naval use; a clause to this effect was even inserted in the Massachusetts charter of 1691.[26] The attempts were ineffective, largely because the prices which the Admiralty paid were too low to compete with a keen local demand for sawn timber. New England produced furs and skins, as did nearly all the mainland colonies – deerskins were exported in considerable numbers from Virginia and the Carolinas; but the more valuable fur-bearing animals of New England, beaver especially, became scarcer as settlement extended, and the trade, though a major factor in Indian relations, was a minor factor in the colonial economy. New England fish and agricultural produce were unsaleable in Old England. It was in the West Indies that the northern colonies found their best market. New England traders, in their own small ships, carried to the islands horses and barrel staves, butter, beef and flour for the planters, salt fish for the slaves. They returned with sugar, much of which they re-exported to England to clear their debts for consumer goods, and rum; about 1700, also, they were beginning to import molasses from which distillers in Boston made their own rum. Having the advantages of a shorter passage and cheaper ship-building materials, they had by 1700 almost entirely squeezed out English shipping (though not, as yet, English capital) from the trade between mainland and island colonies. Without this trade, the sugar colonies could not have existed and the North American colonies could not have developed.[27] Economically it made sense, and there was no legal objection to it. Mercantile theorists, it was true, thought of a colonial empire as a wheel with the metropolis at the hub, and expected that trade would normally move up and down the spokes rather than round the rim; but no English act prohibited intercolonial trade. The effect of English legislation, indeed, was to protect it. The goods which New Englanders sold in the islands did not compete with English products (they did with Irish; but Ireland, in English theory, occupied, like New England, a position on the rim of the

73

wheel). The New Englanders, however, went much further. They bought rum and molasses not only from English planters, but from French who since, rum was unsaleable in France, sold it cheaper. They sold provisions to the French islands in time of war. They bought French sugar and shipped it, as English, through Boston or New York to England. They shipped sugar and tobacco, irrespective of origin, to continental Europe, robbing the crown of revenue and English dealers of their profits. In these and many other ways they not only contravened official theory on the function of colonies in a maritime empire; they broke explicit laws.

The English Navigation Laws have been much studied and written about, and it is unnecessary to describe them in detail here.[28] They formed by 1700 a complex network – 'system' is perhaps too tidy a description – of rules and exceptions, many of which were drafted *ad hoc* to deal with particular situations or to still the outcries of particular groups of people, rather than to realise consistent economic theories. In so far as they dealt with colonial matters, however, they did embody certain clear administrative principles. They assured the colonies of a monopoly in the home market for their characteristic products. Conversely, they pressed the colonies, chiefly by fiscal means, to produce goods which England could not produce, and discouraged them from making manufactured goods which they could obtain from England. They required exports of the most valuable colonial products, the 'enumerated' products, to be sent to England; it seemed reasonable that if colonial producers were to be given a guaranteed market in England, then England should insist on a corresponding monopoly. With some explicit exceptions, they required goods, English or foreign, intended for the colonies to be shipped from an English port. They restricted trade between England and its colonies, and between colony and colony, to British ships, which included colonial ships, and excluded foreigners in general from the colonial market. With somewhat less consistency, they placed the colonies outside the fiscal boundaries of England. Duties on colonial products were usually lower than those levied on comparable foreign goods, but colonial products always paid duties. Colonial trade brought, or was supposed to bring, a steady stream of wealth into England, but it was private wealth, and the only way in which the crown could tap the stream was through its customs. In view of the cost of providing naval protection for the colonies and their trades, no one could reasonably object to these charges. Some liberally-inclined economists criticised the system,[29] but on the whole, the acts represented the conventional economic doctrine of the time, and people in the colonies accepted them, at least in principle.

Enforcement, of course, was another matter. No European imperial government, in seventeenth-century conditions, could hope to enforce consistently, over great distances, rules which conflicted with powerful local interests. Colonial governors did not, as a rule, go deliberately looking for trouble. There was no disciplined, salaried colonial civil service. If prosecutions were brought, local juries would not convict. Infractions, therefore, usually went unnoticed, provided there was no general public defiance. Defiance, however, or something very near it, was not unknown; English colonies were well provided with machinery for obstructing central government. Unlike the colonies of France and Spain, they had grown up in a period when representative institutions were gaining strength in the mother country. The 'rights of Englishmen', which the colonists naturally and repeatedly claimed, included such devices. Most of the colonies (all, by 1700) possessed elected legislative assemblies. These bodies, like parliament in England, represented entrenched interest: that of freeholders. Civil wars in England, and periods of neglect, had encouraged them in independent habits. In dealing with the home government and its representatives in office, their attitude was parochial, often obstinate, sometimes insolent. They were not hostile to England or disloyal to the crown, but they saw no reason why their habits and their interests should have to be adapted to fit a general imperial pattern.

The later Stuart governments in England had made strenuous efforts to achieve centralised control. James II had even tried to establish in New England a viceroyalty roughly on the Spanish model. The attempt ended with the revolution of 1688; probably it would have failed anyway. Restoration lawyers, however, insisted, with a fair measure of success, that colonial assemblies could be required by crown or parliament to pass specific acts;

that parliament itself might, in default, enact measures enforceable in the colonies,[30] and that all colonial acts must be approved by the Privy Council. In 1696 William III set up a permanent Board of Trade and Plantations to replace the Privy Council committees which had hitherto looked after colonial affairs; though executive power remained, as before, with the Privy Council itself. A general customs organisation was created, staffed by officers appointed in England, backed by vice-admiralty courts to enforce the Acts of Trade.[31] The crown already appointed the governors and certain other officials in nearly all the colonies and was successfully reducing, in practice, the formal legal distinction between crown colonies and private colonies, whether chartered or proprietary. The assemblies, however, could not be dislodged or ignored. They held the power of the purse. In some of the old crown colonies – Virginia, Barbados, Jamaica – the assemblies had been induced at an early date to grant to the crown a permanent, though very inadequate, revenue by indirect taxation. Most assemblies, however, steadily refused to do this, objecting suspiciously, but implausibly, that such a revenue might produce a surplus, which might then be used outside the colony. They voted year by year, reluctantly and stingily, the taxes from which the entire cost of government, save only naval defence, had to be met. Most colonial governors were frustrated in their efforts towards sound administration by the lack of an assured revenue. Even their own salaries were at the mercy of the assemblies, to which they were not responsible and which they could control only with difficulty. For another three-quarters of a century in the mainland colonies, for longer still in the West Indies, an uneasy balance of power was to remain characteristic of English colonial government in America. It was not oppressive; but it was always weak, often incompetent, and usually more or less corrupt.

One chief factor held the empire together, apart, of course, from old associations. That was the fear of invasion or encirclement. The Dutch possessions in North America had been swallowed up, but the Spaniards still ruled the largest and richest of the New World empires; the French colonies were growing in power and population and appeared as dangerous enemies in the north and west; the Indians were a perpetual menace on the frontier. At the end of the century it seemed possible that all three might combine against the English on the Atlantic seaboard.

French colonisation in the seventeenth century was less spontaneous, more planned and regimented, than English or even Spanish expansion – for the Spaniards, too, were expanding in New Mexico and up the Pacific coast. The various companies under whose auspices settlement had been organised were all controlled and subsidised by the crown, and in Colbert's time the crown relieved them of their administrative powers and assumed direct responsibility for colonial government. By 1678, Colbert had already done in the French empire what James II failed to do in the English. Each colony was ruled by a military governor appointed by the crown. These soldiers were assisted and at the same time watched by civil governors, *intendants*, who handled all financial and economic business. Governors and *intendants* together were advised by nominated councils which also served as courts of appeal, though they had none of the independent powers of the Spanish *audiencias*. The system was simpler and cheaper than the elaborate bureaucracy of Spanish America, quicker and more efficient than the creaking English representative system. The economic policy of colonial France was a mercantilism even more rigid and consistent than that of the English Restoration governments, and despite shortage of shipping and the persistence of Dutch and New England smugglers in the West Indies, the French government made strenuous efforts at enforcement. Unlike the English government, it had also a positive emigration policy. Colbert retained the system of feudal *seigneuries* established in Richelieu's day, but made them conditional upon effective occupation. The *seigneurie* system had a long life; it was the only feudal order of society in the Americas which outlived the seventeenth century. Irksome and restrictive in many of its detailed demands, it nevertheless combined successfully the necessary provisions for settlement and defence. It was to survive the departure of French officials from Canada in 1763, and to last well into the nineteenth century.[32] The French, unlike the English, never thought of allowing their colonies to be peopled by paupers, felons and religious dissidents. On the contrary, everything possible was done to attract eligible settlers, especially to Canada.

77

Demobilised soldiers were pensioned with land for farms in Canada and settled along the Richelieu River and at other strategic points. Tools, seed and stock were provided at government expense; and the government even provided free passages to Canada for women who were willing to marry settlers there. These provisions were not without effect; the population of French Canada trebled under the Colbert régime. Even so, at his death in 1683, the total number was only about 10,000. The subsequent steady increase was due more to the fecundity of the settlers than to a steady increase in emigration. The military efficiency of the population was very high, despite its political and economic primitiveness. The settlers were at once adventurous and disciplined, and their liability for military service was a reality, in sharp contrast with the English colonial militias, which were divided among a dozen separate governments, seldom mustered, and accustomed to cavil at the orders, or rather the entreaties, of the king's representatives.

As explorers by land or by inland waterway, the French in America at this time far outshone their English contemporaries. By 1673 Jesuit missionaries had visited most parts of the Great Lakes region and were striking southwards to the headwaters of the Mississippi and its affluents. In 1682 La Salle had made his great journey by water down the whole length of the Mississippi to the Gulf of Mexico and opened up a whole vista of strategic and economic possibilities. La Salle lost his life in 1687, while still a young man, in a premature attempt to plant the colony of Louisiana at the mouth of the Mississippi. His adventurous imagination presented to his countrymen the project of connecting Louisiana with Canada by a chain of French settlements. The whole distance could be covered by several alternative water routes, with comparatively short portages. Communications could be safeguarded by forts covering the principal portages and the narrowest stretches of water. Nothing came of La Salle's dream in the seventeenth century, for Colbert's death was followed by a period of stagnation and neglect in the colonial policy of France; but in the eighteenth century the project was pursued with great vigour, and might have set close limits to the slow westward expansion of English settlement had the French in America been more numerous.

The courage and initiative of explorers are not enough, in themselves, to found an enduring empire. Even Colbert failed to make the solid work of settlement attractive to adventurous Frenchmen. Canada was in any event a harsh place to settle; and the restrictive feudal structure of Canadian settled society constantly drove the more enterprising out to the wilder frontiers. Many of these hardy traders and trappers adopted Indian ways, took Indian women, and produced in a generation or two a characteristic type, the half-caste *coureur des bois*. At the same time, the ill-defended monopolies of the trading companies attracted interlopers, who were often the companies' dismissed or disgruntled servants. Two such malcontents were largely responsible for the most severe blow which befell the French monopoly in Canada in the seventeenth century – the foundation of the English Hudson's Bay Company. An overland route to the shores of Hudson's Bay was first discovered by two French fur traders, Radisson and Groseillers. These men tried, but failed, to persuade the authorities in France to develop a trade in furs from Hudson's Bay; but they found a backer in England, in that restless royal adventurer, Prince Rupert. The result was the incorporation in 1670 of the Hudson's Bay Company, trading directly to the bay by sea. This enterprise was the first serious attack on French leadership in the fur trade; and is the only Stuart incorporation which survives as a working concern today.

Twelve years of financial good fortune followed the company's foundation, and in those years forts were established to exploit the trade of the whole southern and south-western shore of the bay. Serious French counter-attacks began in 1682. In the general war following the English revolution of 1688 the French achieved widespread success. Frontenac, able and vigorous governor of Canada, recaptured Nova Scotia, overrun by the New Englanders in 1691, frightened the Iroquois tribes into temporary peace, and kept the frontiers of New England and New York in constant fear of combined French and Indian raids. Much of the bitterness of colonial warfare arose from this habit of employing Indian auxiliaries, with their traditionally barbarous methods of fighting and of torturing prisoners. At the same time a brilliant sea commander, d'Iberville, ravaged the English settlements in Newfoundland and all but destroyed the company's hold in Hudson's bay. The favourable colonial terms secured by France in the Treaty of Ryswyck were due largely to the successes of these men.

By the end of the seventeenth century the general lines of the final struggle for power and trade in America were already apparent. The Dutch were beginning to drop out, weakened by unequal war in Europe. The power of Portugal was localised in Brazil and unlikely to expand elsewhere. To some observers at least, the Spanish empire seemed on the verge of collapse. In fact, despite commercial weakness and a top-heavy bureaucracy, it was to outlast the others as an imperial unity; but its part in the eighteenth-century struggle was to be mainly defensive. Of the major fighting competitors, each had its weaknesses. The English empire obviously suffered from lack of unity and discipline; the French empire had the more serious defect of lack of people. These factors, however, were not decisive. In the end the conflict between them was to be decided by the capacity to build, man and deploy ships.

NOTES

1. P. F. X. Charlevoix, *Histoire de l'Isle Espagnole ou de S. Domingue*, 4 vols, Amsterdam, 1733, iv, p. 267.
2. J. A. Williamson, *The Caribbee Islands under the proprietary patents*, Oxford, 1925, pp. 192–7.
3. On this point see J. B. Labat, *Nouveau voyage aux Isles de L'Amérique*, 6 vols, The Hague, 1724, I, p. 73.
4. From about 1683 the French usually maintained five or six warships permanently in the Caribbean; but they had other tasks than fighting pirates. The Spanish privateer *guarda-costas* cruised chiefly against smugglers, but took some pirates too. The first naval squadron to be sent to the West Indies for the express purpose of suppressing piracy was an English one: four frigates under Sir Robert Holmes in 1687. See A. P. Thornton, *West India Policy under the Restoration*, Oxford, 1956, pp. 231–66.
5. On the development of the Jamaica and Leeward Islands 'stations', see Ruth Bourne, *Queen Anne's Navy in the West Indies*, New Haven, 1939.
6. For a summary, see R. Pares, 'Merchants and Planters', *Economic History Review*, Supplement 4, Cambridge, 1960, pp. 21–3.
7. Labat, *Nouveau voyage*, I, pp. 125–7.
8. *Ibid.*, II, pp. 351–63.

9. *Ibid.*, I, pp. 93–7. The indigo business is further described in *La commerce de l'Amérique par Marseille*, 2 vols, Avignon, 1764, I, pp. 353–9.

10. A *Survey of Jamaica* made about 1670 listed forty-five holdings of 1,000 acres or more. Public Record Office, London, C. O. 138/1, pp. 61–79. Sir Martin Noell, the London merchant, got an initial grant of 20,000 acres; but this was exceptional. Pares, 'Merchants and Planters', p. 59.

11. S. L. Mims, *Colbert's West India Policy*, New Haven, 1912, pp. 273–9. Pares, p. 23.

12. R. Pares, *War and trade in the West Indies*, Oxford, 1936, pp. 329–32.

13. G. Debien, *La société coloniale au XVIIe et XVIIIe siècles*, Paris, 1953.

14. G. Debien, *Les engagés pour les Antilles, 1634–1715*, Paris, 1952, pp. 145–8, and chapter 12.

15. For the complicated story of the English and French slaving companies see K. G. Davies, *The Royal African Company*, London, 1957, and Gaston-Martin, *L'Ère des négriers*, Paris, 1931.

16. R. Pares, *A West India Fortune*, London, 1950, pp. 229–31.

17. This point is argued in K. G. Davies, 'The origin of the commission system in the West India trade', Royal Historical Society, *Transactions*, fifth series, vol. II, 1952, pp. 89–107. For a summary of the whole question, see Pares, 'Merchants and Planters', pp. 33–7.

18. Labat, *Nouveau voyage*, I, pp. 309, 319, 338–9.

19. G. L. Beer, *The old colonial system*, New York, 1933, pp. 13 ff. Percentages are by value.

20. For a summary of the demographic evidence see K. F. Helleiner in *The Cambridge Economic History of Europe*, vol. IV, 1967, pp. 40–58.

21. J. T. Adams, *Provincial Society 1690–1763*, New York, 1927, pp. 2 ff.

22. Pares, 'Merchants and Planters', p. 21.

23. Adams, *Provincial Society*, p. 9.

24. Pares, 'Merchants and Planters', p. 35.

25. Negro slaves were employed on big farms in the Narragansett area, chiefly looking after cattle and horses, or in household service; but their numbers were never large. L. Greene, *The negro in colonial New England 1620–1776*, New York, 1942, p. 76.

26. J. J. Malone, *Pine trees and politics*, Seattle, 1964, p. 10.

27. The best analysis of the trade is R. Pares, *Yankees and Creoles*, London, 1956.

28. The most comprehensive account is L. A. Harper, *The English Navigation Laws*, New York, 1939.

29. Sir William Petty, for one: 'For trade will endure no other laws *nec volunt res male administrari*', *The Petty–Southwell Correspondence*, 1676–1687, p. 59.

30. The 1699 Act against pirates was a clear example of such an exercise of parliamentary authority. *Calendar of State Papers, Colonial*, 1700, pp. 132, 164.

31. The details of the 1696 reforms are summarised in C. M. Andrews, *The colonial period of American history*, 4 vols, New Haven, 1938, I, pp. 160 ff.

32. R. C. Harris, *The seigneurial system in early Canada*, Madison, 1966.

4

The Indian Ocean

On 7 August 1720, the English East India Company's ship *Cassandra* was taken by pirates off northern Madagascar. The news created a considerable stir; the *Cassandra* was a ship of force, pierced for forty guns, and she carried a valuable cargo. The pirate ships which took her were also powerful vessels. They had originally fitted out at New Providence; but in 1718 Woodes Rogers, of privateering and circumnavigating fame, had taken over the government of the Bahamas and had inaugurated a policy of hanging pirates instead of harbouring them. Piracy knew no boundaries; many had removed to remote bases in Madagascar, where there was no government, native or European, capable of driving them out, and where they could ambush merchant vessels coming in, like the *Cassandra*, to wood and water.

The captain of the *Cassandra* and a few other survivors, after a fierce but vain resistance, escaped ashore, and eventually reached Bombay, where they made depositions. The pirate squadron, now including the *Cassandra*, sailed on to the Laccadive islands; it would be interesting to know who navigated them through that maze of atolls, which was not properly charted until more than a hundred years later. In the Laccadives, they captured an English 'country-ship' – a private trader – which they took into Cochin to refit. At the Dutch factory in Cochin they sold some of their loot and bought stores and provisions; and also got information of a powerful squadron sent out from Bombay in pursuit of them, under the command of Macrae, late captain of the *Cassandra*. Macrae actually sighted them off Tellicherry, but failed to come up with them. They made for Bourbon (Réunion), where they took a large Portuguese Indiaman, homeward-bound with the retiring governor general from Goa on board. This functionary had with him a substantial fortune derived from private trade during his period of office, some of it in diamonds. In order to dispose of these to the best advantage the captors discussed a visit to the Red Sea ports; but after a short and convivial stay at Bourbon (where the French authorities, having perhaps no choice, allowed them generous facilities) they decided instead to return to the West Indies.

This was probably a commercial as well as a strategic decision; the West Indies offered a good market for Indian cotton goods, and there might have been a flourishing direct trade, had not mercantile organisation and rules discouraged it. Our pirates paused only at Delagoa Bay, where they destroyed a Dutch trading post and took a Dutch ship, at anchor in the bay loading slaves. The *Cassandra* was last reported in 1723, lying off Portobello, where Taylor, the pirate leader, was said to be negotiating, through the captain of an English man-of-war, for a pardon. This being refused, he obtained a Spanish commission, and probably proved a valuable recruit to the *guarda-costa* service. The dividend to his ship's company, after the deduction of expenses and of very large payments to the Spanish authorities, was said to be £1,200 a man. As for Macrae, he became governor of Fort St George at Madras, served there for six years with distinction, and then retired to his native Ayrshire with £100,000 acquired by private trade.

Piracy was a commonplace in the Indian Ocean, as in most waters where there was shipping worth robbing; the *Cassandra* episode was one of hundreds. It was one of the most notorious, however, and its details happen to be well documented.[1] It is of interest not only as a yarn, but as a convenient illustration of the peculiarities of European commercial enterprise in the Indian Ocean in the early eighteenth century. One striking feature is the calmness with which piracy was accepted as part of the normal commercial scene. Ever since Vasco da Gama, Europeans had operated in the Indian Ocean as predators as well as traders. European groups reacted angrily against attacks on their own ships, as the Bombay Marine did in the *Cassandra* case; but the officials of trading factories were rather pleased than otherwise when their competitors were plundered, and they had no hesitation in doing business with pirates. The suppression of piracy in general was in almost everyone's interest, but it was nobody's specific business. Strong and well-organised on land, the Asian powers on the shores of the Indian Ocean lacked fighting strength at sea. None of them possessed a navy capable of facing, on the high seas, ships such as the *Cassandra*'s captors. Indeed, the Mughal government in India expected the European trading companies, in return for their privileges, to help in patrolling coastal waters against local corsairs. This was one of the reasons for the existence of the East India Company's little private navy, the Bombay Marine. The Marathas, in their long and stubborn resistance against Mughal power, operated a considerable fleet, based on Gheria. The Maratha vessels were light lateen-rigged *gallivats*, not designed for operating on the high seas, but extremely formidable, because of their numbers and their speed, in coastal waters. They might be likened to the tough ponies used by the Maratha cavalry ashore. They preyed upon Mughal and European shipping alike, and at times virtually dominated the Konkan coast, from Cutch to Cochin. At the time of the *Cassandra*'s capture the Maratha fleet was commanded by the famous admiral, Kanhoji Angré. For a time Kanhoji occupied Khanderi Island, only sixteen miles off Bombay, and demanded tolls from all shipping passing through what he claimed to be Maratha territorial waters. Neither the Mughal's maritime vassals, the Sidis of Janjira, nor his European clients, achieved much against Kanhoji; nor could the Maratha princes control him. He made himself, in effect, an independent ruler. He and his sons and grandsons defeated or eluded English, Dutch and Portuguese punitive expeditions for over half a century; until 1756, in fact, when Gheria was taken by a combined force under Clive and Watson, in alliance with the Peshwa against his over-mighty vassal.[2] A somewhat similar situation was created in the Bay of Bengal by *Feringhi* corsairs, of mixed Portuguese and Arakanese origin, operating from Sandwip Island near Chittagong;[3] while on the western shore of the Ocean, the Imams of Muscat, having in 1698 expelled the Portuguese from Mombasa and occupied Quiloa and Zanzibar, maintained a corsair kingdom which preyed upon shipping entering the Red Sea and the Persian Gulf, and defied the attempts of the Persian government, with Portuguese help, to dislodge them.[4] Seagoing traders, menaced by these various predators, had to look after themselves as best they could. Trade in the Indian Ocean was dangerous; Europeans, in order to participate in it profitably, needed well-armed ships and, in some places, fortified, well-manned factories. These had to be provided by the participants in the trade, and paid for out of the proceeds.

Who were the participants? At the beginning of the eighteenth century, trade by the sea route round the Cape was being conducted by one government, four or five chartered companies, and an unknown number of more or less clandestine 'interlopers'. The government was that of Portugal, where the right of trading from Europe to the East was still a royal monopoly. Every year two or three ships left Lisbon on crown account for Goa, on the west coast of India. Goa was a Portuguese possession, acquired in a time of political confusion in India nearly two hundred years earlier. Its governor general, defended by a small garrison of mercenaries from the slums and prisons of Lisbon, ruled over a territory of several hundred square miles, inhabited chiefly by Luso-Indians, Catholic Christians of mixed descent, of Portuguese speech and with Portuguese names. This European colony was, and was to remain, unique in India. From Goa, all the Europeans on the coast recruited *lascars* to man their ships and *topasses* to serve their guns. The other Portuguese footholds in India were the 'Province of the North', the sixty-mile stretch of coast from Bassein, just north of Bombay, to Damão; and the harbour town of Diu in Gujerat, with its immediate hinterland. Diu was heavily fortified – its massive walls still stand – but much decayed, its roadstead more frequented by pirates than by traders. The Province of the North was commercially prosperous, but constantly threatened by land or sea, by one or other of the Maratha rulers; most of it, all except Damão, was finally conquered by the Peshwa's armies in 1739. The stations at Cochin and in Ceylon had been lost to the Dutch in the seventeenth century. Bombay had been ceded in 1661 to Charles II as part of a bid to secure English support against the Dutch. The Portuguese presence in India presented, then, a spectacle of decay; but it was not negligible. Portuguese was still the *lingua franca* of most commercial intercourse in which Europeans took part; every trading factory had a Portuguese 'linguist' on its strength and Portuguese dictionaries as an essential part of its equipment – the Bombay factory in 1722 had two hundred of them in stock.[5]

Goa was exceptional, a long-lived but precarious relic of six-teenth-century audacity. Most European governments in the seventeenth century had shown a prudent reluctance to assume direct responsibilities of this kind. They drew a clear distinction, in this respect, between the Indies of the East and the Indies of the West. All the Americas were actually or potentially within the jurisdiction of one or another European power. The Indian Ocean countries were actually or potentially within the jurisdiction of Asian rulers. Some of these rulers were extremely formidable, sovereigns of great and civilised empires. European governments had neither the will nor the resources to challenge these mighty princes, or even to treat regularly with them on equal terms. They had no wish to become involved in difficult and possibly dangerous political exchanges in the East. On the other hand, they wished to encourage their subjects in the profitable pursuit of Eastern trade, and to draw an indirect profit themselves. Governments, therefore, issued charters, conferring upon selected and accredited groups of merchants such privileges as lay within their power to grant, and leaving to them the conduct of affairs in the East. The chartered company was a device whereby a European government, by granting a monopoly of a particular trade to a particular group among its subjects, could delegate to that group the duties of administration, jurisdiction and defence. In this spirit Charles ii, having received Bombay in full sovereignty as part of his wife's dowry, promptly handed the place over (at a price, of course) to the East India Company. In the later seventeenth century the profits of Eastern trade were so large that a company engaged in it could afford to perform these duties, make substantial payments or loans to its home government on occasions such as renewals of charter, and still pay acceptable dividends to its shareholders. Such a company exercised in fact, and might even claim in form, a delegated sovereignty.[6] The company, not the government, negotiated with Asian rulers. The company provided protection on the high seas and (if need be) ashore, and could, on its own responsibility, make local war or peace; it might occasionally receive diplomatic or naval support in time of war against other European powers, but usually, and always in time of European peace, it employed its own armed ships and its own troops to protect its factories and its trade. The company maintained discipline and exercised jurisdiction, not only over its own servants, but over all persons of its own nationality in the East. The company, in its own name, acquired by lease, purchase or concession, such land as it needed for the conduct of its business. Further, if it operated outside the jurisdiction of any of the larger kingdoms and found itself dealing with weak or financially irresponsible princelings, it might be tempted to acquire territory by foreclosure or open conquest. In such circumstances the step from trade to dominion might be short.

Among the various corporations trading to the East under European charters in the early eighteenth century, two stoood out as giants of their kind: the *Vereenigde Oost-Indische Compagnie* and the United Company of Merchants of England trading to the East Indies. Both were joint-stock companies, their stocks purchasable on the open market. Their constitutions, however, differed considerably. The Dutch company bore, throughout the two centuries of its existence, the marks of its early seventeenth-century origin in an amalgamation of half a dozen independent concerns.[7] It was composed of six provincial 'chambers', each of which traded with its own capital, and distributed to its shareholders the corresponding share of the total profits. Shareholders, as such, had virtually no say in the conduct of affairs. It was not to be expected that a great corporation, probably the biggest commercial concern in Europe, intimately associated with government both as a financial partner and as an auxiliary in war, should risk entrusting important decisions to the chances of democratic voting. The directors of each chamber were appointed by the local municipal or provincial government; and the chambers, in proportion to their size, appointed the seventeen general directors. The 'Heeren XVII' formed the central management of the company; they controlled the administration of factories and territory in the East and the marketing in Amsterdam of the goods which the company imported; they handled the company's relations with the States General; and they laid down from year to year the general trading policy which the several chambers executed. The chambers owned and operated ships; the Heeren XVII decided in broad terms how the ships should be freighted and employed. The organisation by chambers was obviously cumbersome; it made decision-making difficult and accurate overall accounting impossible; it worked only because of the predominance of Amsterdam over all the others. On the other hand, it made the company a national concern in which all the major cities played a part.

The English company, by contrast, had been, ever since its foundation in 1600, very much a London affair, controlled by a small group of City financiers. At the end of the seventeenth century its exclusiveness, its obvious prosperity and its good relations with the Stuart kings, had together nearly proved its undoing; a powerful group of jealous outsiders in 1698 succeeded in getting themselves incorporated as a rival company, with a parliamentary charter, as opposed to the royal charter of the 'old' company. For several years there had been two companies; not until 1709 were differences composed and the 'United' company safely launched.[8] In order to retain the chartered privileges of its seventeenth-century predecessor, this body had had to offer immense loans to the government, and in consequence had embarked on its trading activities without any working capital.[9] It nevertheless became (together with the Bank of England and the South Sea Company) the centre of a developing financial market in London and of the government's political and financial interest there. It was also the biggest and most complicated trading organisation in the country. Its constitution provided for a court of proprietors, comprising all shareholders owning a qualifying amount of stock. The proprietors elected the twenty-four directors, who formed the central management and who ran the company's affairs through an intricate system of overlapping committees. In practice, as before, a relatively small group of major stockholders, prominent City personages, were usually able to control the court of proprietors and to retain the 'direction' in their own hands or in those of their friends. They did this partly by personal influence, partly by collusive 'splitting' of stock to create voting power when necessary,[10] partly by enlisting the support of the 'shipping interest' within the company. By the early eighteenth century the company no longer owned the ships it employed; it chartered them. The ships were designed for the trade and could not be used economically in any other. The 'managing owners' to whom they belonged, the ship-builders who constructed them, the captains who commanded them, were almost all proprietors of company stock. They formed a strong vested interest, opposed to change; they could be relied on to support the 'direction' in the court, so long as the directors pursued a conservative policy. This the directors were, in any event, usually disposed to do. They knew that the charter, on which the company's very existence depended, required periodical renewal; they had recently been reminded that renewal might depend on parliamentary scrutiny. Their obvious policy was to avoid public controversy; to keep down expenses, especially administrative and military expenses; to concentrate on well-tried, reliable lines of trade; to keep the shareholders quiet, by good but not extravagant dividends; above all, to co-operate unobtrusively with the government at home, in order to preserve the company's privileges of delegated sovereignty and commercial monopoly abroad.

Both these great companies were monopolists, the one of Dutch, the other of English trade east of the Cape of Good Hope; but too much should not be made of the term. They competed with one another, in buying Eastern goods wherever their operations overlapped, and in selling them in the European market. They competed with several other similar, though smaller, European companies. They competed with European 'interlopers'; and they competed with their own servants.

None of the other European East India companies operating in the Indian Ocean at the beginning of the eighteenth century was in a position to offer very serious commercial competition. A Danish company had existed more or less continuously, with several reorganisations, since 1616, and had established factories in India; but it was a small concern, with inadequate capital backing. In 1727 an attempt was made to attract the shareholders of the suspended Ostend Company; but after protests from the English,

Dutch and French governments, the proposal was dropped. From the 1730s the company found a profitable line of business in Chinese tea, much of which was smuggled into England.[11] In the Indian Ocean area its rôle was always minor. The *Compagnie des Indes orientales*, established by Colbert, with powerful royal backing, in 1664, was to all appearance a more formidable affair; but in the first half-century of its life its financial situation was precarious. The investing public in France failed to respond to government propaganda, and the company's capital was never adequate to its task. Much of it was provided by the government, and the government largely directed the company's policy, often towards ends which were not strictly commercial. The king imposed upon the company a considerable colonising effort in Madagascar, and an expensive series of naval cruises designed to 'show the flag' in the East, in addition to the central task of establishing a commerce full of risks in itself. In the first decade of the eighteenth century, the privileged position of the French within the Spanish empire drew much French commercial capital away from the Indian Ocean and into the Pacific coast trade. In 1719 the company was absorbed into the vast and comprehensive *Compagnie des Indes*, by whose operations Jean Law hoped to restore the finances of France. It slipped into bankruptcy with the rest of the Law system in 1720. In 1723 it was re-established and reorganised; even then the government persisted in a logical but impracticable marriage of Eastern and Western trade. The *Compagnie des Indes* was to trade to India and the Far East, to West Africa and the West Indies; it was to operate the *ferme des tabacs* and the beaver monopoly; and was to be responsible for the development of Louisiana, including the Illinois territory – this last a heavy military and administrative burden. It got rid of these American responsibilities in 1731. It was still short of capital for its Eastern projects, and incurred large debts in building up its fleet and in constructing dock facilities at Lorient; but by the mid-1730s it was at last able to develop a genuine commercial policy of its own in India, and to become a serious competitor of the English and the Dutch.[12]

For both English and Dutch, interloping presented a far more troublesome problem than the competition of other national

companies. Straightforward, undisguised interloping – direct
trade between Europe and the East by private merchants in
defiance of company monopoly – was a peculiarly English problem; or rather, British, since many of the culprits were Scots. The
company could, and sometimes did, seize interloping ships; but it
was not always physically possible, nor (since interlopers had
powerful friends) always politically expedient, to proceed in this
high-handed fashion. The customs could seize incoming interlopers' cargoes; but some preventive officers were venal, some incompetent, some lazy; smuggling was never very difficult. The
Dutch company suffered less from direct interloping, partly because of its ruthlessness in seizing offenders in Eastern waters,
partly because of its decentralised organisation in the Netherlands.
Dutch private merchants found it more profitable to become
shareholders in one of the chambers, or to smuggle goods in
company ships, than to fit out ships themselves for open interloping.[13] Interlopers, however, could assume many disguises.
They could, for example (despite repeated legislation forbidding
the practice) register their ships under foreign flags. The celebrated Ostend Company, chartered by the Emperor Charles VI in
1722, was little more than an organised 'flag of convenience'.[14] Its
members were a miscellaneous collection of private traders, some
of whom had been operating out of Ostend for years. There were
Flemings, Dutch, English, French, Irish and Scots (including
Jacobite exiles) among them. The English formed the largest
group and most of the ships were English built.[15] Both in England
and in the Netherlands the competition of traders sheltered by this
organisation caused great alarm, both on commercial and on political grounds. The English, Dutch and French governments all
brought strong diplomatic pressure to bear on the emperor, who
agreed in 1727 to suspend the company's charter, and in 1731 to
cancel it. Some of the English members returned to England with
negotiated pardons, for which they paid large sums in indemnity
to the English company; some found, in the following year, a congenial protector in the newly created Swedish East India
Company;[16] some carried on their interloping business privately
as before.

The East India companies had to face competition not only

from one another and from interlopers, but from their own servants. These great corporations, like the governments which chartered them, did not, and could not, pay adequate salaries to the people they employed. Company servants were paid pittances in cash and made their livings – their fortunes, if they were lucky and lived long enough – through their opportunities for private trade. This was not an abuse (though it led to abuses); it was the custom of the time, and in any event it could not have been prevented. In the English company the space allotted for private trade in the early eighteenth century was limited, in theory, to about five per cent of the total tonnage, out or back. The captain naturally got the lion's share; but every man in a company ship, from captain to cabin boy, had his 'privilege', his allotted space, according to his rank, for goods which he might purchase at one end and sell at the other, on his private account.[17] 'Privilege' space inevitably encroached on company space. Similarly, the staffs of the European factories throughout the East supplemented their token salaries by trading locally on their own account; inevitably, they were tempted, in purchasing goods for their employers, to behave as middlemen rather than as agents. All the East India companies, therefore, were served abroad by men whose interests did not wholly coincide with those of the shareholders who nominally employed them, but who needed the cover and protection which the companies gave to their private operations. In the first half of the eighteenth century these two sets of interlocking interests worked together in reasonable harmony. In the second half of the century, in the English company particularly, they diverged. The company was to be dragged by its servants into courses which most of its shareholders greatly disliked.

In the early eighteenth century the principal object of all the European companies operating in the Indian Ocean was still straightforward trade; more specifically, the purchase, the carriage to Europe, and sale there, of 'India' goods: cotton 'piece goods', raw and manufactured silk, pepper, saltpetre, coffee, tea, chinaware, and sundry drugs and spices. Not all these were products of countries bordering the Indian Ocean. Tea and chinaware came from China and Japan; and the finer spices (except for cinnamon, which grew in Ceylon) were products of small islands in the Malay archipelago. Pepper was grown in many parts of the archipelago and also in Malabar; it was one of the most important articles of the 'Europe' trade – an interesting early example of a commodity which had been a luxury and had become an article of general consumption. Silk also came from many places in the East, but its many varieties and qualities were clearly differentiated. There were different markets, and successive fluctuations of fashion, for China silks, Bengal silks, Persian silks. Coffee, at the beginning of the eighteenth century, meant Arabian coffee, marketed at Beit-el-Faki in the Yemen and shipped from Mocha or Hodeida on the Red Sea.[18] The Dutch governors-general introduced coffee trees into Java, and the first small shipment of Javanese coffee reached the Amsterdam market in 1712.[19] In terms of percentage profit, coffee was one of the most valuable articles of trade at that time, surpassed only by the finer spices. Saltpetre was a product of India, an essential raw material in the armament industry; few Indiamen left homeward-bound without hundreds of thousands of pounds of it, stowed in hundredweight bags immediately above the keel. Saltpetre and sundry other bulky and relatively cheap primary products – raw cotton, rice, sugar – were contemptuously lumped together under the name of 'gruff goods'. The great staple of the 'Europe' trade from India was woven cotton: the hundreds of types, varieties and qualities of cotton cloth, colloquially called 'piece goods', coming from all parts of India, ranging from coarse 'Guineas' for Africa and the West Indies to the fine calicoes and muslins, in high and constant demand in all parts of Europe.

The export to the East of articles of European manufacture was a secondary object of the trade. The difficulty was, and had been ever since Vasco da Gama's day, that very few European products commanded ready sale in the East. Firearms always did; but the wisdom of exporting arms was questionable, and not all Eastern rulers wanted their subjects to buy them. The closing of Japan to foreign trade in the middle of the seventeenth century, for example, may have been due in part to a desire to keep foreign firearms out of the hands of the great feudatories, the *daimyo*.[20] There was a market in India for base metals such as iron, copper, lead; and the English East India Company protected its mercantile 'image' at home – as it was, indeed, required by law to do – by half-hearted attempts to sell English woollens, particularly in Persia. The attempts were never very successful, because the company's woollens were undersold by Turkish merchants importing *via* the Levant. The only certain way of securing cargoes of piece goods and pepper for the 'Europe' ships was by paying for them in cash, preferably silver. The *Cassandra*, when she was taken, was outward-bound for Bombay; she carried £10,000 worth of woollens and £25,000 worth of silver coin. The proportion was typical of such cargoes at the time.[21] The coin was part of the 'investment' for the year, to be spent on the purchase of India goods. The *Cassandra*'s shipment, as it happened, was in ducatoons – those great silver discs of distinguished design and (usually) high purity, minted in the Netherlands expressly for the East India trade. Because of their quality, and the high price of silver in the East, these ducatoons tended to disappear when they reached India, to be hoarded, or else re-coined as rupees of one kind or another. Much more usually, the 'investments' were in Spanish or Mexican coins, piastres or 'reals of eight', or an unsorted mixture sold by weight and commonly known as 'mark reals'.[22] These could always be bought in Cadiz (where all the East India companies maintained agencies) or in Amsterdam; and in the early eighteenth century they were the commonest and most acceptable international currency throughout the East. Whatever the actual coins used, the silver in them came mostly from Mexico. The stream of silver which for many years had set from the West Indies across the Atlantic, circulated in the pools and eddies of European commerce and then flowed out again – some of it – carrying European trade to the East. The volume of the trade (due allowance being made for wars and other crises) fluctuated with the volume of silver production.[23] The pack of West Indian predators which ran down the *Cassandra* had followed a familiar scent.

The East India companies habitually raised the working capital for their annual 'investments' by issuing short-term bonds. With the proceeds they bought the silver (sometimes, in smaller quantities, the gold) which they shipped to the East. There were objections to this way of doing business. The old bullionist complaint, that the East India trade drained away the home countries' 'treasure', had become, by the early eighteenth century, an archaism. There was no acute shortage of bullion; the supply of precious metals, both Mexican silver and Brazilian gold, was increasing; some European countries, England especially (but not France), were turning from a silver coinage to a gold one.[24] There was no compelling reason why silver should not be exported. Nevertheless, it was expensive, and often difficult, to collect the requisite sums in bar or coin, in due time for shipment. The companies' constant endeavour was to reduce their bullion exports, and to acquire in the East itself some of the cash needed to buy 'India' goods for shipment to Europe. One way of doing this was by participation, direct or indirect, in 'country' trade; in trade between one place and another in the East.

'Country' trade, as distinct from the cautious, predictable out-and-back of the 'Europe' trade, was trade by Eastern methods and on Eastern terms; a tramping trade, from port to port, wherever a profit could be made. European ships – ships owned by Europeans, that is, usually, but not necessarily, with European masters, and with lascar crews – had penetrated, by the early eighteenth century, into a great variety of local trades. They constituted a small minority of ships in the Indian Ocean and China Seas; how small, it is hard to say, because native merchants often employed European captains, or freighted their goods in European ships, and *vice versa*; there was every variety of partnership or of competition. But Europeans were to be found conveying pilgrims from north India to Jeddah; shipping piece goods from Surat and Bombay to the ports of the Red Sea and the Persian Gulf, from Madras and the Hugli to the many harbours of the archipelago; horses from Arabia to western India; copper from Japan to Surat, Coromandel and Bengal; raw cotton from Bengal, pepper from Sumatra, sandalwood from Timor, to Macao. They took advantage of local gluts and shortages to enter the inter-island trade in rice. They speculated in bullion. They bought gold in Malaya, in Sumatra and in China (where gold was produced but not coined) and carried it to Manila, where Mexican silver was plentiful and cheap, or to India to be coined into 'pagodas'. Some of the European ships engaged in these activities belonged to chartered companies; others to private merchants operating independently;

others, again, to servants of the chartered companies trading in their private capacities (as Macrae of the *Cassandra* did when he became governor of Madras). There was a marked difference in this matter between the policies of the English and Dutch companies. The Dutch company, at least until 1744, interpreted its monopoly strictly. It employed its own ships in the country trades. It forbade, and tried hard to prevent, participation in those trades by any other Dutch vessels. The English company was content to monopolise the English 'Europe' trade. It rarely interfered with privately owned English vessels in the East, and it allowed its servants a very wide latitude to engage in country trade.[25] Indeed, it encouraged them to do so, by issuing (for a fee, naturally) passes authorising their movements and promising them, in effect, the protection afforded by the company's forts, its armed ships and its prestige.[26] This turned out to be sound commercial policy. The Dutch system certainly ensured, at least in theory, that the profits of country trade went into the company's coffers; but in so diverse and variable a business, the individual trader, with his intimate local knowledge, was more adaptable and in general more efficient than the centrally directed company ship. More than anything else, it was the steady growth of country trade which spread English commercial influence round the shores of the Indian Ocean, largely at the expense of the Dutch. The English company, moreover, found in the private 'concerns' of its servants and in the activities of licensed private traders, an important financial convenience. These gentlemen all, or nearly all, wished to remit their profits to England. They usually did so by purchasing, in India, company bills of exchange, payable in London. In this way they contributed to the annual 'investment' to be laid out in Indian goods, and reduced the company's need to send bullion from England. There was a danger to the company in this: that as time went on it might find itself more and more trading on the 'capitals of its servants', more and more in their debt, less and less able to hold them to account; that it might find itself even maintaining factories in the East, at a loss to its shareholders, for the convenience and profit of its 'servants'.

At the beginning of the eighteenth century these dangers were not yet apparent. A much more obvious danger, not only to the

English but to all the European companies, was the steady decline in the military and administrative efficiency of the Mughal empire, under whose nominal protection most European trade in India was carried on. Aurangzeb was the last Mughal emperor strong enough to insist on the obedience of his major vassals. The last twenty-five years of his long reign were years of almost constant campaigning to assert his authority in the Deccan. After his death in 1707, short reigns and disputed successions undid his work. His *subadars* became, in effect, independent rulers. In the north, the Rajput princes, alienated by religious persecution, renounced their allegiance; in the Deccan, the predatory Marathas raided unchecked. India as a whole was slipping, not for the first time in its long history, into an anarchy of contending principalities. The European companies could no longer appeal with any confidence to the imperial authority for protection against extortionate viceroys, against local raiders, or against one another; they had to look after themselves on land, as they had always done at sea. In the seventeenth century most European business in India had been transacted in the great trading cities such as Surat, where the Mughal authorities would never have allowed foreign fortifications. All the companies trading at Surat maintained open, undefended establishments – the Dutch factory, with a European staff of fifty or sixty, being the largest. The mounting political disorder of the early eighteenth century made this way of conducting business more and more unsafe. Company servants, with increasing emphasis, pointed out to their directors the advantages of concentrating trade in towns which belonged to them, which they could control and fortify.

The English company, as it happened, was potentially well placed in this respect. Bombay had a good harbour and a defensible site. It lay near an important weaving area; and through its subordinate factories, Anjengo and Tellicherry on the southern Malabar coast, it participated also in the pepper trade. Bombay was a much less important place than Surat, but its trade was growing, and Parsi shipowners and shipbuilders were already moving there, attracted by the relative safety which it offered. Madras was an older and bigger establishment, acquired by the company by a loose and obscure agreement of feudal type with the former kingdom of Golconda. Like Bombay, it drew upon a weaving hinterland, and had its own satellite stations at Cuddalore and Masulipatam. It was effectively fortified; and though its harbour was only an open road, it was safe enough during the south-west monsoon. Calcutta was still little more than a village on a mudbank in the Hugli; but it could, and eventually did, become, as its founder Job Charnock foresaw, the key to the Ganges basin, the richest region of all India. The company had established itself there by purchasing the *zemindari* of the neighbouring villages. Fort William, impressive rather than formidable, it was said, was completed in 1716. In 1717 the company secured from the Emperor Farrukhsiyar confirmation and extensions of its possession of these three principal settlements.

The Dutch company's establishments followed a similar pattern, though somewhat less conveniently distributed. The biggest outright Dutch possession in India was Cochin, taken from the Portuguese in 1663. Cochin was a harbour of some importance, a crossroads of Indian Ocean trade, and the outlet of a pepper-producing region. There were other sources of pepper, however, and Cochin and Malabar in general were among the least profitable of Dutch enterprises in the early eighteenth century. Ceylon was also unprofitable. The Dutch held most of the coastal towns, but the king of Kandy still governed the interior. Quarrels with this not inconsiderable ruler constantly interrupted the Dutch collection of cinnamon and areca nuts, which were the island's only important exports. At Trincomalee, the Dutch possessed the best harbour in the eastern Indian Ocean; but Trincomalee had no commercial importance and its strategic value had attracted little attention. Its hinterland was a jungle, and since there was no food there it could not easily be made a base for operations, whether naval or commercial. On the Coromandel coast, on the other hand, the Dutch maintained a profitable string of establishments, engaged in collecting piece goods for shipment to Batavia. Most of these were no more than factories; but some were more or less fortified, and the principal station, Negapatam, was a town in Dutch possession, boasting a castle, though a smaller one than Fort St George at Madras.[27] Similarly in Bengal and Bihar: there were Dutch factories, purely trading establishments, at Kasimbazar, centre of the Bengal silk trade, and at Patna; and a fortified factory at Chinsura on the Hugli near Calcutta.

The French company, relatively a newcomer in India, possessed Pondicherry, a small town on the Coromandel coast, obtained by treaty with a local ruler. This was the only outright possession of the company in India at the turn of the century and it remained the administrative centre. The Malabar village which became Mahé was not seized and fortified until the 1720s. Factories were maintained in the familiar areas of European trade: at Surat; at Calicut on the Malabar coast and Masulipatam on the Coromandel coast; and at Chandernagore on the Hugli above Calcutta.

The principal European companies trading to India in the early eighteenth century, then, all possessed small towns and scraps of territory, and each, in addition, maintained trading factories up and down the peninsula. In main commercial centres such as Surat, each company had its own establishment. Most of the territorial possessions were, to a greater or less extent, fortified or in process of fortification. Each principal fort was the capital of a little local commercial empire. From India tentacles of trade stretched across the Indian Ocean. Europeans traded and competed at Gombroon (Bandar Abbas) in Persia; at Mocha on the Red Sea; at Bussorah at the head of the Persian Gulf. Besides these outlying factories, each company possessed also its way-stations, its ports of call for wood, water and provisions on the way to India. The Dutch had their prosperous little colony at the Cape, one of the very few European colonies of settlement outside the Americas, where European farmers produced food for sale to passing ships. The English company was less fortunate or less far-sighted; the only staging point in its possession was the lonely island of St Helena in the South Atlantic, which, because of the peculiarities of the trade wind, was useless on the outbound passage. The French possessed Bourbon (Réunion) – where, it will be remembered, the *Cassandra*'s captors found congenial shelter – and in 1721 they occupied Mauritius, abandoned by the Dutch, and re-named it Île-de-France.

The little forts on the Indian coasts, the scattered outposts on the ocean approaches, obviously had a strategic value; their possessors might use them to bring political and military pressure upon minor Indian rulers or upon European competitors. In the early eighteenth century, however, this was a subordinate consideration. The forts and outposts existed chiefly for the protection and support of trade. The companies were still primarily commercial concerns. They traded, as far as possible, peaceably; to outward appearance, they traded profitably; certainly they paid out handsome dividends in normal years – probably, in the Dutch case at least, excessive dividends.[28] Their directors complained from time to time that administrative and military expenses were eating into the profits, and warned their servants against incurring further charges; nobody had tried seriously to persuade them that political dominion in India might itself be an important source of profit. In the vastness of India none of their activities counted for very much; they were all operating, politically and commercially, on the fringe of Indian life. They were not yet ready to make India their battleground.

NOTES

1. Most of the documents (including the *Cassandra*'s own papers, probably landed at Cochin) found their way into the Dutch archives. *Algemeen Rijkarchief*, The Hague: *Koloniaal Archief*, 1841 and 1907. The story occupies a prominent place in Johnson's *History of the Pirates*, where R. L. Stevenson found some of his ideas. It is related in detail in J. Biddulph, *The pirates of Malabar*, London, 1907, pp. 134–60.

2. The best account of these local naval wars is in C. R. Low, *History of the Indian Navy*, 2 vols, London, 1877.

3. A Toussaint, *Histoire de l'Océan Indien*, Paris, 1961, pp. 145–6.

4. See R. Coupland, *East Africa and its invaders*, Oxford, 1936.

5. Holden Furber, *Bombay Presidency in the early eighteenth century*, New York, 1965, p. 2.

6. An early explicit claim to this effect was made by Sir Josiah Child, in opposing the establishment of a court of Vice-Admiralty at Bombay. J. Bruce, *Annals of the East India Company*, London, 1810, II, p. 592.

7. The standard authority on this complicated arrangement is G. C. Klerk de Reus, *Geschichtlicher Ueberblick der Administrativen, Rechtlichen und Finanziellen Entwicklung der Niederländisch Oostindischer Compagnie*, Batavia, 1894.

8. For a detailed discussion of these developments see W. R. Scott, *The constitution and finance of English, Scottish and Irish joint stock companies to 1720*, 3 vols, Cambridge, 1910–12, II, pp. 150 ff.

9. According to James Mill, 'The vast advance to government, the place of which they feebly supplied by credit, beggared the English Company and ensured their ruin from the first.' *The History of British India*, 10 vols, London, 1858.

10. On this device, and other details of the internal politics of the company, see Lucy C. Sutherland, *The East India Company in eighteenth century politics*, Oxford, 1952, *passim*.

11. L. Dermigny, *La Chine et l'Occident, 1719–1833*, 3 vols, Paris, 1964, I, pp. 180 ff.

12. *Ibid.*, I, pp. 155 ff. For a general account of the company, see H. Weber, *La compagnie française des Indes*, Paris, 1904.

13. K. Glamann, *Dutch Asiatic Trade 1620–1740*, Copenhagen, 1958, p. 9.

14. R. de Roover, 'L'organisation administrative et commerciale de la Compagnie d'Ostende', *Bulletin d'Études et d'Informations de l'Institut supérieur de commerce St Ignace*, Antwerp, 1934, XI, pp. 659–81.

15. N. Laude, *La Compagnie d'Ostende et son activité coloniale au Bengale*, Brussels, 1944, pp. 225–35.

16. Dermigny, *La Chine et l'Occident*, I, pp. 173 ff.

17. For the English company, the rules in force at the beginning of the eighteenth century, as laid down in the court books (the directors' minutes) are summarised in Bal Krishna, *Commercial Relations between India and England 1601–1757*, London, 1924, pp. 160–2. In the course of the century the directors resigned themselves to the inevitable and acquiesced in various expansions of the officers' privilege; but the later regulations say nothing about seamen. See W. Milburn, *Oriental Commerce; containing a geographical description of the principal places in the East Indies . . . with their Produce, Manufactures and Trade . . .*, 2 vols, London, 1813, II, p. 126. The privilege system, as it had developed by the end of the century, is admirably summarised in C. N. Parkinson, *Trade in Eastern Seas 1793–1813*, Cambridge, 1937, pp. 200 ff.

18. Glamann, *Dutch Asiatic Trade*, pp. 183 ff.

19. *Ibid.*, pp. 207 ff.

20. Dermigny, *La Chine et l'Occident*, I, p. 119.

21. *Koloniaal Archief 1841*, fols 119–26. See Furber, *Bombay Presidency*, p. 5. On the proportions of bullion in the outward cargoes of English Company ships in the early eighteenth century, see Bal Krishna, *Commercial Relations*, pp. 216 ff., and Dermigny, *La Chine et l'Occident*, II, p. 689. M. Dermigny summarises in tabular form the changing proportions of goods to money throughout the century, and distinguishes between the India and China trades.

22. Dermigny, *La Chine et l'Occident*, II, pp. 727–30: some examples of individual shipments, p. 729 n. 4. See also T. Dasi, *Estudio de los Reales de a Ocho*, 2 vols, Valencia, 1950.

23. Dermigny, *La Chine et l'Occident*, II, p. 744.

24. A. E. Feavearyear, *The pound sterling, a history of English money*, Oxford, 1931, p. 139.

25. See, for a statement of company policy in this matter, Furber, *Bombay Presidency*, p. 26.

26. *Ibid.*, p. 10, for an example of such a pass.

27. The Coromandel establishments were described in accurate detail by a late-seventeenth-century traveller: D. Havart, *Op en Ondergang van Coromandel*, Amsterdam, 1963. See also: T. Raychaudhury, *Jan Company in Coromandel*, The Hague, 1962.

28. For a brief summary of English and Dutch dividends, see Bal Krishna, *Commercial Relations*, pp. 172–5.

5

The East Indies and the China Sea

The conduct of the various European corporations trading in the East at the beginning of the eighteenth century was determined in large measure by the character of the Eastern states in whose territory they operated. The authority of the Ottoman, Persian, Mughal and Chinese empires still commanded European respect. If the Mughal power in India was showing signs of decay, it was nevertheless strong enough to suppress any European attempt at armed aggression. As recently as 1600, the English company had been reminded of their dependence on Mughal favour. An attempt to seize Chittagong, and to use it as a territorial base for trade in Bengal, had ended in humiliating defeat. The authority of the emperor and of his major feudatories also set limits to armed conflict between one European group and another; Europeans might fortify their factories to defend their property, but active rivalry between them was confined to commercial competition and to insignificant local bickering. Most of the commercial and territorial concessions enjoyed by the companies in various parts of India depended on imperial *firmans*, which were themselves conditional on restrained behaviour. In a less systematic, less highly organised fashion, similar commercial relations were maintained in the Burmese kingdoms and in Siam, by one or other European group. These kingdoms welcomed European traders, but sometimes exacted a price in the form of naval assistance.[1] Japan was more aloof: the government there permitted only one European group, the Dutch company, to trade in its territory, and that in only one harbour, Deshima, off Nagasaki. From time to time it restricted the goods which might be exported. As for China, European trade there was in its infancy. It depended on imperial permission, narrowly limited and revocable. The conduct of European supercargoes towards the Chinese authorities was necessarily one of wary and ceremonious respect. In general, in all the major trading areas of Asia accessible by sea, save only one, where Europeans traded at all, they did so by the permission of the rulers and on conditions which those rulers laid down.

The one exception was the Malay archipelago: that immense area of shallow sea and fertile, mountainous islands, extending in a majestic curve from Sumatra to the Philippines. A hundred years earlier, when the English and the Dutch first entered those seas to challenge a long-standing Iberian monopoly, the East Indian islands had been considered the most attractive area, commercially speaking, in all the East; much more so than India. They produced a great range of gums, metals, drugs and spices. The Moluccas, Amboina and the Banda Islands, at the eastern end of the chain, were the sole source of the most valuable spices used in Europe: cloves, nutmeg and mace. Pepper, a much commoner commodity but still a highly profitable article of trade, grew in most of the islands, Java and Sumatra being the chief producers. Spices were not the only commercial attraction of the area for European traders. There was gold in Sumatra; and Perak in Malaya was one of the few known sources in the world of tin, an essential ingredient of brass and bronze, and therefore in high demand in India, together with copper from Japan, to make guns for Aurangzeb's wars. Spices, nevertheless, were the main attraction. Cloves and nutmeg, cheap enough in their places of origin, could be brought to account in Europe at a profit of thousands per cent. The European market, however, could absorb only a limited quantity of these substances. A very little buyers' competition in the islands, a very little sellers' competition in Europe, could ruin the whole business. The spice trade, therefore, was the subject not of commercial competition in the ordinary sense, but of ruthless fighting and intrigue between rival monopolies, each of which endeavoured to eliminate its competitors. As it happened, the political situation in the archipelago encouraged rivalry of this kind.

The area as a whole was politically fragmented and unstable.

Most of the principalities were comparatively small. Mataram, which occupied about half of Java, was the largest. Most of them had no fixed rules of succession, and so were constantly plagued by harem intrigues and succession wars. War interfered with trade, and the European companies trading in the area often became involved simply because of a desire for definite and stable decisions. Sometimes their intervention was requested, by one or other party to a dispute. Since many of the rulers were merchant princes, who controlled or monopolised the more valuable exports of their kingdoms, intervention in their succession quarrels could be highly rewarding. Even in the absence of any pretext for intervention, the lesser rulers were vulnerable to naval force or threats of force. Europeans, operating in the area with well-armed ships, constantly sought to exclude other Europeans and secure monopolies for themselves, by bullying, bribing or cajoling the rulers with whom they had regular dealings.

In trade, in commercial war and in armed diplomacy, the Dutch company, with more money and more ships in the area, had outdistanced all European competitors in the course of the seventeenth century. In 1700 the only English factory remaining in the archipelago was at Bencoolen on the west coast of Sumatra, an out-of-the-way place where one or two ships called each year for pepper.[2] The Portuguese still held Timor, a down-at-heel island colony chiefly dependent on the sandalwood trade to China through Macao, now much reduced through uncontrolled cutting of sandalwood trees. In the remote Philippines, the Spaniards still ruled Manila, market for the exchange of Chinese silk for Mexican silver, connected with Mexico and thence with Spain by the slow, plodding annual passage of the Manila galleons. European 'country' shipping, it is true, plied throughout the archipelago, picking up cargoes where it could; and everywhere local trade was carried by a throng of local shipping, Malay, Javanese, Buginese, Chinese, which outnumbered European vessels a hundred to one. Nevertheless, in a hundred years of trading and fighting, the Dutch company had achieved its central purpose. It controlled and in many places monopolised the trades which its directors, rightly or wrongly, considered most profitable and desirable; essentially, the pepper and spice trades.

Dutch control was exercised remotely and indirectly from Amsterdam, directly and more effectively from Batavia, seat of the governor general and council, administrative centre not only of the island trade but of all Dutch trade in the East, and general warehouse where most of the Eastern goods intended for Europe were collected. The Dutch company was unique among the East India companies, in thus centralising its operations on a single Eastern capital. Since Dutch commercial interests extended from Nagasaki to the Persian Gulf, the plan of forcing the greater part of the 'Europe' trade through a single port on the north coast of Java involved much unnecessary sea transport by long, indirect routes,[3] but considerations of convenience were expected to give way to considerations of monopoly. A centralised trade was the easiest to control and protect, and few direct voyages were permitted until well into the eighteenth century. Within the archipelago, the monopolised trades were controlled either by actual territorial possession of the productive areas; or by commercial treaties extorted from defeated or indebted rulers; or by a combination of the two.

Amboina and the Banda Islands were company possessions, having been conquered from the Portuguese in the early seventeenth century. In these islands production was ruthlessly controlled. The company bought, at its own price, what it needed of the spice crop, and compelled the cultivators to destroy the rest, sometimes by cutting down the trees.

Ternate in the Moluccas and Macassar in Celebes were typical examples of treaty-controlled principalities. A riot against the Dutch factors at Ternate in 1650 had led to reprisals, and in 1657 the sultan had been compelled to an agreement whereby, in return for a Dutch pension, he undertook to prohibit the cultivation of spices in all islands subject to him, leaving spice-growing entirely to the islands in the possession of the company. The effect of this subjection had been to increase the wealth and prestige of Ternate's rival, Macassar, whose sultan had for some years defied the Dutch, with arms supplied by Portuguese and English traders. In 1669, however, Macassar had been defeated by a Dutch fleet and a large force of Buginese mercenaries under an enterprising commercial *conquistador*, Cornelis Speelman. The sultan had then agreed to sell all the exportable produce of his kingdom to the company, and to grant the Dutch a monopoly of the import of manufactures and of all Chinese goods. By cutting off his supply of European firearms, the treaty made the sultan, in effect, the company's vassal.

In Java, the commercial and military policy of the company was more complicated. It had to provide not only for the control of trade but also for the defence and the provisioning of Batavia. The most powerful states of central and western Java were the sultanates of Bantam and Mataram, both of which had claimed suzerainty through most of the seventeenth century over Batavia and the territory immediately adjacent. In 1675 the Dutch had intervened in a succession dispute in Mataram, and in 1677 had secured from the victor, Amankurat II, a highly favourable agreement. This treaty closed the harbours subject to Mataram to all other foreigners, granted the Dutch a monopoly of the opium trade, and bound the ruler, the *susuhunan*, to deliver annual consignments of rice at a fixed price. In addition – a significant innovation – it ceded to the company outright the considerable territory of Preanger, stretching from the Batavia boundary south to the Indian Ocean. Bantam's turn had come five years later: in 1680 the son of the reigning sultan had risen against his father and called in the Dutch, who had promptly invaded, driven out the father and enthroned the son. The new sultan undertook in 1684 to sell to the company, at its own price, the whole pepper crop of his kingdom, expelled the English from the factory they had occupied for sixty years, and closed his ports to all foreigners except the Dutch. A small company force pursuing partisans of the old sultan into southern Preanger, was the first European party to penetrate that remote and mountainous region, refuge of dacoits and runaway slaves.

The company was not able immediately to exploit its successes. The interventions in Bantam and Mataram shocked Muslim opinion everywhere. Rumbles of displeasure were heard from distant Delhi. There was talk throughout the islands of holy war. In Java itself, and on the Java Sea, pretenders, prophets and soldiers of fortune, including adventurers from Macassar, Bali and Madura, kept up sporadic fighting, and in 1703 a fresh succession dispute broke out in Mataram.[4] This time, however, the company intervened decisively to place a prince of its own choice on the throne. Patiently, inexorably, it foreclosed on the promises exacted from the Javanese princes. By 1705 the situation was clear. The company controlled the Javanese ports, and monopolised their most lucrative trades; independent rulers throughout the island were in effect its vassals, its pensioners or its subordinate allies; and it possessed in full sovereignty a large and, in part, highly productive territory covering about one-sixth of the area of the island. The first decisive step from trade to dominion had been taken.

The company was ill-equipped for such responsibilities. It was a trading corporation, a firm of shipowners. The governor general its paid agent in the East, exercised, perforce, a wide discretion to fight, negotiate and administer; but his powers were ancillary to the organisation of trade. At his elbow, and second only to him in seniority, stood an executive officer known as the director general of trade. The company's other European servants under the governor general and director general, though often working in fact as directors of factories, commandants of forts or residents at the courts of native princes, all held commercial rank, as merchants, junior merchants or clerks. The Heeren XVII on the whole disliked territorial acquisitions, considered them at best a necessary evil, and were unwilling to support the expense of any but a purely commercial administration in governing them.

The only area of Java directly administered by Dutch officers was the *Ommelanden*, the territory immediately surrounding Batavia. Considerations both of security and of food supply made it necessary to govern this area, along with the town itself, as a European colony. It was policed and administered by a district commissioner known as the *Landdrost*.[5] The courts in the *Ommelanden* administered Dutch-Roman law, as modified since 1642 by the Statutes of Batavia; though from the beginning of the eighteenth century they were supplied also with summarised compendia of Muslim and Chinese law, for application in minor cases where Europeans were not involved. Taxes of European type were collected; Europeans paid direct taxes in money and were the chief contributors under most heads of indirect taxation. Chinese immigrants paid, for permission to settle, a capitation tax known as *hoofdgeld*. Javanese in the *Ommelanden* usually paid no money taxes, but were liable to forced labour, particularly for harbour works. The town of Batavia was by 1700 a place of considerable size, laid out with some attention to amenity, with wide streets and intersecting canals. As tropical stations went, apart from the climate and the malaria, it was a pleasant enough place to live in. Many of the Dutch inhabitants were *blijvers* – permanent residents with no intention of returning to Europe. The place had a reputation for convivial hospitality, and was a favourite with visiting ships' companies; 'a glorious place for punch', according to Woodes Rogers, who put in there during his circumnavigation, and wrote a good description.[6] Arrack distilling, indeed, seems to have been the only considerable industry, in a predominantly commercial population. The population was cosmopolitan, including Dutch, Portuguese, Javanese, other Indonesians, and Chinese. Outside Dutch circles, Portuguese was still the commonest *lingua franca*. The Chinese in Batavia and the *Ommelanden* numbered about 10,000 in 1700. They were respected and encouraged by the Dutch authorities because of their industrious habits and their successful attention to business; but disliked and envied, largely for the same reasons, by the Javanese. Racial discrimination as such was unknown in law and slight in practice. Asians, Chinese especially, frequently served as burgess members of the *College van Schepenen*, the appointed board of officials and burgesses which acted as a municipal council. Mixed marriages were common; though the company discouraged Asians and Eurasians from going to the Netherlands. There was sharp discrimination in law against non-Christians. In Batavia and the *Ommelanden*, the public exercise of any worship except that of the Dutch Reformed Church was forbidden; but the company's officers made little attempt to enforce the rule, and in practice, despite the protests of the ministers, Hindus, Muslims and Chinese enjoyed complete freedom of worship immediately outside the town. The company professed no 'civilising mission', still less a religious one. Its officers were unmoved by the steady extension of Islam, which had long displaced Hinduism everywhere in the archipelago except in Bali, and which was still expanding vigorously in the interiors of the larger islands, at the expense of pagan cults. The clergy whom the company dutifully sent to Batavia, went there to minister to the company's servants, not to proselytise.

Outside the *Ommelanden*, the company accepted much less responsibility for its non-European subjects. It governed its possessions in Java through a loose system of indirect rule. Local administrative duties were entrusted to native 'regents', in theory the company's servants, in fact petty feudatories, vassals of the company as many of them had formerly been of Mataram. Their activities were supervised by a Dutch commissioner, the *Landcommissaris*, who had under his command mounted *maréchaussées* recruited from Balinese and other non-Javanese settlers; but the *Land-commissaris* usually left the regents alone, so long as they did their work and gave no trouble. They ruled as little local tyrants, sure of the company's support if their authority were resisted. Their principal duty was the collection and delivery of produce. The tributes formerly rendered to the sultans of Mataram were paid to the company, under the name of *contingenten*, usually in the form of fixed quantities of pepper, indigo and cotton yarn. In addition to these customary tributes, however, the company pre-empted the whole crop of certain products and required the regents to deliver it. *Leveringen*, forced deliveries, were distinguished in law from *contingenten*; they were regarded as commercial contracts, and the crops collected under them were paid for. In practice, however, the company usually fixed its buying prices so low that *leveringen* became another form of tribute.[7] In the company's own accounts, *contingenten* and *leveringen* were confused with one another and with the proceeds of ordinary trade. The rapid increase in coffee exports from Java in the 1720s and 1730s was achieved largely through ruthless application of the tribute and forced-delivery system in the Preanger districts. Regents and *Land-commissaris*, as well as the company itself, battened on the producers and took their toll of marketable produce on its way to Batavia. Throughout the eighteenth century, according to one calculation, for every *picul* of 126 pounds shipped by the company, the cultivator had to supply between 240 and 270 pounds and was paid for fourteen.[8]

Forced deliveries were characteristic not only of the company's policy in its own possession, but also of the treaties governing the company's relations with the independent princes who still ruled most of Java. The monopoly of pepper exports from Bantam, already mentioned, was typical of such treaties. At each major court the company maintained a 'resident' – ostensibly a diplomatic representative – whose main duty was to insist on the fulfilment of these commercial undertakings, but who also exercised criminal and civil jurisdiction over the company's servants and other Europeans living in the principality. Residents rarely tried to interfere in native administration (except when civil disturbance threatened the company's interests) or in the affairs of non-European foreigners. Their business was to restrain the princes to whom they were accredited from overt hostility against the company, and to see that the stipulated quantities of spices were delivered to the company's godowns.

The Heeren xvii acquiesced, albeit reluctantly and suspiciously, in these arrangements. Their servants in the East advised them that without political control, or at least political influence, profitable trade was impossible. They knew that this advice was not wholly disinterested, but they had neither the local knowledge to refute it nor the effective power to overrule it. They were fighting a losing battle against local political circumstances and against the private interests of their own servants. They were right to be querulous. In the seventeenth century both the company and its servants, at least the more fortunate among them, had prospered. By the early eighteenth century the situation had changed. Company servants, the lucky ones, were prospering much more, and some were making great fortunes; but the company was prospering much less. The whole vast corporation, indeed – so powerful, so ruthless, to all appearances so successful – was losing money.

The total disbursements of the company as a whole began to exceed the total receipts in the middle 1690s. The losses were not at first evident, and did not cause alarm until many years later; deficits did not begin to appear regularly in the Netherland accounts until 1736. The company had immense reserves. Throughout the first two decades of the eighteenth century it paid very high dividends, as high as forty per cent in some years.[9] Neither the shareholders nor the general public had any reason to suspect that all was not well. The accounts, it is true, were always kept secret; but even if they had been made public they would not have revealed the true state of affairs. As a commercial enterprise the company at the beginning of the eighteenth century was remarkably old-fashioned and conservative in its organisation. Its accounting system compared unfavourably with that of the English company, very unfavourably with the meticulous practice of their smaller Danish competitor. The regular Netherland accounts were 'factorage' accounts, profit-and-loss calculations of a relatively primitive kind, quite inadequate for so large a concern.[10] They gave no details of the enormous capital expenditure on ships, forts and factories in the East. They did little more, indeed, than compare the trading outlays and receipts at the central Netherland factory. They did not distinguish between factory and factory in the East; losses at particular places were often not detected for years, and unprofitable factories were hardly ever closed down. The accounts did distinguish, it is true, between commodity and commodity; the annual orders sent to Batavia relating to future shipments were based on these classified *rendementen*. Since, however, the prices of Eastern goods generally were high in Europe in the early eighteenth century, and since invoice prices at Batavia, thanks in part to the forced-delivery system, were low, the Netherland accounts presented a highly optimistic assessment of trading profit; an assessment by which the high dividends regularly paid in those years seemed fully justified.

It was a false assessment. No balance-sheet was ever drawn showing the financial situation of the company as a whole. Such a balance-sheet would have been extremely difficult to compile, because of the distances separating the various factories and the time required to collect all the books. Some of the company's directors saw the importance of comprehensive accounting, and Johannes Hudde, president of the Heeren XVII in the 1680s, had actually drawn up a plan for a balance-sheet which anticipated many practices of modern scientific bookkeeping.[11] Hudde's plan was not followed. If it had been, it would have revealed that Batavia was piling up an enormous deficit. The directors were covering this deficit by their annual consignments, which they raised partly from the profits of their Netherland trade, partly by borrowing, and partly by running down their reserves.[12]

An over-generous dividend policy has sometimes been blamed for the steady deterioration of the company's true financial position in the eighteenth century. The dividends may indeed have been a contributory factor, but they were certainly not a decisive one. Much more important was the mounting expenditure on territorial administration, on the regulation of production, on defence, and on frequent – sometimes unavoidable – interventions in local wars. As administrative costs increased, moreover, Dutch inter-Asian trade (as distinct from 'Europe' trade) slowed down, stagnated, or even in some branches actually declined. The directors were aware of these contractions, though not of their full extent, and usually blamed the dishonesty of their own servants. They had reason for this: as their territorial dominion expanded, so did the opportunities for illicit profit, not only in private trade (there had always been plenty of that) nor only in smuggling, but in direct financial speculation or extortion. A *land-commissaris*, for example, could make a tidy fortune by selling settlement licences to Chinese immigrants. More and more, the interests of the company and the interests of its servants diverged, and the company suffered. There were more deep-seated causes, however, of which the directors were only dimly aware, if at all. The deliberate purpose of Dutch administration, in Java and elsewhere, was to regulate production in the interests of the 'Europe' trade; to depress the prices and limit the production of commodities wanted for that trade; to destroy local trades which competed with the company's. The result was a general impoverishment. The Javanese under Dutch rule were forced to become more and more a race of cultivators. Many a merchant prince and his subjects, finding their old trades hampered or prevented, took to piracy; a vocation not without honour among the fighting maritime peoples of the archipelago, then and now. Impoverishment and piracy together reduced the capacity of the Javanese to purchase either European goods or, more important, the fine cotton textiles which the company brought in from India. The flourishing Dutch trade on the Coromandel coast, so profitable in the late seventeenth century, shrank rapidly in the early eighteenth, partly through the contraction of the Javanese market, partly as a result of Aurangzeb's wars; and though the Dutch company took an initiative in opening trade in Bengal, its business there was overshadowed by that of its chief rivals, the English company and the country traders.

In the early eighteenth century the ominous phrase 'onze competiteurs' occurred more and more frequently in the correspondence of the Heeren XVII, usually in connection with the products of India and Persia, but often also in connection with China. It is curious that the company should have developed the cultivation of coffee in Java – where there were no competitors – and should have sold great quantities of it competitively and profitably in Europe, yet nevertheless should have failed for several crucial decades to appreciate the commercial importance of tea. Tea, at the end of the seventeenth century, was launched on the path which sugar, tobacco, cocoa and coffee had already travelled. From being a scarce novelty, an exotic drug, in Europe, it was becoming an article of daily use, at least among the well-to-do. It was a familiar commodity in Batavia, where for many years past it had been imported from South China in Chinese junks for the use of Chinese residents. As the demand for tea grew in Europe in the late seventeenth century, the company itself had begun to buy some of this tea in Batavia for dispatch to Amsterdam, selling to the junks in return Indonesian products, chiefly pepper and tin. The Batavia authorities did not try, however, to send ships to China, apparently because they were doubtful of their reception there; they discouraged attempts to trade directly to China from Holland, because they feared – rightly, no doubt – that their own trade with the junks would suffer; and they ignored suggestions that tea might be cultivated in Java. When, therefore, towards the end of the seventeenth century, for the first time for more than two hundred years, the commercial door to China was set slightly ajar, the Dutch were among the last to enter.

Such an acknowledged opening, by however narrow a crack, was a striking reversal of long-established policy. The later Ming emperors and their senior officials had set their faces against all foreign contacts, except those which fitted readily into the tra-

ditional tribute system. Trade with Europeans or Japanese was
considered not only unnecessary and distasteful, but potentially
dangerous and subversive of good order. There had been a few
loopholes in the general system of isolation. A tolerated trickle of
trade passed through Portuguese hands at Macao. Chinese ships,
as we have seen, traded at Batavia, and in larger numbers at
Manila. There was also considerable semi-clandestine trade
through the island of Formosa. The Dutch had maintained a trading base there, Factory Zelandia, from 1624, and had virtually
governed the place, in so far as it was governed at all, from 1642.
After the fall of the Ming dynasty and its replacement by the
conquering Manchus in 1644, the isolation of China became, for a
time, even more complete. In the general turmoil, Kuo Hsing Yeh
('Coxinga'), a Ming partisan in Fukien turned pirate and maritime
warlord, established himself in 1662 as independent ruler of Formosa, and expelled the Dutch from the island.[13] The Manchu reaction to Coxinga's depredations was a desperate order to evacuate
whole stretches of coast in Fukien and Kwangtung provinces. The
Portuguese at Macao (who had themselves given some small military support to the last Ming emperor) got themselves exempted,
at great trouble and expense, from this order; but their trade
suffered heavy damage, and they were sternly warned against receiving other European vessels at Macao.[14] The Dutch company
offered naval help against Formosa, in return for permission to
trade, but the offer, after long and baffling local negotiations, was
refused.[15]

The only people to snatch an advantage from this confused
situation were the English, and as usual the initiative came not
from the directors, but from the local agents. Dacres, chief at
Bantam, in 1670 secured from Cheng King, Coxinga's son and
successor, licence to trade in Formosa and later at Amoy, the
island harbour off the Fukien coast, which Cheng King momentarily controlled. Cheng King's protection, it is true, proved short-
lived. In 1680 the armies of the Manchu Emperor K'ang-Hi –
whose long and brilliant reign, following upon a destructive
Fronde, has been likened to that of his contemporary Louis xiv[16]
– took Amoy. In 1683 they crossed the strait and conquered Formosa. The kingdom of the sea which Coxinga had founded came to

an end.[17] Manchu policy, however, was supple and realistic. There was no massacre. Cheng King's son entered the imperial service. The English were not punished, except for the seizure of some of their goods at Amoy in 1680, for their association with pirates. Their trading was tolerated, condoned or ignored; more, in 1684 it was, by implication, legalised. In that year K'ang-Hi, confidently in control, proclaimed the China Sea and the South China ports open to foreign commerce; within, naturally, the conventions of the ancient tribute system. When the emperor thus set the door ajar, the English were, so to speak, already on the doorstep.[18]

The emperor's decree owed nothing to European pressures or requests; trade with Europeans was a relatively minor consideration, a small source of revenue. The immediate effect of the decree was to establish, without loss to Chinese dignity, a limited contact with Japan; not, indeed, by inviting Japanese traders to China – the Chinese were far too suspicious of the *Wako*, the 'robber dwarfs', to allow that – but by sending Chinese ships to Japan. Japan produced copper; Ch'ing China used a copper coinage, and suffered from a scarcity of copper. In 1685, then, a fleet of junks left Amoy, by the emperor's personal order, for Nagasaki, to sell silk and sugar and to buy copper. This was the beginning of a new and flourishing Sino-Japanese trade, which was to reduce the supply of silk to Manila and to compete successfully and damagingly with the Dutch trade in Japanese copper.[19] Incidentally, however, the emperor's decree opened new opportunities for European trade, opportunities of particular interest to the English company. Debarred from Japan, lacking (since their expulsion from Bantam) a convenient base in the archipelago, the English were driven by circumstances, and by the perspicacity of some of their factors in the East, to a direct trade with China; a trade chiefly in a single commodity, tea. In these circumstances, they despatched to Amoy in 1685 the appropriately named HCS *China Merchant*, the forerunner of a great fleet.

The opening of the sea in 1684 did not inaugurate a commercial free-for-all on the China coast. K'ang-Hi's relatively liberal attitude towards trade did not communicate itself to local officials. Duties were high, formalities vexatious, and permission to trade by no means automatic. Almost every ship, on arrival at a Chinese port, became the subject of slow and intricate negotiations, terminable only by means of 'presents'. Sometimes a ship or her cargo was held. In 1689 the *Defence*, sent from Madras to Canton to load sugar for Persia, was unable to extract her cargo from the customs, and her captain endeavoured to recover it by force. In the end he had to leave hurriedly to escape arrest, leaving his supercargo and six hands ashore.[20] The brief emergence of two East India companies in England at the end of the seventeenth century introduced new risks and confusions, but also a rapid increase in activity, since the two competed vigorously for the trade in Chinese tea, silk and porcelain; the Old Company concentrating chiefly upon Amoy, the New upon Canton, where its first China ship, the *Macclesfield*, arrived in 1699. The *Macclesfield*'s supercargo rented a house at Canton – a modest forerunner of the palatial *hong* which the United Company later, in the second half of the century, was to maintain beside the river on Thirteen-Factory Street. The United Company from its inception insisted that the tea trade between China and England was to be monopolised in the terms of its charter, and not left open to country ships. Eight company ships put in to China ports between 1690 and 1696; between 1697 and 1703, twenty.

Naturally the English did not have the field to themselves for long. Regular trade between Moscow and Peking, furs one way, silk the other, was authorised by the Treaty of Nertchinsk in 1689 and actually began in the 1690s; but this was carried on by overland caravan and did not compete directly with the business of the East India Company.[21] French competition was more serious. The first French ship to make the direct voyage, the *Amphitrite*,[22] left Port-Louis in 1698. She belonged to a syndicate, the leading member of which was Jean Jourdan, a prominent financier interested, among many other things, in the manufacture and foreign sale of looking-glasses.[23] The *Compagnie de Chine*, as Jourdan's group came to be styled, characteristically endeavoured to sell such articles of luxury and display in China; unlike the less imaginative East India Company, which exported woollens. French interest in China was imaginative in other ways also. It was intellectual as well as commercial. The French Jesuits, whom K'ang-Hi welcomed at Peking to discuss philosophy and mathematics, were not always promoters of French commercial interests, and indeed in a sense competed with them.[24]

The *Compagnie de Chine* became closely associated with another concern in which Jourdan had an interest: Noël Danycan's *Compagnie de la mer du Sud*, also founded in 1698, to exploit the close and ostensibly friendly relations between France and Spain by trading on the Pacific coast of South America. Most expeditions to China in the early eighteenth century went by way of Cape Horn and paid trading visits to the ports of Chile and Peru on their way to Canton. From Canton they sometimes returned to Brittany round the Cape of Good Hope; two centuries after Magellan, voyages of circumnavigation were beginning to appear commercially practicable. Such voyages could not, however, be regularly maintained. They were too long (three or four years) and too costly. The French company lacked reliable financial support, such as the Bank of England or the Wisselbank could give. It had insufficient working capital, and had to borrow at high rates. Its charter saddled it with an over-generous dividend policy. The French market for tea, unlike the English, which seemed insatiable, was limited. In 1716 the company suffered a severe blow, in an edict prohibiting the import of foreign silk into France. In 1719 it was swept, along with others, into Law's gigantic consortium. French commercial contact with China, then, though certainly not negligible, and though sustained from 1702 onwards by resident factors, was intermittent. Between 1698 and 1715 the English East India companies sent forty-three ships to China,[25] not all, it is true, from England – a few sailed from Madras. In the same years, twenty-three French ships were dispatched to Canton, sixteen of them by way of Peru.[26] There were no French sailings to China between 1715 and 1720.

About 1715 the Ostenders began to appear in the East in considerable numbers. Many of them, as we have seen, were in reality English, Scottish, Irish or Dutch interlopers trading from Ostend. In 1722 they received their charter from the Austrian emperor. From its inception the Ostend Company concentrated much of its energy on the China trade. The authorities at Canton paid no attention to the monopolies claimed by the older companies; they accorded to the Ostenders the same consideration, or lack of consideration, as to all foreigners, and there was no form of pressure by which the English could squeeze the Ostenders out. It is impossible to estimate with any precision the scale of the Ostend company's operations; it was probably nearer to the English than to the French. Much of the tea which came to Europe in Ostend ships was eventually smuggled into England, which explains the alarm of the English East India Company; but the Dutch company also complained in 1726 that the Ostenders were glutting Europe with tea.[27] The Dutch at that time were themselves considering entering the direct trade. When, in 1727, the Austrian emperor was induced by vigorous diplomatic arm-twisting to suspend the Ostend charter, it was the Dutch company which emerged as the chief competitor with the English. For some years past the Heren XVII had complained of the inadequate quantity, the high price and the poor quality of tea sent from Batavia. They also complained of the packing; the tea, they said, deteriorated at sea because it was packed in bamboo baskets, unlike tea direct from China, which came in lead-lined chests. In 1729 they finally made up their minds, and sent a ship, the *Coxhorn*, from the Texel to Canton, carrying 300,000 florins in silver ducatoons and pieces of eight. The voyage was a success, and was followed by others. For a few years Dutch imports of tea actually exceeded English; but the effort of exporting, year by year, bullion or specie on the *Coxhorn* scale, was too great for the company's resources. It was the old problem of all European trade in the East; and the solution was on the familiar lines: an effort to find, in other parts of Asia, goods which the Chinese wanted. From 1734 the company embarked on a determined export drive, to sell Indonesian products in China. Outward-bound ships called at Batavia to pick up goods assembled for them there; they proceeded to Canton, where they sold their cargoes and loaded with tea; and then returned direct to the Netherlands. To overcome objections to the direct trade, the company increased the privilege tonnage allotted to its servants in ships sailing to China; and in the 1740s, departing from a long-established rule, it opened large areas of the 'country trade' to privately owned ships, in its endeavours to pay for its tea. It achieved considerable success, but failed to maintain its momentary lead. The commodities it chiefly tried to sell in China were tin, pepper and Japanese copper. Tin sold well; copper was a failure, because the Chinese could get it more cheaply direct from Japan; as for pepper, the quantity which could be absorbed, even by so vast a market as southern China, was limited. The English company did better, by selling in China the products of Bengal: raw cotton, cotton yarn, and later, despite imperial prohibitions from 1729 onward, opium.

The story of European trade in China in the eighteenth century was one of high profits and vexatious cross-purposes. To Europeans, trade was an essential and highly respectable avocation. Peaceful trade between metropolitan countries (colonies, of course, were another matter) appeared to them a normal and basic feature of international intercourse; to deny such trade in times of peace would be unfriendly, outrageous even. The terms and conditions of trade, the duties to be paid and so forth, were matters for negotiation, important enough to be discussed on occasion between governments, at a high level of diplomatic exchange. To Chinese, at least to educated Chinese, trade, however necessary and profitable, was an occupation socially inferior to agriculture, to craft industry, and of course to learning; an occupation normally beneath the attention of scholar-administrators, one to be firmly subordinated to the moral ends of the state and confined carefully within the traditions and customs of the established social order. Foreign trade was not a normal right, but a special privilege. Traditionally the only acceptable relation – the only conceivable relation – between foreign kingdoms and the Celestial Empire was that of vassalage, and the privilege of trading on Chinese territory was accorded to foreigners only as incidental to the rendering of homage and tribute. To fit the visits of European traders into the official category of tribute-bearing embassies was obviously difficult; but the convention, or fiction, was sedulously maintained. When European groups – who naturally neither accepted nor understood the convention – complained of vexatious restrictions or worse, they were usually told that they came by their own wish, that the empire had no need of their goods, and that if they did not like the conditions, they were free to depart.

The authorities at Canton, and those at Peking when they thought of the matter, were in a perpetual dilemma over

European trade. They could not really be indifferent to it. The anomalous standing of Europeans, their powerful armament, their frequently uncouth and occasionally disorderly conduct, the deleterious nature of some of the goods they introduced – all these characteristics combined to make them objects of suspicion, a potential threat to good order. The activities of Christian missionaries, also, and the growth of Christian sects in China, caused increasing uneasiness from the 1720s. K'ang-Hi, like Kublai Khan centuries earlier, treated missionaries with tolerance and respect, and employed resident Jesuits on a number of delicate missions. His successor was less tolerant, more suspicious.[28] Other Christian Orders, it should be added, were less scrupulous than the Jesuits in their respect for Chinese custom. For strict traditionalists, any teaching which encouraged departures from custom was potentially subversive; and though proselytising had no obvious connection with trade, it provoked xenophobic reactions among scholar-administrators against Europeans in general. On the other hand, European trade was a source of welcome revenue to the government and of profit to many in Canton. Probably the central authorities were never informed of the full extent of the trade; but they knew that if it were officially prohibited, it would probably find clandestine channels, and the only effect would be a loss of revenue. The government, therefore, compromised. While permitting the trade to continue, it tried, with increasing success in the course of the eighteenth century, to isolate the traders. Their business was effectively confined to Canton, and to a small group of prominent merchants in Canton, who were nominated by government and organised in a guild or cartel, the celebrated *Co-Hong*. The *Co-Hong* members not only fixed prices; they were made responsible for the payment of duties and for the general good behaviour of their European correspondents. Little social intercourse was allowed. The movement of Europeans was more and more restricted to Wampoa anchorage, where their ships lay, and to the strip of waterfront where their factories were built. Thirteen-Factory Street became what a modern French scholar has aptly called a commercial lazaretto. Here the resident factors, in the long intervals between tea-buying seasons, yawned away their time. They could not, even if they wished, learn the language or study the culture of the great civilisation which hemmed them in; the Chinese were forbidden to teach them. So they quarrelled and gossiped, played cards, and drank to excess; or removed themselves, in the off-season, to the more genial (if soporific) atmosphere of Portuguese Macao.

Company servants hated Canton, as well they might, and had to be paid extra as an inducement to serve there. The Dutch especially, accustomed in Java to a firm exercise of dominion in the interests of their trade, must have felt the frustrations of business in a place where dominion was out of the question and trade itself barely tolerated. The English, the most numerous group, usually took the lead in complaining, but to little or no effect. The Chinese authorities were equally impervious to respectful petitions, to diplomatic pressures, and to commercial and naval threats. Nevertheless, the trade flourished. Europe, and England especially, must have its tea. In the course of the eighteenth century the volume of shipping tonnage sent out by the English East India Company was to increase nearly ten-fold, from an annual average of less than 5,000 tons to one of more than 40,000. The proportion of this tonnage devoted to the China trade was to increase from less than one-eighth to more than a half;[29] an extraordinary commercial phenomenon, in connection with an exotic luxury product and an acquired social habit. The East India Company's China trade was to be carried on throughout the eighteenth century without benefit of dominion; but it was one of the factors, and not the least important, which determined the manner in which expanding dominion would be used in other parts of the world.

NOTES

1. This could be embarrassing. In 1664–5 the Mughal viceroy of Bengal was at war with the king of Arakan, over the latter's support of the *feringhi* pirates of Sandwip and Dianga. Both sides demanded Dutch naval assistance. The Dutch escaped from the dilemma only by abandoning their factory at Mrohaung. The upshot was the annexation of Sandwip to the Mughal empire and a permanent reduction of Arakanese power. D. G. E. Hall, *History of South East Asia*, London, 1964, p. 378.
2. For the history of Bencoolen in British hands see J. Bastin, *The British in West Sumatra 1685–1825*, Kuala Lumpur, 1965.

3. For a list of distances and summary of passage times, see Glamann, *Dutch Asiatic Trade*, p. 26.

4. For a narrative of this complex series of campaigns and intrigues see E. S. de Klerck, *History of the Netherlands East Indies*, 2 vols, Rotterdam, 1938, I, pp. 299 ff.

5. This brief sketch of administration in the Ommelanden and in the Preanger districts follows de Klerck, *History of the Netherlands East Indies*, I, pp. 348 ff.

6. Woodes Rogers (ed. G. E. Manwaring), *A cruising voyage around the world*, London, 1928, p. 286. The best modern descriptive history is F. de Haan, *Oud Batavia*, Bandung, 1935.

7. De Klerck, *History of the Netherlands East Indies*, I, pp. 331-2.

8. J. S. Furnivall, *Netherlands India, a study of plural economy*, Cambridge, 1944, p. 40.

9. Glamann, *Dutch Asiatic Trade*, p. 249.

10. The inadequacy of company accounting was fully analysed by W. M. F. Mansvelt, *Rechtsvorm en geldelijk beheer bij de Oost-Indische Compagnie*, Amsterdam, 1922. Mansvelt's analysis is summarised in J. C. van Leur, *Indonesian trade and society*, The Hague, 1955, p. 233.

11. Glamann, *Dutch Asiatic Trade*, pp. 253 ff.

12. The figures of the company's expenditures and receipts, in so far as they can be reconstructed, are set out in Klerk de Reus, *Geschichtlicher Ueberblick*, Beilage IX (b) and XI (c).

13. W. Campbell, *Formosa under the Dutch*, London, 1903, pp. 65-74 and 383-456.

14. For example, the bad reception accorded to HCS *Surat* in 1664; H. B. Morse, *The chronicles of the East India Company trading to China, 1635-1834*, Oxford, 1926, I, pp. 33-4.

15. Dermigny, *La Chine et l'Occident*, I, p. 135.

16. *Ibid.*, p. 130.

17. C. Imbault-Huart, *L'île Formose, Histoire et description*, Paris, 1893, pp. 94-101.

18. For this series of events see D. K. Bassetts, 'The trade of the English East India Company in the Far East, 1623-1684', *Journal of the Royal Asiatic Society*, 1960, XXIII, pp. 154-6.

19. J. Hall, 'Notes on the early Ch'ing copper trade with China', *ibid.*, XII, 1949, p. 452.

20. Morse, *Chronicles*, I, p. 78.

21. It is described in detail in J. F. Baddeley, *Russia, Mongolia, China*, London, 1919, II, pp. 223 ff.

22. P. Pelliot, 'L'origine des relations de la France avec la Chine. Le premier voyage de l'Amphitrite en Chine', *Journal des Savants*, Paris, 1930, p. 7.

23. E. Frémy, *Histoire de la manufacture royale des glaces de France au XVIIe et au XVIIIe siècle*, Paris, 1909, pp. 192-4.

24. V. Pinot, *La Chine et la formation de l'esprit philosophique en France*, Paris, 1932.

25. Morse, *Chronicles*, I, pp. 308-9.

26. Dermigny, *La Chine et l'Occident*, I, p. 153.

27. Glamann, *Dutch Asiatic Trade*, p. 225.
28. The Emperor Yong-Cheng's doubts and suspicions were frankly revealed to the French missionary P. de Mailla, and reported by him at length in a letter dated 16 October 1724. *Lettres édifiantes et curieuses écrites des missions étrangères*, Paris, 1703–74, III, pp. 363 ff.
29. From the figures in W. Milburn, *Oriental Commerce*, I, pp. xlv–xlviii.

PART II
Collisions and Mutinies

6

The Spanish Succession

Throughout the eighteenth century, the principal European powers interested in overseas trade, or in colonial dominion, or both, were in repeated collision. In itself, this was nothing new; Europeans had fought repeatedly over colonial possessions and distant commercial monopolies ever since the time of Henry the Navigator; but eighteenth-century colonial fighting was distinguished by its scale, its formality, its close connection with declared wars in Europe. The maritime powers of western Europe in the eighteenth century committed to colonial theatres of war a far greater proportion of their formal armaments – especially, of course, their naval armaments – than they had ever done before, or than they were ever to do subsequently. Few European wars, it is true, originated wholly or even primarily in colonial disputes; but every major eighteenth-century war had its colonial aspect; colonial territory and overseas commercial concessions figured prominently in every major treaty of peace.

The great weight of naval armament allocated to theatres of war outside Europe was principally, in the first half of the century almost entirely, employed in American waters, and above all in the Caribbean. Far more force was exerted in attempts to defend or acquire territorial possessions, to protect or extend trade, in the West Indies than in the East. More was at stake there. The colonies and plantations of the New World were living extensions of Europe, as Eastern factories, even Eastern conquests, could never be. They were inhabited by Europeans, who had to be protected. They were commercially valuable. The major maritime states of western Europe maintained with their American colonies (and, where they could, with other peoples' American colonies) a trade which considerably exceeded in value, and greatly exceeded in volume, the corresponding trade to all countries east of the Cape of Good Hope. The following tables give the approximate figures for England, as an example, at the beginning of the eighteenth century:

Total volume of English imports and exports by areas (000 tons)
1699–1701[1]

	Imports	Exports
Scandinavia and the Baltic countries	208	10
France, Germany, Netherlands and neighbouring countries	44	180
Southern European and Mediterranean countries	46	25
West Indies and Africa	33	10
North America	23	10
East India	5	negligible

As might be expected, comparison by value presents a somewhat different picture, since the East India trades dealt largely with imports of small bulk and high value, paid for in money; but still the American trades have the advantage:

Total value of English imports and exports by areas (£000)
1699–1701[2]

	Imports	Exports
Scandinavia and the Baltic countries	583	335
France, Germany, Netherlands and neighbouring countries	1,750	3,312
Southern European and Mediterranean countries	1,555	1,708
West Indies and Africa	765	473
North America	342	378
East India	756	136

Imperial responsibility and mercantile interest thus pointed the same way. Political and naval attention were attracted still further to the West Indies, because the Caribbean offered the easiest and shortest access to Spanish America. Spanish America was always a market for European manufactured goods, and for African slaves to work in its plantations and its mines. It was a limited and difficult market. Purchasing power was concentrated mainly in an upper class of Spaniards and Hispanicised Indians, lavish spenders but relatively few in number. The wholesale purchasing centres were widely separated. There was very little intercolonial commerce; a century of foreign piracy and Spanish restriction had almost killed it.[3] The centres were isolated one from another, and the quantity of goods each could absorb was limited. In conditions of open trade, a relatively small increase in competition among suppliers in any one place would have brought prices tumbling down; but trade was not open. The protective measures designed to maintain an Andalusian commercial monopoly were not very effective, but they constituted enough of an obstruction to keep up prices. The risks of smuggling were well worth taking, especially since a large part of the returns could be had in bullion or specie. At the end of the seventeenth century the rate of bullion production, after a long mid-century decline, was rising, especially in Mexico, and silver was fairly plentiful. In many parts of Europe silver, for domestic coinage purposes, was declining in value and importance, both absolutely and in relation to gold; but it was in high demand as an international trading commodity. Generally speaking, the further from Europe one traded, the higher the value of silver in terms both of gold and of goods. Planters and merchants in the French and English colonies needed it to pay their European debts, and always supported an aggressive commercial approach to Spanish America. In Europe, a steady demand for silver was maintained by people engaged in importing and re-exporting oriental goods: principally, the East India interests.

Trade with Spanish America, then, though not of central concern (except to Spain itself), was important to all the major economies of western Europe. Merchants, politicians and economic pamphleteers believed it – or professed to believe it – far more important than it really was. A combination of exaggeration and illusion was to some extent deliberately fostered by interested parties who wanted government support; but it was also traditional. The myth of El Dorado, modernised and mercantilised, retained its grip on men's minds. In the late seventeenth century, sophisticated politicians and business men in Europe no longer accepted, as Sir Walter Raleigh had done a hundred years before, the story of a Golden Man in the interior of Guiana; nor did they regard the Spanish Indies in crude terms, merely as a treasure-house to be robbed whenever possible. They did, however, think of the Spanish American market as insatiable, of the flow of bullion as inexhaustible. The policies of English, French and Dutch towards Spain and towards one another, were constantly affected by these two illusions. For traders, mercantile theorists and politicians in all three countries, the difficulty was to decide how best to profit by the supposed wealth of Spanish America, in view of the manifest weakness of Spain.

There were a number of possibilities: first and most obvious, the attempt to divert some of the east-bound silver shipments by systematic plunder of Spanish shipping, by naval action in time of war, by employing buccaneers or other auxiliaries in time of peace. This policy of predation had so long a history that it might almost be called traditional; but by the later seventeenth century it had become self-defeating. There was less and less silver at sea in Spanish ships, and buccaneers, long encouraged, had become an unmitigated nuisance to all maritime people. Another possibility was war with Spain, with a view to seizing territory in the Indies. This also had a long history. The Dutch had been the principal land-grabbers in the early decades of the seventeenth century, the English in the middle decades, the French towards the end; but the only permanent acquisitions they had to show for it were relatively marginal islands. There was little prospect of detaching any substantial mainland territory from the empire. Any attempt to do so would meet not only fierce Spanish resistance, but the relentless hostility of all the other powers concerned. The English and the Dutch, uneasily conscious of the growth of French strength in the Americas in the last two decades of the century, found it more prudent to keep on outwardly civil terms with Spain. Illicit trade seemed to offer better opportunities of profit, than open aggression; and here again there were several alternatives. Smuggling to the harbours of the Indies, either directly from Europe, or through French, Dutch or English Caribbean islands, was the most obvious method, and manufactured goods and slaves entered the Spanish colonies in considerable quantity in this way. Alternatively, it was possible to enter the trade at the Spanish end, consigning goods in Spanish ships, ostensibly as the property of Spanish merchants. The Seville firms, which lent their names for the purpose, for a commission, had a reputation for financial honesty. French exporters had long engaged in this kind of business, and had done well at it. Finally, at a time when Spain was hard pressed, there was the possibility of bringing diplomatic pressure on Madrid in order to extract formal commercial concessions. The Spanish government had never yet succumbed to bullying or blackmail on this subject, but might be forced to it.

All these alternative policies depended on two assumptions: that the Indies would remain in the possession of Spain, and that Spanish government would continue irresolute and weak. The first assumption seemed reasonably safe, the second could not be relied on. There was another, more ominous possibility: that the control of Spain itself might be taken over by a stronger power. Carlos II was a childless invalid. In the last three years of the seventeenth century his death was daily expected. Three European princes could advance genealogically plausible claims to succeed: Philip, Duke of Anjou, grandson of Louis XIV; the Archduke Charles, second son of Leopold II of Austria; and Joseph Ferdinand, electoral Prince of Bavaria, Carlos' nephew. Of the three the Bavarian, being the least formidable, was likely to be most acceptable to interested foreign powers, and to offer the best hope of preserving the balance and the peace of Europe. The French candidate, conversely, was the most controversial and least acceptable. It was generally assumed that if Philip succeeded, he would pursue a foreign policy dictated by Louis XIV. Anyone could see what that policy was likely to be; what dangers might threaten English and Dutch territory and trade, from the Spanish Netherlands, the Spanish coast of the Straits of Gibraltar, or the shores of the Caribbean; and how the French capacity for war might be increased by easy access to the Spanish Indies. Louis XIV, however, did not immediately press his grandson's full claim. He had no wish, so soon after Ryswyck, to risk a general war. He agreed with William

III in 1698 to support a partition arrangement, whereby Spain, the Indies and the Spanish Netherlands should go to Joseph Ferdinand, and the Spanish possessions in Italy should be divided in order to compensate the French and Austrian claimants. This reasonable agreement – reasonable for everyone except Spaniards – came to nothing, for three main reasons: the untimely death of the Bavarian prince in 1699; the subsequent refusal of the emperor to accept for his son anything less than the whole Spanish inheritance; and the passionate hostility to any form of partition among Spaniards themselves, who so far had not been consulted but who, according to Stanhope, would 'rather deliver themselves up to the French or the devil, so they may all go together, than be dismembered'. It was left, then, to Carlos on his deathbed – in effect, to his confessor – to choose between two candidates for the succession. He did so in his last will, made shortly before his death in 1700. This famous document, over which much blood was to be spilt, represented more than the arbitrary choice of a dying man and more than the outcome of a struggle between the factions round the deathbed. It represented the determination, which the king shared with his subjects, that the Spanish crown should keep its dominions intact; it accepted, by implication, that this could no longer be ensured by Spanish power alone; accordingly, it named the candidate whose efforts to this end were most likely to be successful, because of the powerful help which he could summon. Carlos bequeathed his throne and all its possessions to Philip of Anjou; only in the event of a French refusal, to the Archduke Charles. Confronted with this all-or-nothing offer, and in the light of the emperor's attitude, Louis XIV had little choice but to accept the throne for his grandson, and Spain as the client of France.

A warlike reaction in Vienna was almost automatic. Apart from the general question of the archduke's claim, the prospect of French dominance of Italy implied a serious threat to the Habsburg rulers of Austria. In England, under a Tory ministry opposed to war and suspicious of William III, reactions were slower. William himself was determined to resist a French take-over; but English opinion supported him only when Louis himself, by an ominous series of actions and pronouncements, demonstrated its dangers. Defoe's forceful pamphleteering,[4] pronouncing the Protestant Succession and the future of English trade to be alike imperilled, helped to rouse alarm in parliament and the City. In September 1701, by the Treaty of The Hague, the Grand Alliance of 1689 was renewed, with the declared purpose of ensuring to the emperor satisfaction for his claims to the Spanish succession, and to England and Holland security for their dominions and for the navigation and commerce of their subjects. More specifically, the emperor was to acquire, *inter alia*, the Italian possessions of Spain. The Spanish Netherlands were to be detached from Spain; a safeguard insisted on by the English and the Dutch, rather than by the emperor. The English and Dutch were to keep, at a successful peace, any territory which they could capture in the West Indies.

Among the French and Spanish words and actions which inflamed English hostility some – the seizure of the Dutch barrier fortresses, the promise to recognise 'James III' as king of England, the unguarded ambassadorial reference to the disappearance of the Pyrenees – concerned only Europe. Others, however, related directly to the future of the Spanish Indies. The war of the Spanish Succession, indeed, was the first major European conflict in which control of colonial territory and trade figured prominently among the aims of the belligerents. French, English and Dutch attitudes towards the Spanish empire were all reversed by the prospect of a Bourbon succession in Spain. Since 1680 or thereabouts, England and Holland had respected Spanish sovereignty in the Indies, because their subjects had found smuggling more profitable than raiding, more feasible than conquest, and because they feared French aggression; but after 1700 they stood for dismemberment. France had been the enemy, trying to seize territory or secure privileges by force; but after 1700 Louis XIV represented the heir. He became determined to strengthen and improve the estate. French efficiency was to be applied to Spanish administration. In the early years of the war Louis pressed many schemes for reform upon his grandson. The Cadiz trade was to be reorganised, to reduce fraud; the cruiser squadrons in the Caribbean were to be strengthened by French officers, to check English and Dutch smuggling; the transatlantic fleets were to be escorted by French warships, to protect them from enemy warships and privateers.

For these services, naturally, a price was exacted. Commercial and naval reforms in themselves favoured the French, who were the chief foreign traders to Cadiz and who ran their own smuggling business in the Caribbean; but more explicit privileges were demanded, and secured. Most prominent among them was the *asiento*, the exclusive contract for the supply of slaves to the Spanish Indies, assigned in 1701 to the French Guinea Company, to run for ten years from September 1702.

The slave trade was the only field of commercial activity in which the Spanish government openly acknowledged its dependence upon foreigners. Throughout the seventeenth century the productive centres of the Indies suffered from a shortage of labour. The supply of African slaves to supplement native Indian labour was a constant preoccupation, both of planters and miners, and of government. Spaniards had no transatlantic slaving organisation of their own. The government usually appointed contractors, who operated a controlled and licensed monopoly and paid heavily for the privilege. For many years these *asentistas* had been Portuguese; after the breach with Portugal in 1640, trustworthy contractors were hard to find. Of the obvious suppliers, the Portuguese were rebels, the English heretics, the Dutch both rebels and heretics, the French implacable enemies. From 1640 to 1662 no official provision was made; the colonists bought their slaves from smugglers; the crown lost both revenue and control. When in 1662, a new series of *asiento* grants began, the contractors were not transatlantic shippers, but middlemen: initially, from 1662 to 1671, two Genoese, Grillo and Lomelin, subsequently a succession of adventurers, dealers and financiers, Spanish and foreign. Whether any of them made a profit, is doubtful. They all bought their slaves, usually in the West Indies, from English, Dutch or French suppliers.[5] Grillo and Lomelin subcontracted – quite legally – to the group of English adventurers who later became the Royal African Company; both they and the adventurers lost heavily on the deal.[6] Indeed, almost everyone who became involved with the *asiento* business burned his fingers sooner or later. It looked attractive. The Spaniards paid, or at least offered, higher prices than did English and French planters, and they paid in silver. The slave trade, however, was always speculative and risky; losses in transit were often heavy; war and piracy interfered with trade. In some years all the slavers trading to Africa – French, Dutch, English, chartered corporations and private traders – together could barely meet the demand in the sugar islands; sometimes island legislatures prohibited export; only rarely was there a substantial surplus. Often, too, the slavers had difficulty in collecting their debts from the *asentistas*. The Royal African Company, for one, warned by the experience of the Royal Adventurers, was usually cautious, though not always cautious enough, about signing long-term contracts with Spaniards.[7] It was the French and English governments, rather than the slavers themselves, who, bemused by the illusion of limitless profits in silver, competed and intrigued to secure the *asiento* for their subjects. Traders were often more interested in the contraband for which slaving gave a cover, than in the slaving itself; but through the importunities of governments the sordid business acquired all the characteristics of an international treaty. When the French concluded their deal with Philip v, the English promptly added the *asiento* to their list of war aims, and secured the promise of a similar concession from the Archduke Charles.

The *asiento* of 1701, in form at least, was a contract freely entered by two independent governments. Other French commercial activities in the Indies were undertaken without even the formality of Spanish consent. Since the early 1680s the French government had permitted and encouraged a smuggling trade from the French Antilles to Spanish Caribbean harbours. In 1698 Noël Danycan de l'Epine, again with royal support, had formed his *Compagnie de la mer du Sud* for the purpose of opening a trade again illicit but certainly no secret – directly with Peru. This concern merged in 1701, as we have seen,[8] with Jourdan's *Compagnie de Chine*; but China voyages formed a relatively small part of the combined business. Voyages to Chile and Peru were much more numerous (eighty-eight of them took place during the war) and as a rule they were more profitable.[9] The ships entered the Pacific by the Cape Horn route, which only recently had come to be considered both technically and economically feasible for regular commercial use. The goods which they unloaded at Callao and other ports had to compete, of course, with other goods, also mostly French in origin, coming by the lawful route over the Isthmus; but in this competition the illicit traders, as usual, had the advantage, because they could sell more cheaply. The Isthmus trade, moreover, soon dwindled to a mere trickle; during the war years, four small official fleets (escorted by French warships) reached Vera Cruz, but only one succeeded in getting through to Puerto Belo. Spanish reactions to the direct trade varied with circumstances. Colonists in Peru welcomed it; *consulado* merchants complained about it; francophile or merely venal viceroys frequently connived at it, or at any rate took no effective measures to stop it. In Spain, reports of the trade caused a great stir in government circles and made it the subject of indignant diplomatic representations. French policy vacillated. Sometimes the interests of Nantes and St Malo were sacrificed, or kept in the background, in order to mollify the Spanish government or stifle the outcry against foreigners in Spain; but more often the merchants' influence and the needs of the treasury overcame the political scruples of Pontchartrain, and the trade was winked at or openly allowed. For the English government it became yet another example of French sharp practice, to be dealt with at a successful peace.

Throughout the war of the Spanish Succession, most of the heavy fighting was in Europe: in Spain, Italy, South Germany and the Low Countries; and in Mediterranean waters. The French, it is true, seemed initially to intend striking at England through the West Indies. In anticipation of the outbreak of war, French naval and military forces based on Martinique had been heavily reinforced. The veteran admiral and marshal, Châteaurenault, was himself sent out in 1701, and by 1702 the total fleet amounted to some forty sail of various rates; though sickness kept many of them in harbour. The duties of these ships were very various. Besides the general strengthening of Spanish Caribbean defences, they were to protect and organise French trade, especially the new *asiento* trade; and provide escort for Spanish transatlantic fleets, whether east- or west-bound, in particular for a *flota* preparing to sail with *caudales* from Vera Cruz early in 1702. Enough forces, it was confidently expected, would be left over from these duties to attack English settlements in the area. To counter this threat,

Benbow was sent out early in 1702, with ten sail. Little came of it all. The *flota* duly sailed, escorted by Châteaurenault with twenty-three French ships, and made an uneventful passage to Spain, the captain-general having refused Châteaurenault's suggestion of putting into Brest; but almost the entire sailing was destroyed, by a combined Dutch and English fleet, after arrival in Vigo Bay.[10] In the West Indies, Benbow's presence deterred the French from attacking Jamaica; but he himself, ill-supported by his captains (two of whom were subsequently condemned and shot for cowardice), was fatally wounded in an inconclusive encounter off Santa Marta, with a French squadron under the ex-buccaneer Du Casse.[11] In the same year, 1702, Codrington from Antigua expelled the French planters from their half of St Kitts. Thereafter, the war in the Caribbean relapsed into mutual commerce-raiding of the familiar uncoordinated kind. English merchant shipping, being the most numerous, suffered most heavily, and so did some of the minor English settlements. The Bahamas colony was almost destroyed in 1703, leaving those islands a refuge for pirates; St Kitts and Nevis were savagely raided in 1706 and Montserrat in 1712. The only serious attempts at retaliation were Wager's successful attack on the galleons at Cartagena in 1708 – a traditional operation, mounted against Spanish property rather than against French forces – and an abortive raid on Guadeloupe. The prescient Codrington, experienced soldier and able West Indian governor, pleaded in vain for a strong force to take Martinique, the main base of French power in the area. Although by 1707 the English had built up their Caribbean war fleet to twenty-four sail, these were not enough to protect trade against a swarm of privateers, and certainly could not be concentrated for a major operation. Elsewhere in the Americas, a similar dispersal of effort and lack of concerted strategic purpose rendered abortive the expeditions sent from Carolina against Florida and from New England against Canada. The only significant outcome of this northern fighting was the British capture, in 1710, of Port Royal in Acadia – 'another Dunkirk', according to the governor of Massachusetts, a base for privateers preying on the New England and Newfoundland fisheries and threatening the trade and safety of New England itself.[12]

Many English pamphleteers attacked their government for neglecting the American theatre of war. Swift, for one, thought it strange '. . . while some politicians were showing us the way to Spain by Flanders, others to Savoy or Naples . . . the West Indies should never come into their heads'.[13] The strategy of attacking Spain through its Indies was old and well tried. The principal enemy now, however, was not Spain, but France; and the notion – characteristic of later eighteenth-century wars between England and France – that the enemy's capacity for war could be crippled by ravaging his sugar islands, had not yet taken hold in England, though it had, to some extent, in France. Marlborough, both as statesman and as commander-in-chief on the main front, disliked distant side-shows.[14] Even Rooke's spectacular destruction of the Indies galleons at Vigo in 1702, he regarded as a side-show, though admittedly a valuable one in that it damaged the enemy's finances and morale. He saw, more clearly than Rooke himself, the great significance of that officer's capture of Gibraltar in 1704, and re-peatedly urged that it should be followed up by seizing Minorca. This was done in 1708. The commitment to support 'Charles III', whose only considerable Spanish following was in Catalonia, en-tailed naval concentration in the Mediterranean. A British fleet operating from Gibraltar and Port Mahon could not only further the central object of the war, but could also, by impeding French fleets from Toulon working out to the open ocean, provide indirect defence for the British West Indies (though not, admittedly, against commerce-raiding privateers). In accordance with this reasoning, the outcome of the war, in the New World as well as in the Old, was decided chiefly by European campaigns and Medi-terranean fleet actions.

The arms of the alliance were almost consistently successful everywhere but in Spain, whose people of all classes (except in Catalonia and Valencia) rallied stubbornly to Philip v as a symbol of Spanish imperial integrity. By 1709 it was clear that Philip could not be turned out of Spain by allied arms. The allies tried, to Swift's sardonic amusement, to bully Louis xiv into expelling him for them. When Louis, not unnaturally, refused peace at this price, the English government decided to make the best of a bad business and exact the highest terms they could get for recognising Philip.

Thereafter the war petered out. Disagreement between the allies over their war aims, and general war-weariness, made possible in 1713 a more rational peace than had seemed likely in 1709. As in the agreements which preceded the war, so in the treaty which ended it, Spain, initially at least, played no direct part. Philip v kept his throne; but until the allies had agreed formally to recognise him, Louis xiv had to negotiate for Spain as well as France. He did so skilfully and realistically. The agreements reached at Utrecht followed more or less the pattern of the Treaty of the Hague of 1701. The archduke, who in 1711 had become the Emperor Charles v, acquired the Spanish dominions in Italy, and was induced to take on the Spanish Netherlands; the Dutch recovered their barrier fortresses; England kept Gibraltar and Port Mahon.

The Treaty of Utrecht was generally thought, then and later, to have established a reasonable and durable equilibrium in European affairs. Outside Europe, however, England and only England secured by it apparently substantial advantages. Among them was the acquisition of Acadia (Nova Scotia) and of sovereignty over Newfoundland. Nova Scotia, rocky and forested, was a modest colony, sparsely inhabited by small farmers and fishermen. In terms of productivity and trade it had little value. It was strategically important; but while the population remained largely French, the English hold on it could not but be precarious, especially as the French themselves, having lost their American Dunkirk at Port Royal, soon began to construct another, more formidable base, as a defence for Canada and a threat to New England, at Louisbourg on Cape Breton Island. As for Newfoundland, the Grand Banks were of high importance, economically, as a source of readily marketable fish, strategically, traditionally, sentimentally, as a maritime training ground. The fishery was exploited mainly by fleets coming each spring from Europe. The crews camped on the beaches during the summer, to dry their catch, and returned home with it in the autumn. The small permanent French and English settlements were unimportant; indeed, from the point of view of the seasonal fishermen, something of a nuisance, competitive, inhospitable and quarrelsome. Territorial possession of the island itself was valuable only in so far as it enabled the possessor to protect and favour his own fishermen and to exclude foreigners; but in the Treaty of Utrecht, English dominion was qualified, and future conflict suggested, by the right which the French retained to cure fish on part of the south shore.

Much more interesting, both to government and to the 'trading part of the nation' in England, was the settlement in the West Indies; not territorially (St Kitts was the only acquisition) but commercially. It was argued that England had paid for the war. To some extent this was true. The Bank of England, the expert practice of the Treasury, the solidly secured National Debt, had enabled a prosperous England to subsidise its allies, who had done the heavy land fighting. It was hoped to recover this expenditure, with interest, through commercial concessions, chiefly in Spanish America. In the full flush of victory in 1707–9, English hopes in this direction had run very high, to include the total exclusion of French goods, and the management of the entire Indies trade by an Anglo-Spanish company. French 'perfidy' being at that time an article of faith in England (and *vice versa*, of course), English politicians wanted these arrangements to be guaranteed by 'real securities', by which they meant the acquisition of key harbours in the Indies. In 1711 the South Sea Company was incorporated to exploit whatever commercial concessions could be extracted from Spain. It was granted a monopoly of English trade with South America. On the financial side, it took over nine and a half million of funded public debt, and so joined the Bank of England and the East India Company as one of the principal props of the financial establishment in the city. Nothing could have shown more clearly the extravagant hopes entertained of Spanish-American trade, than the prominence accorded to this celebrated but shaky concern. Harley, newly appointed lord treasurer, was its first president.

The concessions actually secured by England in the negotiations of 1711–13,[15] though much less than had been hoped for, were nonetheless impressive, at least on paper. France renounced any special privileges of trade with Spain or the Spanish Indies, and promised in particular to prohibit the direct trade from French ports to the Pacific coast of South America. Spain, in return for an

English guarantee of the integrity of its possessions in America, promised not to alienate any territory there, to France or to any other nation. Spain also undertook not to grant any special commercial privileges in America, except as provided in the treaties. The only special provisions which the treaties contained were in favour of England. The *asiento* for the supply of slaves was transferred to England for thirty years; and by the English government was duly assigned to the South Sea Company. The company was to buy its slaves from the Royal African Company. The quality of the slaves to be supplied, and the ports to which they were to be shipped, were specified in the *asiento* treaty of 1714.[16] The company was allowed to acquire land in Buenos Aires for the 'refreshment' of slaves to be landed there (this being the only remaining vestige of the old demand for 'real securities'). Finally, in return for an undertaking to refrain from illicit trade, and for sundry other concessions, the company secured an unprecedented and valuable privilege: that of sending a shipload of general merchandise every year to the Spanish Caribbean. The cargo was to be sold at the regular fair at Puerto Belo or Vera Cruz, and the king of Spain was to have a quarter share.

None of the participants in these agreements was likely to be able, or even willing, to keep his promises in full. French trade to Peru continued. According to Dahlgren[17] sixty-two French ships made this voyage between 1713 and 1724. The Spanish government, in order to check the traffic, had to send out, in the latter year, a considerable naval expedition, officered by Frenchmen. Neither the English nor the Dutch government made any serious attempt to stop Caribbean smuggling by privately owned ships. As for the South Sea Company, its privileges, in practice, virtually constituted a licence to smuggle. Some of the clauses of the *asiento* treaty were obviously drawn with this in mind. Buenos Aires, for example, was not an important market for slaves; the considerable establishment which the company proposed to maintain there must have been intended, at least in part, for smuggling goods overland to Chile and Peru. The same was true of the clauses permitting the company to employ tenders to 'refresh' the annual ship while it traded at Puerto Belo, and to dispatch small vessels from Jamaica with 'necessaries' for factors and Negroes in the

Spanish Caribbean harbours. Any illusion the Spaniards may have had about the company's intentions must have been dispelled by the reputation of the man whom the English government had employed as their chief commercial negotiator in 1712–13. Manuel Manasses Gilligan, in whose fertile brain these clauses originated, was an adventurer of shifting nationality with a long record of smuggling, trading with the enemy in war, and general sharp practice.[18] The very employment of such a man aroused Spanish suspicions of English good faith.

The Spanish government had agreed, under duress and with extreme misgiving – with a feeling, indeed, of bitter humiliation – to an open breach of a long-established principle. At all costs, the breach must be kept from widening. An armed coastguard service operated against smugglers in the Caribbean, but it was not disciplined enough to be consistently effective, and it could not be used against the South Sea Company, whose privileges were embodied in an international treaty. Spanish economists knew that effective commercial control of the Indies could be recovered only by a growth of Spanish industry, making Spanish goods competitive in the trade, and making Spain an attractive market for American products; but this would be, at best, a long-term solution, and the problem was urgent and pressing. Spain was prostrate, desperately in need of capital for reconstruction. Much bullion destined for Spain was dammed up in the Indies. Mercury, essential for the production of more bullion, had to be shipped from Spain. Above all, if communications were not quickly reestablished, the English would secure a virtual monopoly of the Caribbean trade, and might eventually try to seize territorial control. The immediate problem, then, was to get the fleets moving again; but where to find the ships? Spanish shipping had suffered great losses during the war. Warships were required for the reduction of Barcelona, long loyal to the Austrian Habsburgs, to the Bourbon obedience. Spain, moreover, was governed in practice not by a French king but by an Italian queen, and Alberoni, conducting the king's affairs in the queen's interest, was committing men and ships to dynastic adventures in Italy. The best that could be scraped together at the end of 1712 was a minuscule *flota* – two warships, two dispatch vessels, and an elderly merchantman described as the *urca de Lima* – commanded by Captain-General Juan Estéban Ubilla. Ubilla was to land mercury and pick up bullion at Vera Cruz. The whole of the rest of the trade was to be farmed out to a single contractor, licensed to dispatch individual 'register-ships' at the times and to the destinations (other than Vera Cruz) which he thought fit. The contractor was a commercial magnate from the north of Spain, Antonio de Echeverz. Of six ships which Echeverz bought or chartered for the enterprise, two were French and one was Dutch.

On the Isthmus, Echeverz' supercargoes found business very slow. The Peruvian market was glutted with French goods, and the ships had to spend many months in the Caribbean in order to get rid of their goods, mostly at a loss. Ubilla's people had a similar experience in the Gulf ports; the market had been spoilt not only by goods smuggled from Europe, but by Chinese textiles imported from Manila. His ships were not ready for the return voyage until the spring of 1715. The political situation was uncertain and pirates, encouraged by the late war, were active. All the register-ships in the area, therefore, were ordered to join Ubilla at Havana and return to Spain in company. This made more delay; but eventually the combined fleet, eleven sail in all, carrying, besides produce and assorted *chinoiserie*, more than 14,000,000 *pesos* in silver and an appreciable quantity of gold, cleared from Havana on 27 July. It was too late for safety. An early hurricane caught them in the Bahama channel on 30 July. Only one ship, one of Echeverz', the Frenchman *Grifon*, escaped to the north. Two other ships, trying to follow the *Grifon*, foundered in deep water. The rest all broke up in shoal water off the coast of Florida. Over 1,000 men were drowned, including the captain-general, and Echeverz' son, who commanded one of the ships. The luckiest ship, apart from the *Grifon*, was one of Ubilla's dispatch vessels; her whole upper deck came adrift from the frames and floated like a raft, with the ship's company clinging to it, until driven up the beach by the force of the waves.[19]

The authorities at Havana reacted with prompt efficiency to the news of disaster, and divers were quickly put to work. The Havana treasury eventually recovered about 4,000,000 *pesos* from the wrecks. This was certainly less than the amount raised. Spanish officials being what they were, part of the salvage doubtless stuck to their fingers; and other, even greedier fingers were at work. During the salvage operations a temporary blockhouse had been built on Cape Cañaveral, in which the bullion, as it was raised, was stored under military guard while awaiting shipment to Havana. News of these activities soon reached Jamaica, the commercial crossroads of the Caribbean. With the active connivance of the governor, Lord Archibald Hamilton, who was a shareholder in the enterprise, a retired buccaneer named Jennings, who was living on the island, collected several hundred kindred spirits and a flotilla of small vessels, sailed to Cape Cañaveral, surprised the blockhouse, murdered the guards, and got away with nearly 500,000 pieces of eight. Truly misfortune dogged Ubilla's fleet, even after it had been sunk. An angry letter of complaint from the governor of Cuba to the governor of Jamaica merely elicited a bland disavowal of Jennings, as a pirate. Hamilton, it is true, when the facts became known in London, was recalled in disgrace; there were limits to government connivance at this sort of thing; but the Spaniards got no compensation, and had no recourse but indiscriminate reprisal. With the experience of incidents such as this, and the resulting chains of reprisal and counter-reprisal to which they gave rise, it is not surprising that Spanish colonial governors often commissioned as *guarda-costas* men who were themselves little better than pirates.

The loss of the 1715 fleet was, of course, a major disaster. It ruined many merchants, shipowners and creditors of the crown. It was not, moreover, an isolated disaster; rather, a calamitous deepening of existing depression. The hurricane made a total loss of a fleet which would have been a commercial failure in any event. It may seem incredible that other speculators could have been found to take Echeverz' place; yet between 1715 and 1720 several contracts, similar to that of Echeverz, were signed for the dispatch of groups of register-ships. These contractors did not have to contend with hurricanes, but they all lost money, while smuggling competitors were making handsome profits. Their failures emphasised, to percipient Spaniards, the weakness of Spain and the vulnerability of empire. Foreigners watched, with greedy and sceptical eyes, the growth of the prosperity of the Indies and the fumbling, largely ineffectual attempts of the Spanish crown to reassert its control, in the years immediately after Utrecht. Spain was then, indeed, the sick man of America. Yet foreigners, especially Englishmen, who predicted the imminent break-up of empire and looked for a share of the spoil, underrated Spanish tenacity of purpose and Spanish powers of recovery. Fear for the Indies led Philip v's ministers, Patiño especially, to give the rebuilding of the navy priority over most other charges on the royal revenue. From 1717 onwards an increasing number of new and up-to-date warships, designed on French lines, were laid down at Cadiz, Coruña and El Ferrol. A broken and half-forgotten naval tradition could not be rebuilt in a few years, and the ships, initially at least, were better designed than manned; but within a generation much was achieved. The fleets with which Spain was to confront England in the Caribbean in the 'War of Jenkins' Ear' and the Seven Years War were far from negligible. A new navy, a French alliance and strong ties of loyalty in the Indies themselves were to keep the empire intact – contrary to many expectations – for another century.

NOTES

1. From Ralph Davis, *The rise of the English shipping industry in the seventeenth and eighteenth centuries*, London, 1962.

2. *Ibid.*, p. 200.

3. There was still an appreciable volume of coasting trade in small vessels in the Caribbean. One example: the accounts of the Cortés sugar estate near Cuernavaca show that cacao, which formed part of the wages in kind issued to estate workers, was sometimes imported from Maracaibo (personal communication from Mr Ward Barrett). See also E. Arcila Farías, *Comercio entre Venezuela y México en los siglos XVI y XVII*, México, 1950, pp. 70 ff.

4. Daniel Defoe, *Two great questions considered*, London, 1700; *The true-born Englishman*, London, 1701.

5. Georges Scelle, *La traite négrière aux Indes de Castille*, 2 vols, Paris, 1906, I, pp. 105 ff.

6. K. G. Davies, *The Royal African Company*, London, 1957, pp. 43, 327. On the original group, the Royal Adventurers, see G. F. Zook, *The Company of Royal Adventurers trading to Africa*, Lancaster, Pennsylvania, 1919.

7. Davies, *Royal African Company*, pp. 328 ff.

8. p. 118 above.

9. E. W. Dahlgren, *Les relations commerciales et maritimes entre la France et les*

côtes de l'océan Pacifique, vol. I, *Le commerce de la mer du Sud*, Paris, 1909, pp. 156 ff.

10. C. Fernández Duro, *Armada Española desde la Unión de las reinas de Castilla y de Aragón*, Madrid, 9 vols, 1895–1903, VI, pp. 23 ff. Most of the silver was landed before the attack. Some of it belonged to English and Dutch consignees, and was confiscated.

11. The accounts of these confused operations in the standard naval histories – Laird Clowes, La Roncière, Fernández Duro – vary considerably in detail. The story from the English end, however, is fairly clear from *Calendar of State Papers, Colonial Series*, 1702, pp. 147, 71, 110, 216–18, 368, 460, 673–9, 744.

12. *Calendar of State Papers, Colonial Series*, 1706–8, pp. 31, 438, 587–91.

13. Swift, *Prose Works*, ed. Temple Scott, 12 vols, London, 1897–1908, V, 'The Conduct of the Allies', pp. 28–31.

14. For his views on the West Indies see W. Coxe, ed., *Memoirs of John Duke of Marlborough*, London, 1818–19, III, p. 37.

15. The course of the negotiations is traced in detail in A. Legrelle, *La Diplomatie Française et la Succession d'Espagne*, Ghent, 1892, vol. IV.

16. Public Record Office, London, *State Papers, Foreign, Treaties*, 472.

17. E. W. Dahlgren, *Voyages françaises à destination de la Mer du Sud*, Paris, 1907.

18. *Calendar of State Papers, Colonial*, 1702–3, nos. 572, 661, 1065; 1704–5, nos. 108, 203; 1706–8, nos. 53, 777; 1708–9, nos. 126, 134, 180.

19. The most detailed account of this catastrophe is in Fernández Duro, *Armada española*, VI, pp. 121 ff.

7

War, Trade and Plantations

Spain retained its colonial empire intact in 1713 because its chief enemies preferred an extension of their trade, which could be had for the asking (or so they thought), to an extension of their territorial dominion, which might have involved more fighting. The English, however, in accepting commercial concessions as the spoils of victory, were deceived, or deceived themselves, over the value of what they were getting. The South Sea Company was not authorised to trade to the South Sea and (as its enemies repeatedly pointed out)[1] never tried to. In the Atlantic its privileges, though enough to send the price of company stock soaring, were much less than had been hoped for, and the opportunities of lawful profit which they offered were limited. The company's agents, however, soon began to exploit the openings which their privileged position gave them for illicit profit. Under the pretext of selling small numbers of slaves at Buenos Aires, they introduced European manufactures, some of them destined for Upper Peru and Chile. They sold many slaves in the Caribbean ports; but since they could never obtain enough from their official supplier, the Royal African Company, they bought extensively (to the annoyance of the local planters) in Jamaica. The company's slave sloops, sailing from Jamaica to Spanish ports, notoriously carried other goods. The annual ships, also, sailed accompanied by 'provision ships' which carried contraband; and while discharging off Puerto Belo (it was plausibly alleged) were reloaded by night from Jamaica.[2] The profits of all this illicit traffic, presumably, enriched the company's agents rather than the company, which, like all such corporations, was systematically defrauded by its servants. The declared profits were never very large. The restrictive conditions of the *asiento* prevented the company from making much by slaving alone; and though some 'annual' ships (particularly the *Royal Prince* in 1723–4) did very well, the ships were not in fact annual. The trade was twice interrupted by minor wars, in 1718 and 1727, and even in peace the Spanish government made difficulties over issuing the permits which each ship was required to carry. Only eight 'annual' voyages took place in the whole life of the concession. The Spaniards, however, suspected that the company concealed its profits in order to defraud the crown of its dividend, and the company's refusal to produce its accounts for inspection lent colour to this suspicion.

The South Sea Company was not the only cause of West Indian dispute. The colonial shipping of three or four foreign nations plied in the Caribbean, carrying lawful trade with their own colonies or unlawful trade with those of Spain. Law-abiding French traders, by the orders of their own government, usually gave bond not to smuggle. The Dutch went armed for an avowedly illicit trade and were known for smugglers on sight. English ships were more numerous than either, but the English government would never accept the suggestion that their shipping should give bond as the French did. English shipping in the Caribbean included the South Sea Company's ships carrying a lawful, or ostensibly lawful, trade with Spanish America; ships engaged in normal traffic between England or North America and the English islands; and smugglers to Latin-American ports. In order to distinguish between fair traders and smugglers, the Spanish government considered itself entitled, subject to certain explicit exceptions,[3] to stop, search, and where appropriate arrest foreign ships anywhere in the western hemisphere. It entrusted these duties to *guarda-costas*, operating from colonial ports and carrying commissions from the local governors. Most of these ships were manned by ruffians trained in the long war against the buccaneers. They were fitted out privately, and received their remuneration from the sale of the prizes they brought in. They cruised in the regular routes of colonial trade, stopping every foreign ship they met and searching for contraband. Colonial governors received a share of the prize-money; there was an obvious temptation to collusion between the governors, the courts, and the captains of the *guarda-costas*. Colonial courts accepted the presence in a foreign ship of any Spanish colonial product – indigo, cocoa, logwood or Spanish money – as evidence of unlawful trade. It was flimsy evidence, for Jamaica produced indigo and logwood in small quantities, and had produced cocoa; and Spanish money was the commonest means of exchange almost everywhere in the Americas. Moreover, a foreign ship might be seized and condemned merely because its position at the time of encounter was, in the opinion of a Spanish court, off the direct course to a lawful destination. This, too, was flimsy evidence; ships approaching Jamaica necessarily passed close to Hispaniola, and ships leaving there had usually to sail round Cuba and beat out against the trade wind through the Florida Channel.

English merchantmen about their lawful occasions could seek naval protection; there were always some warships on the station; but here the privileges of the South Sea Company presented an obstacle. Because of its official concession, its large stocks and its expensive establishments in America, the company was vulnerable to Spanish resentment. Its directors knew that any action taken by English warships, in reprisal for Spanish attacks on English shipping, might be punished by confiscation of the company's property. They preferred therefore to bring pressure in Madrid, through the British ambassador, rather than seeking direct remedy in the West Indies. They used their influence with the English government to discourage an aggressive naval policy, and sometimes they dissuaded naval commanders from taking perfectly proper action to protect legitimate English shipping.[4] To this extent the interests of unprivileged traders were sacrificed to those of the company. Smugglers, of course, had no claim on naval protection (though they sometimes got it) and had to take their chance with the *guarda-costas*; but the *guarda-costas* often did not discriminate; many peaceful and lawful traders, mostly English, were seized, condemned, and sold in prize.

The result of these seizures was a long list of financial claims; and in the 1730s a mounting wave of national indignation piled up in England against Spain. The South Sea Company demanded compensation for property which had been seized in the brief wars of 1718 and 1727, and the English government supported its claim. The English West India merchants clamoured for redress for arbitrary seizures, and the opposition supported *them*. The Spanish government retorted with complaints about continued smuggling and with demands for payment of the company's debts to the king of Spain – slave duties, share of trading profits (if any) and so forth. Besides these financial disagreements and the perennial dispute about free navigation, there was the problem of the logwood-cutters in the Bay of Honduras, and a boundary dispute between Florida and the newly settled English colony in Georgia. None of these disputes need have led to war; war was forced by the truculence and clamour of the 'trading part of the nation' in England, and by the pressure of opposition groups in parliament. Atrocity propaganda played a part in the proceedings. In 1738 a Captain Jenkins was induced to appear in the House of Commons to exhibit (preserved in brandy) his ear, sliced off by a cutlass blow in a scuffle with *guarda-costas*, who had boarded his ship off the coast of Cuba.[5] The Commons were not told that this celebrated affray had taken place seven years earlier, in 1731. The House, suitably roused, resolved that it was 'the undoubted right of British subjects to sail their ships in any part of the seas of America'. General letters of reprisal were distributed to English merchants – a curiously old-fashioned gesture – and a British fleet cruised menacingly off the coast of Spain. In face of these provocations the Spanish government at first displayed considerable patience. A draft agreement, worked out with Walpole by the ambassador in London, was accepted in Madrid and actually ratified as the Convention of El Pardo. By its terms Spain was to pay £95,000, the estimated excess of Spanish over English depredations; but the South Sea Company and its supporters opposed the agreement because it did not expressly recognise the company's right of navigation nor guarantee a renewal of the *asiento*. The £95,000 was never paid. Extensions of overseas trade, it seemed, no less than colonial dominion, had to be fought for. In 1739 Walpole allowed himself to be pushed reluctantly into war with Spain.

A war against Spain for the sake of free navigation was assured of enthusiastic support in England; but fighting Spain (as Walpole well knew) meant, sooner or later, fighting France as well. Fleury had no great love for the Spain of Elizabeth Farnese; but no French statesman would willingly leave the Spanish *flotas,* and the French goods they carried, at the mercy of England. Moreover, in the mood of greedy and truculent imperialism in which the English entered the war, they were eager also to make permanent conquests of Spanish territory, which would certainly have led to war with France. The great preparations made in 1740 for Lord Cathcart's expedition against Spanish America prompted Fleury to send out a fleet under d'Antin, with very bellicose instructions; but d'Antin lay so long at St Domingue awaiting reinforcements and trying vainly to arrange a junction with the Spanish fleet, that his men fell sick, his stores ran out, and he was obliged to return to France without accomplishing anything. Meanwhile, back in Europe, Frederick II had challenged the Austrian succession and seized Silesia. The leaders of an aristocratic military caste in France persuaded their government that the opportunity was too good to miss. The French, hoping for gains in north Italy and the Netherlands, eager to humiliate an ancient enemy, joined the Prussians in the hounding of the Habsburg empire. Official France momentarily forgot America, and the Spaniards were left to defend their Indies as best they could.

Here, it seemed, was an English opportunity; but in the event, Spaniards in the Indies displayed a new and unexpected capacity for looking after themselves, and for England the war went limpingly. Vernon's initial success in capturing Puerto Belo and destroying its fortifications was not repeated. He was obliged to spend part of 1740 looking for d'Antin's fleet The great force sent out under Ogle and Cathcart to join him suffered from ambiguous orders and divided counsel. Havana, now protected by a naval squadron permanently based there, was (probably rightly) deemed too strong to be taken. The combined naval and military attacks on Cartagena, and afterwards on Santiago de Cuba, were both failures. As usual, the English took many prizes and seriously interrupted the normal lawful trade of Spanish America; the Puerto Belo galleons, indeed, were never restored and that part of the trade was left to a few 'register-ships' sailing singly and taking their chance. The smugglers throve by the war; the English government characteristically ordered Vernon to do all he could to protect and convoy English trade with the enemy's colonies. Nevertheless the admirals commanding the Havana squadron succeeded not only in protecting their own base, but also, on four separate occasions, in getting substantial treasure shipments home to Spain: Torres' squadron to Santander in 1741, Torres, again, to Ferrol in 1744–5, Reggio to Cadiz in 1747–8 and again in 1749.[6] Outside the Caribbean, Anson's foray in the Pacific, and his subsequent circumnavigation, were famous feats of arms and seamanship, and of successful plunder.[7] Had his ships been better found and manned, had he arrived earlier, Anson might have effected a junction with Vernon on the Isthmus, and established an English toll-booth on the old silver route to Peru; or he might (as the Spaniards greatly feared) have effected a lodgement on the coast of Chile. Either of these projects, if they could have been maintained, would have caused the Spaniards great inconvenience. The strategic assumptions on which they rested, however, were already becoming old-fashioned. Panama was already on the way to becoming a ghost town. In the later eighteenth century Buenos Aires, not Cape Horn or the Isthmus, was to be the main gate to Upper Peru. Anson's achievement, in the event, was a brilliant raid and no more. In general, the 'War of Jenkins' Ear', embarked on lightly and for relatively trivial causes, in itself produced relatively trivial results.

A maritime conflict between England and Spain in the Indies, however, could not be treated as an isolated episode; the resumption of hostilities with France was only a matter of time. Anglo-French armed rivalry in America was endemic. The settlers of each nation felt threatened on many fronts by the planting and trading activities of the other. Every move had a military implication. Planters were expert at communicating their fears to their respective governments. Both governments, moreover, sought constantly, whether by alliance, by cajolery or by bullying, to exploit the relative weakness of Spain. Every outbreak of war in Europe brought latent hostility to the surface and led to overt fighting in America. The War of the Austrian Succession, with its frequent and sharp reversals of military fortune, offered, or seemed to offer, many opportunities for a swift colonial *coup*. Yet neither government could simply and cynically use the war in

Europe as an excuse for commercial and colonial aggression. France was very heavily extended in Europe and most French statesmen naturally regarded overseas commitments as secondary. England, though considerably less involved in the vicissitudes of the Austrian crown, could not ignore Europe. The king was committed to the defence of Hanover; ministers worried perpetually over French designs on the Netherlands; government and people – at least most substantial people – dreaded a Jacobite rising with French support. England, though militarily weak, entered upon a land as well as a sea war in Europe in 1742, to protect Hanover, to support Austria, and to forestall the consequences of French military success in Europe. Not until 1744 did the French government retort by rallying, under the Second Family Compact, to the support of Spain in America. The agreement was on familiar lines: the Spaniards were to have French help in recovering Minorca and Gibraltar and in driving the English out of Georgia; the French were to be rewarded by privileges in the Cadiz trade. America, however, remained perforce a distant side-show, for English and French alike; Carteret's dictum, 'look to America ... Europe will take care of itself',[8] mere words. When fighting began in earnest in America, the forces which could be spared for it on both sides were limited; and in the event, not much came of it.

The war between England and France in the Caribbean was governed not by desire to acquire new territories or new trades, but by commercial rivalry between two existing sets of sugar colonies. The French Caribbean islands, larger in area and with soil less exhausted, were competing more and more successfully with the English islands in the production of cheap sugar and in trade with Europe and English North America. War offered the English an opportunity to cripple French sugar production, since they could not defeat it in open competition. Planters on both sides disliked the acquisition of fresh sugar-producing territory; they feared that increased imports into their protected markets would lower prices. Each side hoped not to acquire and exploit the enemy's colonies but to destroy and depopulate them; to burn the canes, to wreck the machinery and, above all, to carry off the slaves, who were the most necessary, most valuable and most mobile part of the planters' capital. Failing the destruction of the enemy's colonies, the next-best thing was to cut off their trade, starve them of provisions and slaves, and prevent them from selling their sugar. In this war naval activity was, in practice, largely confined to this second type of operation, and in it the English achieved considerable success. The main weakness of their position was colonial indiscipline. The dependence of the French islands upon North America for timber and provisions, upon Ireland for beef, should have given the English an important tactical advantage; but in war as in peace the shippers of New England continued to trade with the enemy, either directly or through the neutral Dutch harbours in Curaçao or St Eustatius. The privateers which sailed from Martinique to prey upon English shipping were often stored with American provisions; meanwhile the English islands went short, and sometimes had to be supplied with food from England. It was largely the profit-seeking of the New Englanders which prevented the British navy from fully achieving its object: the commercial isolation of the French in the Caribbean.[9] The North American colonies, with their scattered (but fast growing) populations, were much less vulnerable to commercial wrecking tactics than were the West Indies, and the fighting there took more account of purely strategic considerations. The key to it was the powerful fortress of Louisbourg on Cape Breton, on which the French had spent great sums since 1713, but which they had neglected to garrison adequately. Here (as Shirley, the energetic governor of Massachusetts, perceived)[10] was an opportunity. Louisbourg guarded the St Lawrence, and served also as a base for a considerable privateer fleet. In French hands ships based there could dominate the Banks fishery, threaten the trade route between Europe and New England, and make the English hold on Nova Scotia, with its predominantly French population, precarious. In English hands it could throttle Quebec. Shirley thought the place could be taken by colonial land forces if adequate naval support were given, and to this Newcastle agreed. The New England assemblies provided 4,000 militia (the other colonial governments characteristically refusing to participate). A small naval squadron – too small to break the deadlock in the Caribbean – was ordered north from Antigua, despite local protests, and proved adequate to compel the surrender of the undermanned fortress.[11] An eminent English divine proclaimed that only eternity would be long enough for due thanksgiving;[12] but Louisbourg was handed back at the peace.

A mutual restoration of oversea conquests was an obvious formula for suspending hostilities, in a situation where the main contenders were all, for the moment, financially exhausted. Louisbourg was balanced – most inadequately, in New England opinion – by Madras. No West Indian territories changed hands. Dominica, St Lucia, St Vincent and Tobago were formally declared 'neutral' and not to be settled; though the Caribs were dying out, and the squatters, mostly French, who drifted in to take their place could not, in practice, be evicted. Between England and Spain, matters were left in the air. Nothing definite was said about freedom of navigation, in whose name the war had begun, or about the logwood camps, which continued to expand with backing from Jamaica. The South Sea Company no longer traded, and in a supplementary commercial agreement in 1750 it accepted £100,000 for the surrender of its Spanish privileges. Private smuggling, though no longer cloaked by the *asiento,* went on as before. The peace of Aix-la-Chapelle, then, was a truce rather than a definitive treaty, and settled no major question at issue, whether in Europe or abroad. The basic hostilities and suspicions, Anglo-French, Austro-Prussian, the mutual irritations between England and Spain, all remained; no one doubted that war, sooner or later, would be resumed. The Seven Years War, however, was to be more than a mere resumption. In the uneasy interval between 1748 and 1756 the combatants regrouped themselves, and some at least revised the order of priority among their objects. In England the attractions of an aggressive colonial, commercial and naval policy overseas gained ground steadily, at the expense of European considerations. This shift of emphasis was supported by a heterogeneous and outspoken public opinion, with bases in the financial 'City', the port towns, and the London mob; and found political expression through the personal ascendancy of Pitt. In parliament the foxhunters and the place-hunters, while as always resenting all taxation, could be cowed, if not persuaded, by his terrifying eloquence; and traditionally, if money had to be spent, they would rather spend it on ships than on armies. Anson, at the

Admiralty, saw to it that they got more ships, and better found, for their money. Pitt saw to it that as many ships as possible were employed where dramatic successes could be had, in the Americas.

There was solid reasoning behind all this. The profitability of the American colonies, to settlers, merchants, and indirectly the treasury, was evidently increasing. The West Indies in particular, far from suffering by the late war, appeared to have thriven by it. War had incidental disadvantages – privateering losses, high freight and insurance rates, and so forth, which offset wartime rises in the price of sugar; but war crippled the commerce of the productive French islands; it raised national anti-French feeling; it caused people in England to shelve the economic question of the merits of British dependence on British-grown sugar. In the interval between the wars the disadvantages disappeared, but some of the advantages remained. Prices remained fairly steady and fairly high – the average was fifty per cent higher than that for the decade before the war.[13] Production was increasing, but so was the capacity of the English market, which now absorbed the whole product of the British West Indies and demanded more. Grocers and refiners in England might murmur at the high price of British West Indian sugar, and ask leave, failing an adequate increase in British production, to import foreign; but no one in authority in mercantilist England, with a new war in prospect, paid much attention to such unorthodox proposals. Jamaica, with its large area of virgin land, was the chief beneficiary of the steady expansion of a protected market; the economies of Barbados and the Leeward Islands were propped up rather than expanded, for they had no room to expand; the possibility of acquiring more islands, desirable anyway on strategic grounds, was economically less repugnant than it had been. War, then, for colonies protected by an efficient navy, was by no means necessarily a disaster. Expanding trade might well be backed by expanding dominion. In England, no one doubted that West Indian islands were worth fighting for.

As for North America, between the wars fighting there hardly stopped, and French and English governments, whatever their own preferences, could not easily keep out of it. The root of the trouble was an extraordinarily rapid growth of population in most of the English settlements, swollen by emigration from Scotland, Ireland and Germany as well as from England itself, and by natural increase. Population multiplied six- or seven-fold in the first half of the eighteenth century, and probably approached 2,000,000 on the eve of the Seven Years War.[14] These increasing numbers made English North America more and more valuable as a market for manufactures and for re-exported East India goods – its imports from England had increased about eleven-fold since 1700 – more and more essential as a source of supplies for the pampered West Indies, and as a producer of 'colonial' goods, tobacco especially, for Britain and, by re-export, for Europe. Even neglected and underrated New England enjoyed a vastly increased demand for its most characteristic product, mast timber, now increasingly and urgently needed by English and West Indian dockyards for masting and sparring an enormously swollen navy.[15] Throughout the colonies, land prices mounted, and with them land speculation on a very large scale. Pioneer settlers seeking land were forced to move further and further west. A number of land companies were formed between the wars, particularly in Virginia – the Loyal and the Ohio in 1749, the abortive Greenbrier in 1754 – to acquire and distribute land west of the Alleghenies; wild forest country, hitherto known only to Indians and a handful of explorers and fur traders.

The French were already interesting themselves in this area, and for them the prospect of ant-like processions of English settlers crossing the mountains and spreading out in the Ohio valley was distasteful and alarming. Their own settlements along the St Lawrence and its confluents were modest; but since a high proportion of the population was concerned, as trappers or as dealers, with the fur trade, access to wild country was for them a necessity. Even in those vast expanses, they felt a claustrophobic dread of confinement. Unlike most English settlers, they were aware of a community of interest with the Indians they dealt with. This sympathy, as well as the more cynical tactic of using any available auxiliary, led them to encourage Indian raids on English outlying settlements. Probably little encouragement was needed; on the New York frontiers, especially, in the Mohawk valley and about Lake Champlain, such raiding had long been endemic and each contestant had its Indian clients. Raiding, however, was necessarily inconclusive; it hardened the attitude of English colonists, without relieving French fear of isolation. This fear was real enough. Sea communications were precarious. In 1749 the English had established, as a counter to Louisbourg privateering, a rival base at Halifax in Nova Scotia. If Louisbourg should again be successfully invested by a British fleet, Canada could be cut off from France. In view of this danger, and in view of the small numbers of the Canadian population (about 55,000 in 1754)[16] the French maintained in Canada a formidable army of regular troops, and a chain of forts along the St Lawrence and the Great Lakes, stretching from Louisbourg to Michilimackinac. Further, with a characteristically wide strategic vision, which often exceeded their tactical reach, the governors of New France endeavoured both to limit English westward advance and to secure river communications with their sally-port, New Orleans on the Gulf of Mexico, by fortifying key points in the Ohio valley: Fort Duquesne, founded in 1753 on the site of modern Pittsburg, and its satellite stockades, in the territory claimed by Virginia.

The Virginia government made attempts, in which George Washington participated, to eject the French from the Ohio; but no other colony, except North Carolina, would support them, the French were locally too strong, and the attempts failed. Responsibility fell back on the government in England. Should it acquiesce? To do so would be to forfeit colonial confidence, already shaken by the retrocession of Louisbourg, and probably to abandon most of North America permanently to the French. Should it negotiate, and so give the French time to build up naval strength? Or should it fight, and run the risk of having to fight as well in the West Indies, in India and in Europe? A little reluctantly, at first somewhat ineffectually, with many disclaimers of aggressive intention, it fought.[17] Braddock, appointed in 1754 as the first commander-in-chief of all British land forces in America, was sent out to Virginia with a thousand regular troops, to march against Fort Duquesne the following year. Boscawen was ordered to intercept at sea French reinforcements on their way to Canada. Combined regular and provincial forces, under Shirley's general direction, were to attempt Fort Niagara, Crown Point on Lake Champlain, and Forts Beauséjour and Gaspereau at the heads of the Bay of Fundy, on the isthmus connecting Nova Scotia with the mainland. All these operations were conceived as defensive measures, as attempts to counter French encroachments and pierce the tightening chain of French positions which threatened and confined the English colonies; but all were nonetheless acts of undeclared war. The Niagara project was especially provocative and risky. It was to be launched from a very inadequate base, the flimsy English fort at Oswego on Lake Ontario; both Niagara and Oswego were supposed, by tacit agreement with the powerful Iroquois confederation, to be peaceful, neutral posts under Iroquois protection – a primitive analogue with the situation of rival East India companies trading in the territory of the Mughal empire. The Iroquois were not strong enough to maintain this protection in the face of organised armies; but despite their long association, as fur-trading middlemen, with the English in the Hudson valley, their reaction to English military operations against the French was likely to be hostile and dangerous. Shirley planned an even bolder stroke, against Fort Frontenac, in an area which the English had never penetrated or claimed, in order to cut French communications down the St Lawrence; a proposal strategically sound but politically quite unacceptable. Shirley's tendency to run ahead of his masters in England was an important factor in his subsequent recall and his supersession as commander-in-chief by the more cautious, equally able, equally unlucky Loudoun.

Nearly all the English projects failed. Boscawen, through bad luck and worse weather, missed the main French fleet and took only two stragglers; enough to provoke the enemy, not enough seriously to weaken him. This failure, and the safe arrival of heavy French reinforcements in Canada, was crucial for the land campaigns. Braddock's army was ambushed and dispersed, and himself killed, by a mixed French and Indian force near Fort Duquesne. The French held Niagara and Crown Point, and subsequently took the opposing English posts, Oswego, and Fort William Henry on Lake George. Only one of the English operations was successful, that against forts Beauséjour and Gaspereau. The attackers had the help of a well-informed spy, Thomas Pichon, who entered British service partly in resentment against slow promotion, partly, it seems, from conviction. He was a rationalist, an anti-clerical free-thinker, who thought his own government guilty of a breach of faith in seeking to undermine the Treaty of Utrecht, by encouraging Indian raiding and by persistent encroachment in Nova Scotia.[18] He was an interesting early example of the phenomenon, commoner now than then, of treason for ideology's sake. A force of 2,000 New Englanders and 250 regular soldiers, acting on Pichon's detailed advice, took Beauséjour in 1755. This was a serious breach in the French chain; it isolated Louisbourg, except by water, from any hinterland capable of furnishing supplies, and it cut off the Acadians from Canadian support. The Acadians, influenced by French priests, had retained their French loyalties through more than forty years. They had been wooed rather than repressed by the government of Nova Scotia, to no effect. Some of them served in the defence of Beauséjour, and after its capture the government, for its own security, decided to expel them. An oath of allegiance was administered, and those refusing it – as nearly all did – either took to the woods or were deported to other colonies. Their lands were subsequently occupied by immigrants of English speech. The pitiful dispersal of these obstinate, simple people, happy nowhere but in Acadia, greatly intensified French indignation against England. The French retort, methodically prepared, came in 1756. An ultimatum, which was rejected, demanded the return of French shipping seized, in America and elsewhere, by British cruisers. Formidable naval squadrons were dispatched to Canada, to St Domingue and to Martinique. A large army was concentrated about the Channel ports, for an invasion of England should opportunity offer. In the first formal engagement of the war, the Toulon fleet, commanded by la Galissonière, who had been governor of New France, seized Minorca; a loss which Byng, commanding British naval forces in the Mediterranean, failed to prevent or retrieve. Once again a series of colonial skirmishes had developed into a worldwide Anglo-French war.

Most of the advantages appeared to lie with France. The English in 1756–7 were threatened with invasion at home (though, admittedly not, since the collapse of the Forty-five, with internal rebellion); their situation in the Mediterranean was seriously weakened; in the Caribbean they had reason to fear the loss of vulnerable and valuable islands; in North America they had been pushed back east of the Alleghenies and cut off from the Great Lakes. The explanation commonly offered, then and later, that of faltering leadership, reflects Pitt's contempt for his fellow men, rather than considered judgment. True, Newcastle's ministry was better fitted to manipulate than to decide; but with the available resources, it is difficult to see what other decisions ministers could have reached. To have given Shirley his head in 1755 would have been to admit publicly the certainty of war, which few, either in England or France, then wished to do. As for commanders in the field, Shirley lacked tact and caution, but certainly not ability. Byng was neither a coward nor a bungler; he failed because his fleet was inferior in fire power to the French, his ships were foul from long sea-keeping, his most crucial signal was misunderstood, and he feared, properly, to leave Gibraltar unprotected. He was court-martialled and shot because mobs, unaccustomed to naval reverses, howled for an expiatory victim, and ministers were afraid to protect him. Nor was Braddock an incompetent general; Washington – no habitual flatterer of English generals – served under him, and respected him. His army was too small for its many tasks, and his men had no training in Indian warfare; but how could they have? Forest fighting had to be learned by experience. Provincial troops did no better at it than European regulars. The deficiency was remedied, in time, by recruiting frontiersmen into Ranger companies attached to the regular army, for scouting duties, just as the French had long employed Indians. All in all, the French record of success, the English of defeat, between 1754 and 1757, reflected less a difference in the quality of leadership, than a real disparity of military strength. France in 1755 maintained a standing army of some 200,000 men.[19] Against these, there were not more than 30,000 troops in the British Isles. To send 1,000 men with Braddock, then, and others to stiffen Shirley's local levies, was a serious sacrifice of home defence. The superior numbers of the English population in North America represented a great potential advantage, but one of limited military significance, because of the difficulty of mobilising it. Most colonial assemblies were reluctant to raise local troops for operations outside their own areas of interest. All demanded regular forces when trouble appeared, and even then some grudged the expense of providing barracks or billets. The French tolerated no local nonsense of that sort, nor did they need to. Their Canadian militia was unified and relatively well-drilled. They could usually reinforce Canada with regular troops at need, provided that the troops could be transported. At sea, English superiority was throughout the eighteenth century an article of English faith. In fact, in 1755 France had about sixty ships of the Line in commission, and Machault hoped soon to raise the number to eighty.[20] The number of English ships of comparable class was variously estimated; the best informed estimates range from seventy-five to eighty.[21] French warships at that time were generally thought to be better designed than English, and so faster.[22] The English, also, always had to employ more ships in commerce protection than did the French, having more commerce to protect; and so long as invasion threatened, many ships had to be kept permanently in the Channel. English naval superiority, then, though real, was far from overwhelming. There were grounds for thinking that the naval and military duel between England and France might prove as inconclusive as its predecessor; might even, in North America, end in a substantial French victory. Matters were in this state when European events forced themselves on the attention of the combatants.

Frederick II's invasion of Saxony in 1756, like his invasion of Silesia in 1740 (and like it, unexpected), precipitated a general European war, distinct from the Anglo-French war overseas, but linked with it by the network of European alliances. The strands of this network had changed significantly since 1748. The French government, increasingly alarmed by the growing military power of Prussia, had abandoned a traditional animosity and entered into agreements with Austria and Russia to oppose – indeed to reverse – Prussian aggression. The English government, in the interest of European 'balance', and on the general principle that any enemy of France was a friend to England, therefore reached a corresponding defensive understanding with Prussia. This celebrated reversal of alliances worked, in the long run, to the military advantage of England. It relieved England of responsibility for defending the Austrian Netherlands and eventually committed France to a dangerous war on two fronts. Many people in England, including the king, it is true, distrusted Frederick II and deplored the invasion of Saxony; but Hanover could not be ignored. If the French could overrun and hold Hanover, England would have to pay a heavy ransom at a peace, probably in the form of cessions of territory overseas, to secure its release. Initially, therefore, British action in Germany was restricted to an unsuccessful effort to protect Hanover from French invasion, and even that expenditure was challenged in parliament. In 1757, however, in the apprehension of defeat, these scruples were overcome and Frederick became something of an English hero. The Methodist preacher Whitefield, from the pulpit of the London Tabernacle, with unconscious cynicism acclaimed Rossbach as a victory for the Protestant cause. Pitt, long opposed to European adventure and expense, came when in office to favour a massive German diversion against France and to appreciate for that purpose the services of an incomparable *condottiere*. Men would be better employed and money better spent in supporting Frederick, he maintained, than in tip-and-run raids on the French coast. From 1758 to 1761, a small but not negligible British army campaigned in Germany. Much more important, immense sums, far beyond what was needed for the mere defence of Hanover, were paid in subsidies to Hanover, Hesse Cassel and Prussia. France similarly, though less generously, subsidised the Austrians; but England, with an expanding commercial economy, better financial organisation, a more flexible tax system, was better equipped for a war of subsidies.[23] For four years Pitt persuaded parliament to pay Frederick annually, in order to keep him fighting, a sum equal to the entire revenues of Prussia.

Pitt, like any successful war minister, rallying public opinion behind him in fear and hatred of the enemy, felt impelled to strike at that enemy wherever the blows might hurt. Later, in defending his European policy against mounting criticism, he went so far as to claim that 'America had been conquered in Germany'; to which George Grenville replied that 'it had not been the German war but the want of seamen that had disabled France from prosecuting the war in America and from invading England'.[24] There is, in fact, very little evidence that in the two distinct wars in which France and England were engaged, the progress of the one greatly affected the outcome of the other. Victory, in a worldwide war for trade and dominion overseas, depended on the ability to build, man and deploy great numbers of ships, enough ships to maintain a simultaneous superiority in all the major theatres of the war. In 1755, as we have seen, the French navy was inferior in numbers to the British, but not decisively so, and the rate of construction was comparable. This, admittedly, was in very favourable circumstances, in time of official peace, under an exceptionally able and energetic minister. If at that time Spain could have been persuaded into war on the side of France, the two navies together would have possessed a decided superiority; but Spanish foreign policy was directed by Wall, the Irish Jacobite exile who had been ambassador in London and was Newcastle's friend; England was served in Madrid by an outstanding and well-liked ambassador, Keene; every effort was made to avoid offence, and Spain remained neutral. After the declaration of war in 1756, the English rate of naval construction rose rapidly, the French remained steady, and after a time declined. This was not the result of conscious choices between land and sea armament; it was inherent in the economic organisation of the two countries. It was not simply a matter of money. England had more shipbuilding ports, more slips, more trained shipwrights – however conservative, however rule-of-thumb their methods. Both countries were deficient in some kinds of native timber; but England had better access to foreign supplies; and lying athwart the routes by which timber must be brought from the Rhine, the Baltic, and North America, to Brest, Rochefort and Le Havre, it could in large measure deny these supplies to France.[25] England, with a much larger merchant marine, was less dependent on timorous neutrals for the carriage of timber and had a much larger reserve of seamen for manning the warships, once they were built. No doubt if the French could have reduced their European commitments, whether by abandoning the Austrians or knocking out the Prussians there would have been more money for their navy; but that would not immediately have produced more ships or more men. Shipwrights required a long apprenticeship; ships took time to build – between one and two years for a ship of the Line; and a lack of seamen could not be remedied by drafting soldiers to fill their places. The tide of maritime war began to turn in favour of England in 1758, before Pitt's subsidies to Prussia had taken effect. The German war had nothing to do with it: it was a matter of numbers of ships, of trained seamen, of experienced sea commanders. In the spring of 1759, the crucial year of the maritime war, England had a hundred and thirteen ships of the Line in commission, thirty building; France, not more than half those numbers; and the disparity was growing monthly.[26]

The years 1758 and 1759 were of almost consistent victory for England, and of defeat for France, in the colonies and at sea. The story has been told in detail many times[27] and need only be summarised here. In 1758 the economic weakness of the French in North America began seriously to affect their military strength. A relatively small population could barely produce enough food, beyond its own normal needs, to supply a relatively large army. The heavy demands for labour and military service made upon the *habitans* increased the difficulty. The harvests of 1756 and 1757 were both bad. The army in Canada became increasingly dependent upon supplies from France; but as the English blockade of French harbours was strengthened and tightened, an ever-increasing proportion of supply ships bound for Canada was intercepted.[28] In the early months of 1758 the entire province was faced with critical shortage. Soldiers' rations were progressively reduced. Indian auxiliaries, always improvident with food and greedy in their demands, drifted away, some to join the English. Problems of food distribution aggravated the personal differences between Vaudreuil, the governor general, and Montcalm commanding the troops. A starving and quarrelling New France awaited, though still with high military confidence, the offensive operations, planned by Loudoun for 1758 and adopted by Pitt, to recover the ground which the English had lost in the previous two years. Montcalm's confidence was misplaced. Of the four principal assaults mounted by the English, only one failed: the proposed invasion of Canada by way of Lake Champlain, led by Abercromby, who (through one of Pitt's rare errors of personal judgment) had just superseded Loudoun as commander-in-chief.

Abercromby's large force was heavily defeated by Montcalm before Ticonderoga. Almost at the same time, Louisbourg surrendered to the combined land and sea forces commanded by Amherst and Boscawen. This action, an outstanding and rare example, in the history of combined operations, of friendly co-operation between the services, had been very thoroughly prepared in Europe by a series of naval engagements, in which French fleets which might have saved Louisbourg were disabled or destroyed: Osborne's defeat of Duquesne's squadron in the Mediterranean and his blockade of the rest of the Toulon fleet in Cartagena; the destruction of the Canada convoy and its escorting fleet out of Rochefort, by Hawke at Basque Roads. With Louisbourg gone (and later, by Pitt's order dismantled) the French army in Canada was effectively cut off from France. After Bradstreet's successful surprise attack on Fort Frontenac a few weeks later, it was cut off also from the Great Lakes; and towards the end of the year the link with Louisiana was snapped by Forbes' expedition against Fort Duquesne; no forced march like Braddock's, but a deliberate, methodical advance, every step consolidated, with an army of more than 6,000 men, regulars, provincials and Indians. On Forbes' near approach the French garrison, already much reduced, evacuated the place and blew it up. Early in the following summer (1759) the forts at Ticonderoga and Crown Point suffered a similar fate, and Niagara surrendered. Everywhere French forces at the outposts fell back on Canada. The army which defended Canada – isolated, lacking regular reinforcement, its numbers increasingly recruited from untrained provincials, its equipment deteriorating and now markedly inferior to that of the enemy[29] – was nevertheless formidable and ably led; and in adversity its leaders sank their differences. The dramatic capture of Quebec by Wolfe and Saunders in September 1759 was not the end of the matter, for the British army soon found itself shut in the city during a bitter winter and early spring. Had even a small French fleet been able to enter the river before the English in May 1760, the situation in Canada might have been retrieved; but French action at sea had been almost entirely paralysed at the end of 1759 by two more major defeats in European waters; the Brest fleet under Conflans – twenty-one fine ships, but manned largely by impressed agricultural labourers – had been virtually destroyed by Hawke in Quibéron Bay; and the Toulon fleet under de la Clue, on its way to join Conflans, was heavily mauled by Boscawen in Lagos Bay, in the lee of Cape St Vincent. Both fleets had been moving to support the long-projected invasion of England. With the wreckage of the Brest fleet strewn along the coast of Brittany, England could not be invaded nor Canada relieved. Even so, it was not until September 1760 that Montreal capitulated and Amherst received from Vaudreuil the surrender of his devastated province.

Campaigning in Canada was necessarily seasonal. Apart from minor forays on snowshoes, the troops remained in winter quarters for six months of every year. Most ships were then withdrawn from the area, and could be employed in warmer waters; chiefly in the West Indies, 'where' according to William Beckford, 'all our wars must begin and end'.[30] It was rarely possible, however, to maintain a regular movement of squadrons between North America and the Caribbean because of the time needed for cleaning and refit, and down to 1757 the warships which could be spared for the West Indies were employed mainly on the routine chores of a war for trade: coastal forays, commerce raiding and blockade, convoy escort duty, operations against enemy privateers. Privateers were everywhere. Port Royal in Jamaica and Fort Royal in Martinique alike, New York even more, lived largely by them throughout the war. At first sight the French did the better at this game of beggar-my-neighbour, and in 1757 they kept Jamaica in constant fear of raids. Their privateers captured many more English ships than English privateers did French;[31] but this was because there were many more English merchant ships at sea than French. The British replaced their losses much more rapidly than did the French. In fact, by 1757 nearly all French merchant ships trading to the West Indies had been either captured, laid up, or fitted out for privateering. The trade of the French islands – what little survived – was in the hands either of neutrals, or of British colonial shippers, often using flags of truce or other devices for trading with the enemy.[32]

From the end of 1758 the British took a new initiative in the Caribbean, and the character of the fighting changed. Pitt, determined to keep Cape Breton Island and not to be forced to ex-change it for, say, Minorca, set about making other conquests which might serve as ransoms at a peace. He picked naturally on the West Indies. Large forces, much larger than had been em-ployed in the previous war, were sent there; and their com-manders were instructed to annex the enemy's sugar colonies, not merely to pillage them. The West India interest, once so fearful of such a policy, now supported it; indeed their most influential spokesman, Alderman Beckford, urged Pitt to adopt it.[33] It was the lesser of two evils. Constant alarms reminded planters of their small numbers and of their vulnerability against an enemy fleet or a slave mutiny, and forced upon them a more strategic, a less purely commercial appreciation of their position. Their properties would be safer if Martinique, Guadeloupe and the neutral islands were in English hands while the war lasted. If it were decided at a peace to keep any islands captured from the French, then the dan-ger of the admission of their sugars to the English market would have to be faced; but even that danger might be avoided by evict-ing the French inhabitants (had not the Acadians been successfully evicted?) and by forbidding their English successors to plant sugar.

Two attacks, one direct and one indirect, were launched against the French West Indies late in 1758. The indirect attack, by Keppel, against the French stations in Senegal, culminated in the capture of Gorée. It crippled the French slave trade and seriously hampered the working of the plantations in the French West Indies. In the direct attack, the combined naval and military forces under Moore and Barrington found Martinique too strong for them, and took prosperous Guadeloupe instead, in the spring of 1759; a French fleet under Bompar arriving just too late to raise the siege. The planters of Guadeloupe were allowed to capitulate on very favourable terms. After the initial damage of the fighting had been repaired, the island enjoyed a renewed prosperity, for English and North American merchants rushed in to supply the food, the timber and the slaves for which it starved. Feckless planters escaped from their debts to French *commissionaires* and were allowed to run up new debts to English factors. Best of all, they found at last a safe European and North American market for their sugars. This was precisely the kind of conquest most disliked by the English planters; it struck directly at their profits without giving them any permanent promise of security. The flooding of the London market with Guadeloupe sugars was one of the reasons for a sharp drop in prices in 1760, and explains the bitter complaints of the West India interest, not against the conquest, but against the terms of the capitulation.

In 1761 ensued a period of complex and abortive negotiation over peace terms. Choiseul, a military realist as chief minister, wanted peace; failing peace, he wanted a Spanish alliance in prosecuting the war; he carried on both sets of negotiations simultaneously, not without dexterity. Pitt, who expected further victories and thought little of Spanish fighting capacity, refused all terms which Choiseul could offer; but Choiseul achieved his Spanish alliance. Spain had long-standing grievances against England – Gibraltar; the Honduras logwood camps; English intrigues with the Mosquito Indians; and the perennial maritime disputes. These last became more acute in this war, and assumed a new form. The Admiralty either could not or would not control the activities of privateers. When the hard-pressed French (in practice, not in law) opened the trade of their starving Caribbean colonies to neutral shipping, any Spanish ship suspected of having touched at a French colonial port became, under the 'rule of the war of 1756', liable to seizure.[34] Many were molested, some in Spanish territorial waters; indeed a turning of the tables. Wall's friendly feelings towards England and Newcastle's attentiveness to Spanish complaints, for long postponed a break; but Wall's patience was not endless and Pitt would fight anyone. As the war moved in favour of England and against France, moreover, it appeared that Pitt intended, if he could, to seize all the French possessions in the Americas, and the neutral islands, to which Spain made some shadowy claim. If peace were made upon such conditions, Spain would be left alone to deal with an England all-powerful in the West Indies. It was in these circumstances that the Spanish government agreed to the Family Compact of 1761, which bound Spain to declare war before May 1762 if peace had not been made between France and England. Peace was not made, and the English government anticipated events by declaring war on Spain in January.

In that same month, Rodney, fresh from England with a powerful fleet, took Martinique. Again a strong French squadron, this time under Blénac, was hurried out from France, and again, because of interruptions of stores on their way coastwise to Brest, arrived too late to achieve anything, beyond causing the customary panic in Jamaica. To the annoyance of the English West Indians, Martinique was allowed a capitulation similar to that of Guadeloupe. Blénac found himself, short of provisions and with half his men sick, blockaded in Cap Français, while Rodney passed on to reduce St Lucia, St Vincent and Grenada. Dominica had already surrendered to a North American force. Of all the French possessions in the West Indies, only St Domingue remained; it was a question, for the French, of where the next English blow might fall – in St Domingue or in Louisiana.

Meanwhile the Spaniards, far from helping to save the French colonies, began to lose their own. There was no contact between French and Spanish commanders. Rodney's fleet was now so strong that he needed only half his ships to stand watch over Blénac; the rest could be sent cruising profitably and safely for Spanish prizes off the Main, away from the hurricane zone. A fresh and powerful combined expedition from England under Pocock and Albemarle, carrying 12,000 regular troops, arrived in Barbados for an attack on Cuba. This force, augmented by two American regiments from New York, took Havana in August 1762. Havana had long been thought by the Spaniards to be impregnable. Its fall made a great stir; the invaders captured in harbour some of the best ships in the Spanish navy, and collected great sums in prize money; and for nine months Cuba was thrown open to English trade, to the great advantage both of traders and inhabitants. Two other misfortunes befell Spain in the same year. An English fleet sailing from the East Indies captured Manila; and a Spanish invasion of Portugal, intended as a diversion, proved an unexpected failure. In October 1762 Charles III capitulated. The French had been pressing him for some months to make peace. It had become obvious that France and Spain together, in the then state of their finances and armament, were no match for England at sea; France could not much longer face the financial strain of war; Choiseul, apparently, really believed that if Charles insisted on an heroic last-ditch resistance, Spain might lose some major province – Mexico, perhaps – and so embarrass France still further.

English ministers were almost as eager for peace as Choiseul, though for somewhat different reasons. George III was anxious to be rid of responsibility in Germany. In England, grumbles about taxation were growing louder. Some political leaders, Bedford, for example, were for peace on principle. Others, who had long resented Pitt's bullying ways, were ready to make political capital out of the general war-weariness. Many, too, felt nervous about the tremendous ascendancy achieved in the colonial field, which they feared would provoke a permanent combination of all the other colonial powers against Britain. These fears were justified; but, as usual, it was not in mortals to countermand success. For Pitt – the only man then in the first rank of English politics who consistently thought in terms of strategic and economic value, who considered colonial acquisitions as something more than debating-points for or against the ministry – the best insurance against future danger was to deprive the French of all oversea bases from which English colonies and trade could be seriously threatened. He dismissed as nonsense the objection that continued war to that end would lead to bankruptcy; during the last four years of the war, English shipping figures increased by twenty per cent and the slave trade almost doubled.[35] Trade had indeed, in his phrase, 'flourished by means of war'. But Pitt, at last failing to carry his colleagues with him, had resigned at the end of 1761. Bute, his successor, wanted a speedy peace, for popularity's sake, and hoped to reconcile the French and Spanish governments to their defeat by appeasement and concession.

For an early peace, something must, of course, be sacrificed; yet something beyond the original objects of the war must be kept, to satisfy popular clamour. The principal object of the war had been to safeguard the North American colonies, and to achieve this end Canada, or at least part of it, would have to be retained; but the trade and revenue of Canada were small, and the public reasonably expected the acquisitions at the peace to pay part of the cost of the war. The French West Indian islands, if retained, would bring an immediate revenue. Retained or not, moreover, they would undoubtedly go on buying provisions from North American traders, and paying in sugar and molasses; much better that this trade should be brought within the British mercantile system, than continue in contravention of it. During the 1761 peace discussions many people in England (though probably no responsible statesman) had thought Guadeloupe alone a more valuable acquisition than Canada.[36] France certainly would not cede all the conquered islands, but some of them might and should be kept. Which? Guadeloupe was the most productive; Martinique, with its good harbour and windward position, the most important strategically. Exporting merchants, refiners, confectioners, distillers, all pointed out the need for more sugar land, since the British islands were not producing enough sugar to allow for re-export to the Continent. They were for Guadeloupe. So, naturally, were the slave traders. The West India interest wanted Guadeloupe to be handed back, to keep up the price of sugar in London; if any French island were to be kept, they preferred Martinique, the Dunkirk of the Caribbean. Rodney also was strong for Martinique, on strategic grounds. Bute, however, apparently thought that France would not yield any settled colony. He agreed to restore both Martinique and Guadeloupe, and as a necessary adjunct, the French laving station at Gorée in West Africa (but not the factories on the Senegal, whose trade in gum was important to the London silk throwers). He demanded the cession of Grenada, all the neutral islands and the whole continent of North America east of the Mississippi. The territories to be ceded were all nearly empty, open to English enterprise, containing few Frenchmen to make trouble for the government; the least controversial cessions that could be devised. With the acquisition of territory was to be included the right of navigating the Mississippi itself. In the final peace terms all these demands were agreed,[37] except that France insisted on possession of St Lucia, on the ground that the island was essential for the defence of Martinique – a very good reason, as Pitt complained, for England to have kept it; and France retained, also against Pitt's strenuous objections, the right to participate in the Newfoundland fishery.

Bute's proposals were the least his countrymen could be expected to accept and the best the French could hope for; but they ignored the claim of Spain to be considered. Spain had been dragged into the war in the interests of France, had suffered heavy losses, and was now being urged to make a hasty peace, also in the interests of France. Charles III dreaded the prospect of Englishmen in the Gulf of Mexico, running their smuggling trade under cover of the Mississippi navigation, intercepting the Mexican *flotas* with greater ease than ever. Choiseul was obliged to recognise the force of the Spanish arguments, and to buy Spanish acquiescence by ceding Louisiana to Spain; thus adding, in Rodney's phrase, another desert to the Spanish empire. The direct disputes between England and Spain were settled, or shelved, without much difficulty. The logwood settlements in Honduras received for the first time a precarious recognition. Spain agreed to tolerate the presence of the cutters and to respect their property; England promised not to fortify the camps; nothing was said about boundaries. England restored Cuba to Spain and received Florida in exchange. This was thought in London to be a poor exchange. Florida was another desert, Cuba a flourishing colony, or at least one about to flourish. Ten thousand slaves had been carried to Havana during the British occupation, to work on Cuban sugar plantations; and officers returning to England spread there the taste for fine tobacco, in snuff and cigars, which has made England a major market for Cuban products from that day to this. As for Manila, the news of its fall arrived too late to affect the negotiations; after two years of very profitable English occupation, it too was quietly restored to Spain.

So a decisive war led to a much less decisive peace. To have peace quickly, the English made great concessions, and made them deliberately. As victors in the war, they were in a position to choose what they would offer. Their choice was in itself significant. By placing the safety of the mainland colonies at the top of their list of aims, ministers discharged a clear duty to their countrymen overseas; but they also recognised an incipient change of emphasis in the English assessment of the value of colonies generally. Shelburne, defending the treaty as President of the Board of Trade, was explicit on this:

> Wherever sugar grows population decreases. . . . Our sugar islands weaken and depopulate our Mother Country. . . . On the contrary the Northern

Colonies increase population and of course the consumption of our manufactures, pay us by their trade with foreigners . . . thereby giving employment to millions of inhabitants in Great Britain and Ireland, and are of the utmost consequence to the wealth, safety and independence of these kingdoms, and must continue so for ages to come.[38]

These views were not universally accepted, of course, either in the City or the country at large; but for the moment they prevailed. French ministers took the opposite view. They were less concerned with the export of manufactures, more impressed with the value of West Indian islands, their islands were indeed, in general, more productive than the British ones. This difference of emphasis made it easier for the French to give up Canada, and for the British to restore Guadeloupe, Martinique and St Lucia, despite the strategic threat which Martinique offered to the British islands and mainland harbours. In discounting this threat, British statesmen made two tacit assumptions. One was that British naval superiority over any foreseeable combination of enemies could be guaranteed, in the Caribbean as elsewhere; this assumption was, on the whole, to prove justified, though with very serious temporary lapses. The other was that old colonies, colonies which had been British before the Seven Years War, were safely British for ever. In fact, within a few years, loyalty was to evaporate and imperial government break down in a major portion of the British colonial empire. The British were not the only Europeans to miscalculate; within a few decades the same thing was to happen in a significant part of the French empire and throughout the greater part of the Spanish. In the last quarter of the eighteenth century and the first quarter of the nineteenth, collisions between the European seaborne empires were to be greatly complicated, sometimes occasioned, by mutiny.

NOTES

1. Malachy Postlethwayt, *The universal dictionary of trade*, London, 1751, s.v. 'South Sea Company'.
2. Jorge Juan and Antonio de Ulloa, *Relación histórica del viaje a la América meridional*, Madrid, 1768, I, p. 142.
3. See chapter 1, above.

4. For a notorious instance in 1730, see Pares, *War and Trade*, p. 15.

5. H. W. V. Temperley, 'The causes of the War of Jenkins' Ear, 1739', *Royal Historical Society Transactions*, 3rd series, III, 1909, pp. 197–236. On Jenkins and his subsequent career see chapter 9 below.

6. These considerable Spanish naval achievements have escaped the attention of historians. Fernández Duro mentions only the first (*Armada Española*, VI, p. 252). The evidence is in *Archivo General de Simancas*, 399 and 400. On the operations of the Havana Squadron in general see J. C. M. Ogelsby, 'Spain's Havana Squadron and the preservation of the balance of power in the Caribbean, 1740–1748', *Hispanic American Historical Review*, XLIX, 1969, p. 473.

7. They were so recognised at the time, and worthily chronicled: R. Walter, *A voyage round the world*, London, 1748.

8. *Cit.* E. Charteris, *William Augustus, Duke of Cumberland*, London, 1925, p. 88.

9. Pares, *War and Trade*, pp. 395 ff.

10. *Correspondence of William Shirley, Governor of Massachusetts and Military Commander in America, 1730–1760*, ed. C. H. Lincoln, 2 vols, New York, 1912, I, pp. 161–77.

11. *Ibid.*, I, pp. 215–79. H. W. Richmond, *The Navy in the War of 1739–48*, 3 vols, Cambridge, 1920, II, pp. 200–16.

12. C. G. Robertson, *England under the Hanoverians*, London, 1962, p. 11.

13. Pares, *War and Trade*, pp. 512–13.

14. There are no reliable figures. For a critical summary of the best guesses, see L. H. Gipson, *The British Empire before the American Revolution*, vol. X, *The Triumphant Empire; Thunder-clouds gather in the West 1763–1768*, New York, 1961, pp. 12–13. Gipson gives a total of 2,000,000 in 1763, including Virginia 350,000, Pennsylvania 300,000, Massachusetts, including Maine, 250,000, North Carolina 200,000, Connecticut, Maryland and South Carolina 150,000 each, New York 100,000.

15. On the growth of the mast trade, see Malone, *Pine trees and politics*, pp. 124–5.

16. Gipson, *The British Empire before the American Revolution*, V, p. 5.

17. For the attempts at negotiation and the mutual retaliations which led to war, see P. L.-R. Higonnet, 'The Origins of the Seven Years War', *Journal of Modern History*, XL, no. 1, March 1968.

18. Gipson, *The British Empire before the American Revolution*, VI, pp. 212 ff.

19. R. P. Waddington, *La Guerre de Sept Ans*, 3 vols, Paris, 1899–1904, I, p. 438.

20. *Ibid.*, p. 246.

21. W. C. B. Tunstall, *Admiral Byng and the loss of Minorca*, London, 1928, p. 34.

22. See chapter 11 below, n. 4.

23. John Entick, *General History of the Late War*, London, 1765, III, p. 96.

24. Horace Walpole, *Memoirs of the Reign of King George the Third*, London, 1845, I, pp. 96–7, 104.

25. P. W. Bamford, *Forests and French sea power*, Toronto, 1956, pp. 61 ff.

26. R. Beaston, *Naval and military memoirs of Great Britain from 1727 to 1783*, London, 1804, vol. III, appendix.

27. Notably by J. S. Corbett, *England in the Seven Years' War*, 2 vols, London, 1907; by L. H. Gipson, *The British Empire before the American Revolution*, *op. cit.*, vol. VII, *The Great War for the Empire – The Victorious years, 1758–1760*, New York, 1949; and on the French side by Waddington, *op. cit.*

28. Gipson, *The British Empire before the American Revolution*, VII, p. 168–9.

29. *Ibid.*, p. 419.

30. Walpole, *Memoirs*, I, p. 307.

31. According to Lloyds' figures, between June 1756 and June 1760, 2,539 British (including colonial) ships were taken by the French, 944 French ships by the British. Gipson, *The British Empire*, VIII, p. 71.

32. The flag-of-truce trade was notorious. Flag-of-truce commissions could be bought from some colonial governments for as little as £20. Some traders employed Frenchmen to ship, so to speak, as professional prisoners of war, to lend colour to the commissions in the event of encounter with British cruisers. Pares, *War and Trade*, p. 448.

33. Beckford to Pitt, 11 ix 1758, *Correspondence of the Earl of Chatham*, edited by W. S. Taylor and J. H. Pringle, 4 vols, London, 1838–40, I, p. 353.

34. Because by engaging, with the connivance of the French authorities, in trade forbidden by French law in normal times, it became, so to speak, quasi-French. See on this subject, R. Pares, *Colonial blockade and neutral rights, 1739–1763*, Oxford, 1938, pp. 180–204.

35. Figures in Public Record Office, C.O. 325/2.

36. For the arguments used in the Canada–Guadeloupe debate, see W. L. Grant, 'Canada v. Guadeloupe', *American Historical Review*, XVII, July 1912, pp. 735–43; and C. W. Alvord, *The Mississippi valley in British politics*, Cleveland, 1917, I, pp. 49–74. For City opinion on the subject, and its influence on Pitt, see K. Hotblack, *Chatham's colonial policy*, London, 1917, pp. 12–17.

37. For the best detailed study of the actual negotiations, see Z. E. Rashed, *The Peace of Paris, 1763*, Liverpool, 1951.

38. *Shelburne MSS*, University of Michigan, Ann Arbor, vol. CLXV, speech of 9 December 1762; these extracts are not in Hansard, but are quoted by H. W. V. Temperley, 'The peace of Paris', *Cambridge History of the British Empire*, vol. I, Cambridge, 1929.

8

The First American Revolt

Decisive though the Seven Years War had been in a military sense, and moderate though the terms of the treaty appeared, at least to the victors, the settlement of 1763 had little chance of permanent acceptance. As contributions to a durable peace the British concessions were wasted. Bute and his associates failed to grasp – mere politicians as they were – that defeat itself, rather than the extent of the losses consequent upon defeat, prompted revenge. Choiseul began planning to that end before the signatures were dry, working to rebuild a shattered navy and urging his Spanish colleague Grimaldi to do the same. Not all French leaders were as eager for revenge as Choiseul; Louis xv was not. Nor did all Spanish ministers share Charles iii's obsessive resentment of England; Grimaldi was no fire-eater, and was more concerned than his master with the financial sums. Nevertheless, France and Spain between them could draw up a long and plausible list of *irredenta* in the Mediterranean, West Africa, North America, the West Indies and India. Both had grounds for fearing and resenting English maritime predominance, and for suspecting that some future English government might plan further conquest. Chatham's return to office in 1766, sick man though he was, caused a flurry in Versailles. In the 1760s, moreover, European seafarers were entering a new age of discovery in the Pacific: an area in which Spain still claimed a monopoly of navigation, but in which the British Admiralty was showing an ominous interest. For both France and Spain, to forestall English activity in that region might well be worth a war.

France and Spain were both financially exhausted in 1763; but too much should not be made of that. Most eighteenth-century wars (the Seven Years War was no exception) were undertaken by governments for measurable, material ends: territory, trade, colonies, revenue. Limited ends were pursued with limited means. Armies were professional, and small in relation to populations: navies, though immensely costly in terms of material, were smaller still in terms of men, and even more professional. Civil populations were concerned, except in territories actually invaded, mainly as taxpayers. Eighteenth-century tax systems were too inefficient, and in most countries too riddled with exemptions, for more than a small fraction of a nation's income to be collected for war or any other public purpose. A government at war could totter towards bankruptcy, as the French government did, with its subjects' wealth largely untapped. When its revenue and its credit were exhausted and its fighting men could not be paid, it had to make peace; but conversely, in a relatively few years of peace it could recover sufficiently to be ready for another war of the same limited unemotional kind. Chaotic though French and Spanish public finances were in the years immediately after the war, by 1766 Choiseul could write confidently that the Bourbon allies should be strong enough to challenge England again by – ironic date – 1770.[1] He was encouraged in this belief by the reports which came from agents in England. Over-confidence there, and resistance to continued high taxation, caused a rapid rundown of naval and military strength in the later 1760s, and government was paralysed, to a degree unusual even in the eighteenth century, by political faction. England, moreover, had no allies. In 1762 the Bute administration had stopped the Prussian subsidies, and subsequently moved towards a separate peace with France. Despite Pitt's indignant protests, their action had been reasonable in the circumstances; it was not in the British interest to subsidise a Prussian invasion of Saxony; but Frederick the Great never forgave England, and in 1766 he rejected Chatham's suggestion of a renewed alliance.

If Choiseul was correct in his estimate of the time required to rebuild French and Spanish financial and military strength, he might be expected from about 1770, to be looking for a favourable occasion. He would have to find, at some moment when England was embarrassed and at a disadvantage, a *casus belli* seriously affecting the interests both of France and of Spain. Despite the Family Compact, the interests of France and Spain did not always coincide. Typical of the relation between the two countries was their divergence over the affair of the Falkland Islands. Lying close to the sea route from Atlantic to Pacific, these bleak uninhabited islands acquired, in the third quarter of the century, a new strategic importance. Anson had drawn attention to their value in the 1740s. The first actual settlement, however, was French. Bougainville (who had been Montcalm's A.D.C. in Canada) planted settlers on East Falkland in 1764, as a private investment with government approval. Byron, in the course of his circumnavigation, carried out a cursory survey of West Falkland a few months later. Each commander, unknown to the other, 'took possession' of the archipelago. The first English settlers, a party of marines, arrived at West Falkland in 1766. Meanwhile Grimaldi had heard of the French settlement, and formally asked the French government to give it up, on the ground that its existence would encourage their common English rivals to penetrate the same area. To this Choiseul very reluctantly agreed; and in 1767 the Spaniards took over East Falkland. To evict the English from West Falkland, the Spanish government wanted an assurance of French support; but Choiseul, whose timetable had been rudely anticipated, blew hot and cold and played for time. He had his own list of grievances over which he was willing to make trouble: the Newfoundland fisheries; the exclusion of the French from their former trade in gum and slaves on the Senegal; and the action of the British in India, who had, he said, insulted the French flag by stopping an attempt to fortify Chandernagore in contravention of the Treaty of Paris;[2] but he could not rely on Spanish support on these issues, and for his own part was unenthusiastic over a war to establish Spanish possession of the Falkland Islands. The Spanish government eventually decided to force the issue. In 1770 a strong expedition sent from Buenos Aires compelled the English garrison to surrender. The British government, when they heard of it, demanded disavowal and restitution, and an Anglo-Spanish war, in which France might be expected to support Spain, became an imminent possibility. In the event it was Louis xv himself who prevented war, by dismissing Choiseul and telling Charles III that France would not fight.[3] The crisis collapsed. In 1771 the Spanish government restored West Falkland to Great Britain and disavowed the action of Bucareli, the governor of Buenos Aires. The Spaniards did not renounce their claim to the island, and the British government, as Pitt and others complained,[4] did not press the point. Britain was unready for war, and North, now in office, did not think the islands worth fighting for, so long as the general right of navigation in the Pacific was maintained. In 1776, the British garrison was quietly withdrawn, leaving a flag flying in token of territorial claim. It was widely alleged – and vehemently denied by British ministers – that this withdrawal had been promised in secret and verbal communications in 1771, and so formed part of the agreement. Whatever the truth of these rumours, the inhospitable reality of the Falkland Islands obviously belied the enthusiastic reports of Anson and Byron. The Spaniards remained in tenuous but undisputed possession of East Falkland until 1811, when they too withdrew, leaving the islands for some years to the shearwaters and the seals.[5]

If British imperialism was to be curbed by French and Spanish action, a more propitious occasion would have to be found. Choiseul's dismissal did not entail the permanent rejection of his policy. Vergennes, who became Louis XVI's minister for foreign affairs in 1775, was an apt pupil as well as a successful political rival. He was one of those prescient Frenchmen (Turgot was another, though he drew different conclusions) who, at the time of the Treaty of Paris, foresaw the consequence of complete English victory in North America.[6] Local indiscipline, no longer restrained by fear of French invasion, would make the British colonies there ungovernable. They had never been easy to govern, and English attempts to govern them had been, since 1688, no more than half-hearted. If the colonists' habitual dislike and suspicion of authority were now provoked by, for example, a serious attempt to re-assert metropolitan control, British colonial rebellion might provide a French opportunity.

Such an attempt was almost inescapable. In all the American empires, the war had revealed administrative weaknesses which strikingly belied authoritarian principle. All the metropolitan governments set to work after the peace to remedy this situation:

to strengthen colonial defences, to rationalise and tighten colonial administration, to encourage and expand colonial productivity and trade, in general to make colonies more profitable to governments, to investors and (where this did not conflict with metropolitan plans) to their inhabitants. The Spanish government, in particular, embarked on a drastic programme of reorganisation. A standing army, established in the Indies for the first time in 1762, was kept in being after the war; the commanding officers were usually peninsular Spaniards, but many Creoles took commissions, and the rank-and-file were recruited largely by local impressment. San Juan in Puerto Rico, at the windward extremity of the Greater Antilles, was developed as a major fortress; a logical retort to the loss of Florida and the evident vulnerability of Havana. Communications were improved; from 1764 a monthly dispatch service operated between Havana and Coruña. Many administrative boundaries were redrawn on more rational and more defensible lines. In 1776, a whole new viceroyalty was created in the Rìo de la Plata basin, and Upper Peru, still an important source of silver, was included in its jurisdiction.[7] José de Gálvez, as *visitador* in New Spain from 1765 to 1771, and subsequently as minister for the Indies, inaugurated a drastic reform of the administrative service, designed to make it more centralised, better disciplined, a more effective instrument of the royal will.[8] The Church, always an essential instrument of colonial government, was brought more closely than ever under royal control. The regular orders in particular came under attack as rich and useless, and in 1767 the most independent of them, the Society of Jesus, which had maintained a rustic state-within-the-state in the Paraguay valley, was summarily expelled.

All this, of course, cost money. The principle that the crown was to draw financial tribute from the Indies had been established from the beginning of American settlement, and had never been seriously challenged; nor was it challenged now. Revenue was freely transferred from the colonies to Spain, to defray naval and other expenses, or from colony to colony. The immense fortifications of Puerto Rico were paid for by subsidies from New Spain. The silver production of New Spain was increasing rapidly at this time (the famous Valenciana mine was opened in 1767) and with it the *quinto*. Strenuous efforts were made to increase revenue under other heads of taxation, and to encourage trade by getting rid of unnecessary restrictions. Many of these measures were based on suggestions made in Campillo's celebrated *Nuevo sistema de gobierno para la América*.[9] Campillo had predicted that if trade were made freer its volume would increase; and that if duties were reduced and simplified, but more efficiently collected, their yield, from an increasing volume of trade, would increase also. Events proved him right. Shipping was at last allowed – encouraged – to follow economic routes. Shipping for the harbours of Peru now came mostly round Cape Horn; the old, inconvenient route across the Isthmus was abandoned, and the convoys which had used it discontinued. The trade of Upper Peru was redirected through Buenos Aries, to the intense indignation of the Lima *consulado*, and the discomfiture of the *peruleiro* smugglers, who lost a great part of their business.[10] Restrictions on intercolonial trade were progressively removed; the stranglehold of the *consulados* on transatlantic trade progressively relaxed. In 1778, these successive relaxations were collected in the so-called Free Trade Decree, a widely celebrated charter of prosperity, which opened the trade of much of the Indies (all save Venezuela and New Spain) to the shipping of all the harbours of Spain. By traditional Spanish standards, this was a bold move; and in general, the government was risking trouble. All its innovations, financial, commercial, administrative, offended long-entrenched interests. Naturally they elicited fierce complaint and protestations of ruin, especially in the Indies, from those whose privileges were invaded; but as yet, resistance was mainly passive. Risings, it is true, Creole and Indian, were fairly frequent and sometimes locally dangerous; but they had always been frequent. Now, as always, they were ill-prepared, uncoordinated, and usually quickly suppressed.

In the French colonial empire the most pressing problem was one of adjustment to reduced circumstances. With Canada gone and the use of the Newfoundland fisheries restricted, French interests in the Americas were virtually confined to the Caribbean. One of Choiseul's first endeavours at the end of the war was to expand this Caribbean empire, *La France Equinoviale*, by the

establishment of a strong colony in French Guiana, employing displaced settlers from Nova Scotia and Cape Breton Island. The
attempt failed, partly because of inadequate preparation, partly
because most of the settlers died of yellow fever and malaria. On
the other hand, the French islands, St Domingue especially, entered after the war upon a period of great prosperity, assisted by
natural fertility, by the Spanish alliance, and by the smuggling
trade carried on by the British North American colonists. This
trade ceased to be illicit, as far as the French authorities were concerned, in 1763; in that year the French colonies received permission to import foreign provisions and to pay for them in rum
and molasses, which were unwelcome in France. About the same
time, certain harbours in Martinique, Guadeloupe and St Domingue were declared free ports, open to foreign traders. Like the
Spaniards, the French hoped, by concessions in minor trades, to
strengthen metropolitan monopoly of the major ones. The whole
export of sugar was still required to be sent to France. Its volume
considerably exceeded that of the British islands;[11] the re-export
of sugar from France to other parts of Europe, after refining, was
one of the main factors in the favourable French international
trade balance. 'The labours of the people settled in those islands,'
wrote Raynal, with characteristic hyperbole, 'are the sole bases of
the African trade; they extended the fisheries and culture of North
America, afford a good market for the manufactures of Asia, and
double, perhaps treble, the activity of all Europe.'[12] Like the
Spaniards, the French endeavoured after the war to strengthen
both the administration and the defence of these valued possessions. The Jesuits – those international scapegoats – were expelled in 1743, with some reason; their commercial speculations in
Martinique before and during the war had caused much confusion
and distress. A start was made on the creation, for the first time, of
secular dioceses and parishes. In 1762 a standing commission or
bureau for colonial legislation was established in France, and leading colonists were summoned before it to give evidence. Efforts
were made to define more precisely the duties of colonial officials,
to eliminate overlapping jurisdictions, and to separate civil from
military authority.[13] In the field of defence, the French, like the
Spaniards, decided after the war to keep regular troops per-

manently stationed in the West Indies. The island militias, unlike the very efficient militia which had existed in Canada, were unreliable bodies, more concerned with protecting their members' families and property against servile mutiny than with defending the islands against foreign attack. Regular garrisons, on the other hand, were expensive. The French government, unlike the Spanish, had never established a right to tax the colonies at will for the benefit of the metropolis. Long-standing convention required revenue raised in a colony to be spent in that colony; in most colonies, indeed, tax receipts covered less than half the cost of administration and local defence; the rest of the cost was borne by metropolitan France.[14] Attempts to make the colonies bear a larger share often led to trouble. It was hardly to be expected that an absolutist Bourbon government should put taxation into the hands of elected assemblies, especially in view of British experiences of these refractory bodies; but taxation by naked decree was recognised to be unworkable. Tax increases could be had in practice only through recourse to the *conseils supérieurs* in the major provinces. These advisory councils, comprising officials, magistrates and leading colonists, were nominated, not elected bodies. Like the *parlements* in France, however (to which they considered themselves analogous), they too could be refractory.[15] Their position was a difficult one; they were called upon to perform a quasi-representative function, without any clear definition of whom or what they represented; their consent to new taxation, therefore, did not always effectively commit those who were to be taxed. In St Domingue, for example, in 1763, an establishment of regular troops having been decided on, the French government agreed to abolish the militia and the hated system of conscription by which it was manned. A little later, a joint meeting of the *conseils supérieurs* of Port-au-Prince and Cap Français was asked to agree to additional taxation of 4,000,000 *livres* annually, to defray the expense of the garrison. After some bargaining, they agreed to this in 1764, as a *don gratuit* for five years. The *octroi*, the export duty, was increased accordingly. A year later, the crown, alarmed by the high death rate among the regular troops, thought it necessary to reimpose the militia requirement; but the troops had still to be paid and the additional *octroi* was retained.

At the same time, those liable to militia service were offered the alternative of paying a money composition, the proceeds of which were to be used to raise and pay a regiment of *gens de couleur*. The *conseils* protested vigorously; and though eventually they were persuaded or bullied by the governor into agreeing once more, their agreement was widely repudiated. Everybody was alienated – the *grands blancs* on whose property the *octroi* fell, the *petits blancs* who could not afford to compound for militia service, the mulattoes and free Negroes who were to be drafted into the new regiment. Many people refused either to serve or to pay. For several years there were mutterings of rebellion, nocturnal conspiracies, collectings of arms and surreptitious drillings in the mountains, until the government took fright, and used its regular troops to end the business brutally, by a series of military executions in 1769–70. Conspiracy died down, order was maintained, but under the surface of general prosperity discontent with French metropolitan government smouldered on.

The problems of imperial organisation which confronted the British government after 1763 were much more complex and more formidable than those faced either by the Spanish or the French. The sheer diversity and geographical extent of British success invited improvisation, hasty decision and muddle. In the Caribbean, in North America, in India, and in a dozen minor theatres of war, victory created more dilemmas than defeat. As usual in the tale of trade and dominion, moreover, the difficulties encountered in widely separated places were interconnected; the solutions attempted in one region often produced fresh problems in another. There was, nevertheless, an order of urgency. In the minds of the British government and of politically minded public opinion in England, after the affairs of Great Britain itself, and the unending struggle for political survival, the situation in North America most immediately demanded ministerial attention. Three problems, or rather groups of problems, were outstanding. The first was one of assimilation. Vast areas of new territory had been acquired, some inhabited by other Europeans, French or Spanish, some by almost unknown Indian tribes. Organs of government had to be provided for these territories, and policies formulated for their future development, which would be acceptable to their inhabitants without being, on the one hand, repugnant to British constitutional ideas, or, on the other, dangerously insecure. The second problem was that of defence, more specifically the cost of defence, past and future. The central government had spent vast sums in fighting the recent war; sums much larger than could be covered by current revenue. The colonial governments – some of them, at least – had similarly spent large sums in proportion to their local revenue; but for more than half of this expenditure, they had been reimbursed by the central government.[16] The very heavy public debt so incurred by Great Britain and the proportionately much smaller debts incurred by the colonies to pay for the war, had to be serviced and if possible reduced; meanwhile, the Atlantic and Caribbean seaboards had still to be defended against European enemies, the Indian frontier garrisoned and policed. It was necessary, or at least highly desirable, from the point of view of the metropolitan government, to raise the money in such a way that the colonists themselves should bear a reasonable share of the burden. Thirdly, the machinery of civil administration: the diversity, the fragmentation and the weakness of colonial government had been all too evident during the war. The local particularism of some colonies had hampered the raising of troops and had prevented the coordination of their activities when raised. Illicit trade to Louisbourg and the French West Indies had been of material help to the enemy, and had been difficult to prevent or punish, because elected local magistrates had connived at it. Governors in the colonies and ministers at home naturally wished to end this dangerous indiscipline, to render royal administration more unified, more effective in serving imperial interests as a whole, as they understood them. They sought, therefore, to free it from its dependence upon the goodwill of local assemblies, sometimes capricious, often obstructive, and nearly always parochial in their policy and interests.

Of all these problems, the government of the new territories was the most urgent, so urgent that the Grenville ministry, which took office in 1763, decided to deal with it by the summary method of royal proclamation rather than the slower, more careful procedure of parliamentary enactment. By the proclamation of October 1763, the conquests bordering the Caribbean were erected into the two new colonies of East and West Florida; the territory south of the St Lawrence estuary was absorbed into the existing colony of Nova Scotia; and the French-settled areas along the river, with their two centres of Québec and Montreal, were combined in the new colony of Québec. This colony was provided with the usual system of representative institutions, in the expectation that its French inhabitants would soon be outnumbered by English-speaking immigrant settlers. This expectation was never fulfilled; but at the time the arrangement seemed tidy and logical.

A much more intractable problem was presented by the wild forest area south of the Lakes and west of the Appalachians, and by the wild people who inhabited it. Ministers felt a responsibility for the Indians; and some of their agents, notably the Indian superintendents John Stuart and Sir William Johnson, had already displayed the affection for primitiveness, the urge to preserve it intact, which was to be characteristic of many colonial civil servants in later times. But Indians were not only picturesque and appealing; they were unreliable and could be dangerous. At the very time of the proclamation, a widespread alliance, engineered by the able warrior-politician Pontiac, was making war on the settlements all along the Ohio frontier. English ministers exaggerated the power and the numbers of the Indian tribes, understandably; Pontiac's war-parties killed more than 2,000 settlers. They believed, rightly, that Indian belligerence arose from fear of territorial encroachment and from resentment against cheating traders. They thought that the tribes would never settle down in peace, without firm reassurance on these points. They therefore proclaimed the Appalachian watershed to be the western boundary of British settlement. Settlers were to be directed, instead, to Québec or to Florida, both of which needed more people. The Ohio forest region was to be administered by the military commander-in-chief, and all trade there was to be confined to places where it could be licensed and supervised. Government thus took on an immense task of policing and surveillance which, for lack of money, it could not perform, and from which it was obliged step by step to retreat. In 1768 the regulation of trade with the Indians was handed back to the colonies, with the result that virtually all attempt at regulation ceased; and a new line of settlement was drawn

187

somewhat further west than the Proclamation line. In 1771 the garrisons at Fort Pitt and Fort Chartres were withdrawn; Virginians began to move in, and an Indian war followed. Finally, under the Québec Act of 1774, the home government gave up direct responsibility for the coveted wilderness, and included it, provisionally at least, within the boundaries of Québec. The decision was not, on the face of things, unreasonable, since in most of the disputed area the only European inhabitants were French-Canadian fur-traders; but the act was widely and fiercely resented. The next result of the government's endeavours was to make enemies of thousands of would-be settlers and, more serious, of powerful land speculators and the interests they represented throughout the middle colonies.

The frontier policy of government offended powerful interests, and was a failure. The goverment's attempts to raise revenue in the colonies, for purposes of defence, by means of imperial taxation were also, in the main, failures. They were undertaken because there seemed to be no other way of securing an adequate contribution. The old method of requisition, colony by colony, which had been employed during the war, was unsatisfactory. Even in the face of common danger, some colonies had evaded their obligations, and more would do so in peace time, whatever the possible future dangers. The colonies could not be persuaded to agree on a common policy in taxing themselves; so the imperial government decided on direct action, and offended nearly everyone. The successive stages in the development of conflict are well known. The first major move by the government was the Plantation Act of 1764, commonly known as the Sugar Act; at once a revenue measure and an act of economic war against the French in the Caribbean. In drafting the Act, the Grenville administration made a genuine attempt to balance conflicting interests, and some of its clauses offered significant advantages to North American producers. Revenue, however, was the primary consideration; the most important clause provided for the punctual collection (albeit at a reduced rate) of the duty on foreign molasses, originally imposed in 1733 but never effectively enforced. This clause provoked protests from several colonial assemblies and cries of ruin from the New England rum distillers; exaggerated cries, probably, coming as they did from an industry noted throughout its history for its capacity to absorb taxation.[17] More cogent and more clearly justified were the objections to the administrative regulations for enforcing the act, which caused real hardship and inconvenience, especially to coastal shipping.[18] The Act was obeyed and the duties paid, but with a very ill grace. A much more vigorous protest greeted Grenville's attempt, in the following year, to levy stamp duties on a wide range of business and legal transactions. The imposition of internal taxation upon the colonies by the authority of the imperial government might well be regarded as an innovation; for though there were precedents for it, none of them was recent. It is evidence of the archaic legalism of parliament, that no member expressed any doubt about the constitutionality of the Stamp Act;[19] though some, notably the old campaigner Barré, who knew his America, doubted its wisdom. The colonists, when they learned of it, had no doubts. The cry went up immediately, 'no taxation without representation', and a general resistance was organised, using a familiar eighteenth-century technique, intimidation by riotous mobs.[20] No one would pay the duty or use the stamps, and Grenville's successors in office repealed the Act; with, however, a reservation, in the Declaratory Act, of the sovereign rights of parliament, indicating that the government had not retreated in principle. In 1767 a new administration returned to the charge with Townshend's Revenue Act, a too-clever attempt to take the colonists at what was believed to be their word; to raise revenue not by internal taxes but by duties on imports into the colonies.[21] To the leaders of radical opinion in America, this was a distinction without a difference; they shifted their ground nimbly, in protest against any raising of colonial revenue by parliamentary enactment. Resistance again took the form of rioting, violence against individual officials, and a fairly general agreement not to import dutiable articles. In 1770 the government again retreated, again with a face-saving gesture. The duties were repealed, with the exception of the fiscally unimportant tea duty, which remained as a symbol of the parliamentary right to tax, and as a focus of colonial resentment. In general, parliamentary taxation raised little revenue; its chief result, because of the resentment it caused, was to increase the influence, in local politics, of extremists such as James Otis and Samuel Adams the Boston rabble-rouser.

Tax riots were not unknown in England. Ministers, while condemning the riots in America, could comprehend them; could even minimise their significance, by attributing them to the simplest and most obvious cause, to dislike of paying taxes. But the situation was not simple. The attempts to levy taxes by parliamentary authority reflected a general desire in English government circles to improve the administration of the empire as a whole, and to strengthen metropolitan control. Characteristic moves to this end were the measures taken in the 1660s to tighten enforcement of the Acts of Trade: the requirement that customs officers should reside at their posts, instead of relying on local deputies; the instructions to captains of HM Ships, in 1762, to assist the preventive officers, and to the judges to furnish them with writs of assistance; the reorganisation of the vice-admiralty courts and the extension of their jurisdiction.[22] Characteristic also was the determination to provide governors and other senior civil servants with fixed salaries, in order to make them less dependent on their assemblies and freer to carry out their instructions. Part of the revenue expected from the Townshend duties was intended for this purpose; even after the repeal of the duties, the central government persisted, by making provision in 1772 for the payment of salaries, out of revenues drawn from America, to the governors and the judges of the Superior Court of Massachusetts.[23] The implications of this move were obvious, the reaction of the Massachusetts radicals immediate and angry. It was the reaction, not of oppressed colonists demonstrating against burdensome taxation, but of men of substance, patricians, defending their local power, influence and freedom of action. With sound and comprehensive strategy, they directed their resentment not against particular enactments, but against the authority by which the enactments were made.

Benjamin Franklin wrote in 1770 that the American provinces were 'so many distinct and separate states' and that parliament 'had usurped an authority of making laws for them, which before it had not'.[24] This was nonsense. Parliament had long possessed authority to legislate for the colonies, as many statutes testified.

Between 1688 and 1763 this authority had never been challenged. In the two generations before 1763, however, it had been little used, at least in peace time. The legislative vigour of the 1760s might plausibly be regarded as innovation – innovation for which, in the opinion of most leading colonists, there was no necessity. They had no interest in administrative efficiency for its own sake; indeed, like most local patricians in most colonial empires, they preferred inefficiency and fragmentation to centralisation and control. Their commerce and shipping, which had grown and flourished under the protection of the Navigation Acts, were now so strongly established that no protection was needed; the Acts – so the argument ran – protected only English and British West Indian interests; in the northern and middle colonies they survived only to restrict and irritate. Similarly with defence, which had always been the main contribution of imperial government to colonial welfare: the principal danger seemed to be permanently removed. Responsible British ministers could not safely rely on this assumption, but the Americans did, and events were to prove them right. French vindictiveness was aimed against England, not against the colonies; French irredentism looked to the Caribbean, not to North America; Gibraltar, not Florida, was the conquest most desired by Spain. As for the Indians, British ministers had always exaggerated their warlike strength. Some colonial radicals believed, or affected to believe, that the exaggeration was deliberate. The seaboard communities were far enough removed from the frontier to ignore any Indian menace, and the western pioneers were willing to take the risk. For colonial politicians, there was no defence problem. Eighteenth-century Americans, like the seventeenth-century Englishmen whose political attitudes they inherited, distrusted standing armies. If the British government, so they argued, insisted on stationing regular troops in the colonies, quartering them on peaceful citizens, taxing people in order to pay them, it must be for a sinister purpose.

By 1770 many colonial leaders were speaking and writing of the need to resist metropolitan encroachments, if need be by force. By this, they meant more than mere inspired rioting by urban mobs, but less, as yet, than a war for independence. Complete and formal separation from England had no obvious positive advantages to offer, except perhaps in Virginia, where many planters were permanently in debt to English merchants and saw in independence a possibility of escape.[25] Most colonial spokesmen were essentially conservative in their aims, or thought themselves so. They wished that the British government, in dealing with their affairs, would return to its pre-war inertia; they professed, and many of them sincerely felt, a traditional loyalty to the crown; they demanded no other than 'the common unquestionable rights of British subjects'; but they wanted those rights made explicit in America. Some – Franklin, Governor Bernard of Massachusetts, even James Otis – proposed from time to time unworkable schemes for colonial representation in parliament. Many more demanded a clear recognition that the colonial assemblies possessed, within their respective provinces, an authority analogous with that exercised by parliament in England. Some politicians in England – Burke, Fox, even Chatham – were prepared to go a long way to meet these demands, at least in practice. There was no lack of well-meant suggestions for accommodation. Accommodation was prevented and an armed breach made certain, by mutual suspicions; by a recurrence of provocative incidents which constantly inflamed those suspicions; and by a ceaseless barrage of oratory and pamphleteering.

Whatever the failings of the leaders of colonial opposition, reticence was not among them. They were vigorous-minded men, able, well-read, articulate. They inherited from England a strong tradition of political and religious polemic. They set out their opinions in newspapers (of which there were thirty-eight in the mainland colonies in 1775) in sermons, in commemorative orations, above all in pamphlets. More than 400 pamphlets bearing on the Anglo-American controversy appeared in the colonies between 1750 and 1776;[26] over 1,500 by 1783. Many of them were serious, substantial and closely-reasoned explanations of the stand which their respective authors were taking on the controversial issues of their day. They represented and combined many trains of thought: the anti-authoritarianism bred in the upheaval of the English Civil War and carried to America by many of the early settlers; the more fashionable, more contemporary notions of natural rights philosophy – natural law, social contract,

During the seventeenth and eighteenth centuries much time was devoted to the development of ship design in order to discover the most practical and economical shape. 1 (*above*) The Dutch *fluyt*, *c*.1700, achieved a deserved popularity and fame because of its simple lines and serviceability. 2 (*below*) An English snow at anchor, 1759. Medium-sized, two-masted vessels first entered the colonial trades in large numbers in the mid-eighteenth century

3 (*above*) The *Princess Royal*, East Indiaman, 1770; a big ship for her day, 864 tons. 4 (*below*) The *Thomas Coutts*, East Indiaman, 1817; a ship of the flush-decked type introduced in the Company's service in the early nineteenth century. In 1826-7 she made a round trip to China *via* Bombay in 10 days under the year, the fastest passage then recorded for a sailing vessel

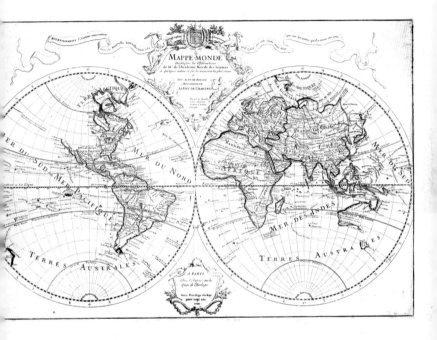

5 In the eighteenth century the French were pre-eminent in cartography as shown by this engraving of Delisle's *Mappe-monde*, 1700. Delisle set new standards by the accuracy of his continental outlines, and his willingness to leave the map blank in the absence of reliable information

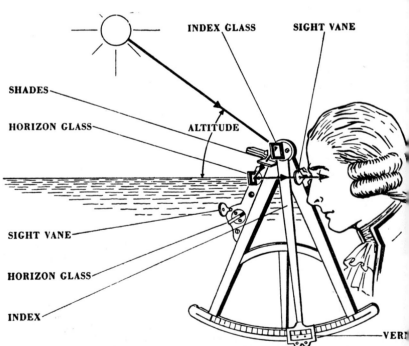

Navigational instruments: 6 (*right*)
The use of the Back-Staff, 1681, to take
solar altitudes. 7 (*below*) The use of the
Hadley Octant, a more sophisticated
instrument of the 1730s

between page 248 and 249

SHADES

HORIZON GLASS

INDEX GLASS

SIGHT VANE

ALTITUDE

SIGHT VANE

HORIZON GLASS

INDEX

VER

Fig. 7. Hadley's Reflecting Quadrant or Octant

8 Azimuth compass, *c.*1720

9 Station pointer, *c.*1820

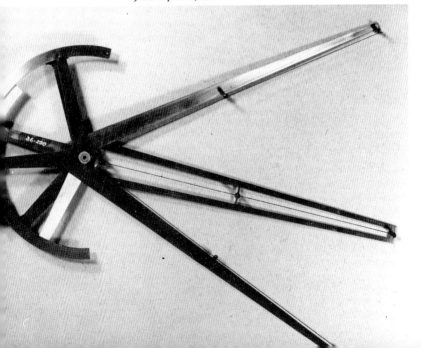

10 View of Batavia, 1721

11 Kanhoji Angre's stronghold: the fort at Geriah, 1756

12 The rock fortress of Trichinopoly, 1773

13 Fort St George, Madras.

14 The writers' building at Calcutta

15 The river bank at Calcutta

inalienable rights, the contractual nature of government; and a nostalgic respect, among men educated in the classics, for the supposed virtues of republican Rome. Here was an apposite analogy and warning. Many of the pamphleteers believed, or talked themselves into believing, that they were the victims of a conspiracy against freedom. The English constitution, which they admired and whose advantages they shared, was being subverted, as the Roman Republic had been subverted, by power-seeking politicians, using corruption on a vast scale to achieve their ends. Many feared that in England the process had gone too far to be arrested; but in America there was hope. Americans retained their rustic simplicity and virtue, the marks not of a primitive society, but of a chosen people. 'The liberties of mankind and the glory of human nature is in their keeping', wrote John Adams, in the year of the Stamp Act. The alternative to resistance was to be dragged down, along with England, into slavery. Slavery, to colonial patricians, was more than a figure of speech. Washington – normally no scaremonger – wrote to a friend in 1774: 'The crisis is arrived when we must assert our rights or submit to every imposition, that can be heaped upon us, till custom and use shall make us as tame and abject slaves as the blacks we rule over with such arbitrary sway.'[27]

These fears, in retrospect, seem grotesque. English ministers throughout this period were at their wits' end for revenue, plagued by factious opposition, ill-informed about America, and able to give only intermittent attention to American affairs. It would be hard to find, in their irresolute fumblings, evidence of a systematic determination to oppress. Yet the conspiracy illusion was widely believed, among radicals in England as well as in America, and the course of events, for minds already suspicious, seemed to confirm it. From 1770 increasingly serious outbreaks of violence in the colonies provoked increasingly severe measures of repression. After the rioting over the Townshend duties, troops were sent to Boston to restore order. The baiting of a sentry by an abusive crowd led to the street brawl described as the Boston Massacre.[28] The troops were prudently withdrawn to the island fortress of Castle William; but even there they were regarded by the townspeople as a potential threat. In 1772 an armed party organised by prominent Rhode Island merchants captured and burned the naval schooner *Gaspée*, engaged in preventive duties. The commission of inquiry into this affair was instructed – understandably, in view of the attitude of local juries – to send the culprits to England for trial; a proposal which aroused far more colonial indignation than the crime itself. The culprits were never officially identified. In 1773 came the Tea Act and its explosive consequences; a curious mixture of the trivial and the tragic. The British government, engaged in regulating the affairs of the East India Company, apparently had no other thought in passing the act, than to help the company over an awkward financial crisis. Economically, the Act was sensible; by withdrawing export duty and reducing the number of middlemen in the business, it would have reduced the price of tea to the American consumer, encouraged consumption, and increased the revenue from the import duty.[29] Obtusely, ministers overlooked the political dangers of a measure which offended at once powerful commercial interests and deep-seated constitutional prejudices in the colonies. The 'Tea Party' took them by surprise and proved to be the breaking-point of their (hitherto considerable) patience. They retorted in 1774 with the series of punitive measures, directed against the town of Boston and the province of Massachusetts, and known as the Coercive Acts. They sent General Gage as governor to Massachusetts, with troops (but not nearly enough troops) and instructions to enforce the Acts. Gage was a genial man, popular in America. He was civilly received in Boston; but he found people determined on resistance, the militia mustering and drilling, the Acts clearly unenforceable.

In drafting Gage's instructions, ministers assumed that they were dealing with a rebellious movement restricted to New England, and even in New England confined to a political faction. Both assumptions were false. The Committees of Correspondence and the first Continental Congress ensured that Massachusetts would be supported by most of the other colonies. As for the loyalists, they were numerous, and included in their number many solid and prosperous citizens; but most of them were moved more by respectable dislike of rebellion and upheaval, than by dynamic enthusiasm for king and empire. In some places, particularly

Boston, they were already cowed by vituperation and violence, and had little political influence. Radicals controlled the town meetings and provincial congresses, which in many places by then were the only bodies able to command obedience. Imperial government, always tenuous, effectively came to an end in most of the mainland colonies in the autumn of 1774. By the spring of 1775 it was clear to ministers that only two courses were open: virtually complete concession, leaving only a token ceremonial association, or a war to reconquer America. In retrospect, the first course might seem to have been the more realistic. It was advocated by a small but vocal group in parliament, the same group which had opposed the Coercive Acts; but their voices raised no echo without doors. King, ministers, a large parliamentary majority, and the general public, all agreed on the second course. They were moved partly by the natural indignation of affronted authority; partly by the conviction that British prosperity and maritime power, British 'greatness', depended in great measure on colonial trade, and that colonial trade could be maintained and developed satisfactorily only through political control. This, like the colonists' belief in a conspiracy against freedom, was an illusion. It had been exposed repeatedly over a decade by Dean Tucker,[30] and was to be exposed more magisterially by Adam Smith in the very year of the Declaration of Independence; but few people attended to the arguments of *avant-garde* economists. England went to war in America, because ministers and people feared that without control of America (including, of course, the West Indies) England might become a minor power in Europe. How they would manage, in the event of military success, to maintain permanent control of an America which was doubling in population and wealth every thirty years or so, ministers apparently never gave themselves the trouble to inquire.

In a purely military sense, the outcome of the war was by no means a foregone conclusion.[31] To conquer so vast a country, in the face of resistance by a united population, would indeed have been impossible; but the population was not united. British success depended first upon rapid movement by powerful regular forces, to destroy the continental army before it could acquire confidence and experience; and secondly upon organising and supporting the loyalists, to whom the task of policing the country would have to be entrusted. The first object might have been achieved; Washington, before Saratoga, gave Howe several opportunities to destroy the main body of the rebel army. Had the war been boldly and ruthlessly conducted, the rebel population might have been reduced, for a time at least, to resigned and war-weary acquiescence. But boldness and ruthlessness were almost always lacking. Professional soldiers and sailors disliked the war. Admiral Keppel went so far as to refuse to serve against the Americans. Commanders in the field were inhibited by the knowledge that the enemy, when defeated, would have to be reconciled. Howe, in his successful New York campaign in 1776, was lavish in proclamations of pardon for those who submitted and parole for those who were captured. At the taking of Fort Washington, he was much criticised by loyalists for not loosing his Hessians upon the rebel garrison; yet some at least of his English officers thought he was right 'to treat our enemies as if they might one day become our friends'.[32] It was impossible at the same time to reconcile the rebels and rally the loyalists; Howe's and Carleton's policy merely undermined the loyalists' confidence in government, without in the least affecting the rebel will to fight. The rebel leaders, as eighteenth-century gentlemen, on the whole preserved the conventions (except, indeed, in robbing and persecuting loyalists); but they fought with more conviction and determination than their opponents. They were a hard core of revolutionaries, with everything to lose by submission and nothing to gain by conciliation. After 1776, they were fighting for clear and much-desired objects. The British and the loyalists were fighting, at best, to restore an uneasy *status quo ante*.

The British generals were run-of-the-mill professionals, none of them (except perhaps Cornwallis) men of outstanding capacity or initiative. They suffered, moreover, from a lack of firm direction and leadership. Germain, the 'American Secretary', has often been blamed for this, probably unjustly. He was not a great war minister, certainly, but he was a competent and conscientious administrator.[33] The trouble lay in the weakness and disunity of the government as a whole. The ministry contained no statesman of Pitt's calibre. North, at the Treasury, had his hands full with running the financial machine, which he did on orthodox and parsimonious lines, and managing the House of Commons. The army was constitutionally the king's responsibility; there was no secretary of state for war, and until 1778 no commander-in-chief. The navy was the concern of the First Lord, Sandwich, who knew his business, but who treated North with contemptuous indifference and co-operated only grudgingly with Germain. Departments went their own way, and so did influential private concerns. The East India Company, at a time when ministers were at their wits' end to find men, flatly refused to suspend its own competitive recruiting. In the absence of firm direction, the forces of political faction and personal patronage took over. A preposterous number of senior serving officers were members of parliament. If they did not get the commands they wanted, they might go into opposition. Keppel, the very type of politician-admiral, instead of being left unemployed on the beach as he should have been, got the Channel fleet. It was difficult for individual ministers to resist pressure to make unsuitable appointments; more difficult still to recall unsuccessful commanders, once appointed. Could one have imagined, in Pitt's day, a Clinton retaining his command for four fumbling years? Worse still, it was difficult to agree on strategic planning and to coordinate the activities of commanders in the field. Generals, like their political masters, each went their own way. Burgoyne's plan of advancing from Canada to seize Albany was strategically sound. Control of the lower Hudson would have cut off New England, the heartland of rebellion, from the wavering Middle Colonies. It might have won the war; but Burgoyne, like most of his colleagues, underestimated the difficulties of the terrain and the fighting strength of the New England militia. His plan would have required, to ensure its success, a strong garrison at Ticonderoga in his rear, and a powerful supporting thrust from New York to meet him at Albany. Carleton, commanding in Canada, refused to provide the garrison, and Howe, at the time when Burgoyne began to get into difficulties, was away with most of his army on an expedition of his own devising against Philadelphia. The New Englanders closed in on Burgoyne's rear communications, no help could reach him from New York, and he was entrapped. In October 1777 he surrendered at Saratoga.

Saratoga has often been called the turning-point of the war, and so in a sense it was. It caused the British virtually to abandon the northern theatre of war, except for the defence of Canada, and to concentrate their efforts in the middle and southern colonies. Perhaps they should have done so from the start. The southern colonies were not only more vulnerable in a military sense; they were considered to be more valuable commercially; and they contained a large loyalist population. A more significant aspect of Saratoga, however, was its effect on European opinion. It confirmed the view which Vergennes and other Frenchmen had long held, that the country of North America, if not the population, was unconquerable by conventional armies; it proved, at the very least, that colonial rebellion could not be put down quickly. The British were clearly committed to a long and difficult struggle and Vergennes decided that this was the opportunity he had been waiting for. It was not in all respects an ideal opportunity; the king of France had no wish to appear as a public champion of natural liberty, popular sovereignty and inalienable rights, nor was it wise for one colonial power to lecture another on constitutional principles. The French government had no interest whatever in American independence for its own sake. They welcomed the war as a military and naval embarrassment to the British and they believed, as did most British statesmen, that the loss of colonies would materially reduce British power; but they could not use the rebellion itself as a *casus belli*. Nor did the French want to provoke another European reaction against themselves, by mounting an all-out attack on Great Britain. Vergennes walked warily. He began by arranging, early in 1778, a treaty of commerce and alliance with the United States. This was not yet war, and when war actually broke out, as in time it inevitably must, he was careful to limit his objects to the acquisition, or the recovery, of colonial possessions. Similarly the Spanish government, which entered the war against Great Britain in 1779, limited its objects. It had no wish to encourage its own colonial subjects in thoughts of rebellion. If, by a sharp blow against Britain, it could recover Gibraltar and perhaps Florida, it could then make peace and leave the North Americans to sink or swim.

Whatever the ultimate objects of French and Spanish intervention, the American rebels were the immediate gainers. British pressure upon them in 1778 was maintained from a series of bridgeheads. The British controlled no extensive territory from which supplies could be drawn; everything had to come in by sea. The available naval strength was fully extended in guarding and supplying the bridgeheads and in escorting convoys. But now ships had to be found for the West Indies, which were, by common consent, more valuable than all the mainland colonies. The Channel fleet was the only available strategic reserve; but Sandwich and Keppel were both obsessed by fear of an invasion of England, and grudged every ship detached from the Channel. Some, at least, of the ships for the West Indies, had to come from North American waters. Some British politicians, including, for a time, North himself, thought that the mainland should be abandoned altogether, and peace made there at any price. The king would not hear of this; but something had to go, and in the event it was decided to withdraw from Rhode Island and Philadelphia. Later British operations were directed from New York, and later still from Charleston, which Clinton took in 1780. Cornwallis thereafter achieved considerable successes in South Carolina and Georgia. They were deceptive successes, however. By 1780 substantial French forces were fighting alongside the Americans, the strain on British strength was steadily increasing, and Cornwallis' bold offensive against North Carolina and Virginia slowed to an ignominious halt.

In the Seven Years War the British navy had defeated both the French and the Spanish, but it had defeated them separately, in succession. In 1778–9 it faced them almost simultaneously, with their fleets and finances intact, and in 1780 they were joined by the Dutch. To defeat such a combination the British needed a navy of more than two-power force, and this they failed to achieve. Sandwich, despite his strategic timidity, was a good naval administrator, and the administrative machinery of the British navy was, in general, better than the French and far better than the Spanish. Ships were brought forward from ordinary in rapid succession, were repaired and commissioned, and dropped down the rivers to join the fleet. Sandwich had taken care to collect vast stocks of timber; new ships were built as fast as the availability of slips and the numbers of shipwrights would allow. All this took time, however, and fleets comparable in size with those which had ensured English victory in the Seven Years War were now too small to establish continuous command at sea; French and Spanish fleets could move about the Atlantic at will, could maintain a strategic initiative, and select the areas in which they would fight. Only one attempt was made to invade England; a half-hearted combined affair in 1779. The Spaniards made repeated attacks on the Mediterranean fortresses, and though they failed at Gibraltar they succeeded, with the help of scurvy, in reducing Minorca at the very end of the war. Apart from these European operations, the French, in accordance with tradition, selected the western Atlantic as a major battleground, operating in the Caribbean, as a rule, in the spring and early summer, on the continental seaboard in the late summer and autumn, returning to the West Indies with the end of the hurricane season and the onset of the North American winter, and remaining there until relieved from Europe. It was a neat and economical plan, one which kept the British islands in constant alarm.

In 1776 the British West Indians had had to make up their minds which side they were on. The American rebels had tried hard to persuade them to join in the rebellion. There were many connections, cultural and sentimental as well as commercial, between the two groups of colonies, and their constitutional arrangements were similar. Like the rebellious thirteen, the West Indies had representative government, but not responsible government. They had largely the same grievances – taxation without representation, interference with their legislative freedom, an adverse trade balance, the inconveniences and restrictions of the Acts of Trade. Many West Indians were taxed to pay part of the cost of imperial defence; but there lay the difference. The North Americans believed that they did not need the defence for which they were asked to pay. The West Indians did need it, and knew they needed it. The islands were rich and vulnerable; their free population was small and many of their leading landowners lived in England. For all these reasons, as well as from loyalty, the British West Indians refused to join the American rebels. The only colony, other than the thirteen, to send representatives to congress was Bermuda, where a few enterprising people made a business of stealing munitions from the royal arsenals and selling them to the Americans. In the West Indies proper, people smuggled and grumbled and hoped that the war would be short.

They were disappointed. For more than four years the West Indies suffered all the dangers and hardships of a major international war. Their trade was interrupted, and they were cut off from their main source of food. In Barbados the price of flour doubled in the first year of the war. Between 1773 and 1783 the slave population fell from 68,000 to 57,000, and in the last three years many were near starvation.[34] Jamaica, which grew a larger proportion of its own food, and could to some extent be supplied from areas under British control in Georgia and South Carolina, was less hard hit, but even Jamaica suffered severe distress. The planters had difficulty not only in obtaining supplies but in getting their sugars away. In the first year of the war the quantity shipped to London fell by nearly half, insurance rates reached twenty-three per cent, and freights rose similarly. British rates of duty doubled in the course of the war. Prices rose too, but with violent fluctuations (due in part to sales of prize sugar) so that planters could have no certainty of covering their costs at any given moment; and in any case there were limits to what grocers and refiners in England would pay. War against France had long been regarded as a panacea for the economic ills of the British West Indies; but war against France and North America together was a major disaster.

While Jamaica and Barbados thus experienced the commercial strangulation which in former wars had been the lot of Martinique and Guadeloupe, most of the other islands suffered actual capture. Dominica was taken by the French in September 1778. The British fleet under Byron replied by seizing St Lucia three months later – a considerable victory, won against D'Estaing's fleet as well as the land garrison. St Lucia became, as Rodney had always predicted, the base from which the British could watch the movements of the French at their centre, Martinique; but even from this point of vantage the British forces were inadequate to prevent the French capturing St Vincent and Grenada in the early summer of 1779. A final, perhaps decisive, blow against Jamaica was expected to follow; but this would have required a large fleet sent direct from Europe, and the effective operating season for such fleets in the Caribbean was inconveniently short. The great armament which de Guichen brought out in 1780 achieved little but an indecisive battle against Rodney's fleet off Martinique.

During all this time the comparative weakness of the British at sea had greatly favoured neutral trade; but the habitual high-handedness of the British navy, in dealing with such neutral ships as it caught trading with the enemy, as usual exasperated neutral governments. The Dutch were the people most concerned. Most of the timber and other naval stores imported into France from the Baltic came in Dutch ships; Dutch St Eustatius in the Leeward Islands was a free port and a vast entrepôt for the supply of munitions to North America. In 1780 John Adams visited The Hague and persuaded the Dutch government to recognise North American independence. The British, in what was almost the only firm stroke to the credit of Lord North's cabinet, declared war. Holland was much less dangerous as an open than as a secret enemy, and St Eustatius was almost undefended. Rodney took the place, with hardly a shot fired, early in 1781, and found there over a hundred and fifty sail of contraband traders and a vast stock of goods – a greater haul even than Havana twenty years before. The island never recovered from its devastation. Rodney might have done more, had he not characteristically preferred to lie at St Eustatius supervising the sale of prizes, until his return to England, sick, a few months later.

Meanwhile Cornwallis had surrendered at Yorktown. He had been entrapped there and cut off from reinforcement by the promptitude of the French, who had out-manoeuvred the English admiral on the station, Graves, and had occupied Chesapeake Bay for several crucial weeks with a powerful fleet. The surrender released this fleet for West Indian operations under its able commander de Grasse. There began, late in 1781, a systematic French and Spanish offensive. The Spaniards, operating from New Orleans, took Pensacola, reconquered Florida, and shortly afterwards captured New Providence. The French recaptured nearly all the recent English conquests and took several other islands in addition. The fate of St Kitts was typical of this phase of the war, in which the French seriously hoped to retain their conquests. St Kitts fell early in 1782. Its small British garrison was shut up in the fortress of Brimstone Hill by an army of 8,000 men landed by de Bouillé, and Hood's bold and successful action against de Bouillé's ships in Basse-Terre road came too late to affect the issue ashore. The inhabitants did nothing to help the garrison. Their capitulation to the French was unheroic, but it was prudent common sense; and by it they secured terms very like those granted by the British to Guadeloupe in the previous war. The terms were so favourable, indeed, that men of property, whose plantations had been saved from plunder by the surrender, chiefly feared that their good relations with the French commanders might be endangered by the patriotic indiscretions of the Negroes and the poor whites. In Nevis and Montserrat, which surrendered shortly afterwards, events followed much the same course. The final crushing blow against Jamaica was expected almost daily.

It was at this critical juncture that Rodney returned from England with a fleet which, joined to Hood's squadron, made him approximately equal to de Grasse in strength. He brought de Grasse to action in April 1782 near the Saintes, the small rocky islets between Guadeloupe and Dominica, and in the battle which followed, his genius as a tactician more than redeemed the negligences of which – in pursuit of prize-money – he had been guilty in the past. De Grasse and seven of his ships were taken, and his fleet scattered. The attack on Jamaica was put off and eventually abandoned, for towards the end of the same year the combatants, compelled by their financial exhaustion and their enormous commercial and maritime losses, began to treat for peace. In the Treaty of Versailles, ratified in 1783, Great Britain recovered Grenada, St Vincent, St Kitts, Montserrat, Nevis and Dominica. The right to cut logwood in Central America was restored on the former ambiguous and precarious terms. New Providence had already been recaptured. France recovered St Lucia and acquired Tobago; trivial results of years of destructive fighting.[35] The Spaniards were reluctant to make peace while Gibraltar still held out, but after Howe's relief operation in the autumn of 1782 they had little prospect of capturing the place. Vergennes on the whole preferred to leave it in British hands, in order to keep anti-British feeling alive in Spain; while for the general public in England the Rock had become a symbol, prized beyond all proportion to its real value as a naval base. Eventually Aranda was persuaded by French pressure to give up his demand, and to accept Florida and Minorca instead; an agreement upon which the British possession of Gibraltar still rests.

As for the thirteen colonies, few people in England after Yorktown thought it worth while, or even feasible, to persist in efforts to reduce them. The idea of American independence was hailed with positive enthusiasm by Fox and his friends; by most other people with a kind of sour-grapes resignation. Even the king saw no practicable alternative, and Shelburne as first minister was in no doubt that of the members of the enemy alliance, the Americans were the ones to whom concessions should be made. The Americans, no more concerned with French interests than the French with theirs, conducted their negotiations separately, without consulting or even informing the French.[36] They bargained stubbornly and secured most of their major demands: political independence; an advantageous and geographically reasonable boundary with Canada and Nova Scotia, which gave them unrestricted access to the unsettled lands to the west; fishing rights in the Gulf of St Lawrence and on the Newfoundland Banks, and drying rights on unsettled stretches of the coast of Labrador and Nova Scotia. They agreed that all private debts should be honoured; but they escaped, in practice, any liability to compensate loyalists for their losses of property. This liability fell upon the British government, as a series of acts and treasury payments over the next twenty years bore witness.

The war of American Independence was the first successful major revolt of a colony, or group of colonies, against a European metropolitan government. For Great Britain, it was a major defeat. It led to fierce recriminations over the conduct of the war, and in this aspect of the matter lessons were learned which were to be applied in the wars against revolutionary France. Yet on the whole, the reaction to the loss of America was conservative. There was no real reappraisal, no fundamental change in British imperial policy. Shelburne, it is true, had absorbed the ideas of Tucker and of Adam Smith. As he put it himself, he preferred trade to dominion. He saw that the North Americans, whoever governed them, were tied commercially to Great Britain. He hoped for a corresponding political *rapprochement*, even perhaps for some kind of voluntary reunion. To further this end he was willing, after conceding independence, to admit the Americans to all the commercial privileges which they had enjoyed as British subjects.[37] In the circumstances this was rational as well as radical; but it was altogether too much for most of Shelburne's fellow politicians. It would be, they complained, to reward rebellion with generosity, loyalty with neglect. It would weaken British naval strength, by abandoning the control of vital 'nurseries of seamen'. It would make an irreparable breach in the Navigation system. In particular, it would hand over the West Indies trade to foreign Americans. Most responsible people who studied such matters still preferred the rigid logic of Sheffield's *Observations*,[38] with its vigorous defence of the old colonial system and its emphasis on naval strength, to the free-for-all road to wealth associated with Adam Smith.[39] Parliament rejected Shelburne's proposals. His successors in office set themselves to strengthen and invigorate the old system; to encourage the development of British North America, in order to fill the gap created by the defection of the thirteen colonies; to support attempts to find new markets and open new entrepôts in other parts of the world.

Empires breed illusions, and the political disputes about English imperial policy in the post-war years were, in part at least, a competition in illusion. Shelburne was probably deluded in supposing a quick *rapprochement* between England and the United States to be possible. Certainly the Americans could not do without English manufactured goods; they continued to offer a big and expanding market. But for more than two generations, diplomatic relations between the two countries were bedevilled by misunderstandings, suspicions and quarrels, including a minor war. Shelburne's political opponents were certainly deluded in thinking that British North America could, in a short time, take the place of the thirteen colonies in a closed imperial system. The attempt to maintain that illusion merely made life more difficult and more expensive for the British West Indies. The greatest illusion of all was that an empire of trade could be established throughout the East, without

Great Britain being saddled with a burden of political responsibility. Trade and dominion were not so easily separated. At the very time when British statesmen were washing their hands of a great part of their American empire, they were acquiring and confusedly trying to organise a new territorial empire, equally extensive and even more difficult to administer, in India.

NOTES

1. Choiseul to Guerchy, 11 August 1766, in E. G. P. Fitzmaurice, *Life of William Earl of Shelburne*, 2 vols, London, 1912, I, p. 282.
2. The Chandernagore affair might have led to serious consequences; Choiseul's memorial on the subject was bellicose. H. St. Paul, ed., G. G. Butler, *Correspondence*, 2 vols, London, 1911, II, pp. 98 ff.
3. Duc de Broglie, *The King's secret: being the secret correspondence of Louis XV with his diplomatic agents*, 2 vols, London, 1879, II, pp. 293–6. Shelburne attributed the fall of Choiseul and the avoidance of war to a 'miraculous interposition of Providence'. W. Cobbett and J. Wright, *Parliamentary History of England*, XVIII, p. 675.
4. *Ibid.*, XVIII, pp. 167–8.
5. The exchanges summarised here are described in detail in J. Goebel, *The struggle for the Falkland Islands*, New Haven, 1927, pp. 326–405, and more briefly in V. T. Harlow, *The Founding of the Second British Empire*, 2 vols, London, 1952 and 1964, I, pp. 24–32.
6. G. Bancroft, *History of the United States*, 6 vols, New York, I, p. 525.
7. O. Gil Munilla, *El Río de la Plata en la Política internacional. Génesis del Virreinato*, Seville, 1949, pp. 309 ff.
8. H. I. Priestley, *José de Gálvez, Visitador General of New Spain*, Berkeley, 1934, pp. 289–92.
9. See above p. 42 and notes. For a general account of these changes and a select bibliography of the subject, see J. H. Parry, *The Spanish Seaborne Empire*, London, 1967.
10. See G. Céspedes del Castillo, *Lima y Buenos Aires, repercussiones económicas y políticas de la creacion del virreinato del Plata*, Seville, 1947.
11. Seventy-seven thousand tons as against 72,000 tons in 1767, the first year for which comparable figures are available. The French shipments, moreover, included nearly 30,000 tons of clayed sugar, whereas the English product was nearly all raw muscavado. The same general comparison held good for other crops – indigo, cacao, coffee. See L. J. Regatz, *The decline of the planter class in the British Caribbean*, Washington, 1928, pp. 123–32.
12. G. T. F. Raynal, trans. J. Justamond, *A Philosophical and Political History of the Settlements and Trade of Europeans in the East and West Indies*, 5 vols, London, 1777, IV, p. 409.

13. G. Debien, 'Esprit colon èt esprit d'autonomie à Saint-Domingue au XVIIIe siècle', *Notes d'Histoire coloniale XXV*, Larose, 1954, pp. 18 ff.

14. A. Girault, *Principes de colonisation et de legislation coloniale*, 2 vols, Paris, 1927, I, p. 219.

15. G. Debien, 'Gouverneurs, magistrats et colons. L'opposition parlementaire à Saint-Domingue, 1763–69', *Revue d'histoire d'Haiti*, 1946, nos. 59 and 60.

16. For the details of this complex financial operation, quite unprecedented in European colonial empires, see L. H. Gipson, *The British Empire before the American Revolution*, X, pp. 38–52.

17. L. H. Gipson, *The Coming of the Revolution, 1763–1775*, New York, 1954, p. 3.

18. E. S. and H. M. Morgan, *The Stamp Act Crisis*, New York, 1963, p. 46.

19. *Ibid.*, p. 76.

20. G. Wood, 'A Note on mobs in the American Revolution', *William and Mary Quarterly*, no. 23, 1966, p. 632.

21. Sir Lewis Namier, *Crossroads of Power*, London, 1962, pp. 194–212.

22. Gipson, *The British Empire before the American Revolution*, vol. XI, pp. 130–5.

23. *Ibid.*, vol. XII, pp. 139–44.

24. *The writings of Benjamin Franklin*, ed. A. H. Smyth, 10 vols, New York, 1907, pp. 259–60. On the general question of parliamentary authority, see R. L. Schuyler, *Parliament and the British Empire*, London, 1929.

25. Persistent attempts by the Virginia Assembly to legalise the payment of sterling debts in depreciated local currency, had been frustrated by the Legal Tender Act of 1764 (4 Geo. III, *c.* 34). This had produced the customary outcry against 'tyranny'. How far indebtedness affected the attitude of Virginians in the War of Independence cannot be precisely determined; but certainly there were few loyalists in Virginia. See B. Knollenberg, *Origins of the American Revolution, 1759–1766*, New York, 1961, pp. 57, 66, 131–2.

26. Bernard Bailyn, *The Ideological Origins of the American Revolution*, Cambridge, Mass., 1967, p. 8.

27. *The writings of George Washington*, ed. John C. Fitzpatrick, 39 vols, Washington, 1931–44, III, 242.

28. On this episode see John C. Miller, *Sam Adams, pioneer in propaganda*, Boston, 1936, pp. 167–88. The soldiers involved were tried, ably defended by local counsel, and acquitted of murder by a local jury; striking evidence of the durability of legal tradition in a time of great popular excitement.

29. For a detailed discussion of the act and its results see Gipson, *The British Empire before the American Revolution*, vol. XII, pp. 72 ff.

30. Especially in *The Case of Going to War for the sake of Procuring, Enlarging or Securing of Trade ...* by Josiah Tucker, London, 1763; and *The True Interest of Britain, set forth in regard to the Colonies: and the only Means of Living in Peace and Harmony with them*, London, 1774. See R. L. Schuyler, *Josiah Tucker, A selection from his Economic and Political Writings*, New York, 1931.

31. For the arguments supporting this opinion, see Piers Mackesy, *The War for America, 1775–1783*, London, 1964, pp. 510 ff.

32. *Ibid.*, pp. 33–4.

33. For a recent judgment on this question, see Gerald Saxon Brown, *The American Secretary*, Ann Arbor, 1963, pp. 177–9.

34. L. J. Ragatz, *The Fall of the Planter Class in the British Caribbean*, Washington, 1928, p. 30.

35. Harlow, *The Founding of the Second British Empire*, I, pp. 324 ff.

36. *Ibid.*, I, 287 ff.

37. *Ibid.*, I, pp. 448 ff.

38. John Baker Holroyd, 1st Earl of Sheffield, *Observations on the Commerce of the American States*, London, 1783, especially pp. 297–8.

39. Though Adam Smith himself had justified the Navigation Acts on the ground that national security must come before 'opulence'. *Wealth of Nations*, ed. E. Cannan, London, 1904, I, p. 429.

9

The New Conquistadores

Captain Robert Jenkins – Jenkins of the Ear – despite an early career in the illicit Madagascar slave trade, was neither a rascal nor a ruffian, but a capable and conscientious seaman. At the time of his brush with the Spaniards off Cuba, he was about his lawful business; his indignation at the treatment he received was genuine and justified. His demand for redress, when he got back to England, could not be ignored; but ministers in 1731 were anxious to keep on good terms with Spain, so Jenkins had to be kept quiet. This was managed in a manner characteristic of the time: someone who possessed the appropriate patronage was persuaded to nominate him to an East India command.[1] His ship was launched in the autumn of 1732 and two months later he sailed in the H.C.S. *Harrington* for St Helena, thence to Bencoolen for pepper. Here indeed was a jump in the world for the one-time slaver. An East India captain was a considerable personage, with access to many opportunities of profit and entitled, while in the East, to a nine-gun salute. Jenkins had reason to be grateful to the *guarda-costas*; and for some years he seems to have carried the bottled ear about with him as a talisman or memento. It was, perhaps, the habit of dining out, so to speak, on his ear, which prompted the revival of the story as anti-Spanish propaganda in 1738. That was after his return from his second East India voyage – Port Dauphin in Madagascar for slaves (some intended for Bencoolen, some for St Helena), thence Bombay and Calcutta, and home by St Helena. He was back at sea when the war which bears his name began. His third voyage was on the coveted China run: Bombay for cotton, Tellicherry for pepper (both for sale in China), then Canton for tutenague, chinaware and tea. On the return passage in 1740, in company with four country ships, he engaged and dispersed off the Konkan coast a Maratha fleet commanded by Kanhoji Angré in person. This made him a captain of note. He was sent as acting governor for a year to clean up the administration of St Helena; and then went on again to Bombay, where he died of fever at the end of 1742, and was buried with company's military honours.[2] A varied career, then; typical, in its later years, of the life of a successful company captain; unusual, in that Jenkins became an East India captain by accident; but also symbolic of the complex interaction between East and West, in the European circles which dealt overseas. About the time Jenkins died, the running armed rivalries and territorial aggressions between Europeans which had long been characteristic of America were becoming overt in India also; India, like America, was to become a European battle-ground.

Until the outbreak of war with France in 1744, the English United Company had developed its business in India steadily and profitably without much interference from European rivals. The Dutch company was its chief commercial competitor, but – quite apart from the fact that the two governments were at peace – the main centres of Dutch interest were elsewhere in the East, and neither company had anything to gain from political conflict in India. Quarrels between the staffs of Dutch and English factories never went beyond periodical bickering and brawling, and occasional posturing over such matters as flags and salutes. The French company was a younger and smaller concern; until the late 1730s it had neither the capital nor the shipping to offer very serious competition to the two giants, and until the 1740s its behaviour in the East was remarkably pacific. Even when the French and English governments were at war, during the War of the Spanish Succession, the representatives of the companies had found it prudent to observe an informal truce, and there had been no fighting in the Indian Ocean. Throughout this period, the chief problems confronting the English company in India, apart from its normal business preoccupations, were those of controlling the activities of its own servants, and of maintaining peaceable relations with the Indian rulers – the 'Country Powers' – with whom it came in contact. Both tasks were becoming steadily more difficult; the first, because of the expanding range of the company's activities, which gave increasing scope for private rackets; the second, because of the political disintegration of the Mughal empire, accelerated by invasions from outside India, Persian and Afghan, and by the constant raiding warfare maintained against the empire by the Hindu Maratha kingdoms in west-central India. As more and more territory slipped from the Mughal grasp, the political situation throughout India became more unpredictable and violent; the task of maintaining good relations with one prince without offending another became harder and harder.

The territorial and commercial standing of the English company in this period was regulated by a series of *firmans* granted by the Emperor Farrukhsiyar in 1717, to an embassy headed by John Surman.[3] The decrees were addressed to the officials of the three provinces – Gujerat, Hyderabad and Bengal – in which the English were settled. Their terms included the right to trade anywhere in Bengal free of all dues, subject to a customary payment of 3,000 rupees a year, and an enlargement of the area round Calcutta where the company acted as *zemindar*. In Hyderabad, similarly, the privilege of trading free of dues was confirmed, the only payment required being a rent for Madras; the areas under company rule, both at Madras and at Vizagapatam, were enlarged; the company was allowed to compound, in the annual sum of 10,000 rupees, for all duties payable at Surat; and its own rupees coined at Bombay were declared legal tender throughout the Mughal dominions. The various territories, under various forms of tenure, thus held by the company, were very small, the largest, that of Madras, only fifteen square miles; there was no disposition on the part of the directors, in the first half of the eighteenth century, to turn the company into a territorial ruler. Nevertheless company servants in India emphasised, and the directors reluctantly accepted, the necessity of controlling some territory. The company's trade involved the collection, and storage over extended periods, of large quantities of valuable goods; the godowns had to be protected in disturbed times by the company's own efforts. The company also raised, in its little territorial enclaves, a revenue which helped to defray the costs of administration and defence; and as landlord, it could to some extent control the activities of local weavers, who contracted with native middlemen to produce cloth for the company, and receive advances of raw material for the purpose. The concessions made to Surman's embassy, therefore, were, at least on paper, of great significance for the company.

Enforcement was another matter. The emperor's *subadars* and many minor vassals demanded their own tolls on the company's trade, while the company permitted, or failed to prevent, abuse of its corporate privileges by its servants for their own private ends. In Bengal the company lived in a state of scarcely veiled hostility with successive *nawabs*, and was prevented for many years from taking possession of its additional villages in the neighbourhood of Calcutta. Some of these, indeed, were not handed over until Clive's treaty with Siraj-ud-Daula in 1757. On the other hand, the company enjoyed some protection against disorder. When the Marathas invaded Bengal in 1742 and 1744, Fort William, its walls cluttered with warehouses and private dwellings, was in no condition to resist them. It was the Nawab 'Ali Wardi Khan who took the field against the invaders and drove them out.

On the west coast the emperor's feudatories counted for much less, the Marathas for much more, in the company's affairs. This was one of the main reasons for the steady migration of business from Surat (where the company's people had to rely on the protection, and endure the exactions, of imperial officials) to Bombay, where they could make their own dispositions for defence. Many Indian businessmen, particularly prominent Parsee shipowners and shipbuilders, also found it safer and more profitable to remove from Surat to Bombay.[4] But Bombay itself went in fear of the Marathas; until the fall of Gheria in 1756, company shipping and private shipping alike were liable to interference and attack in coastal waters. The Marathas, moreover, controlled most of the forest areas on the slopes of the Ghats and the edge of the tableland, upon which the Bombay shipyards depended for their supplies of teak and poon. All in all, the safety of Bombay depended less on its fortifications, than on the maintenance of civil relations with the Peshwa.

At Calcutta and Bombay the company's people knew more or less where they stood. At Madras, the largest of the company's bases, the situation was more complicated and less predictable. The Carnatic, the territory between the Bay of Bengal, the Eastern Ghats, the Kistna and the Coleroon, in which Madras lay, was in theory subject to the nizam of Hyderabad, in his capacity as subadar of the Deccan. By the 1740s the title of subadar was an anachronism; in fact, the nizam was an independent and hereditary prince. The nawab of the Carnatic, with his capital at Arcot, was subject only to occasional and ineffectual interference from Hyderabad; but his power in turn was weakened by the existence of a group of independent and hostile Hindu principalities in the southern Carnatic, south of the Coleroon. The most important of these were Tanjore, which had been created by a Maratha invader in the previous century, and Trichinopoly, a rock fortress of great strength, with its surrounding territory, the last surviving remnant of the ancient empire of Vijayanagar. The balance of power between the nizam, the nawab and the Hindu states was unstable and precarious; and each of the princes involved was beset by ambitious rivals, claimants to his throne or to part, at least, of his dominions. Troubled waters in which to fish; as might be expected, it was here in the Carnatic that the European groups first abandoned the peaceful attitude, one towards another, enjoined upon them by the 'Country Powers'. The principal contenders, also as might be expected, were the English and the French.

The *Compagnie des Indes* had been a slow starter in the Indian Ocean trades, but by the 1730s it had got rid of many of its entanglements elsewhere, had handed Louisiana back to the French crown, and had passed on most of the West African slave trade to the West Indies to licensed private traders. It was free to concentrate on its Eastern business, and by 1734 fourteen of its ships were reported trading in the East.[5] In India, the company was served by exceptionally able representatives: Dumas at Pondicherry, and Dupleix, who in twelve years as factor at Chandernagore amassed the great private fortune which was to provide a basis for his subsequent spectacular career. About the same time, La Bourdonnais, as governor of Mauritius, began organising there a base for French naval power in the Indian Ocean; and when, in 1740, war between France and England seemed likely, he was encouraged to cruise against English shipping off the coast of India.

His small expedition was the eastern counterpart of the great fleet which d'Antin took to the West Indies in the same year. The crisis passed, and La Bourdonnais went back to Mauritius; but the English company, thoroughly alarmed, asked its own home government for naval support in the event of the threat recurring. When the actual outbreak of war in 1744 became known in India, there were no French warships in Indian waters. Dupleix, who had become governor of Pondicherry in 1742, proposed to his English counterparts a truce similar to that in the previous war; they replied civilly that they themselves had no hostile intentions, but that they could not answer for any king's ships which might arrive. In fact, unknown to either party, Commodore Barnett's small squadron was already on its way – the first English naval force to operate in Indian waters – and on arrival seized a number of French ships, including some country ships in which Dupleix had an interest, and which he had tried to protect under the nawab's flag. Dupleix retorted by sending to Mauritius for help; La Bourdonnais quickly improvised, from the company's ships in the area, a fleet considerably stronger than the English squadron, and much more ably commanded; and the combined French forces proceeded in 1746 to invest Madras. Fort St George, designed to withstand cavalry raids, not combined siege operations, could make only a token resistance. The English appealed for protection to the nawab, who first sent orders to the French to desist, then an army, which arrived after the English surrender, and which was defeated at Ambur and dispersed by the much smaller, but better armed, better disciplined forces of the French company, fighting under French officers. Dupleix and La Bourdonnais then fell out over the spoils. La Bourdonnais, knowing that with the onset of the north-east monsoon he would have to withdraw his ships from a dangerous lee shore, wanted to restore Madras immediately to its owners, for a ransom which would have included a handsome payment for himself. Dupleix wanted to keep the place, plunder it – also, of course, with great profit to himself – and divert its trade to Pondicherry. In one respect Dupleix had his way. La Bourdonnais was driven off by the monsoon, and returned to Mauritius; Madras was plundered; and eventually Dupleix was able to engineer the recall of La Bourdonnais to France in disgrace.[6]

The Madras campaign was fought on a very small scale, by comparison with the concurrent operations in the West Indies; India was still a distant affair of merchants. It had small direct results, for Madras was handed back at the peace in 1748. Nevertheless, it set ominous precedents. For the first time, Europeans had made war among themselves on Indian territory; they had defied the authority of their overlord, a major Indian ruler; they had defeated, with surprising ease, a formidable army which the ruler sent against them, so demonstrating that cavalry, elephants and large numbers were no match for small forces possessing heavy fire power and (relatively) good discipline; and finally they had settled by treaty among themselves the future of an important town, without any reference to the overlord's wishes. All this had been done chiefly on the initiative of men on the spot; their employers, in supporting them, had truckled to success. After 1746 the two groups of company servants could not return to their earlier state of mutual forbearance. They could not trust one another. In time of European peace, however, they could not wage open war upon one another in India. Each group tried, therefore, to protect its own position and to damage that of its rival, by local alliances. In the violently disturbed state of southern India, princes and pretenders welcomed such alliances. In effect, the Europeans offered themselves, with the company forces they commanded, as *condottieri*; as the 'mercenary troops of these polished barbarians'.[7] As with mercenaries everywhere, the more ambitious among them were tempted to turn *conquistador*. It was easier to report conquests after the event than to obtain authorisation beforehand, and the new conquistadores did not always trouble to inform their masters fully of the nature of their activities.

The uneasy peace in Europe from 1748 to 1756 was a period of almost continuous fighting in the Deccan and the Carnatic. It was the heyday of the European *condottieri* in India. The French took the initiative in this confused and indirect warfare, and for several years they had much the best of it, thanks to the imagination, skill and daring of their leaders Dupleix in the Carnatic, and Bussy (who was not only an able soldier and a consummate diplomat, but also a distinguished oriental scholar) in the Deccan. By 1751, through an adroit combination of diplomacy and war, one ally and protégé of the French had been installed as nawab of the Carnatic, another as subadar of the Deccan. These princes had made extensive grants of territory and revenue, both to the French company and to Dupleix personally. Dupleix was created memsebdar of the eastern Carnatic, and so became in his own right a considerable hereditary prince. The English at Madras, more commercially-minded and less daring, could boast no comparable success. They had tried, in 1749, to strengthen their position in the southern Carnatic by threatening to back a pretender to the throne of Tanjore, and had secured the cession of a minor harbour, Devi-Kotah on the Coleroon. For this – 'an unjust and rash Enterprise and concerted and carried on without Authority and contrary to the True Interest of the Company' – they were reprimanded. 'You seem,' observed the directors, 'to look upon yourselves rather as a military colony than the Factors and Agents of a Body of Merchants.'[8] At about the same time, the directors of the French company were writing to congratulate Dupleix on 'la glorieuse action de nos troupes'.[9]

English directors were not unaware of the dangers of a situation in which Madras and Fort St David might be cut off from a trading hinterland controlled, directly or indirectly, by the French. They still thought, however, that the remedy lay not in military countermeasures, certainly not in territorial aggression, but in support of reigning Indian rulers and in reliance on their protection of legitimate trade. As late as 1754, a confidential analysis of the French danger stated: 'The credit of the English as merchants is superior in India to that of the French, and they will always have the Preference in all India Governments who are their own masters, so long as they preserve their mercantile reputation.'[10] The directors misjudged both the temper of their own servants and the character of the princes – mostly military adventurers – with whom they had to deal. The English in the Carnatic had already begun to take matters into their own hands, and were already resisting French threats by French methods. Dupleix' noose round Madras was cut unexpectedly by Clive, who, late in 1751, captured Arcot by a bold dash, and held it, while Dupleix' nawab, Chanda Sahib, was away on a campaign against Trichinopoly. An English ally and protégé replaced a French on the

Carnatic throne. This was indeed a 'rash Enterprise and concerted and carried on without Authority'. To the French at Pondicherry it was 'le commencement de nos désastres'. But even if Dupleix had not met, in Clive, a *condottiere* as bold and resolute as himself, his system probably could not have lasted long. A single bold stroke of diplomacy might place a prince upon a throne; but to keep him there required constant vigilance and continued heavy expense. The resources of the French company were much smaller than those of the English. Dupleix' military reach exceeded his financial grasp. To meet the cost of war, he spent his own personal fortune, borrowed from his associates, and contracted immense debts in the company's name. He repeatedly assured the directors that all was well; that the revenues of the territory he acquired, and the profits of expanding trade, would amply meet the costs and eventually yield great profits; but in a Carnatic ravaged by constant fighting, revenues could not be collected nor normal trade pursued. Bussy could do little to relieve Dupleix' need; the Deccan never had revenue to spare. By 1754, the directors had discovered the true state of affairs and recalled Dupleix in disgrace; without, however, abandoning his policy.

A successful conquistador is a man who not only conquers, but makes his conquests pay for themselves; as did Hernán Cortés, Affonso d'Alboquerque, Jan Pieterszoon Coen; as did Clive, the company's writer 'of martial disposition', who turned soldier in earnest in 1751. The reasons for Dupleix' failure in this respect, and for Clive's success, are not to be found in any difference of character or ability between the two men. Both possessed all the attributes of the conquistador: imaginative daring, tenacity of purpose, ruthlessness on occasion; lightning grasp of a situation, the power of quick and bold decision; personal magnetism, the capacity to lead and to dominate. Nor was the difference principally one of backing; for though the resources of the French company were inferior to those of the English, its directors were much less reluctant than their English counterparts to support martial enterprises. Dupleix, however, was obliged by circumstances to apply his energy and his resources in the wrong part of India. India, from the standpoint of an invader, consists of an immense, fertile, populous valley, with high mountains to the north of it, and relatively unproductive uplands filling most of the peninsula to the south. The river valley, the alluvial plain of the Ganges and its confluents, were worth conquering, the rest was not. Compared with Bengal and Bihar, the narrow strips of productive territory along the Malabar and Coromandel coasts, where Europeans first set up as traders and first fell to fighting over territory and influence, were as nothing in themselves. To the perceptive invader, they were chiefly valuable as stepping-stones to Bengal. The most direct access to the heart of Bengal was by sea and up the Hugli. It was not a very easy access; the river mouth was guarded by formidable shoals, the notorious Sandheads; the river itself was a maze of shallows, and the central channel had only seven fathoms of water at low tide; in the south-west monsoon ships came surging into the river like corks in a mill-race; in the north-east, they had a tedious and dangerous beat, with the floodtide and against the wind, going about every ten minutes or so between the mudbanks. Once these intricacies were mastered, however, a seaborne invader possessing a secure base – Madras, for instance – in south India, had shorter and better communications than any enemy marching overland. Job Charnock, when he founded his trading post at Calcutta, a hundred miles up the Hugli, presumably had these geographical facts in mind; but until the 1750s no one tried seriously to exploit them. Bengal had not suffered the kind of political disintegration which, in the Carnatic, had led the European groups into competitive intrigue and undeclared war. The companies had remained content with trade. Clive was the first European to enter Bengal by sea with an army at his back, and to establish himself there as a conquistador.

The occasion of Clive's expedition was the attack on Calcutta in 1756 by the nawab of Bengal, Siraj-ud-Daula, who had succeeded his grandfather, the Tartar adventurer 'Ali Wardi Khan, only a few weeks earlier. Relations between the nawabs and the English company had always been difficult. The company enjoyed privileges conferred by an imperial authority, to which the later nawabs accorded no more than formal deference. The dispute about the territorial extent of the company's holdings round Calcutta has already been mentioned. The company's right to trade free of tolls throughout Bengal also caused disputes. The company's servants, in their private capacity, used this privilege to cover duty-free internal trade in such commodities as salt, tobacco and betel, so placing native traders at a disadvantage and diminishing the nawab's revenue. The company had no direct interest in this trade and, in order to avoid trouble with the nawab, forbade it; but the prohibition was widely ignored. The nawab's officials collected duties on the trade whenever they could, the company's servants complained of the exactions of the nawab's government, and the nawab accused the company of conniving at the smuggling activities of its servants. These were perennial disputes, inherent in the nature of the company's business. They became more acute in the 1750s, because the disturbances in the Carnatic made it impossible for the company's ships to make up their cargoes at Madras; they were sent on to Calcutta instead, and as the company's business in Bengal increased, so did the opportunities for abuse. At the same time, reports from the south gave rise to fears that European rivalries might spread to Bengal and disrupt that province as they had disrupted the Carnatic; or that one or another European group might try its hand at kingmaking. Siraj-ud-Daula may have been thinking in terms of a preventive strike; he may have been moved merely by vanity, hope of plunder, and expectation of an easy victory. The expectation was plausible; Fort William, with its neglected fortifications and its comatose garrison, largely of Portuguese mercenaries, was indefensible.[11] Its batteries, such as they were, commanded the river, not the landward approaches. Siraj-ud-Daula took the place in five days; the chief episodes were the desertion of most of the council and their flights to ships in the river; the plunder of the liquor godowns by the soldiers of the garrison; the sack of the town by the nawab's troops; and the Black Hole.

A prompt counterstroke could come only from Madras, where the company's forces had lately been supplemented by a small fleet of king's ships and by a royal regiment. An expedition was being planned against Bussy at Hyderabad. Formal war with France was imminent. The Madras council had to decide whether their first duty was to preserve the situation in the Carnatic and ensure the safety of Madras; or to try to recover Calcutta and retrieve the situation in Bengal. By a narrow margin, they chose Bengal; probably indignation over the Black Hole helped to turn the scale. The colonel commanding the king's regiment refused to command the expedition, because the company's rules on the sharing of plunder were not to his liking;[12] another interesting sample of eighteenth-century discipline. Clive, though still a junior officer, was given the command, and a large sum in silver for the expenses of the expedition was consigned to him personally. By the time this decision had been reached, the north-east monsoon had set in, and Clive had a long and troublesome passage to Calcutta; but he reoccupied the town without much difficulty. Siraj-ud-Daula – who, after plundering the place, had no idea what to do with it – had withdrawn to his own capital, Murshidabad. At the time of Clive's arrival he was preoccupied with a potential threat in his rear, from an Afghan adventurer who had captured Delhi and was engaged in plundering it. He agreed, early in 1757, to a treaty whereby all English privileges under the 1717 firmans were restored.

Clive should then have returned to Madras, in accordance with his instructions. Meanwhile, however, news had arrived of the renewal of war with France. Clive, reluctant in any event to give up his independent command, turned on Chandernagore, the French headquarters in Bengal, and with the help of Watson's ships in the river, captured it. Siraj-ud-Daula, who had done nothing to protect the French, then took alarm. He refused to implement his recent treaty with Clive, began to reassemble his own army, received French fugitives from Chandernagore at his court, and wrote to ask Bussy to come from Hyderabad to his help.[13] There was little likelihood of Bussy being able to accede to this request; he was tied down in the Deccan, with a formidable little army but no money to pay it. Meanwhile opposition to Siraj-ud-Daula's policy, or lack of it, was growing among his own subjects. He had a gift for alienating everyone whose support he needed. The government of the Mughal empire in its great days had been based upon an alliance between the martial Muslim princes who ruled the empire and its major provinces, and Hindu magnates who accepted, on terms, the status of feudatories and who also manned the upper ranks of the civil service. Minor officials were also mostly Hindus. This was Akbar's legacy; an arrangement by which the Mughal rulers ceased to be foreign conquerors and became accepted as Indian. Aurangzeb in his later, more fanatical years, had persecuted Hindus, and had run into much trouble as a result; but in general the arrangement stood, both in the empire and in the successor states as they gradually split away. 'Ali Wardi Khan in Bengal had followed Akbar's example, but Siraj-ud-Daula in his short reign followed that of Aurangzeb. Outraged Hindu notabilities, such as the Seth brothers, bankers of Murshidabad, who had helped to finance 'Ali Wardi Khan's government, were now subjected to discriminatory taxation and threatened with circumcision. They had good reason to desire a revolution; and a plausible candidate for the nawab's throne was available, in 'Ali Wardi Khan's nephew Mir Ja'far, whom Siraj-ud-Daula had also insulted. Clive himself, despairing of any dependable understanding with Siraj-ud-Daula, now became a king-maker. He made secret agreements with Mir-Ja'far and with the Hindu magnates, and marched towards Murshidabad. His victory at Plassey resembled Dupleix' success at Ambur eight years earlier; the victory of a small but well-disciplined, well-equipped army over a large but ill-coordinated, ill-armed force, further divided by treachery. Siraj-ud-Daula was put to death by Mir Ja'far's people, and Mir Ja'far succeeded him – the first nawab of Bengal to owe his throne to European support. He was not, initially, ungrateful. His agreement with Clive had stipulated large concessions to the company: extensions of its commercial privileges; a monopoly, militarily vital, of the trade in saltpetre; and a promise of reimbursement for all the expenses of the war. In addition, Clive and his associates received lavish personal presents. Clive's share was worth more than £200,000; and in 1759 he received a further favour, the transfer from the nawab to himself of an honorific imperial office, accompanied by a princely *jagir* of some £27,000 a year. The income was charged upon the quit-rents of lands near Calcutta, in the possession of the company; the nawab simply directed that the quit-rents should be paid to Clive instead of to himself. This was unexampled; it made Clive, while still a salaried servant of the company under the orders of the Madras council, a direct feudatory, like the nawab himself, of the Mughal emperor. It also made him, of course, a very rich man. Clive, characteristically, made no attempt to conceal the transaction or explain it away; nor, apparently, did he foresee the trouble it was to cause, when the directors heard of it.[14]

By 1758 the company, though making no claim to rule, was the most influential body in Bengal; Clive, though without any office entitling him to govern, was the most powerful person. The nawab was his client. The French, as an organised political force, had been driven out. The turn of the Dutch came in 1759. The Dutch company had big interests in Bengal, chiefly in the piece-goods trade to Batavia, and its servants ran a lucrative, though clandestine, monopoly of opium going in the same direction. They had some reason for fearing that Clive might serve Chinsura as he had served Chandernagore, and tried to forestall him by reinforcing their garrison there, in defiance of the nawab's prohibition, which was really Clive's prohibition. They were met with English force. For many years, Dutch military operations in the East had been directed against rulers much less formidable than the Indian princes. Their Malay troops, armed with muskets and plug bayonets of a type long obsolete in Europe, were no match for the English company's forces in Bengal.[15] They were heavily defeated, and sued for peace. From 1760, Dutch trade in Bengal continued only by courtesy of the English company. Clive's control of the province, though informal and indirect, appeared complete. In 1760 he returned to England to lay out his loot in purchasing political influence, and to counter as best he could the alarm and jealousy which his lightning successes had aroused among his employers.

The relative immunity of Bengal from inter-European fighting was due not only to Clive's successes, but also to the course of events in the Carnatic. The change from informal fighting to declared war in 1757 brought battle fleets, French and English, into Indian waters for the first time. The essence of naval strategy in India was to control the strip of water, some 200 miles long, off the Coromandel coast between Point Calimere and Madras, if not continuously, then at least during the south-west monsoon. Eight or nine significant fleet actions took place in Indian waters in the second half of the eighteenth century; all were in this strip of water, and nearly all during the south-west monsoon. None was decisive in itself; the fleets were comparatively small, and were usually handled with some degree of tactical timidity. Knowing the difficulties of relief at so great a distance from home, admirals tried to preserve their fleets from the risk of major losses. The French especially preferred to fight at long range, and to cripple the enemy temporarily by cutting his rigging. During the Seven Years War, the English fleets usually had the best of the Coromandel fighting. Their success was due partly to the worldwide superiority of English naval strength, which increased as the war progressed; partly to the ability of Admiral Pocock, who was a bolder tactician than his opponent d'Aché; partly to the jealousy, amounting almost to hatred, between the French naval and military commands. More fundamentally, however, it was a question of bases. Bombay, the only good harbour in the possession of either combatant, was on the wrong side of India, but it was nearer the scene of action than Mauritius, and with its Parsee-run shipyards was much better equipped as a base. In 1758, for example, d'Aché, after two inconclusive encounters with Pocock's fleet, felt obliged, despite fierce reproaches from his military colleagues, to withdraw to Mauritius for refit; he failed to find adequate stores there, and had to send to the Cape to provision his ships, spending for the purpose large sums intended for the army in the Carnatic. He was absent from the station for a whole year. On his return he again encountered Pocock patrolling off Pondicherry, was badly mauled in the ensuing action, and again had to withdraw. The constant presence of an English fleet off the coast during the main operating season of each year prevented any attempt on the part of the French to retrieve their losses in Bengal; it also prevented reinforcements, money and supplies, other than those procurable locally, from reaching the French armies in south India. French military superiority in the Carnatic was steadily reduced, despite Clive's continued absence in Bengal. The initial run of French successes, which included the capture of Fort St David in 1757, was checked by the end of 1758. Bussy had to be called in from Hyderabad, where he had been for years the power behind the throne; his departure left the field clear for an English invasion of the 'northern Circars', linking the Carnatic with Orissa and Bengal. This operation, planned by Clive and led by Forde, took

Masulipatam early in 1759, and shortly afterwards the siege of Madras was lifted. In 1760, Eyre Coote's victory at Wandiwash dispersed the main French army and opened the road to Pondicherry. Pondicherry itself, blockaded by sea and invested by land, surrendered in 1761, and work was started immediately on the demolition of its fortifications. This was effectively the end of the war in India. At the Peace of Paris, the French gave up all acquisitions and all claims originating since the beginning of 1749, in exchange for the return of the factories in their possession before that date. They also engaged to erect no fortifications and maintain no troops in Bengal. From 1763, then, the French company ceased to be a significant territorial power in India. It still traded there, but like the Dutch company, traded on sufferance. The terms of the treaty caused a vindictive outcry in France. Lally, the military commander-in-chief – who had held both the king's and the company's commission, and who had quarrelled with the company's officials, with the naval commanders, and with Bussy – was beheaded, without even Voltaire writing a word in protest.

From 1763 the English company was the dominant power in the richest part of India. It was ill-equipped to shoulder such a burden. Its agents there were not trained civil servants. Few of them felt any responsibility towards the people of India; officially, indeed, they had no responsibility, for the nawabs still reigned and ruled and the emperor was still, at least nominally, suzerain. Their loyalty to the company which employed them was less than wholehearted. They were sent to India to serve the company's interests; but they also expected, as they had always done, to make money for themselves. For this, they now had many new opportunities, which they exploited on a scale to appal even Mughal officials. They fleeced the local populations, through their assumed privileges of duty-free internal trade in Bengal, which threatened to put local traders out of business. They defrauded the company, by collusive contracts to supply, in their private capacities, goods which it needed; the prodigious numbers of bullocks, for example, continually demanded by the army. They fleeced the rulers in many ways: by lending them money, against land or revenue assignments – the nawab of Arcot and the raja of Tanjore were notorious and feckless debtors; by many varieties of bullying and blackmail – the nawab of Bengal, owing his very throne to the company's military support, was always vulnerable to 'squeeze'. Three times in five years a nawab, rendered viciously desperate, turned on the company, was deposed by the Calcutta Council, and replaced by another, who in turn was forced to hand over huge sums as the price of his enthronement. The third of these revolutions, in 1763, involved the company in war outside Bengal, with the nawab of Oudh, Bengal's neighbour on the west, and with the Emperor Shah Alam II, both of whom supported the dethroned Mir Kasim. Hector Munro's victory at Buxar in 1764 broke up this confederacy, but also threatened to widen the area of danger; it suggested to the Bengal conquistadores the possibility of dominating the whole of northern India and controlling the imperial throne – to the directors of the company a dangerous megalomaniac frenzy.

The company, in short, having captured the richest part of India, seemed likely to lose it through the shortsighted rapacity of its own servants. The new conquistadores were as contumacious, as powerful, in their own way as dangerous to authority, as the merchant princes and sea-lawyers of New England, whose rebellious stirrings at precisely the same time were beginning to cause alarm. The directors' repeated prohibitions of military adventures, of private trade, of the taking of presents, were ignored or openly defied. The offenders could not easily be disciplined or dismissed; most of them had friends and interests in the company and could make trouble for the Direction. The situation invited intervention by government, whether to support or to control the company. Clive himself had suggested this on several occasions, and it might be argued that the war, the peace, and events immediately following the peace, supplied precedents for it. The war had been won in India with the help of royal forces. The peace had been negotiated by the government, not by the company – the first Anglo-French agreement on India to be so negotiated. Ministers, to be sure, had consulted with directors; they professed to be acting on behalf of the company, and indeed made a favour of it;[16] but it was their peace. Embarrassed as they were by Opposition clamour against the treaty in general, they could not afford to have the company complaining about it. Some people, prominent in the company but not privy to the negotiations – Clive was one – would have preferred stiffer terms, including the total exclusion of the French from Bengal. It was important to the Bute ministry that the Direction should remain in the hands of the company conservatives, mostly followers or associates of the old spider of Leadenhall Street, Laurence Sulivan; men who believed in keeping on good terms with government and who still persisted in regarding the company as a 'body of merchants'. Clive, the rich conquistador, moving with a sullen awkwardness about the corridors of power, rallying the 'gentlemen of Bengal' behind him, was a national hero and a political menace. In 1763, for the first time, the treasury intervened obliquely in the internal politics of the company. In the election of directors of that year Sulivan was kept in and Clive out with the help of ministerial support, and of a large sum advanced from the Pay Office for the purpose of 'splitting' votes. The Sulivan party then moved for the company to take over Clive's *jagir*. This was not only a manifestation of personal spite; Clive's position was highly equivocal; and for the directors it was exasperating to hand over the nawab's quit-rents to a company servant, when the nawab himself claimed to be unable to discharge his debts to the company. Clive defended himself by a political *volte-face*, offering the support of his connection to the new (Grenville) ministry. The treasury intervened on his behalf in the 1764 company election, in which the Sulivan party was defeated, though narrowly.[17] In the next twenty years, as company affairs became more closely entangled in national politics, such interventions were to be frequent.

Influencing company elections in London, however, was a long way from controlling company policy in India. For the time being, the company was left to deal as best it could with an Indian situation fast becoming desperate. In 1765 Clive himself – poacher turned gamekeeper, his enemies said – went back to Bengal as governor, with wide powers to restore discipline. He certainly was the man for it, with his decisiveness, his abrupt and bullying ways. The 'Augean stable' was his own favourite metaphor in describing his task. During his short stay, less than two years, he concluded the treaties which recognised Shah Alam's title as emperor, and stabilised the province of Oudh as an allied, and in some degree protected, buffer state on the western frontier of Bengal; he pulled back the army and the traders to within the Presidency of Bengal; he suppressed a mutiny among younger officers in the army, who had seriously thought of becoming a kind of Varangian Guard at Delhi and who resented the loss of their field allowances; he made strenuous efforts to enforce the rule against private internal trade, dismissing many offenders and sending some to England for prosecution. More significant for the future, he induced the powerless emperor to take from the nawab, and grant to the company, the *diwani*, the revenue administration of Bengal. This, as events proved, was a long step towards territorial sovereignty. It was not so intended; its purpose was rather to avoid, or at least limit, the company's responsibility for detailed administration. It was an early experiment in what later came to be known as direct rule; contemporaries called it the Dual System. Clive insisted that the company should not meddle with the actual work of tax-collecting; it had no civil service capable of such work, and Clive made no move to create one – he was much more concerned to keep the company's servants' fingers out of the till. The collecting was to be done, as before, by native officials, but under the direction of a deputy-nawab approved by the company. The proceeds of collection were to be paid to the company's government at Calcutta, which was to make necessary disbursements for administration and defence and pay agreed annual sums (as subsidy, pension, tribute, according to one's point of view) to the emperor and to the nawab. After these payments a substantial surplus – over £2,000,000, so Clive, with great exaggeration, assured the directors – would accrue to the company as a return for its services. Some of this surplus could be used to pay adequate salaries to company servants, thus removing any excuse for them to engage in private trade, a point to which Clive rightly attached great importance. The rest would augment the annual 'investment' to be laid out in buying India goods and Chinese tea, and so reduce the need to export specie from England. This was the Dutch prescription for oriental trade; as Horace Walpole commented, 'We are Spaniards in our lust for gold, and Dutch in our delicacy of obtaining it.'[18]

The news of the *diwani*, when it reached London, produced two unintended consequences: the first, a rush to buy East India stock (led by Clive, who had foreknowledge), and a steep rise in its price; the second, a move by government to secure a share of the proceeds. One of the chief preoccupations of government at that time was the search for colonial contributions towards the cost of colonial defence. The news of the *diwani* – 'a gift from Heaven', Chatham called it – came within a few weeks of the repeal of the Stamp Act. This body of merchants, it seemed, was levying, contrary to its charter, a political tribute on territory acquired with the help of government forces. The Bengal revenues, according to Chatham and his colleagues, accrued to government, which by their means could make good from the East the deficit it was incurring in the West. Naturally the directors disputed this interpretation; it came to bargaining, and in 1767 the company agreed to contribute £400,000 a year. (In that year, it may be noted in passing, the supplies voted by parliament on account of American and other colonial charges amounted to about £428,000.) This transaction made further interventions inevitable; government had acquired a vested interest in the financial stability of the company and in the orderly administration of its affairs, at a time when both were being undermined by the company's own servants.

During these contentious years considerable numbers of these men, having made fortunes in India by licit or illicit means, returned to England, bringing their money with them. Some of them had been disciplined or dismissed by Clive, and were full of resentment; not entirely unreasonably, since they had been censured for doing what others, including some who were now directors, had done before them; how were they to know that standards of conduct were to become stricter? Many remitted money home in company bills, in itself a serious embarrassment, since the proceeds of the London sales were not enough to meet the bills, and the company had to borrow in the City for the purpose.[19] Arrived in England, the 'nabobs' invested in company stock and acquired a voting strength in the General Court sufficient on occasion to overwhelm the Direction, even when it had ministerial support. They made common cause with speculators interested in 'bulling' the stock, and to this end forced through in 1766–7 two successive (and wholly unwarranted) increases in dividend in less than a year. They compelled the Direction to drop its impending prosecutions, and so encouraged their colleagues still in India to further defiance. Neither of Clive's successors in Bengal was a Clive, and discipline there again disintegrated. When in 1769 the province was devastated by famine, the company's organisation could do nothing to relieve its distress; some company servants, indeed, made matters horribly worse by cornering rice for their own profit. Millions starved to death, and the revenue surplus almost disappeared. Bad news came also from the south. Hyder 'Ali, the military adventurer who had recently usurped the throne of Mysore, invaded the Carnatic in 1767, and the company's natural allies, the nizam and the Marathas, stood aside. A destructive war was followed, in 1769, by a humiliating peace. In that year, the 'bull' market in London collapsed; the price of stock dropped alarmingly; some contemporaries gloomily recalled the South Sea Bubble. That was an exaggeration; but some proprietors were ruined; Sulivan, the ablest and most experienced man in the company's Direction, lost £15,000; Shelburne, who had always been his political supporter, lost £20,000, and withdrew from the company's affairs, believing, rightly, that his connection with them damaged his political reputation. In all responsible circles indignation arose from the belief that company rule in India was oppressive and extortionate, and so damaging to national reputation and conscience; but this was still a relatively minor complaint; Burke's rhetoric had not yet aroused public opinion in defence of the hapless *ryot*. More serious was the complaint, coming loudly from those who had burned their fingers, that the company was reckless in its financial management, and was damaging the national credit. Perhaps most serious of all was the feeling that the company's returned servants were a corrupting influence in English political and social life. The landed magnates who, for the most part, ran the archaic racket which then passed for government in England, were themselves no strangers to corrupt practices. They dealt in rotten boroughs. They used patronage of all sorts in seeking power, in supporting faction, and in furthering the interests of their relatives, friends and clients. Yet they were not without public spirit or sense of responsibility, and convention among them set limits to what was allowable. They resented bitterly the intrusion of upstart nabobs who knew nothing of limiting conventions; whose motives seemed purely selfish; who were taking over the East India Company and seemed bent on destroying it; who fought or bought their way into parliament; who applied to dishonourable ends prodigious sums acquired by extortionate means.

If the company could not control the new conquistadores the government must, or lose India. North, whose mosaic of a ministry was botched together in 1770, hesitated. Meddling with chartered corporations was politically dangerous; any measure likely to increase crown patronage was bound to raise a storm; the flimsy framework of British public administration could not be expected to carry the weight of an Indian empire. But pressure increased; stop-gap – though sensible – bills introduced by Sulivan in parliament in 1771 were contemptuously rejected; the Commons' Select Committee on the subject, formed early in 1772, contained men like Burgoyne, Barré, Lord Howe, and Lord George Germain who were already concerned over American affairs, and emphasised the belief that Britain was threatened not with one colonial rebellion, but two. They called for drastic measures. In 1772 a severe financial crisis in the City paralysed general credit. The company, having rashly declared a dividend of 12½ per cent, sought to postpone distribution, and approached government for a loan, which was made the following year, very grudgingly, subject to the future limitation of dividends and the regular submission of accounts to the treasury. North at last accepted that the ministry must itself introduce a comprehensive bill to regulate Indian affairs, and got Jenkinson, that prodigy of administrative industry, to prepare one. In the Regulating Act of 1773 government asserted, somewhat tentatively, its authority over the company in respect of political and administrative activities in India, and revised the company's constitution in order to make the assertion effective. The Act was a half-measure, drafted in haste, intended to be amended and strengthened in the light of experience;[20] but within a few weeks of its enactment the respectable merchants of Boston employed their hoodlums to tip the company's tea into the harbour; parliament retorted with the Intolerable Acts, and the American rebellion began. Warren Hastings was left to wrestle with the ambiguities of the Act and to manage the affairs of India despite them. Apart from temporary tinkering in 1780–1 to postpone the expiry and renewal (or abrogation or alteration) of the company's charter, the Act stood, shakily, until it was superseded by Pitt's famous India Act of 1784.

The Regulating Act and the India Act were both based on the tacit recognition that the company's purely commercial activities in India had become relatively unimportant. The company's main business there was to collect revenue – tribute. This in itself was new in British imperial experience. The fact that the tribute was exported in the form of goods made no difference in principle. Government wished to ensure, in India, that the tribute was actually received by the company and did not disappear into the pockets of its servants; that the company did not spend excessive sums on administration and defence, or allow its servants to embark on further adventures of conquest and plunder, which devoured money and might involve government in unexpected wars. In Europe, it wished to ensure that the company distributed moderate, not excessive dividends; that it constituted a stabilising, not a disturbing element in the stock market; and above all that it made regular and substantial contributions to the needs of government. At the London end, under the 1773 Act, government was to be kept constantly informed; all communications from India dealing with financial or political matters were to be laid before the treasury or a secretary of state, respectively. The conduct of policy was left to the directors; it was hoped (optimistically, as it turned out) that their power and their independence of the proprietors would be increased, by lengthening their term of office from one year to four; by sharply raising the voting qualifications of those by whom they were elected; and by rules making 'splitting' prohibitively risky and expensive.[21] Ministerial control over the directors was to be maintained, as before, by the mixture of pressure and favours commonly described as 'influence'. In India, there was to be a governor general at Calcutta, with loosely-defined powers of supervision over the other presidencies. He was to be guided by a council of four, and was to be bound by the vote

231

of a majority. Ordinances of the governor general in council were to be subject, like colonial legislation in America, to the royal prerogative of disallowance. For the enforcement of discipline among the company's servants, there was to be a supreme court for Bengal, its judges appointed by the crown. The court's relations with the council, the precise extent of its jurisdiction, the nature of the law it was to apply, were left undefined.

The whole scheme, with its ambiguities, its checks and balances, its built-in friction, might have emanated from the chancery of a Spanish Habsburg. It never worked smoothly. The proprietors in London kept up a stubborn rearguard action against changes pressed upon the company by government, and were still able, on occasion, to overrule the Direction. The councils at Bombay and Madras, jealous of their independence, pursued their local, and often irresponsible, policies without consulting the governor general; though he was expected to rush to their help when they got into trouble. The supreme court interpreted its instructions as conferring the blessings of English justice, along with the savageries of the English penal system, upon natives who were company's servants only in the sense that they collected revenue for the company, or British subjects only in the sense that they lived in Calcutta. These invasions of local jurisdiction produced a long series of recriminations between judges and council. Worse still were the quarrels within the council itself. Its members were named in the Act. The governor general was Warren Hastings, already governor of Bengal, the ablest and most respected of company servants then in India. Three of the others were not company men at all, but were appointed from outside and had Clive's Augean stable metaphor implanted in their minds before they left England. Two of them – the thick-headed martinet Clavering, and Francis the clever, self-righteous, vindictive climber – were exceptionally difficult characters. Hastings could not overrule them; he outlived one and outstayed the other; but Francis continued to pursue the vendetta in England and later played a prominent part, with Burke, Fox and Sheridan, in Hastings' impeachment.

Francis' opposition to Hastings was not only a matter of personal spite and thwarted ambition; there were diferences of principle as well as of temperament. Francis was a doctrinaire, Hastings a practical administrator and a pragmatist. Francis was a disciple of Clive, like him utterly indifferent to Indian culture and ignorant of Indian ways; Hastings a student of Sanskrit, fluent in Persian and Bengali, aware of the complexities of Indian society and sensitive to Indian reactions.[22] Francis wanted the English crown to rule in Bengal as a distant overlord, handling only external affairs and defence, leaving trade to the company, leaving internal government to Muslim officials – 'considerable Moormen'[23] – leaving the 'Gentoos', the cultivators of the soil, to the paternal care of the *zemindars*, that heterogeneous class of hereditary tax farmers and landlords whom Francis, and other Whiggish Englishmen, persisted in regarding as Indian counterparts of English country squires. If Francis had had his way, the British India of the nineteenth century would never have come into existence. Hastings, first of a long series of dedicated proconsuls, thought of himself as the ruler of an Indian kingdom, responsible for its good government and its economic rehabilitation as ends in themselves, as well as for its development as the chief base of English trade throughout the East. Acutely conscious of the breakdown of Mughal administration, he believed that the English, if they were to remain in Bengal, must govern it openly. They must govern, to be sure, through remodelled native institutions and in accordance with native law and custom; Hastings was not an advocate of direct rule. Direct rule, however, was implicit in much of what he did. Effective supervision required that native law and custom, particularly the intricacies of land and revenue law, should be studied and mastered. Once involved in that labyrinth, the company's servants would not be able to escape responsibility. Eventually, a heterogeneous collection of commercial and military adventurers would have to be converted into a professional civil service; something which Britain itself did not yet possess. Hastings took the first steps; he stopped the worst scandals in Bengal; he created the essentials of a sound administrative machine; he averted breakdown. The prosperity both of Bengal and of the company revived under his government. More he could not do, so long as the Regulating Act kept him the prisoner of his own council.

The divided counsels encouraged by the Act were frustrating enough in the internal affairs of Bengal; in the relations of the company with the other Indian powers they were potentially very dangerous. The directors in London were apt to assume that if their servants in India would refrain from 'military adventures', the company's business could be carried on in peace. This was an over-simplification. Certainly the greed and irresponsibility of would-be conquistadores could, and sometimes did involve the company in war which the directors would have preferred to avoid; but this was only one of many possible causes. The company had become one of the major 'Country Powers'. It had to defend itself against possible hostile combinations; it had its allies and its jealous enemies; yet its relations with other country powers were seldom conducted on any consistent and rational plan, because of its lack of internal unity. Even after the Regulating Act, there were in India not one company government, but three; not one, but three foreign policies; sometimes four, if one counts the policy laid down in London. During Hastings' period of office, the company was almost constantly at war, here or there in India. The Rohilla war of 1774, for which Hastings was much criticised, might be called a military adventure; or it might be called the fulfilment of a treaty obligation to a friendly prince, the nawab of Oudh, to rid him of a predatory Afghan group threatening his northern marches; in any event it was a purely Bengal affair. So, at first sight, was the more complicated matter of relations with the Mughal emperor. The emperor – insignificant as a ruler but highly significant as a symbol – was at once the company's suzerain and pensioner; it might be serious for the company if he accepted the protection of some other power – the Afghans, say, or the Marathas. This happened in 1771, when the Marathas removed the old man from Allahabad where Clive had settled him, and installed him once more at Delhi. The Maratha confederacy was territorially the largest, and potentially (but for its chronic disunity) the most formidable of the powers of India. Good relations with the Peshwa had long been a cardinal principle of the company's policy, and the Calcutta government, though worried, reacted mildly. They merely ceased to pay the emperor's pension. Their pacific intentions were defeated, however, by the

234

Bombay council, who in 1774, in order to strengthen the defences of Bombay, attacked and captured the neighbouring Salsette island and Bassein fort and harbour. In 1775 they offered their support to a pretender to the Peshwa's throne at Poona in return for a promise of title to these new acquisitions. The governor general had not been informed or even consulted, and naturally complained; but to everyone's surprise the directors, always concerned over Bombay, supported the council's military adventure, so that when the Bombay forces got into difficulties Hastings had to send an army right across India to rescue them. The Maratha war lasted from 1778 to 1782. It was the cost of this war which drove Hastings to some of his most unscrupulous acts; to extorting money with menaces from Chait Singh of Benares, and from those retentive old ladies, the Begums of Oudh.[24]

The most dangerous storm-centre of India, however, was as usual in the Carnatic. Most of the councillors and other senior company servants at Madras, and a mixed collection of private adventurers, including some very shady characters, had lent money, or claimed to have lent money, to that prodigious borrower the Nawab Muhammad Ali of Arcot. The nawab's revenues were pledged several times over, and his creditors' only hope of satisfaction lay in his acquiring more. The Madras council, therefore, again without consulting the governor general, supported an attack in 1773 on the raja of Tanjore, as a result of which that ruler's territory was annexed by the nawab and its revenues passed, in effect, to the Arcot creditors. This 'military adventure' was disavowed by the directors, who sent out Lord Pigot – former Madras nabob, and like Clive poacher turned gamekeeper – as governor, with instructions to return Tanjore to its raja. Pigot was deposed on arrival by a conspiracy to which the nawab and the leading creditors were parties, arrested, and placed in confinement (where subsequently, to everyone's embarrassment, he died). This was in 1777, the year of Saratoga; government's attention was elsewhere, but the Pigots had a considerable parliamentary and City connection, and the Opposition took the matter up. It was the Pigot episode, rather than Francis' vituperation against Hastings, which initially set Fox and Burke off in full cry after the East India Company. In India, the seizure of Tanjore, and Pigot's failure to return it, was much resented by the raja's Maratha kinsmen, and helped, with the Salsette affair, to unite the Maratha confederacy against the company. Next, the Madras conquistadores proceeded to quarrel with the nizam over territory in the Northern Circars, and despite an attempt at intervention by Hastings, to withhold the nizam's tribute. Finally, in 1779, after the outbreak of war with France, they sent an expedition to seize the French settlement of Mahé on the Malabar coast. Mahé was not a place of much importance, but its seizure provided Hyder 'Ali of Mysore (who claimed, by virtue of conquest, a general suzerainty in Malabar) with a *casus belli*. In 1780 that formidable predator invaded the Carnatic for the second time. The company found itself, in Hastings' words, at 'war either actual or impending in every quarter and with every power in Hindustan'.

The company disposed of considerable armed forces of its own, though few of its soldiers were Europeans. It was supported, from the beginning of 1780, by a small royal fleet spared, with difficulty, from Atlantic operations. Its predicament was perilous (and of course ruinously costly), but not yet desperate; though being deficient in cavalry it could not prevent Hyder from doing a great deal of damage. The outcome depended on whether the French government would move, and could move quickly enough, to exploit the situation. The *Compagnie des Indes* had been wound up in 1769, and the trade of India thrown open to private French traders. French stations were unfortified; armies had been disbanded. The English had seized Pondicherry and Chandernagore, as well as Mahé, in 1779. Many French adventurers remained in India, however, and experienced French mercenaries ('amas de bandits', according to Bussy, but formidable nonetheless) served with the armies of every major prince. If a French army could support Hyder 'Ali; if, above all, a French fleet could destroy, or even challenge, British superiority off the Coromandel coast, then the verdict of 1763 might well be reversed. The moment was doubly propitious, not only because of Hyder's successes, but because of the entry of the Dutch into the war in 1780, which promised to the French the use of Dutch harbours at the Cape and Trincomalee. Hughes, commanding British ships on the station, promptly occupied Trincomalee; but Suffren, arriving early in

1782 with superior force, took it from him. Suffren had twelve sail of the Line to Hughes' nine (still small fleets; de Grasse and Rodney had thirty-three and thirty-six, respectively, at the Saintes). He had a safe refitting base off southern India, whereas Hughes had none nearer than Bombay. He was the bolder and more imaginative tactician; and he knew that additional ships had left Cadiz late in 1781, bringing an army under the veteran Bussy to reinforce Hyder 'Ali. To all appearance southern India would soon be at the mercy of the French. Time, however, proved their enemy. Bussy was delayed, first by harassing engagements in the Bay of Biscay, then by a plague epidemic at Mauritius. Dutch ships, expected to join Suffren, were held back to defend Batavia and the Cape. Hastings extricated himself from the Maratha War by an agreement with Sindhia, ablest and most independent of the Maratha princes. The Treaty of Salbai confirmed Salsette to the company – an insignificant outcome of four years' fighting; more immediately important, it released company forces for the south. Meanwhile British reinforcements, military and naval, began to arrive at Madras. Royal land forces had never before played much part in fighting in India; but by 1783 their numbers there grew to approximately the same strength as the garrison of Jamaica.[25] Suffren and Hughes, now reinforced, fought a series of stubborn engagements off the Coromandel coast, in which Suffren generally had the better of it, but was never able to establish definite command by destroying Hughes' fleet.[26] When Bussy finally reached Trincomalee in the spring of 1783, Suffren put him and his army ashore safely at Cuddalore; but by that time Hyder 'Ali had died and Tipu, his son and successor, had withdrawn to the Malabar coast. Shortly afterwards news arrived of the preliminaries of peace in Europe; a peace which in most respects was to restore, for Europeans in the East, the arrangements of 1763.

The war which began in a leafy village in New England had ended outside a dusty town in south India. In the last two years India had ceased to be a distant side-show and had become a major theatre of European war. For the English it had been a near-run thing. With the peace came the recriminations: recriminations against a system which confused trade with territorial dominion and seemed to produce nothing but financial crises;

recriminations against the policies which had brought India into the combat zone, at a time when the weariness of the nation with an unsuccessful and expensive war was reaching a climax; recriminations against the abuses of British rule in India and the extortions and oppressions practised there by the company's servants, or some of them. As yet another Select Committee turned out its voluminous reports in 1782–3, and as the torrent of Burke's oratory poured over the House, public indignation became a force driving government to action. For the first time, voices were heard lamenting that Englishmen had ever set foot in India, or asking why trade with India could not be carried on 'in like manner as we now carry on our trade with China'. The answer to that came pat: that trade with China depended on dominion in India, and that in India, if the English abdicated, the French would take their place.[27] That was not to say, however, that things could go on as they were – far from it. Amid cries for root-and-branch reform and a vindictive search for scapegoats, leading politicians – Dundas, Fox, Pitt – produced their Bills, their 'systems' for redressing the past, guiding the future, and limiting the extent of British rule in India.

Pitt's India Act, in the end, was considerably less than a root-and-branch reform. Too much patronage was at stake for the government of the day to be allowed to seize it all. There were too many interests to be safeguarded, too many political opponents to be conciliated. Fox's failure to recognise this necessity cost him twenty years in the political wilderness.[28] Pitt was wilier. The nabobs knew by 1784 that they were, at best, fighting a rearguard action against the forces of change; but they fought stubbornly, and they had money to burn. Most of the India 'interest' in parliament – both the City interest and the 'Bengal squad' – supported Pitt, as a lesser evil than Fox, but they exacted their price for it.[29] The India Act, therefore, like its predecessor, was a compromise. The company was neither abolished, nor restricted to purely commercial functions. It remained an administrative agent of government, as well as a trading corporation paying dividends to its shareholders, and its directors retained the patronage which was by far their most valuable emolument. Nevertheless, the Act had 'teeth'. It provided both the machinery and the sanctions necessary for decisive government control. A committee of the Privy Council – the Board of Control – was to approve, and might amend, the directors' dispatches for India. The proprietors were deprived of any power to annul or suspend resolutions of the directors so approved. It was a cumbersome device; but as the board's powers came to be exercised mainly by its president, and as the president for a decade was the able and ambitious Dundas, in effect if not in title secretary of state for India, the system worked. In India itself the governor general, virtually a king's minister, corresponding directly with the president of the board, was given full and clear authority over the political activities of all three presidencies. He was given also what Hastings never had: power to override his own council. This was not, indeed, in the Act; but Cornwallis, Hastings' successor, refused to go to India without it, and he had his way. It was crucial and unprecedented; for many years, ever since the first establishment of royal colonies, it had been assumed that governors were not to be trusted, that their power must always be limited and balanced, that they must be required to act in association with their councillors whom, in most cases, the crown appointed. To make a governor responsible directly (in effect) to a secretary of state, and then to entrust to him virtually full powers, was a revolutionary precedent, but one which was to be widely followed. It had a corollary: that the governor general, from Cornwallis onward, should not, as a rule, be a company man.

Naturally the company's servants in India resented the act, especially the clauses which affected them directly. Hastings resigned and returned to England, to be vindictively pursued by the Fox–Burke–Francis party as a scapegoat for the company's failings. Meetings were organised, resolutions adopted, petitions forwarded, all in ominously familiar terms: His Majesty's subjects overseas were entitled to the protection of the laws of England in common with other subjects of the realm; the obligation of servants to deliver upon oath an inventory of their whole property under penalties of excessive severity was grievous and oppressive, as was their liability to be sent forcibly to England to stand trial for offences alleged to have been committed overseas; the New Court of Judicature established for trying such charges was 'a tribunal unrestrained by the settled rules of Law, and subject to no appeal, depriving them of their undoubted Birth right, the trial by Jury'; all these were 'Violations of the Great Charter of our Liberties and infringements of the most sacred Principles of the British Constitution'.[30] One has to remind oneself, with a slight effort, that the year was 1785, not 1774; that these resolutions were drafted not in Boston or Philadelphia, but in Calcutta; that the legislation complained of was not the Intolerable Acts, but Pitt's India Act. A dichotomy already familiar in America had made its appearance in India: on the one hand the demand of British subjects overseas for 'liberty'; on the other the British government's desire for effective administration and regular tax collection, and its sense of obligation on behalf of indigenous peoples.

In India there was no rebellion. The 'settlers' were too few, their roots in the country too shallow. Politician and proconsul in combination tamed the company's adventurers and turned them into civil servants. The day of the conquistadores was over. Not, of course, the day of European conquest: in many parts of India that had only just begun. The conquistadores, sent out for trade, and in defiance of orders to the contrary, had acquired dominion. Dominion, even under reluctant governments, could be defended only by the proconsular acquisition of still more dominion. After 1784, moreover, private traders – the commercial successors of the conquistadores – wherever they found their business interest restricted by local political conditions, pressed the company's local government to extend its political authority; and under Cornwallis, still more under Wellesley, the government complied.[31] This was the inescapable legacy of enterprise and indiscipline.

> It is notorious [as Macaulay put it], that the great men who founded and preserved our Indian Empire treated all particular orders which they received from home as so much waste paper. Had not these men had the sense and spirit so to treat such orders we should not now have had an Indian Empire.[32]

NOTES

1. *Gentleman's Magazine*, 1731, f. 265. William Coxe, *Memoirs of Sir Robert Walpole*, I, 579.

2. Jenkins' East India career, unlike the ear episode, has been little studied. It is summarised in Furber, *Bombay Presidency in the early Eighteenth Century*, pp. 47–53. On his successful reorganisation at St Helena, see P. Gosse, *St Helena, 1502–1938*, London, 1938, pp. 176 ff.

3. The story of Surman's negotiations with the emperor is told in detail in C. R. Wilson, ed., *Early annals of the English in Bengal*, 3 vols, Calcutta, 1895–1917, II, part 2.

4. R. A. Wadia, *The Bombay Dockyard and the Wadia Master-builders*, Bombay, 1957.

5. A. Anderson, *An historical and chronological deduction of the origin of Commerce*, 1764, rev. ed., 4 vols, London, 1787–9, III, p. 474.

6. H. H. Dodwell, *Dupleix and Clive, the beginning of Empire*, London, 1920, pp. 5 ff., 18–19.

7. Colonel M. Wilks, *Historical Sketches of the South of India*, 2 vols, London, 1817, I, p. 262.

8. India Office Letter Book 28: 52–4, 23 January 1750.

9. Bibliothèque Nationale, N.A.F. 9145: 24, 15 July 1750.

10. India Office, Home Series, Misc. 93: 146–60.

11. C. R. Wilson, *Old Fort William*, 2 vols, London, 1906, II, p. 25.

12. Adlercron to Fox, 21 November 1756. India Office, Home misc. 94, p. 210.

13. These moves are recorded from the French end in Jean Law, ed. A. Martineau, *Mémoire sur quelques affaires de l'empire mogul*, Paris, 1913.

14. The fullest account of the *jagir* business is in Sir John Malcolm, *Life of Robert, Lord Clive*, 3 vols, London, 1836, II, p. 216.

15. *Ibid.*, p. 74–90.

16. Lucy S. Sutherland, 'The East India Company and the Peace of Paris', *English Historical Review*, 1947.

17. For a detailed account of these contests see Sutherland, *The East India Company in Eighteenth Century Politics*, chapters IV and V.

18. *Letters*, ed. Paget-Toynbee, VIII, p. 149.

19. The company's rules limited the issue in India of bills on London to £200,000 a year. From 1766 this figure was regularly exceeded. In 1771 it reached £1,063,067. *Parliamentary History*, XVII, 677, and Sutherland, *The East India Company in Eighteenth Century Politics*, p. 226.

20. It was so regarded by North, Jenkinson and the king. Harlow, *The Founding of the Second British Empire*, II, pp. 68–9.

21. Sutherland, *The East India Company in Eighteenth Century Politics*, pp. 254 ff.

22. See Sir Keith Feiling's sympathetic biography: *Warren Hastings*, London, 1954, *passim*.

23. Francis' views are set out in *6th (Select) Committee Report on the Administration of Justice in India*, App. 14. *Reports from Committees of the House of Commons*, vol. V, pp. 193–240. Those of Hastings on the same topics are in the same Report, App. 12. *Reports*, vol. V, pp. 903–7. On the 'considerable Moormen', Francis was sometimes in the right of it; he supported, while Hastings (on instructions from the directors) prosecuted, Mohammed Reza Khan, Naib Nazim and Naib Diwan of Bengal from 1765 to 1772, a notably able administrator. See Abdul Majed Khan, *The Transition in Bengal, 1756–1775*, Cambridge, 1969.

24. For a clear account of all these events, see *The Cambridge History of India*, vol. IV, Cambridge, 1929, chapters 14, 15 and 16.

25. Mackesy, *op. cit.*, p. 495.

26. For the details of these operations see Sir Herbert Richmond, *The Navy in India, 1763–1783*, London, 1931.

27. *Parliamentary History*, XXIII, 801, 1231, 1301–2.

28. For the character of Fox's bill, the shifts and defections it occasioned, and the fall of the North–Fox ministry, see Sutherland, *The East India Company in Eighteenth Century Politics*, pp. 395 ff.

29. In 1784 about sixty Members of Parliament had a direct interest in the company, as directors, proprietors, ship-owners, ship's 'husbands', or returned company servants. For a detailed analysis see C. H. Philips, *The East India Company, 1784–1834*, Manchester, 1940, pp. 307 ff.

30. The Calcutta Resolutions, 25 July 1785. Public Record Office, c.o. 11/25.

31. On this aspect of the company's activities see Pamela Nightingale, *Trade and Empire in Western India, 1784–1806*, Cambridge, 1970.

32. In his speech on the war with China, 7 April 1840.

The French War and the Second American Revolt

'The time in which we live will constitute an awful period in the history of the world; for a spirit of subversion is gone forth, which sets at nought the wisdom of our ancestors and the lessons of experience.' So Bryan Edwards, the urbane planter-historian of the West Indies, speaking in the House of Commons in 1798. He knew what he was talking about. No one who had lived in a slave-worked colony could be ignorant of the dangers of a 'spirit of subversion'. Edwards had visited Cap Français in 1791 and been an eyewitness of savage and widespread servile mutiny. He had felt the chilling fear that revolution might spread through the Caribbean to his Jamaica. Returned to England, he had watched, from across the Channel, the progress of revolution in France. There, the pedantic constitutionalism of the National Assembly had given place to missionary fervour, to a determination to spread the doctrines of 'liberty' beyond the borders of France. Within France, the initial collapse of government opened the way to domination by the clubs, to the street fighting and the executions of the Terror. The Terror had served its purpose: an enforced and disciplined unity at the service of the revolution, at home and abroad. The threatened and outraged monarchies of Europe, in the ensuing general war, had tried to stem the revolutionary tide, and failed. England, counting on control of the Channel to keep French armies out, had been alarmed into war less by horror of regicide than by the French seizure of the Austrian Netherlands and the opening of the Scheldt to French shipping in 1792. It had become urgently necessary, from the English point of view, to prevent the United Netherlands going the same way; but in this, British policy also failed. The Batavian Republic had been established as a satellite of France in 1795, a political *coup* which put into French hands the whole Channel coast facing the Thames, and might well – if the captors could follow it up at Batavia and the Cape – reopen much of the East to revolutionary France. Once again the English had only their navy between themselves and their colonies, and French belligerence. In purely naval terms the balance of advantage was difficult to calculate. The French navy was only a little inferior in numbers to the British – seventy-six serviceable Line ships in 1793, against ninety-three British;[1] as usual English critics proclaimed the French ships to be faster and more powerful, class for class, than the British; certainly they had fewer stations to cover and less commerce to protect. On the other hand, most professional naval officers in France were royalist in sentiment; they came chiefly from royalist areas – Brittany and Provence; many had been guillotined, or had fled into exile. By 1793 many ships, even Line ships, were commanded by merchant skippers or by promoted petty officers, often elected by their own ships' companies and liable to be deposed if their orders were unpopular with their constituents. Single-ship mutinies were frequent. Citizen armies have often proved effective instruments of war, citizen navies rarely. The British advantage should have been decisive, on the face of it; but the British government was uneasy about the temper of its own people. Englishmen had their grievances, and were not immune to egalitarian slogans. Even the navy – indispensable, admired, but too much taken for granted, could not always be counted on. In 1797 it was paralysed for months on end by ugly and dangerous mutinies at Spithead and the Nore. A conservative Englishman with colonial interests might well think that the 'spirit of subversion' had placed the whole empire in danger.

In fact it was the French empire which, in the colonial field at least, was in the greatest danger. The British mutinies were isolated incidents; for most Englishmen, fear and dislike of France far outweighed any attractions offered by French political theory. The British government in 1793 had found itself involved in a new type of European war, of which it had no experience and only a limited

244

understanding. Ministers had no idea of how to counter the ideo-logical propaganda, the universal conscription, the mass enthusiasm which made the revolutionary armies unexpectedly dangerous, and they reacted in conservative, eighteenth-century fashion. They were willing to hire mercenaries and, within limits, to subsidise allies; but the coalition against France which they endeavoured to organise had neither cohesion, common determination, nor even a common purpose. Pitt himself was not eager for war, and proceeded cautiously. English forces acting independently, whether in naval raids or military landings, could make only a peripheral impression on metropolitan France or upon its recent conquests. The landing at Dunkirk and the occupation of Toulon (at French royalist invitation) in 1793 were failures; the invasion of Corsica in 1794 lasted only two years. The French, conversely, with their disorganised navy, could not launch an effective direct attack on England while the Channel fleet remained intact; nor could they dislodge the English from the Mediterranean. As often before in the eighteenth century, though now in different circumstances, war between England and France in Europe produced deadlock. As often before, both belligerents turned to colonial theatres of war, initially to the West Indies, where each had threatened interests to protect and each could hope, by sudden assaults on undefended islands, to impoverish the enemy, increase its own commerce and revenue, and acquire territories for bargaining at a peace. The plan of weakening the enemy by capturing his sugar islands was traditional, almost automatic, and no doubt its effectiveness, as always, was exaggerated; but it had a real basis. Refined West Indian sugar was among the biggest and most lucrative of French exports to the rest of continental Europe. England had a new and important reason for cherishing the West Indies, which in the 1790s supplied directly or indirectly most of the raw cotton for a booming textile industry. Both belligerents thought that without West Indian revenue the machinery of war could not be maintained. Neither at first appreciated the extent to which West Indian circumstances had been altered by the contagion of revolution in Europe.

St Domingue had been the first casualty. The planters of St Domingue had their grievances,[2] and saw in the meeting of the

Estates General in 1789 an opportunity of airing them. The colonial assembly – itself established, by royal decree, only two years earlier – was badgered into electing delegates. The assemblies of Martinique and Guadeloupe did the same. Eventually, after much argument, six colonial deputies were admitted to the Estates General in their tennis-court days – the first occasion in European history on which colonial representatives sat in a metropolitan legislative assembly. Their object, naturally, was to demand greater local autonomy, greater freedom from metropolitan control. There was nothing inherently remarkable in the spectacle of a land-owning, slave-owning oligarchy raising the cry of 'liberty', in the sense of liberty to run their colony in their own way; something of the sort had already happened in some of the English North American colonies and was soon to happen in Spanish America. The St Domingue planters, however, were vulnerable, and in calling public attention to themselves at that juncture they made a serious error of judgment. The 'liberty' they sought obviously meant, among other things, liberty to proceed more drastically than before against slaves and free persons of colour. They encountered immediate resistance and alarming counter-proposals from the *Amis des Noirs*, a body recently formed in imitation of Clarkson's abolition society in England, but considerably more radical. The National Assembly, after much oratory, came down – albeit timidly – on the side of the *Amis des Noirs*, in a decree empowering persons of colour born of free parents, if otherwise qualified, to vote for the colonial assemblies. A relatively modest proposal, considering the source from which it came; but it was too much for the white planters, who saw in it the thin end of the egalitarian wedge. They refused to obey the decree, the governor refused to enforce it, and there was much wild talk of secession from France. Mulattoes and free Negroes, many of them property owners, demonstrated in arms, demanding the rights they had been granted. No one appeared to reflect that talk of natural rights had implications for slaves. Both parties were taken by surprise when in August 1791, in answer to signals conveyed by drumbeats or through nocturnal ritual gatherings, the slave population of the northern plain rose in revolt, systematically setting fire to houses and canefields and murdering the white inhabitants. Within a few

246

weeks the whole plain was a smoking ruin roamed by plundering bands.

The only hope of restoring order lay in the dispatch of troops from France; but the Jacobin party in the National Assembly opposed any move in support of slave-owning planters and a royal governor. When, late in 1792, after the Jacobins had gained control in Paris, an army reached St Domingue, it was a revolutionary army, under the orders of Jacobin 'commissioners' sent out to enforce the rule of liberty, equality and fraternity. They proclaimed a conditional emancipation and encouraged a force of freedmen to enter and sack the town of Cap Français. Most of the surviving whites fled, either to the United States or to other islands, British or Spanish. These events naturally alarmed the Spanish government in Santo Domingo and the British government in Jamaica. The miseries and resentments of slavery were international. Among the slave leaders of St Domingue, Boukman came from Jamaica, Christophe from St Kitts. Colonial governments might well fear the contagious spread of rebellion, especially rebellion fomented by the agents of the new French government. When in 1793 both Spain and England declared war on revolutionary France, both governments sent expeditions to invade St Domingue. The purpose of these invasions was to rescue the white planters and help them to suppress the rising; incidentally to embarrass the French government; and ultimately – for the English at least – to annex all or part of the colony. The enterprise failed. Spain made peace with France and withdrew from the contest in 1795. In Jamaica, in the same year, government attention was distracted by a dangerous rising among the mountain Maroons[3] inspired by the example of the French islands and, it was believed, by actual French agents. After four years of wasting war the British troops withdrew from St Domingue, defeated by force of numbers, by yellow fever, and by the guerrilla skill of François-Dominique Toussaint.

Toussaint, the first of a series of gifted Haitian leaders, was left in control. He made strenuous efforts to revive the broken economy of the colony, and to give its virtual independence a constitutional basis as '... une seule colonie qui fait partie de l'Empire française, mais qui est soumise à des lois particulières'. Laws, that is, promulgated by Toussaint as governor general for life. There was no room in the French empire, however, for two dictators. In 1801 Toussaint defied Bonaparte's orders by invading and conquering Spanish Santo Domingo, at a time when Bonaparte was cherishing Spain as an ally. Bonaparte had no liking for the 'spirit of subversion'. He intended, as soon as he could, to reintroduce the old order, slavery and all, in the French islands. Geographically and strategically, St Domingue was the centre from which he could best set about rebuilding the French colonial system in the Americas, including Louisiana, recently recovered from Spain. St Domingue must be reduced to obedience and 'gilded Africans' put down. The Peace of Amiens provided a convenient opportunity, and a formidable army was assigned to the task in 1802. It failed, as the British had failed, and for similar reasons. In 1803, upon the breakdown of the Peace of Amiens, Napoleon resumed the war in Europe, and washed his hands of the St Domingue affair – indeed of the whole scheme of American empire, for Louisiana was sold in the same year. The ragged, starved, fever-stricken and forgotten remnant of an army surrendered to the British. St Domingue never recovered. Twelve years of fighting and neglect had destroyed the elaborate and cruel organisation which had made it rich. Prosperous, brutal St Domingue became brutal and poverty-stricken Haiti.

Elsewhere in the West Indies similar patterns of conflict developed, with servile mutiny employed on a large scale as an instrument of war for the first time in West Indian history. The Windward Islands, as usual, were the scene of heavy fighting, in which both sides made serious miscalculations. French Jacobin commissioners underestimated – or at times welcomed – the destructive forces let loose by hasty declarations of emancipation and equality. English naval and military officers overestimated the effective support they would get from royalist French planters. The French had a battle-cry which rallied the forces of social and economic discontent; the English had the superior force at sea. The French could make revolutions but not always control them; the British could capture islands but not always hold them.[4] St Lucia, for example, changed hands three times. Guadeloupe was taken by the British in 1794 but recaptured a few months later by the able Jacobin commissioner Victor Hugues, who proclaimed emancipation and engineered a successful rising against the planters and their British friends. From Guadeloupe Hugues set on foot intrigues with the Maroons of Jamaica and the 'black' Caribs of St Vincent, which contributed in each island to a desperate outbreak in 1795. The British authorities suppressed these risings with difficulty, and were so alarmed by them that, to prevent a recurrence, they resorted to wholesale and pitiful deportations: the Trelawny Maroons to Nova Scotia, the St Vincent Caribs to Ruatán. By 1798 Guadeloupe was the only important West Indian colony left to France; but the French derived small benefit from it. Its sugar production dropped, because of the disturbances; and of the sugar which was produced, little reached France, until 1801 when an expedition sent out by Bonaparte restored both slavery and metropolitan control. Martinique, also captured in 1794, remained in British hands until 1801; slavery and internal peace were maintained, and with access to the British market the sugar industry of the island entered on a period of notable prosperity.

The inclusion within the French system of the Netherlands (in 1795) and Spain (in 1796) gave the British an excuse to take over their West Indian colonies also. Demerara, Essequibo and Berbice were seized in 1796, Trinidad in 1797. These were valuable possessions. Trinidad was a fertile and sparsely populated island, needing only labour to make it productive; and the saline mud of the Guiana coast was very well suited to cotton growing. Partly as a result of these various acquisitions, imports from the West Indies into Great Britain, despite the attrition of war and the attentions of privateers, increased by more than twenty-five per cent between 1792 and 1798.[5] The Pitt–Dundas–Grenville administration was often accused by its critics of squandering resources on West Indian adventures and neglecting the main threat in Europe. The West Indian operations were touch-and-go affairs, in which the fortune of war might easily have gone the other way; but the ministry could reasonably retort that they yielded value for money.

After the *coup d'état* of 1797 which brought the Directory to office in France and Bonaparte to effective command, French overseas policy turned increasingly towards the East, directed there both by Bonaparte's ambitious imagination and Talleyrand's reasoned assessment of possibilities. India seemed to be the only remaining theatre where French arms could seriously damage British interests. In the second half of 1797, the naval mutinies ended, Jervis at Cape St Vincent and Duncan at Camperdown had put the Spaniards and the Dutch respectively out of naval fighting for the time being, and so had greatly weakened the French position in Atlantic waters. Any plan for an invasion of England had to be put aside or postponed. India, then: in the Indian Ocean the subordination of the Netherlands and the value and vulnerability of British trade could profitably be exploited.

Some such move had been expected, indeed anticipated, in England. Early in 1795 Baring, then chairman of the East India Company, had warned Dundas of the danger of French influence at the Cape of Good Hope. The Dutch East India Company had perforce accepted the Republic and the French alliance; but the Cape settlers were known to resent the company and its restrictive, bankrupt rule. The stadthouder, who had fled to England, was persuaded to instruct Dutch governors, including the company's governor at the Cape, to place themselves under British protection; and an expedition was sent to the Cape to enforce the order. It was a small expedition and might never have reached its destination, but that the French at that time were concentrating most of their naval forces in the Mediterranean. The transports sailed past Brest and across the Bay almost unescorted; and although neither governor nor burghers at the Cape accepted the stadthouder's order, the colony was captured after a short campaign. At approximately the same time, a small fleet from Madras by Dundas' order seized Trincomalee, the splendid harbour which the Dutch had neglected, and whose value had first been fully appreciated during the previous war, by Suffren. A fleet based on Trincomalee could command the Coromandel coast and the Bay of Bengal for most of the year. The Cape was less decisive as a base; Table Bay is not an entirely satisfactory anchorage. Useful though it was as a calling station for refreshment, moreover, it was not indispensable, since coppered ships could make a direct passage to India without calling; and its possession did not automatically neutralise the Isles of France, from which frigate squadrons harried the East India Company's shipping. The Malabar coast, except for whatever protection a fleet at Bombay could provide, lay open. Still, the British position in India had been made as safe as orthodox naval strategy, with the ships available, could make it.

Bonaparte's plan for an invasion of India in 1798 was unorthodox and bold; too bold, perhaps, for his resources. It postulated French command of the Mediterranean, which appeared secure at the time the plan was hatched, but which could not be relied on permanently. Communications were to be guarded from Malta, seized by a swift *coup* from the moribund Order of St John. The next step was the occupation of Egypt. From there, a French army could be ferried, by ships based on Mauritius, to India, where it would join the forces of Tipu Sultan of Mysore, who had inherited from his father Hyder a determination to drive the British from south India. The plan leaked out, however, and was defeated by quick anticipation. Marquess Wellesley, governor general in India, struck promptly and successfully at Tipu's capital Seringapatam; Nelson's action at Aboukir Bay broke the French line of communication, destroyed a powerful French fleet, and marooned a French army helpless in Egypt. Thereafter Malta was blockaded and, in 1800, taken; and in 1801 the French army was driven from Egypt. Again, it had been touch and go. British ministers knew next to nothing about Egypt, and Dundas' policy in the Levant and the Red Sea had been a gamble. Nelson himself, at the Nile, had taken an alarming risk, not only of grounding his ships, but of placing them within boarding range of that French *corps d'élite*, the Army of the Marine. The gamble succeeded and French dominance in the Mediterranean was ended; but it might have gone the other way.

In 1801 Nelson defeated at Copenhagen the most dangerous French attempt, up to that time, to cripple British naval power: the attempt, through the Armed Neutrality of the North, to cut off the supply of Baltic shipbuilding timber. The steady run of British naval victories from the second half of 1797 onwards reflected the accelerating pace of naval construction in England, due partly to the incipient industrialisation of the dockyards, partly to the steady increase in British overseas trade which provided much of the necessary revenue. It reflected also the professional abilities and the innovating boldness of an outstanding generation of flag officers; more ships, in short, and better commanded. The French were falling behind in naval construction, and were paying the price of the revolution which had demoralised and decimated their corps of naval officers. Yet none of this seriously affected the French domination of continental Europe; none of the blows which France and England aimed at one another touched a vital spot. If the French wished either to retain and enlarge their colonial empire, or to stop the British interfering with their European plans and subsidising their European enemies, they must cripple British naval power at home and abroad; and this they patently could not do by direct means, even with the help of the Dutch and Spanish navies. If the British wished to end the recurring menace to their Channel coasts and to rescue Europe from general subservience to Napoleon, they must be prepared to fight, and equip and pay others to fight, on continental soil on a greater scale than any British government had contemplated since Marlborough's day. Their prospects of success, against big, well-equipped armies commanded by generals of genius, seemed doubtful at best; yet there was no real alternative. Successful colonial campaigns were well enough, as far as they went; but colonies lost much of their value, without assurance of access to the European markets in which their products were sold. Moreover, so long as Austrians and Prussians, intermittently in receipt of British subsidies, felt they were being asked to fling themselves on French bayonets in order that Great Britain might grab more sugar islands, a reliable and effective anti-French coalition was impossible.

As these lessons sank in, the character of the war changed; but not suddenly or immediately. The Peace of Amiens, initiated six months after Copenhagen, was not a turning point but a pause, a peace of stalemate and financial exhaustion. Its terms, hastily negotiated, provided for the return of all colonial conquests except Trinidad and the Dutch posts in Ceylon, which Great Britain retained. These colonial concessions were sharply criticised in England, as might be expected, and failure to implement one of them was the immediate cause of the renewal of war. The strategic value of Malta had only very recently been brought to British attention. Under the treaty it was to revert to the knights, who were clearly incapable, even with Neapolitan help, of manning the great fortifications of Valletta. Early in 1803, alarmed by reports of a revival of Napoleon's designs upon Egypt and India, the British government demanded, as a safeguard, the retention of Malta for a further ten years; and this demand being rejected, declared war on France. Initially the renewed war followed traditional precedents. Napoleon prepared interlocking and complementary plans for an invasion of England and an assault on the British West Indies. Pitt set about constructing yet another European coalition, offering subsidies as before, but more generously and more indiscriminately.[6] This coalition, momentarily promising, drew Napoleon's Grand Army away from Boulogne. Instead of invading England, Napoleon marched to the upper Rhine, to inflict crushing defeats on the Austrians and Russians at Ulm and Austerlitz. The third coalition collapsed within a year of its formation; but meanwhile Nelson had delivered an equally damaging blow against the combined French and Spanish fleets at Trafalgar. Trafalgar, and accompanying lesser victories elsewhere, ended any possibility of serious French operations in the West Indies, or against India by the Mediterranean and overland route; and a few months later Popham's recapture of the Cape of Good Hope virtually secured the sea route to the East. After 1805 the French – who, with their allies, had lost thirty-one ships of the Line in six months[7] – could make little impression on Great Britain or its colonies by direct naval assault, nor could they land an invading army. They could not defend their own colonies; British squadrons, having reoccupied the colonial conquests given up in 1802, set about acquiring others.[8] The British, however, could not rid themselves of the menace across the Channel; it was always there, awaiting a chance opportunity, a moment of relaxed vigilance. They could not undertake a landing in continental Europe with any hope of success, nor could they shake French domination there, merely by the time-honoured method of paying others to fight.

After 1805, then, began a search for new ways out of an old deadlock. For Napoleon, the new way to defeat the shopkeepers – since he could not wreck their shop nor cut off their supply of merchandise – was to reduce them to bankruptcy by preventing their deliveries. After 1805 the war against England became more strictly European in scope and more economic in character. The continental system inaugurated by the Berlin decree of 1806 was an attempt to close the harbours of Europe to British exports. It was comprehensive: Italy, since Marengo, was politically French; Jena, in 1806, enabled Napoleon to dictate the economic policy of Prussia; Spain was virtually taken over in 1807, Portugal invaded; the participation of the Baltic powers, except Sweden, was secured by alliances or agreements. A large part of British exports consisted of re-exported colonial goods, for which Europe was the only significant market; their exclusion, if it did not in itself reduce the British government to financial impotence, would at least prevent the building up of credits, out of which timber imports were paid for and subsidies to Napoleon's enemies provided.[9] It would be satisfyingly appropriate, as the British seized more and more colonies, to render those colonies worthless by making their products unsaleable. English writers might retort that their European customers would not put up with beet sugar, acorn coffee and cabbage-leaf tobacco (all three expedients were tried in France at this time); the genuine goods, of which Great Britain possessed a virtual monopoly, would find a way in, either by licences, or by smuggling though such places as Malta, Anholt and Heligoland. This was true, so far as it went; but the value of British exports to northern Europe fell in fact from £10,320,000 in 1805 to £5,090,000 at the end of 1807, to less than £3,000,000 in 1808; great quantities of sugar accumulated from time to time in London warehouses; at the height of the system the price of sugar in Paris was nine times that in London.[10] The threat to British commercial prosperity was serious, then; but it was never decisive. The somewhat old-fashioned economic arguments on which the system was based, overemphasised colonial re-exports and underemphasised the growing importance of manufactured goods, the product of Great Britain itself. For these exports, Europe was not the only market; there were many alternatives. At the beginning of the nineteenth century Great Britain was exporting perhaps thirty-five to forty per cent cent of its total manufactured product, chiefly iron and steel goods and textiles.[11] In 1805, only thirty-three per cent of these manufactured exports went to Europe.

About twenty-seven per cent went to the United States and forty per cent to 'all parts of the world', which meant chiefly British overseas possessions, but also included Latin America. British exporters had thus a variety of options. Closure of the continent, even if it were complete, would be disastrous only if it coincided with closure of the United States. This, of course, was a possibility, and in 1808–9 it actually occurred, though the embargo and non-intercourse acts were widely evaded. In general, the effect of the continental blockade was not to cripple British export trade, but to inconvenience it, to diversify it, and to drive it into a greater variety of overseas channels.

In these circumstances the attention of government naturally turned, as it had often turned before, to Latin American. The Spanish empire, at the beginning of the nineteenth century, was no longer the Naboth's vineyard or the commercial El Dorado it had seemed to be a hundred years before. Not that it was less prosperous; some of its provinces – New Spain, Venezuela, Cuba, the Río de la Plata – were more productive than they had ever been; trade was more vigorous; and the empire as a whole had undergone, since 1763, a notable overhaul of its administrative, military and commercial machinery. It was, however, more familiar. After 1763 foreign, particularly British, merchants had found ways of participating in its prosperity surer, less hazardous than plunder, contraband or conquest. The Free Ports Act of 1766 had opened certain harbours in the British West Indies to such foreigners as wished to purchase British goods, or to sell their own colonial goods to British purchasers, and were willing to risk the displeasure of their own authorities. The volume of trade through these free ports was considerable: some £500,000 in 1792, it was estimated, and probably more than double that by 1807.[12] As for direct trade between Europe and the Indies, licences to break the rules could usually be obtained from both governments, even in wartime, by big concerns shipping to Buenos Aires, Lima or Vera Cruz.[13] Illicit trade continued as well. An appreciable volume of goods went via the Brazilian ports to the Río de la Plata; some, even, through the minor Pacific harbours. The capture of Trinidad was a convenience to smugglers, whose trade to Venezuela was encouraged enthusiastically by Picton, the first British governor.

In the same year, 1797, Spain, cut off from its colonies by maritime war, opened the ports of the Indies to neutral shipping. This decree was the end of effective Spanish control of the Indies trade. Naturally it facilitated British trade as well as neutral. At Buenos Aires a situation developed in which British contraband traders sustained severe competition from lawful French, German, Portuguese and United States shipping, but in which, irrespective of flag, a high proportion of the goods brought in was British.[14]

All these contacts enabled commercial observers to make a much more realistic assessment of the Spanish American market than had been possible, say, at the time of the Austrian Succession War. Economic growth, though impressive, had been much slower than in North America. Slaves were no longer a major item of import from British sources; the slave trade was falling into disrepute, and was to become illegal for British subjects in 1807. There was a brisk demand for manufactured goods; but the possibility of expansion was limited by the concentration of purchasing power in relatively few hands. Spanish America produced no single commodity essential to British industry. Spanish American trade, then, was valuable, but not vital, to Great Britain; it was considerably less important, even potentially, than the trade of North America, the West Indies or India; and many informed observers thought that the existing channels were adequate. Whenever war with Spain threatened (in 1790, in 1796–7, in 1801–3) the familiar eighteenth-century proposals were trotted out for Spanish American conquests, to expand trade by extending dominion, to weaken Spain, to forestall France; but, except for the special case of Trinidad, these schemes received only passing attention.[15] Few responsible people in England thought such conquests worth the risk and expense. Many doubted even their military feasibility. Much would depend, clearly, on the attitude of the inhabitants, on their willingness to exchange imperial masters, and Popham's unauthorised seizure of Buenos Aires in 1806 – an exploit in the old buccaneering tradition – put an end to optimism on this subject. After a swift initial success, and despite substantial reinforcement, the British forces were expelled by a concerted rising among the local population.

Conquest, however, was not the only form which intervention

in Spanish America might take. There was another possibility, which also had been canvassed for some years: a plan to expand trade by encouraging colonial rebellion. There were plenty of discontented people in the Spanish Indies. Indian discontent, of the kind which flared up in the rebellion of Tupac Amaru, was understandable, though rarely effective; but many Creoles were discontented too. Educated urban groups resented the suspicious obscurantism of colonial government: the Inquisition censorship of printing – inefficient, dilatory, capricious; the periodic attempts to suppress books which in Spain itself were readily available. There was much surreptitious reading of Rousseau and Raynal. Local magnates resented the steady tightening of metropolitan administration, which trenched upon their own patrician authority. Consumers resented commercial regulation, which kept up prices and hindered, though it could not prevent, the introduction of cheap and desirable foreign goods. Office-seekers resented the preference accorded to peninsular Spaniards in appointment and promotion, in the army, the civil administration and the Church. Creole patricians, while willing to respect the viceroys and judges who represented royal authority, both despised and envied the sharp, pushing young *gachupines* who came to the Indies to make their fortunes. Everybody resented taxation; though Creoles paid lower taxes than Spaniards in Spain. Creole society on the whole was conservative, traditionally loyal, in a general and distant fashion, to Church and King; and whether its diffuse and varied discontent amounted to a readiness for revolt, might well be doubted. Discontent, however, had self-appointed emissaries abroad. Since about 1790 a number of disaffected Creole émigrés had been touring the major capitals, airing their grievances and seeking support for conspiracies against Spanish imperial government. The most plausible and persistent of them, the Venezuelan Miranda, who had been dismissed from the Spanish army for embezzlement, among other offences,[16] had met Pitt in 1790, and maintained intermittent contact with British ministers over the next eighteen years. He convinced Dundas, at least, of the commercial and political advantages to be gained by backing Spanish American independence. There were, of course, both political and psychological obstacles in the way. Revolution was in itself repugnant to most responsible Englishmen of the time. The risk of turning Venezuela into a second Haiti was daunting to contemplate. The Duke of Wellington probably expressed the general feeling – as he often did – in discussing the matter in retrospect years later: 'I always had a horror of revolutionising any country for a political object. I always said, if they rise of themselves, well and good, but do not stir them up; it is a fearful responsibility.' There were doubts also of Miranda's own credibility and competence. It was not clear whom or what he represented. His own attempt to lead a rising in Venezuela was a failure; the local Creoles declined to 'rise of themselves'. The failure did not, however, discredit the policy of intervention for the purpose of 'liberation', for Miranda had received little or no effective British support. The Buenos Aires episode in the following year revealed the pitfalls of the alternative, the conquest policy, and convinced most informed people that the only intervention likely to succeed was one which proclaimed independence as its object.

The arguments for an intervention of some sort were greatly strengthened in 1807–8. If Napoleon's continental system worked, Great Britain would have to subsidise such allies as it could find, and pay for its timber imports, in specie or not at all – a powerful reason for establishing intimate contact with some part of Spanish America; not Venezuela, which produced no silver; but Mexico, perhaps? None of the devices for pushing British exports in the Indies had so far had much success in Mexico. Strategic arguments for an intervention were stronger still. In 1807 the Portuguese court, threatened by French invasion, fled in a British fleet to Brazil; a removal which opened that country wide to British trade, but which also gave it a firm claim to British naval protection. Meanwhile Spain fell more and more under French control; in 1808 the country was invaded by a French army, the king induced to abdicate, the heir-apparent exiled, and Joseph Bonaparte proclaimed 'king' of Spain. Here, again, was the prospect which caused such alarm in England, at the beginning of the eighteenth century; that the resources of the Spanish empire might be placed at the disposal of France. To prevent it, an army was hastily assembled in Ireland, under Sir Arthur Wellesley; its probable purpose the promotion of independence, its probable destination Mexico.[17]

The plan was overset and the situation abruptly transformed in the summer of 1808 by an unexpected event: a spontaneous series of national risings in Spain against the Bonaparte, and a beginning of guerrilla war. Here was the opportunity long awaited in England: the opening of a front in continental Europe. Great Britain immediately made peace with Spain – that is, with the agents of the resistance movement – promised support, and undertook not to weaken or dismember the empire. Wellesley's army sailed, not to secure the independence of Spanish America, but to restore the independence of Spain. Thus began the long attrition of the Peninsular War, which was to drain and overextend Napoleon's resources and contribute powerfully to his eventual defeat. No commercial sacrifice was involved; British merchants could and did extend their business in the Indies under Spanish licences and by virtue of somewhat equivocal agreements between the British government and the resistance *junta*. But who was actually to govern the Indies? Colonial officials were in a cruel dilemma between their national loyalty and their professional duty. Properly concerned to maintain order and to keep the administrative machinery working, they inclined at first to take their instructions from the government actually ruling in Madrid: the Bonaparte and his ministers. To Creole patricians, the orders of Jacobins and French military adventurers were wholly unacceptable; yet the central junta – the Regency government, as it came to be called – commanded little more respect. It was, at first, an itinerant and hole-and-corner affair, dependent on British support; and when, with money and weapons obtained from England, it gradually acquired territory and power, it began to propound liberal and anticlerical ideas deeply offensive to conservative Creole opinion. Creole loyalty gathered sentimentally round Ferdinand, the exiled prince, a potent symbol, impotent to rule. In effect, from 1808 to 1814 the Indies were temporarily independent of Spain. In some provinces the senior officials kept control; in others they were expelled by risings led by local juntas; in yet others they negotiated agreements as best they could with assemblies of local notables, and awaited better times. Each province went its own way, and many fell prey to civil war.

The Spanish empire was not the only colonial empire whose

centre was invaded by the French, whose throne was occupied briefly by a Bonaparte, and whose provinces, threatened by the 'spirit of subversion', attracted British attention. The Dutch, in the course of the war, enjoyed the protective friendship both of France and of England; the one overran their home territory, the other took their colonies and trade. The revolution of 1795, which drove out the stadthouder and established the Batavian Republic, had been the work mainly of Dutchmen with French revolutionary sympathies. The republic was from its beginning a satellite of France; but the successive constitutional devices employed in governing it left too many openings for internal initiative and disagreement to suit the aims of Napoleon. In 1806 he declared the United Netherlands a monarchy and placed his brother Louis upon the throne. In 1810, dissatisfied with Dutch participation in the continental system, he removed Louis and annexed the Netherlands as provinces of France. With them, he annexed what remained of the Dutch colonial empire.

Between 1795 and 1810 Great Britain, with the consent of the exiled stadthouder, had seized, restored, and again recaptured all the Dutch colonies which appeared to be of immediate strategic or commercial value. By 1810 only Java, with its dependencies Timor, Macassar, Bandjermasin and Palembang, remained in Dutch hands. The authorities at Batavia, cut off for long periods from The Hague, semi-independent, and without enthusiasm for revolution in general or French rule in particular, had carefully avoided giving offence to the British. The directors of the English East India Company, who in the event of hostilities would have had to provide ships and troops, had seen no great advantage in an annexation of Java. The Batavia Dutch, left to themselves, had enjoyed some years of commercial prosperity, chiefly because of a boom in coffee sales. The collapse of coffee production in Haiti had caused a serious shortage, and neutral ships, chiefly Danes and Americans, had converged on Java. The involvement of Denmark in war with England in 1807, and the American embargo on foreign trade, brought the boom to an end; but at the time of the inauguration of Napoleon's continental system the finances of the colony were in good order.

Meanwhile in Holland the *Oost-Indische Compagnie*, bankrupt and impotent, had been relieved of its administrative powers in 1796. In 1800 it was dissolved, bequeathing to the republic its assets, its responsibilities and its debts; and the government of the republic had to devise a new system of colonial administration. There ensued a period of complicated discussion and of legislative enactments, ranging from the pamphlets of Van Hogendorp,[18] embodying the liberal principles of the French Revolution, to the much more conservative 'Nederburgh' charter,[19] which in 1804 was actually adopted. The whole debate was somewhat academic, and was cut short by the establishment of the Bonaparte 'kingdom' in 1806. The governor general who was finally selected, in 1807, to restore effective metropolitan control in Java was a Bonaparte choice, the old Jacobin and old soldier, Marshal Daendels. Daendels applied himself to his task with Bonaparte zeal and thoroughness. He organized the government in prefectures on the French model; converted a hierarchy of commercial employees into – on paper at least – a graded civil service, with fewer opportunities of illicit private profit; terminated the quasi-feudal privileges of the Javanese regents, converting them also into civil servants subordinate to the prefects; and created a new and independent system of courts. His principal task, however, was to put the island into a state of defence. He built roads and fortifications with the same ruthless energy he used to put the Javanese in their place, and with a free use of forced labour. In 1810, upon learning of the annexation of the Netherlands, he duly hoisted the French flag. Naturally these activities attracted the attention of the British government in India. A quiescent, semi-independent Java was one thing; a fortified Java at the disposal of France, quite another, especially since Napoleon had ominously subordinated its government to the captain general of Mauritius. For once, the British government, the directors of the East India Company and their officers in India were of one mind, and in 1810–11 British forces occupied both Mauritius and Java. There was little resistance. Daendels had been recalled shortly before the invasion, apparently because Napoleon thought him too independent. His next employment was in the 1812 expedition to Moscow. His successor Janssens had already, as governor at the Cape of Good Hope, surrendered one Dutch colony to the British; now he was to surrender another.

He did his best, as he had done at the Cape; but he reported that Daendels' unwelcome zeal had made French rule so hated, by Dutch and Javanese alike, that the British were welcomed by many residents almost as deliverers.[20]

Neither the British government nor the East India directors thought of Java as a permanent acquisition. Despite their eagerness, over the past decades, to acquire trading stations and bases in the East Indies,[21] they had no wish to be saddled with the administration of a large and populous island. Their main object was strategic: to protect India from the possibility of French encirclement. The orders issued to the invading force were 'to expel the enemy from all their settlements, to destroy all their forts, to take possession of all arms and ammunition, and to demolish all stores and magazines, wishing to leave the possession of these settlements to the occupation of the natives';[22] but Minto, governor general in India and commander-in-chief of the expedition, rightly pointed out that to disarm the Dutch and leave them at the mercy of the Javanese might be their death sentence. The proclamation which he issued described the English intention as 'merely to annul the unlawful annexation of Java by the power of France and take it under the protection of Great Britain'.[23] Protection implied administration. The responsibility was government's, as Minto insisted: 'It seems to be understood that territories conquered from European powers, although locally situated within the Limits of the Company's privileges ... are nevertheless acquired exclusively for the Crown.'[24] Obviously, however, the actual work of governing Java would have to be done by the company, and Minto was less clear than were his employers about the temporary nature of the occupation. The administration which he set up was civil, not military, and the lieutenant governor to whom it was entrusted appeared less concerned with rescuing the Dutch from the French, than with rescuing the Javanese from the Dutch system as it had operated in the eighteenth century.

Raffles had been employed, before the invasion, in preliminary negotiations to secure the support of the Javanese princes. He knew the country and was determined, once it had been taken over, that it should be retained. The history of India over the previous fifty years revealed many examples of men-on-the-spot making unauthorised territorial acquisitions, which a reluctant company or home government had often no option but to confirm. Raffles, however, was no conquistador, but a very talented civil servant; and Java in 1811 was not Bengal in 1756. His only hope of persuading his masters to keep Java lay in demonstrating that the place was commercially valuable and that it could yield at least enough local revenue to pay for its own administration and defence, preferably a surplus. Of this, Raffles was confident.[25] He embarked immediately on a drastic reorganisation of the general, judicial and revenue administration, on lines partly suggested earlier by Daendels, partly drawn from British experience in Bengal. Java was to be as British as Raffles could make it, not only in its mode of government, but also in its commercial contacts. In Daendels' time the place had been economically in a state of siege; the British invasion reopened trade, naturally mainly in British ships, other shipping, indeed (including Dutch), being as far as possible excluded. The process was greatly assisted by events in England in 1813, when the enemies of the East India Company at last succeeded in getting the company's commercial monopoly abolished. In India, the company gave up almost all pretence of being a trading corporation, and settled down to the rôle of an administrative agency. Except for China, where the company retained its privileges for another twenty years, English ships might trade directly to any part of the East. Lancashire cottons could reach Java direct. All in all, Raffles achieved much, as his Dutch successors acknowledged, in quickening the trade of Java, in improving the efficiency of its administration, in pushing the Javanese towards a more flexible cash economy, in replacing tributes in kind and labour by a land revenue in money; but he never succeeded in balancing the books. The surveys necessary to build up the land revenue could not be accomplished in time; the administrative reforms were costly; the treasury was saddled with the obligation of redeeming vast quantities of worthless paper money issued by Daendels. Each year showed, not the promised surplus, but a mounting deficit. According to the directors of the East India Company, Raffles 'rendered the occupation of Java a source of financial embarrassment to the British government'.[26]

Moreover, Lord Hastings, who had succeeded Minto as governor general in 1813, was instructed to discourage expansion in the archipelago; not unreasonably – there was trouble enough in India itself in his time. In 1816 Raffles was recalled. His next appointment clearly indicated his employers' displeasure: Bencoolen. But Raffles was irrepressible. He immediately became involved in an unauthorised search for a more suitable site for a British base. This was a long-standing ambition; over the previous thirty years many attempts and many proposals had been made, all frustrated by Dutch belligerence or by British official preoccupation with India. In 1819, however, Raffles, on behalf of the company, bought from the sultan of Johore the inconsiderable island which was to become the harbour-city of Singapore.

Meanwhile in Europe the long wars had dragged to a close. From 1812 the fortunes of battle had turned against Napoleon all across Europe, from Moscow to Madrid. In 1815 he had suffered his final defeat and had surrendered, to be sent off to ignominious island confinement at St Helena. The statesmen of Europe, recovering the polished manners of an earlier generation, met in congress to seek a settlement. In so far as the settlement regulated the transfer of colonial territories, the British government was in a position, in many parts of the world, to take its choice. It had attained, in the field of overseas trade and dominion, a pre-eminence over other Europeans even more complete than in 1763, and was determined to safeguard its position by appropriate acquisitions. The total number of British colonies increased, accordingly, from twenty-six in 1792 to forty-three in 1816. The choice was discriminating; there was no rush to acquire territorial dominion for its own sake, no vindictive demand to rob the French of all they had possessed; merely a calculated resolve that sources of revenue or essential materials, valuable markets and major trade routes should be protected against any possible recurrence of French or other interference. Most of the acquisitions were made for strategic reasons; some were, in themselves, mere worthless rocks; the persistent nightmare of a Bonaparte escape from St Helena, for example, dictated British insistence on Tristan da Cunha and Ascension.

Outside Europe, the chief strategic preoccupation of British statesmen was no longer the West Indies, but India; a pre-occupation which, throughout the nineteenth century and the first half of the twentieth, was at times to amount to obsession. The most serious threats to the British in India had always arisen from hostile alliances between Indian and European powers; alliances such as that which Napoleon had proposed with Tipu Sultan. That particular threat had been averted, but similar threats might recur. The British still had powerful enemies in India. Their position was secure in the east and, since Wellesley's defeat of Tipu, in the south; but they had not seriously challenged Maratha control of most of central India, nor adequately protected the Ganges valley against the raids of predatory mountain peoples, such as the Gurkhas in Nepal. The Maratha confederacy was at this time the most formidable of the country powers. Some of its princes, notably Sindhia, still maintained armies officered by Frenchmen. Their frequent civil wars kept central India in anarchy, and gave cover for raids on British India by armies of organised bandits, the Pindaris. Any British operation against the Pindaris might unite the Marathas on the only ground they all had in common: fear and hatred of the British. Minto's policy had been to leave the Marathas (and the Gurkhas) alone, and put up with the raiding, except for periodic expostulation. Hastings resumed the offensive, and fought two major wars, the Gurkha War (1814–16) and the third and last Maratha War (1816–18). In both he eventually achieved his principal objects, but at the cost of heavy fighting and some serious reverses. At the time of the peace negotiations in Europe, therefore, it appeared that the East India Company was committed to a policy of extending its political and territorial authority, and that this policy involved war with various 'Country Powers', the outcome and duration of which could not be predicted with any certainty. It was essential, from the British point of view, to preclude the possibility of European interference. Hence, the British insistence on retaining the strategic points on the routes to India, which had been seized during the French war: Malta, the Seychelles, Mauritius; the Cape of Good Hope and Ceylon.

Strategic considerations apart, the French overseas were treated with some forbearance. They retained their footholds in India –

Pondicherry, Karikal, Mahé, inconsiderable scraps of territory, unfortified – and Senegal in Africa. In the West Indies they recovered Cayenne, Martinique and Guadeloupe; a drastic restoration. Louis XVIII re-established the administrative arrangements not of 1789, but of 1763. The islands were less valuable, relatively, than they had been – there was no world shortage of sugar, and the strategic value of Martinique was reduced by the British retention of St Lucia. In the course of the nineteenth century they were to become problem areas, imperial slums; but at the time the restoration seemed generous. There was policy, of course, in generosity. The British government was anxious to build up a strong federate state of all the Netherlands. For this, the acquiescence of the major European powers, including France, was necessary and had to be paid for. To keep Flushing and Antwerp permanently out of the hands of France was worth, as Harrowby put it, 'twenty Martiniques'.

Similar considerations affected the disposal of the Dutch colonies. The British government throughout the war had officially regarded the Dutch as victims rather than accomplices of Napoleon; and the new Netherlands state, if it were to fulfil its function as a buffer on the North Sea coast, must not be weakened or impoverished. The Dutch recovered Java and its scattered dependencies without much fuss, and Amboina, Banda and Ternate, in 1816. Significantly, they retained the essential features of Raffles' administrative reorganisation. In the course of the nineteenth century Java was to develop as a highly productive Dutch plantation; though the commercial capital of the archipelago was to be not somnolent Batavia, but booming Singapore. The Dutch islands in the West Indies, similarly, remained Dutch, and so did Surinam. The British government, however, was determined to keep not only Ceylon and the Cape, but the Guiana settlements of Demerara, Essequibo and Berbice, which were important sources of high-grade raw cotton. The retention of these places posed a problem in Anglo-Dutch relations, which the British government solved, to Dutch satisfaction,[27] by buying them.

Two other colonial powers found themselves, at the end of the war, on the winning side: Portugal and Spain. The Portuguese possessions in the East – Goa, Timor, Macao – were no longer of much significance, economic or political. The African settlements were significant only in so far as slavers operating there could elude British cruisers – as they usually could. All remained Portuguese, and little attention was paid to them. Brazil was another matter. The removal of the court from Lisbon to Rio had stood the empire on its head, and powerful vested interests had been created in Rio. After the return to Lisbon in 1821 a spirit, not perhaps of subversion, but of rivalry and separation, remained alive; the genie had been loose too long to be stuffed back into the bottle from which it had emerged. The outcome was more or less amicable: the creation of an independent 'empire' in Brazil ruled by a prince of the Portuguese royal house. This arrangement owed something to British good offices, something, too, to British naval mercenaries; and independent Brazil throughout the century retained close commercial ties with Great Britain.

The Spanish government, after Ferdinand VII had been hoisted on to his throne by Wellington's army, set to work to reassert control over Spanish America, which the Council of Regency had largely lost. In this, it had the goodwill of most other European governments. In England, it is true, there was considerable sympathy in some quarters for Creole aspirations to independence, on romantic grounds, or grounds of doctrinaire liberalism, or in hope of commercial advantage; but the British government could hardly place obstacles in the way of its allies recovering their own colonies. It could, however, and did, place obstacles in the way of other European powers assisting in the process, and its threat of displeasure, backed by unexampled naval force, limited Spanish hopes to what their own forces could achieve unaided. They could not, for example, reassert authority in Buenos Aires; the United Provinces of the Río de la Plata seemed gone for ever – not very united, and commercially to some extent provinces of Great Britain, but unquestionably independent of Spain. Elsewhere, Spanish armies, fresh from their experiences in the Peninsular War, made rapid progress. By 1816 major rebel groups remained only in Venezuela and western Mexico, bands of *guerrilleros* not easily distinguishable from bandits. The 'spirit of subversion', however, was still abroad, another genie which refused to re-enter its bottle. It now found its embodiment in Bolívar, a military leader of genius and a prophet of magnetic power. Ferdinand VII, on whom such high hopes had rested, was much less appealing as an absolute monarch than he had been as an exiled prince; Goya's pitiless portraits reveal why. Reconciliation, an orderly settlement, would have required time, wisdom and forbearance. Something might have been achieved. Spaniards were not necessarily intransigent; Apodaca, the last effective viceroy of New Spain, showed himself both realistic and magnanimous. Nor were Creoles necessarily irreconcilable; most were conservative, many still sentimentally loyal. Even among the revolutionary leaders there were those who would have welcomed an arrangement of the Brazilian type. Ferdinand, however, lacked forbearance and wisdom and was allowed little time. Another revolution in Spain shook his throne in 1820. It was put down, but not until 1823, and then by the hated French. During those three years the Indies were lost. Spanish ministers affronted Creole opinion not only by their radicalism and anti-clericalism but by their indifference. Colonial affairs were rarely debated, or even discussed in the press. Viceroys received no instructions, generals no reinforcement, loyal subjects no encouragement. Visionaries, military adventurers, or local chieftains took over, employing cowboy armies and mercenary fleets. By 1825, only Cuba, Puerto Rico and the Philippines were left. The first, and once the strongest, of the European colonial empires dissolved into twenty or so disorderly republics, looking to France for imported European culture, to England for European goods.

NOTES

1. W. James, *Naval History of Great Britain*, London, 1902, I, 51–3, appendix 1, and appendix 6.
2. See p. 184 above.
3. The descendants of former Spanish slaves. They were a formidable force in eighteenth-century Jamaica. See R. C. Dallas, *History of the Maroons*, 2 vols, London, 1803.
4. For the actual course of the fighting see Sir J. W. Fortescue, *History of the British Army*, 13 vols, London, 1899–1930, IV, pp. 370 ff.
5. Bryan Edwards, *History of the West Indies*, V, appendix 18.
6. The sum allocated for this purpose in 1805 was the record figure of £7,000,000. This should be compared with the service estimates for the

same year: army £18,581,127, navy £15,035,630, ordnance £4,456,994. Pablo Pebrer, *Taxation, Revenue, Expenditure, Power, Statistics and Debt of the Whole British Empire*, London, 1833, p. 154.

7. *Barham Papers*, III, p. 274.
8. 1806, the Cape of Good Hope; 1807, Heligoland, Curaçao, the Danish West Indies; 1808, Mariegalante and Désirade; 1809, Senegal, Martinique and Cayenne; 1810, Guadeloupe, St Martin, Ile de France (Mauritius), Bourbon, Seychelles, Amboina and the Banda Islands; 1811, Java.
9. John M. Sherwig, *Guineas and Gunpowder, British foreign aid in the wars with France*, Cambridge, Mass., 1969, p. 185.
10. Eli Hecksher, *The Continental System, an economic interpretation*, ed. H. Westergaard, Oxford, 1922, pp. 245, 292-4.
11. François Crouzet, *L'Economie Britannique et le Blocus Continentale*, 2 vols, Paris, 1958, I, pp. 68-9. Somewhat lower estimates are given in Phyllis Deane and W. A. Cole, *British Economic Growth, 1688-1959*, 2nd ed., Cambridge, 1967, pp. 196, 225: 25 per cent for textiles, 23.6 for iron and steel goods.
12. Frances Armytage, *The Free Port System in the British West Indies. A study in Commercial Policy, 1786-1822*, London, 1953, pp. 69-70, 92-3.
13. John Lynch, 'British policy and Spanish America 1783-1808', *Journal of Latin American Studies*, I, 1969, p. 28.
14. Enrique de Gandía, *Buenos Aires colonial*, Buenos Aires, 1957, pp. 35-55.
15. Lynch, 'British policy and Spanish America', pp. 2 ff.
16. J. H. Parry, 'Eliphalet Fitch', *History*, June 1955.
17. Neither purpose nor destination is certain, because the final orders were never given. Lynch, 'British policy and Spanish America', p. 23.
18. J. S. Furnivall, *Netherlands India*, Cambridge, 1944, pp. 56 ff.
19. J. S. Furnivall, *An introduction to the history of Netherlands India*, London, 1934, p. 35.
20. *Ibid.*, p. 45.
21. Harlow, *The Founding of the Second British Empire*, p. 45.
22. M. L. van Deventer, *Het Nederlandsch Gezag over Java en onderhoorigheden sedert 1811*, The Hague, 1891, p. 4.
23. Proclamation of 11 August 1811. *Encyclopaedie van Nederlandsch-Indië*, 7 vols, The Hague, 1917-35, II, p. 19.
24. Minto to the Board of Control, 6 December 1811. Van Deventer, *Het Nederlandsch Gezag*, p. 4.
25. (Sir) Thomas Stamford Raffles, *Substance of a minute recorded on 11 February 1811*, London, 1814, p. 168.
26. R. Coupland, *Raffles*, London, 1926, p. 58.
27. To judge by a secret minute by Falck, soon to become minister for colonies: 'Of course our own interest ought to have brought us to abandon properties that are always onerous and already compromised by the least chance of war. What good fortune to find people complaisant enough to pay us for abandoning them.' H. T. Colenbrander, *Gedenkstucken der algemeene geschiednis van Nederland*, p. 606.

PART III

The Second Age of Discovery

Ships and Sailors

Si l'industrie et l'audace de nos nations modernes ont un avantage sur la reste de la terre et sur toute l'antiquité, c'est par nos expéditions maritimes. On n'est pas assez étonné peut-être de voir sortir, des ports de quelques petites provinces inconnues autrefois aux anciennes nations civilisées, des flottes dont un seul vaisseau eût détruit tous les navires des anciens Grecs et des Romains.[1]

So wrote Voltaire, with only slight exaggeration. The ship of the Line of Voltaire's day was a not inconsiderable monument to human industry and ingenuity. It was extraordinarily impressive to the eye, the massive lines of its fortress hull relieved by the intricate tracery of its spars and rigging. It was bigger than most country houses, and far more complex in construction and design. It took two years to build. Its fabric incorporated over 3,000 loads of oak[2] – each load of fifty cubic feet, the yield of a big tree – to say nothing of the elm for its keel and garboard strakes, the pine trunks which formed its masts and yards. It took a hundred tons of wrought iron, forty tons of copper, thousands of feet of hempen rope and cable. It housed from 600 to 800 men, in some discomfort, and could carry food and water to supply them, somewhat unhealthily, for about six months. Each of its broadsides could throw, every few minutes in battle, half a ton of metal with lethal force against targets a quarter of a mile away. When adequately manned it was reliable, efficient and deadly. Yet it had a short life, usually not much more than twenty years (though some ships served much longer). Damp wood is perishable; dry rot, and in warm waters the secret tunnelling of the ship worm, destroyed more ships than all the raging of the sea and the violence of the enemy. Ships had constantly to be replaced or rebuilt;

great fleets of timber carriers plied to the Baltic, fetching the plank, frames and masts and spars which naval dockyards constantly demanded. Despite the difficulties and the cost, navies increased in size throughout the century. In each successive conflict, the maritime powers of Europe sent to sea a greater number of these ponderously beautiful engines of war, and employed an ever-increasing proportion of them in distant colonial or commercial theatres.

The ship of the Line changed little in essentials throughout the eighteenth century; a curious circumstance, considering its crucial importance as a weapon, and the shortness of its life. Worn-out ships were replaced by new ships of almost identical design – if, indeed, the word design can properly be applied to a process so firmly tied to tradition and rule-of-thumb. Naval campaigns were won partly by strategic foresights or good guessing, naval battles partly by tactical skill, though it was skill of a somewhat crude kind, limited – at least during the first three-quarters of the century – by the rigidity of conventional battle formations, the rudimentary nature of signal systems, and imperfect fleet discipline. Captains often failed to grasp what the admiral wanted them to do, especially if he wanted them to do something not precisely covered by Permanent Fighting Instructions.[3] Sometimes they simply disobeyed, and might or might not be court-martialled for it. Not until the War of American Independence were these matters sufficiently tightened up and developed, to allow scope for the tactical genius of a Rodney, a Suffren or a Nelson. In any event, when two fleets actually engaged, battle became a mêlée, a series of individual fights between single ships or small groups; the admiral to some extent lost control of his ships, and individual captains came into their own. It was then that victories were won, by ships pounding one another at short range until one or the other struck, ran, burned or sank. Neither at this stage, nor at any stage in eighteenth-century naval war, were technological considerations decisive. Superiority in construction, inventiveness in design, hardly entered the question; the same types of ship were common, with only marginal variations, to all the major navies.[4] The issue of battle was ultimately decided, partly by the *condition* of ships, their time out of dockyard, which affected their speed and handling qualities; partly by courage and determination, by sea-manship and gunnery, which determined their fighting capacity. Gunnery was not a matter of scientific design, or even of superior accuracy. With smooth-bore muzzle-loaders firing solid shot, ac-curacy was hardly to be hoped for; effective fire was point-blank. What mattered was rate of fire, and this could be improved only by relentless drill. It did improve; by Nelson's time a well-drilled ship could hope to get off a broadside a minute, in a brief en-gagement.[5] Above all, however, when all that drill could do had been done on both sides, the issue of battle depended upon the superiority of one fleet over another in total weight of metal.

This meant, essentially, superiority in numbers: more ships, not better ships, nor even bigger ships. The weight of metal a ship could carry depended admittedly on its size: its length on the gun deck, and the number of decks; but in size, as in design, ships of the Line varied comparatively little from navy to navy and from decade to decade. Among British first-rates – three-decks mount-ing a hundred guns or more – the first to be built in the eighteenth century was the *Royal Ann*, launched at Woolwich in 1706: 172 feet on gun deck, a hundred guns; the second, the *Royal Sovereign*, Chatham 1719: 175 feet on gun deck, a hundred guns; the last, and biggest of the century, the *Ville de Paris*, Chatham 1795: 190 feet on gun deck, 110 guns.[6] It may be noted in passing that the *Sov-ereign of the Seas*, flagship of Charles I's ship-money fleet, built in 1637, was only a little smaller than the *Royal Ann*.[7] The French were more adventurous than the English in building very big ships, but they overreached. The *Commerce de Marseille*, built in 1792 and taken at Toulon, was 206 feet on the gun deck, and so flimsy as to be considered unsafe by her captors. The limiting factor was the size of the available timber. The modest increases in the size of big warships in the eighteenth century were achieved by ingenuity in scarphing, by piecing together smaller lengths to make the largest members of a ship's frame. Acceptable keels, ribs and even stem-posts could be built in this way; but the members which bore the greatest strains – the stern-post, on which the rudder was hung, the catheads which supported the anchors, the wing-transom knees – had to be solid single pieces. England, despite the chronic inad-equacy of its forests and its heavy reliance on Baltic plank, was relatively well supplied with big free-standing hedgerow oaks, from which 'great' and 'compass' timber could be cut; the French, with much more extensive forests of their own, nevertheless relied heavily for the largest pieces, especially for large forked and curved pieces – knees, futtocks, and so forth – upon foreign sources of supply: Italy and Albania for Toulon Guipúzcoa for Rochefort and Brest.[8] A similar difficulty affected the masting of big ships. There were many sources of mast and spar timber, from the Baltic round to the Adriatic; but trees big enough for the lower masts of first-rates, or even seventy-fours, were scarce everywhere in Europe. They were commoner in North America, but difficult, expensive and dangerous to transport. 'Made' masts, the only alternative (masts pieced together, that is, from several segments, like a split-cane rod) were unreliable, or thought to be so. Over and over again dockyards, with their stores full of ordinary timber (though that, too, often ran short), were obliged to hold up the construction of big ships for lack of a few special pieces. Charnock summed up the situation at the end of the century: 'The size of our ships seems now to have reached its ultimatum,' he wrote, 'for nature itself in some measure fixes its limits . . . Timber, the growth of nature as much as man, cannot be made to grow larger.'[9]

Growing navies reflected a growing volume of merchant shipping, which the warships were supposed to protect and with which, in war time, they competed for men and material. The most rapid growth, among European fleets, was in English shipping, which more than trebled in total tonnage in the course of the eighteenth century. The rate of growth was uneven. In the first half of the century foreign-going trade expanded slowly; it was damaged by two protracted wars, of the Spanish Succession and the Austrian Succession, both, in their naval aspect, largely wars of attrition against merchant shipping; the net increase in the total volume of shipping was small. Between 1748 and 1775, however, growth was very rapid, despite the Seven Years War. The mounting demand for tonnage during this period was partly met by extensive purchases from North American builders. It was stated in 1774 that nearly a third of British owned ships were American-built[10]– mostly smallish ships, cheaply built (though not necessarily cheap to operate), employed largely in trade with North America. Expansion of business was especially rapid in the distant trades – East Indian, West Indian, North American – which between them employed some 150,000 tons of shipping in 1748, nearly 300,000 tons in 1775;[11] and in the timber trade from the Baltic, which expanded steadily in direct response to the demand for shipbuilding timber, for commercial as well as naval purposes. The American war caused serious interruptions, both to the supply of ships and shipbuilding material, and to trade itself; obviously it stopped the purchases of American-built ships; but the English shipbuilding industry responded to renewed demand after the peace, and growth was resumed, though at a somewhat less rapid rate, to the end of the century and beyond. The French wars again interrupted European trade and slowed the rate of shipping growth; but they also had the effect of pushing a higher proportion of English shipping into distant trades. The other major merchant fleets of western Europe, in so far as the vicissitudes of war allowed, followed much the same pattern of development as the English, though in lesser degree: they increased in size in the course of the eighteenth century, some more, some less, and they too increased the proportion of their shipping employed in distant waters.

Merchant ships, throughout the sixteenth, seventeenth and eighteenth centuries, were usually much smaller than men-of-war. In the eighteenth century, East Indiamen formed a partial exception to this generalisation; they performed some of the functions of warships, resembled them in construction, and were much larger than any other class of merchantman. In most other trades, the size of ships was held down not by technical difficulties but by market possibilities; the larger the ship, the greater the risks of underlading or of delay in securing a full lading. The advantages of size in reducing running costs per ton had to be balanced against the increase in the risk of under-utilisation. In the middle and later decades of the eighteenth century the general growth of trade, and the increasing regularity and predictability of certain major trades, gradually reduced that risk; so there appeared a marked tendency towards bigger ships, particularly in the East Indian, West Indian and West African trades, and in the bulk-carrying trades – coal, grain and timber. The tendency should not be exaggerated, however. In England, where the tendency was very marked, there are no reliable figures before 1788, the first full year of compulsory registration; in that year 9,355 ships were registered as English-owned, and 7,756 of them were still under 200 tons. In the two years 1790–1, 1,156 ships were built in England; only 150 were over 200 tons,[12] and ten or a dozen of these were Indiamen of over 600 tons. It was in a small but growing class of medium-sized merchantmen, from, say, 150 to 450 tons, that the main innovations in design, construction and rig were made, in the first three-quarters of the eighteenth century. Only in the last quarter of the century did the biggest ships, Indiamen and warships, take the lead.

One of the most important eighteenth-century innovations was an improvement in steering gear. Steering a ship of any size with a tiller, even with relieving tackles, demanded considerable physical effort, sometimes by a number of men, especially in a following sea; in the steerage, moreover, a helmsman was prevented by the overhang of the quarterdeck from watching the sails. The characteristic seventeenth-century appliance, the whipstaff on the quarterdeck, was mechanically unsatisfactory.[13] The solution was to fit a yoke to the head of the rudder, and run the lines through leading blocks to a drum mounted on the quarterdeck and rotated by a wheel. The ship's wheel was introduced shortly after 1700 and spread very rapidly. It permitted much more accurate steering than the tiller, and could be handled by a single man, or by two at most in heavy weather.

Eighteenth-century developments in rig can be followed in some detail, from pictures and drawings, from descriptions in Admiralty passes and from the inventories which accompanied Admiralty court appraisements.[14] There were no revolutionary changes; rather, a continuation of trends two and a half centuries old. The rig of all save the smallest ships was standardised in essentials by 1700 throughout western Europe. Almost all ships of more than sixty tons or so had three masts. They were square-rigged on fore and main, with foresail, foretopsail, sometimes (especially in large ships) foretopgallant, mainsail, maintopsail and maintopgallant. Courses and topsails usually had two or three rows of

278

reef points; the old practice of lacing bonnets to the foot of the course had almost disappeared. Studding sails were known, but were not yet in very general use. The mizen carried a lateen, sometimes surmounted by a square topsail. The little lateen jigger, known in the sixteenth century as the bonaventure mizen, had disappeared by the middle of the seventeenth. For headsails, our ship of 1700 set a fair-sized square sail, the spritsail, on a yard below the bowsprit. It was a troublesome sail, necessarily baggy and loose-footed, difficult to control and to sheet hard home. In Spanish ships it was appropriately nicknamed *cebadera* – nosebag. It was supplemented in most big ships by a spritsail-topsail, whose yard was hoisted on a small mast stepped at the end of the bowsprit. This too was an awkward little sail; it could be furled only by men scrambling out along the bowsprit, and lowering the yard, and the staying of its mast was complicated and precarious. Its main purpose was to swing the ship's head when getting under way or going about; it contributed little to driving the ship. The principle and the advantages of fore-and-aft sails, originally developed for Dutch inland craft, were generally known, and in 1700 most sea-going ships possessed two such sails, usually maintop and fore-staysails.

The most important advances in rig in the eighteenth century were refinements and extensions in the use of fore-and-aft sails, especially as aids to steering. The special virtues of fore-and-aft headsails began to be appreciated in the first decade of the century, when the jib made its first appearance. To make the most of this valuable sail, its tack had to be boomed out by a slender spar, the jib-boom, projecting from the end of the bowsprit. This interfered with the stepping of the spritsail-topmast, and with the sail it carried. The two sails coexisted for a time, sometimes in the same ship, if contemporary pictures can be believed; but jibs were general by the 1720s and by 1740 the spritsail-topsail had become an archaic curiosity.[15] The spritsail lasted longer, and survived in big ships to the early nineteenth century; having by then outlived its usefulness. Equally slow and tentative was the adoption of the gaff-headed spanker in place of the lateen on the mizen. Gaff-headed sails had been used in small craft, especially in the Netherlands, since the early seventeenth century; they began to appear in numbers in seagoing ships in the 1740s. As an after-sail in a square-rigged ship the spanker had many advantages over the lateen. Its gaff, fitted with jaws working up and down the mast, was easier to hoist and lower than the long, heavy lateen yard. Its boom gave it a flatter set, and so greater turning effect, than the loose-footed lateen. Lacking the high peak and long projecting foot of the lateen, it left more room for the after-mast to carry a full, or nearly full tier of square sails as well, a point of particular importance in two-masted vessels. In going about, it could be controlled by means of its sheet, without laborious hauling on lifts and vangs or fiddling adjustments of tack-tackle. Yet lateen mizens, with a long history of usefulness, died hard. Some warships still carried them in the 1790s. Drawings of the late eighteenth century sometimes show a curious compromise: an aftersail cut like a spanker, but bent on a lateen yard. The lower third of the yard, projecting forward of the mast, carries no sail; it is a mere vestige without useful function.[16]

The practical effect of all these changes in sail plan was to make ships lighter on the helm and easier to handle; to give them better performance when closehauled on a wind – a matter of great importance for English and Dutch shipping beating out of the Channel against prevalent sou'westerlies; and to save labour. Labour-saving considerations also affected the distribution of square sails, particularly in merchant ships. The subdivision of total sail area became more complicated. The number of sails on each mast tended to increase; foretopgallants became almost universal, mizen topgallants became common, and by the end of the century 'royals' had appeared above the topgallants in some big ships. Sails tended to become more nearly equal in size and cut, longer and squarer in the head, and shallower; this made it easier to gather them in by the clewlines and buntlines, and to furl them on the yards with a small number of hands. With these changes, appeared a tendency to reduce the number of masts in merchant ships of small to moderate size, and to increase the size of ships which could be adequately canvassed with only two masts. In 1700, in England at least, two-masted ships of more than sixty tons were very rare; by the 1770s two-masted ships of 150, even up to 200 tons were common.[17] The brig and the snow (the two types differed only in details) became, in the middle decades of the century, the typical small seagoing merchant ships of northern Europe. Their most attractive feature was the small number of hands needed to work them. Even navies, towards the end of the century, used brigs mounting twelve or fourteen guns for inshore work. Gun-brigs were later to play a notable part in suppressing the slave trade. It was in the late eighteenth century that the practice first became general of classifying merchant ships by their rig, not only by their size or hull design. Brigs, schooners (favoured by North American shipowners), 'ships' (which spread square sails on the mizen above their spanker or lateen) and barques (which usually did not) all became recognised types. Navies, characteristically, continued to use their own nomenclature, based on the numbers of guns carried. *Endeavour* and *Resolution* were barque-rigged, but when taken into the navy they were classed as sloops-of-war.

Developments in hull design are harder to trace than changes in rig. Builders' models of warships have survived in considerable numbers; but commercial shipwrights rarely bothered with models, except for building Indiamen, and few drawings have survived. Frequent references in the middle decades of the century, however, to 'cat-built' ships indicate that the English had become heirs to the Dutch in the construction of the simplest and most economical type of bulk-cargo carrier. 'Cats' were the speciality of the shipbuilding ports of the north-east of England. They were big ships, as merchantmen went; of the 150 ships of over 200 tons built in England in 1790–1, eighty-eight were built in that region, probably all cats. They were admirably designed for the jobs they had to do, but were versatile with it. The most efficient shape in which to stow bulky cargo, in trades where speed is unimportant, is that of an oblong box. The seventeenth-century Dutch *fluyt* had approximated this shape, and had achieved a deserved popularity and fame. *Fluyts*, however, had their defects; flimsiness, due to economy of material; excessive length, which caused hogging; too much 'tumble-home'; and the weakness of the round-tuck stern. Cat-built vessels, particularly those intended for the coal trade, avoided most of these defects. Coal is a heavy cargo; it was carried winter and summer, in great quantities, through treacherous waters; colliers had to be strong. They were solidly built of oak; their proportions were moderate; their tumble-home relatively slight; and they had robust transom sterns.[18] They retained, on the other hand, some of the virtues of the *fluyt*: their full section (i.e. flat floor); their capacious, almost rectangular hold; their simplicity and economy of rig. They had bluff bows and straight stems, with no beakhead and only a modest cutwater; they were built for strength and carrying capacity, not for speed, certainly not for looks. Their qualities were widely appreciated; when Cook used Whitby-built collier barques for his exploring voyages, no eyebrows were raised at the Admiralty. The *Endeavour*, indeed, had been selected for the service before Cook's appointment to command her. Cook himself chose the *Resolution* for the second voyage, and the only public complaint came from (Sir) Joseph Banks, who fancied a frigate or an Indiaman. It was, perhaps, fortunate that no one listened to him. *Endeavour* struck on the Great Barrier Reef, was kedged off, beached, and repaired by her own carpenter and company; no Indiaman could have been so treated. *Resolution* and *Adventure* performed as honestly, in making the longest ocean voyage ever made till then, as they had formerly done in carrying coals.

Indiamen were at the other end of the seagoing social scale from the humble north-country collier. English, French or Dutch, they were all much bigger than other merchant ships. The English company throughout the first half of the eighteenth century employed ships of 400 or 600 tons, smaller than it had sometimes used in the seventeenth century, smaller than many Dutch Indiamen, but still big ships for their day. For charter purposes, throughout the first three-quarters of the century, they were all reckoned at 499 tons. Such a ship could mount, though it did not necessarily man, as many guns as a frigate; but it stood higher out of the water than a frigate and looked like a miniature ship of the Line. After about 1750, actual tonnage came more and more to exceed charter-party tonnage. In the last quarter of the century, the company began to operate much bigger ships, and towards the end ships of the biggest class, from 1,200 to 1,500 tons, approximated ships of the Line not only in appearance but in actual size. Such a ship might be a little longer than a seventy-four, but narrower and deeper, in order to profit by a tonnage measurement rule which ignored depth.[19] The similarity between Indiamen and men-of-war sometimes deceived experienced officers. In 1804 the French Admiral Linois, with a ship of the Line and four frigates, sighted the English China fleet off Pulo Aor: five Indiamen of the largest class, under the company's senior captain, Commodore Dance, and a number of smaller vessels. Dance, knowing that the French frigates could overhaul him if he ran, put a bold face on it and stood towards the enemy. The bluff succeeded. Linois, concluding that he had to deal with ships of the Line, himself bore away, whereupon Dance hoisted the General Chase and pursued the French until they were out of sight. There were other similar episodes. For aping warships, the companies paid a price. Part of the price was small stowage space in relation to size; since the companies were monopolists, however, and since their chief trading profits came from transporting commodities of relatively high value in proportion to their bulk, this did not greatly matter in itself. True, it was symptomatic of a general stagnation of design; but even this should not be exaggerated. Conservative though they were, in the later eighteenth century both navies and East India companies themselves initiated some valuable innovations, and these have now to be considered.

By far the most important was copper sheathing. The search for suitable sheathing against shipworm had been going on intermittently since the sixteenth century, and copper had been suggested as early as 1708. The first serious experiments with it, made on the English frigate *Alarm* in 1761–3, demonstrated its efficacy not only against worm, but against weed and barnacle. The *Dolphin*, in which Byron and Wallis made their circumnavigations, was also coppered. Her sheathing presented serious maintenance problems, difficult to deal with when far from dockyards. Cook's ships – which, of all ships, needed protection – were not coppered, but 'sheathed and filled'; the sheathing of thin deals, the filling of broad-headed nails hammered in close together all over the bottoms. The chief trouble with copper, observed in both *Alarm* and *Dolphin*, was corrosion of the iron fastenings of keel and rudder. It was caused (though the cause was not fully understood till later) by electrolytic action between the copper and the iron. It could be avoided only by the substitution of copper for the iron bolts below the water line, and this took time. By 1776, twelve English warships, all frigates or smaller, had been coppered. The rush to copper the major European navies began in 1779–80. Coppered ships were faster than similar ships without copper, and the advantage increased the longer the ships were off the ground. Rodney off the Spanish coast in 1780 and at the Saintes in 1782, Suffren on several occasions off the Coromandel coast, owed their success largely to the use of coppered squadrons to bring a reluctant enemy to action on advantageous terms. For merchant ships the main attraction was not speed but durability. Copper, in this respect, was not infallible; it could, indeed, conceal the progress of dry rot under the sheathing, as it did in the *Royal George* in 1782. In general, however, coppering not only increased the efficiency of ships, but prolonged their life. In the last two decades of the eighteenth century the English East India Company usually retained its ships for six voyages, instead of four as it had done formerly; that is, for twelve or fourteen years instead of eight or ten, an advantage which amply repaid the builders for the initial cost of coppering.[20]

The East India Company repaid its technological debt to the navy in a number of ways. Its shipwrights, when they served in India, encountered a shipbuilding tradition very different from that of Europe, much older, in its own way certainly no less distinguished. Even ships of European type built in India incorporated many native Indian features. They were built of teak, a material greatly superior to oak in most respects. It is an oily wood, not susceptible to dry rot; *teredo navalis*, which thrives on oak, avoids teak; it preserves iron, instead of corroding it, as oak does, and is far more durable than oak. Men familiar with Indian-built ships were less tied to European tradition than were their European fellows, more willing to discard time-honoured archaisms; and from 1798, Wellesley's policy of admitting Indian-built ships to the company's trade to England made these stoutly-constructed vessels a familiar sight in the London river.

One of the most influential and practical ship-designers of the late eighteenth century was Gabriel Snodgrass, who served the East India Company as surveyor, latterly chief surveyor, from

1757 to 1797, and who had spent his early working years as a shipwright in Calcutta. Among the many innovations suggested by Snodgrass and gradually adopted in the company's ships were: iron knees, standards, breast-hooks and crutches, all of which took up less space than wooden ones, were cheaper, and saved compass timber; iron spindles and pawls for capstans; round-headed rudders; movable boards in the hold. More important still, he was responsible, more than anyone else, for the disappearance of two time-honoured archaisms, the 'tumble-home' topside and the open waist. Ever since the introduction of heavy guns in the sixteenth century, big ships had been built narrower on the upper deck than on the waterline. The purpose was to discourage boarding, and by keeping the weight of the guns as far inboard as possible, to improve stability. Its efficacy, for the latter purpose, was doubtful. It was inconvenient and wasteful of space, and it rendered the ship 'tender' when heeled; some warships, for this reason, could not open their lower lee ports in anything of a wind. The vertical side advocated by Snodgrass – drawing, no doubt, upon his Indian experience, especially with big rice carriers – economised on scarce curved timber for the futtocks, increased stowage space, gave greater security to the masts by increasing the spread of the shrouds, and made the ship stiffer when heeled. This improved stability in turn made possible a flush upper deck. Until the very end of the eighteenth century the upper deck of most big ships had been discontinuous. Fo'c'sle and quarterdeck had been connected by gangways along the sides. The space between the gangways, from foremast to mainmast, had been left open, or covered over by gratings. The purpose of this arrangement had been to reduce topweight; but sometimes it had the opposite effect. If a big sea came on board, the water pouring down to the main deck was difficult to get rid of, and might put the ship in danger of capsizing. In the 1790s, under Snodgrass' influence, exercised through construction contracts and inspection, Indiamen were built with a continuous upper deck strong enough to bear the weight of guns and boats amidships. Snodgrass could then write, with considerable justification, that 'the East India Company's ships, as now constructed, are the first and safest ships in Europe. . . . If the improvements adopted in those ships were extended to the navy, much labour and expense would be saved to the Nation.'[21] Naval constructors never adopted improvements hastily, and they took their time in adopting flush decks and vertical sides. Even in the company's fleet, which then usually numbered about a hundred ships, the process of re-equipment took some years. It was hastened by an unprecedented run of losses in 1808–9, when fourteen Indiamen, all of the old deep-waisted type, were lost in violent storms. The newer ships were seen to make much better weather of it. They also displayed on occasion, despite their bluff and deep holds, a creditable turn of speed; but this was due less to technical developments than to changed circumstances. In the eighteenth century, East India captains had not been in the habit of driving their ships. They served a leisurely monopoly, and they had the comfort of important passengers to consider; so they snugged down at night, and even by day ran no risk of splitting their sails. After the opening of the India trade in 1813, however, competition made greater speed desirable, and the ships proved capable of it. In 1817 the China fleet – thirteen heavily laden Indiamen – astonished the shipping world by sailing from Canton River to the Channel in 109 days.

The eighteenth century, then, was a period of steady growth in the total shipping tonnage of western Europe; in the proportion of shipping employed in long voyages to distant places, whether for purposes of trade or of dominion; in the average tonnage of individual ships; in their seaworthiness; in their business efficiency. It was a period of detailed development in build and rig, but not of revolutionary changes. The industrial revolution, it is true, had a considerable impact on dockyards during the French wars. The basic job of sawing planks, for example, which in the Netherlands, Scandinavia and the Baltic ports had long been done by reciprocating saws worked by wind or water power, was all done by hand over sawpits in England until the end of the century, when the steamdriven circular saw began to take the hard work out of it. Steam engines, at about the same time, began to replace horses for pumping out dry docks, and men for laying and twisting hempen cable in the ropewalks. Steam drove the ingenious team of machine tools devised by M. I. Brunel for the mass production of blocks.[22] On board ship, however, there was as yet no industrial revolution. The actual work remained much as it had been for centuries. Sails, spars, boats, cables and anchors, all had to be man-handled with the help of elementary mechanical devices – capstans and tackles. A glance over the *Victory* at Portsmouth illustrates what this meant in terms of labour. Her hempen cable was twenty inches in circumference (chain cable did not come into naval use until 1811) and was brought in by a 'messenger' travelling between two capstans. The capstans and the nippers on the messenger were all worked by manpower. So were the massive purchases which hoisted the anchor to the cat-head, and tackles with which the guns were run out. Examples could be multiplied. The *Victory*, of course, was a big warship; but even in the humblest merchant packet, there was still, at the end of the eighteenth century, no avoiding a great deal of hard manual work. Throughout the century, with the total shipping tonnage of all Europe increasing much more rapidly than the total population, the most intractable problem facing navies and merchant fleets was how to find enough men to do this work. The most desirable of all developments were those leading to improvements in the manning ratio.

In this respect the middle decades of the eighteenth century were a period of significant change. The number of tons of shipping which could be worked by one man increased; the crew needed to man a ship of a given size was drastically reduced. The extent of the change differed with the size of ship: a big ship on a regular run was easier to man economically than a small one engaged in 'tramping', and the advantage of size increased throughout the century. Both the extent and the speed of the change varied from one trade to another. The bulk trades of northern Europe, especially the timber and coal trades, achieved very economical standards of manning quite early in the century: as high as twenty tons per man in the Norway trade in the 1720s, for example, and about the same for big ships in the Baltic trade (though the Baltic average was reduced because of the many small ships still operating there). Improvement in these trades thereafter was relatively modest, though still considerable. In 1757 the owners of a 300-ton collier, which had been involved in a collision, could claim that she was adequately manned by eleven men, including officers.[23] In the distant trades with which this work is concerned, manning ratios remained fairly steady through the first three decades of the century; there was a steady improvement in the 1730s and 1740s; and after the War of the Austrian Succession a very rapid improvement down to the eve of the American War.[24] Ships trading to Barbados and the Leeward Islands, for example, were manned at an average rate of about $9\frac{1}{2}$ tons per man at the beginning of the century, $10\frac{1}{2}$ after the Austrian Succession War and $13\frac{1}{2}$ shortly before the American War. The Jamaica trade followed a slightly different pattern from the rest of the British West Indies; at the beginning of the century its average manning ratio was less favourable – under 9 tons per man – and it actually worsened slightly in the 1720s; by 1750, however, it had overtaken the other West Indian trades at $11\frac{1}{2}$ tons; and on the eve of the American War it was well ahead at $14\frac{1}{2}$ tons. For the Virginia and Maryland tobacco trade, whose shipping was very efficiently run, the corresponding figures at the same dates were roughly 10, 13 and 16 tons, respectively. In more concrete terms, over about seventy years the normal crew of a 200-ton Virginia trader dropped from twenty-one men, to about thirteen. These ratios were certainly no worse than those of Dutch ships in similar trades, and may have been slightly better; they were much better than French ratios, largely because French law required all merchant ships to carry a proportion of apprentice seamen.

The improvement of manning ratios in eighteenth-century merchant ships was too big and too continuous to be entirely explained by the relatively modest increases in size and improvements in rig, which have already been noticed. There were other factors at work, and of these by far the most important was the improvement in the policing of the seas by warships. In western European waters, piracy was almost extinct by the early eighteenth century, except off the Barbary coast, where local rulers continued to prey intermittently on passing shipping down to the early nineteenth century. Special measures had to be taken from time to time, to abate this nuisance. In general, merchant ships had no enemies to fear in peace, and in war they relied on convoy. They no longer needed to carry guns or guns' crews. The same was true, by the 1720s, of the Atlantic seaboard of North

America. In the West Indies there was a dangerous increase in piracy immediately after the Spanish Succession War, when many privateers turned pirate. During the 1720s determined and increasingly successful action was mounted against pirates, and merchant ships, though they still carried some guns, made in peacetime less generous provision for manning them, except in the dangerous slave trade. Slavers always needed big crews. The curious difference between ships plying to Jamaica and ships for the lesser Antilles in the 1720s and 1730s, is probably to be explained by a difference in defence needs. Pirates had ceased to be a serious menace by 1730, but off Jamaica the *guarda-costas*, often little better than pirates, were very active. In the Austrian Succession War, convoy became the usual defence against *guarda-costas* and privateers; and the *guarda-costas* became better disciplined and controlled. The Jamaica ships were than able to take full advantage of the economies in manning made possible by technical improvements and increased size.

In the Indian Ocean, piracy and organised predation by native corsair rulers both lasted much longer. In wartime also, there were rarely enough warships in the area to provide adequate and regular escort. Partly for these reasons, partly because of the important passengers they carried, the big Indiamen maintained heavy manning throughout the century; heavy, that is, by commercial standards, not at a level comparable with men-of-war. A big Indiaman, as big as a naval seventy-four, would usually be pierced for thirty-five or forty guns; but even in wartime would rarely mount so many, and with her normal crew of 130 or so could not man more than half that number at any one time. The lower ports shown in contemporary paintings of such ships were usually dummies, and of the upper ports some, at the after-end, were usually empty. Passengers did not care to have the after-cabins cluttered with guns. Even the midship guns, though mounted, might be so buried in goods and stores as to be unusable. Indiamen, in short, were not warships, but armed merchantmen which superficially resembled warships. Nevertheless, their armament prevented them from sharing significantly in the general tendency to reduce costs by employing smaller crews.

Real warships were quite unaffected by this general tendency.

For them, the significant ratio was not tons per man, but men per gun, and that remained constant. The size of warships' companies was governed almost entirely by the number of guns; the size of each gun's crew, by the necessity for man-handling. A big gun, loaded and run out, could be fired by one man; after the gun had recoiled, the same one man, at a pinch, taking his time over it, could sponge out, re-load and ram; but then the gun had to be run out again, and this required at least six men straining at the tackles. There were some technical improvements in gunnery in the eighteenth century. Improvements in iron-making enabled iron guns definitely to supersede guns of expensive bronze or brass; goose-quill primers filled with fine powder and ready-use charges packed in flannel cartridges, both improved the rate of fire; the introduction of training tackles made 'oblique' fire possible. The three last innovations were important factors in Rodney's victory at the Saintes in 1782. In 1790 flint-locks came into official service in British warships, and gradually replaced the old linstock or slow match; the French following a few years later. But none of these developments was of major significance, and none affected manning. The activities of navies, as we have seen, were prominent among the factors which enabled merchant ships to reduce their crews; but any surplus which resulted was promptly snapped up, in wartime, by the navies themselves. As navies increased in size, their demand for men increased in direct proportion. Hence, in England, the press; the French managed better, by maintaining, from 1689 onwards, a register of seamen; but compulsion, in one form or another, was an essential feature of recruitment in all major navies. Hence, also, as more and more resentful and potentially mutinous recruits were dragged on board, the increasing severity of naval discipline towards the end of the century and throughout the French wars. This discipline involved not merely more frequent and more savage floggings, but also – and probably much more resented – long, indeterminate commissions, and the close incarceration of men on board ship when in harbour, to prevent their running away.

Navies not only absorbed men, they destroyed them; and that not only – not even mainly – in battle, but by disease. Like the ships, the men in them rotted. In the best of circumstances, shipboard life was unhealthy. It was difficult to keep ships dry; wet clothes and bedding encouraged rheumatoid complaints which, if they did not kill men, slowed their movements. In bad weather it was difficult to keep fires alight to cook hot meals. Extra spirit issues, though doubtless welcome, were an unsatisfactory substitute. Significant improvements were made in both these respects in the course of the eighteenth century: flush-decked ships were drier than waisted ones: permanent brick-built hearths between decks were vastly more reliable than the old, primitive fire-box in the break of the fo'c'sle; and much ingenuity was exercised in devising more efficient galley equipment.[25] There were worse dangers, however, than rheumatism and general discomfort. Throughout most of the eighteenth century ships' companies, especially the crowded crews of warships, were repeatedly devastated by killing disease. During the American War the British navy raised 171,000 men. Of these 1,240 were killed in action, 42,000 deserted and 18,500 died of disease.[26] The main killers were the mosquito-borne diseases, malaria and yellow fever, which attacked men in tropical harbours, especially in the West Indies; typhus in home waters; and scurvy everywhere, in ships which spent long periods at sea. Quinine had long been used as specific for malaria; for yellow fever there was no known cure; and nothing could be done to prevent either disease in harbour until, more than a century later, the rôle of the mosquito as carrier came to be understood. Meanwhile, the best remedy was to put to sea.

Putting to sea gave no immunity from typhus. This, the dreaded 'gaol fever', often devastated fleets after a year or two of war, when the reservoir of merchant seamen was exhausted and the press-gangs began to bring in verminous recruits from the slums of big cities. There was an appalling epidemic of typhus in the British Channel fleet in 1780, when the flood of new entry overwhelmed the rudimentary hospital organisation. The fleet could scarcely be got to sea. Everyone in England concerned with manning problems was thoroughly scared; and perhaps for that reason, a striking and continuous improvement in the handling of fleet epidemics began after that calamitous year. Much of the improvement was due to the influence of the great naval physician James Lind, who, though he had no notion of the significance of lice and fleas, did understand the importance of cleanliness. Lind insisted in 1781 on the establishment of Receiving Ships, where new entries could be examined, issued with new clothes, and quarantined.

Scurvy, the worst killer of all, presented problems of a different kind. No one in the eighteenth century had heard of vitamin C; but everyone knew that men fed on fresh food did not suffer from scurvy. It was impossible, with eighteenth-century methods of storage, to keep most kinds of food fresh for more than a short period; and in many parts of the world where European ships went, it was difficult to obtain fresh supplies. Some officers, therefore, shrugged off scurvy as an inescapable hazard of the sea; others pursued the search for anti-scorbutics which could be preserved. According to Gillespie[27] the French navy issued its men with a mash of sorrel leaves, carried pulped and barrelled; Dutch ships in the East and West Indies carried whole limes barrelled in brine; Gillespie recommended both. There were endless experiments with half-measures and useless nostrums. Sauerkraut and 'portable soup'[28] probably did some good, extract of malt little, elixir of vitriol none. Cook achieved a resounding triumph in 1775, when he returned from his second world voyage without losing a man from scurvy, and proved that careful victualling could eliminate the disease. Cook, in his determination to keep his men healthy, had tried virtually everything; it was not clear, even to him, which of the many reputed anti-scorbutics carried in his ships had really been responsible for his success. Probably several of them contributed. During the twenty years after his return, however, informed opinion gradually fixed upon the best of the various remedies, a remedy so simple that it seemed too good to be true; namely lemon juice. (Orange juice would do equally well. West Indian limes were an inferior substitute.) The therapeutic value of citrus fruits had been known at least since the beginning of the seventeenth century. Fruit was expensive, and whole fruit was difficult to keep in good condition; whole fruit, moreover, even whole juice in cask, was bulky; it was difficult to carry enough of it to meet the needs of a heavily manned ship on a long voyage. The problem was, therefore, to find a method of concentrating lemon or orange juice without impairing its efficacy; to induce naval authorities to insist on its issue and use, regardless of its cost; and to persuade the owners of merchant ships that dead men cost more than lemons. So far as the British navy was concerned, the Admiralty, persuaded by Sir Gilbert Blane, who had been Rodney's physician, ordered, in 1795, a regular issue of lemon-juice concentrate, daily, to all hands. Within five years, scurvy was almost unknown in the fleet.

The conquest of scurvy was a striking example of the gap between scientific recognition of a technique and its administrative adoption. However tardy, it was probably the most important single advance in nautical management in the whole period with which we are concerned. It made possible the long blockades which broke the naval power of Napoleon. During the American War Keppel and Hawke (who agreed about few things) both maintained that a large fleet could not be kept continuously at sea for more than six weeks.[29] The next generation of admirals thought nothing of six months. Progress in merchant shipping is more difficult to trace, depending there as it did on the initiative and enlightened self-interest of owners. On the whole, the East India companies were ahead of the navies in this matter; but they were not consistent, and sometimes tried to economise on the wretched soldiers they transported. Commanding officers of troops being carried to India had to insist on the company providing adequate lemon juice for their men.[30] These failings were due to culpable meanness or negligence, however, not to ignorance. By 1800 no one doubted that scurvy could and should be prevented. For sailors, soldiers and emigrants alike, long sea passages lost much of their horror (though none of their tedium). One more limitation on European trade and dominion overseas had been removed.

NOTES

1. *Cit.* F. Grenard, *Grandeur et décadence de l'Asie*, Paris, 1947, p. 193.
2. R. G. Albion, *Forests and sea power*, Cambridge, Mass., 1926, p. 20.
3. For a concise account of the Fighting Instructions and successive Signal Books in the British navy, see Michael Lewis, *The Navy of Britain*, London, 1968, pp. 536 ff.

4. It was fashionable among British naval officers during the eighteenth-century wars to complain that both Spanish and French ships were superior in design to British. Charnock echoed the complaint (vol. III, chapters 5 and 6, *passim*) but there is not much real evidence to support it. Gabriel Snodgrass, chief surveyor to the East India Company, a ship-designer of great ability and originality, derided it as a francophile superstition. G. Snodgrass, 'On the mode of improving the Navy', 1796, *cit*. C. N. Parkinson, *Trade in the Eastern Seas*, Cambridge, 1937, p. 136. It is true that French ships were often in better condition than British; probably because they spent less time at sea. The French may have paid somewhat more attention to questions of design – to 'improvement' rather than 'augmentation' – especially in the middle decades of the century, but the advantages they derived from it seem to have been only marginal. On Spanish design, see G. de Artiñano y de Galdácano, *La arquitectura naval española en madera*, Madrid, 1920; a distinguished and beautifully produced book.

5. Peter Padfield, *Guns at Sea*, London, 1973, p. 116.

6. Charnock, *Marine Architecture*, III, p. 245.

7. *Ibid.*, II, p. 271.

8. P. W. Bamford, *Forests and French Sea Power, 1660–1784*, Toronto, 1956, pp. 103–12.

9. Charnock, *Marine Architecture*, III, p. 234.

10. Richard Champion, *Considerations on the Present Situation of Great Britain and the United States*, London, 1784, pp. 14–15.

11. Ralph Davis, *The Rise of the English Shipping Industry in the Seventeenth and Eighteenth centuries*, London, 1962, pp. 41, 395 ff., and *passim*.

12. *Ibid.*, p. 70.

13. Parry, *Age of Reconnaissance*, p. 79.

14. Davis, *English Shipping Industry*, p. 75, n. 1.

15. For the details of this process see R. C. Anderson, *The rigging of ships in the days of the Spritsail topmast, 1600–1720*, Salem, 1927.

16. The *Victory* was so rigged in the 1790s. The yard is shown clearly in a picture of her, in the National Maritime Museum at Greenwich. For the subject-matter of this paragraph see David Steel, *Elements and Practice of Rigging and Seamanship*, 2 vols, London, 1794.

17. Davis, *English Shipping Industry*, p. 77.

18. *Resolution*'s dimensions were: Keel 94′, length on lower deck 110′, extreme breadth 30′, depth in hold 13′, tons (measure) 461. Her sheer draught is reproduced in *The Journals of Captain James Cook*, edited by J. C. Beaglehole, vol. II, Cambridge, 1961, p. xxviii. For *fluyts* see B. Hagedorn, *Die Entwicklung der wichtigsten Schiffstypen bis ins 19 Jahrhundert*, Berlin, 1914, p. 102.

19. *Length of keel × breadth × half-breadth ÷ 94*. This formula usually produced, in the later eighteenth century, slightly less than tons burden (the weight of goods which the ship could carry). It encouraged the building of crank ships. For a lucid discussion of these complexities see C. N. Parkinson,

Trade in the Eastern Seas, 1793–1813, Cambridge, 1937, pp. 130 ff. and David Steel, Elements and Practice of Naval Architecture, 2 vols, London, 1805.

20. C. Singer, E. J. Holmyard and others, eds., A History of Technology, 5 vols, Oxford, 1958, IV, p. 579.

21. Parkinson, Trade in the Eastern Seas, p. 137.

22. History of Technology, IV, pp. 426, 437, 580 ff.

23. Davis, English Shipping Industry, p. 72.

24. Ibid., p. 71 ff. The figures on which this paragraph is based are all to be found in chapter IV of Mr Davis' book. There are interesting comparisons in G. W. Walton, 'Sources of Productivity Change in American Colonial Shipping, 1675–1775', Economic History Review, 2nd Series, vol. XX, 1967, p. 67.

25. W. N. Boog Watson, 'Alexander Brodie and his fire hearths', Mariner's Mirror, LIV, no. 4, November 1968, p. 409.

26. C. Lloyd and J. S. L. Coulter, Medicine and the Navy, 4 vols, London, 1961, III, p. 137.

27. Leonard Gillespie, MD, Observations on the Diseases which prevailed on board a part of His Majesty's squadron on the Leeward Island Station between November 1794 and April 1796, London, 1800. See also A. Reussner, 'L'hygiène navale à la fin du XVIIIe siècle', Revue d'histoire des colonies françaises, XIX, 1931, p. 35.

28. J. C. Drummond and Anne Wilbraham, The Englishman's Food, London, 1939. Cook reported favourably on both sauerkraut and portable soup. The latter seems to have been made by evaporating clarified broth to dryness. It resembled slabs of glue.

29. Lloyd and Coulter, Medicine and the Navy, III, pp. 124–6.

30. There are several examples in Public Record Office, W.O. 34/138, especially f. 202 (1781).

12

Charts and Navigators

In October 1707 a British fleet, returning from the Mediterranean under the command of Sir Clowdisley Shovell, ran foul of the Scilly Islands in thick weather. Seven ships of the Line, of a total sailing of twelve, went ashore on the Gilstone Ledge. Five became total wrecks. Two thousand men were drowned, including the admiral, whose body – stripped by the islanders, as was their wrecking custom – was subsequently recovered and brought to London for Abbey burial. The disaster was the result of navigational error; Shovell believed his ships to be further east, further into the Channel, than in fact they were; and no chart then available showed the islands in their true position. It was not only an occasion, therefore, for national mourning over the loss of men and ships; it was a stern reminder that seafaring was a dangerous trade; that navigation, even in a well-equipped and well-commanded fleet, was still largely a matter of hazardous guesswork.

After 200 years of oceanic voyaging, seamen had still, in the early eighteenth century, no reliable way of fixing a ship's position out of sight of land. They could measure latitude; this was an ancient skill, and several methods were available. The easiest and oldest was by meridian altitude of the Pole Star, with the simple corrections necessary to allow for the star's small polar distance. Pole Star sights were possible, of course, only in the northern hemisphere, but other stars would serve, provided that their declination was known. Latitude from the meridian altitude of the sun was somewhat more complicated, because the sun's declination, unlike that of a star, varies with the time of year and with the longitude or local time of an observer's position; but the necessary corrections were well known. Declination tables had been in use since the late fifteenth century; mathematically accurate tables of the declination of the sun and of a number of fixed stars became available, as a result of Kepler's discoveries, in the course of the seventeenth century, and were carried in all well-equipped ships. The accuracy of observed latitude at sea was limited, however, by the coarseness of the instruments in general use. The cross-staff used for star sights was a primitive instrument, and difficult to use accurately, because the upper and lower extremities of its transom had to be aligned with the star and with the horizon, respectively, at the same instant. Sun sights were taken with the backstaff or David quadrant – the 'English quadrant', as the French called it. This was a more sophisticated instrument fitted with an upper arc, on which a shade vane was mounted. The observer stood with his back to the sun, aligned the horizon vane on the horizon, and adjusted his sight vane until the shadow cast by the shade vane fell upon the horizon vane.[1] The instrument was about three feet long, and had to be held steady with one hand while the sight vane was adjusted with the other. In conditions of clear horizon and calm sea a skilled observer could fix his latitude within, perhaps, a quarter of a degree. Of course the navigator kept an 'account', a dead-reckoning. From compass and log-line he knew his courses steered and (roughly) his progress through the water; his line (if he were up-to-date in his profession) being knotted at fifty feet according to Norwood's rule,[2] so that, run with a half-minute glass, a knot was the convenient equivalent of a sea-mile of 6,000 feet in an hour. He applied corrections for compass variation (which he could get from tables or an isogonic chart)[3]; for leeway (which he could judge by experience or, crudely, observe); and (to the limited extent they were known) for ocean currents. With the aid of traverse tables he translated the resulting course and distance made good into difference of latitude and of longitude, and plotted an estimated position on his chart. His only check on the accuracy of this estimated position, when out of soundings and out of sight of land, was his observed latitude. Longitude was purely a matter of dead-reckoning; there was no known practicable way of checking it by observation while at sea.

The indefatigable Flamsteed, the first Astronomer Royal, who ran the Greenwich Observatory from 1675 until he died in 1719, and who devoted his years to compiling a magisterial catalogue of the fixed stars, complained that seamen accepted too easily the limitations of the haven-finding art; they were all too ready to assume that the problem of observing longitude was insoluble, or that any solution proposed was too difficult to be used at sea. The learned world was more optimistic. In that age of scientific speculation and self-conscious learned societies, the persistence of so intractable a problem was a constant intellectual challenge. The disaster to Shovell's fleet made it, in England, an affront, a matter of grave public urgency. The central figure in the public outcry which followed was William Whiston, who had succeeded Newton in the Lucasian Chair of Mathematics at Cambridge. Whiston was already a personage of some notoriety. He had been turned out of his chair because of his heterodox religious beliefs, and in other respects was generally regarded as a crackpot. In his portrait, which hangs in Clare College, he certainly looks like one. Whiston himself proposed a scheme for anchoring large numbers of hulks, in precisely charted positions along the main trade routes, emitting simultaneous sight and sound signals from which passing ships could get their longitude.[4] The proposal (though Newton commended it) was widely ridiculed as impracticable, but it aroused great public interest, and Whiston – partly, perhaps, in order to advertise his scheme – organised a petition to parliament seeking positive encouragement for the 'discovery of longitude'. An act of 1714, accordingly, established a Board of Longitude, empowered to offer research grants and very handsome money prizes for a reliable method of finding longitude at sea. In 1715 similar prizes, the Prix Rouillés, were established in France under the auspices of the Academy. The French, it may be noted in passing, were more systematic than the English in navigational training and research; 'professors' were maintained and paid by the state in the major ports. In England these matters were left to private enterprise. Eventually, both in France and England, methods were to be found and the prizes claimed; the eighteenth century, so conservative in the design of ships, was to be an era of striking advance in the art of navigation and in the design of navigational instruments.

All this took time. The longitude problem was not to be solved by a flash of scientific intuition. The general principles involved were already, in the early eighteenth century, well understood, and had been for many years. The difficulties were those of practical application. The difference between the longitude of two places is equivalent to the difference between their local times, reckoning 15° of difference of longitude to one hour of difference of local time. The problem of finding longitude, therefore, is one in which the local time on the observer's meridian at a particular instant is to be compared with the local time on a datum or standard meridian at the same instant. Each of the major maritime nations of Europe used a standard meridian which passed through its own territory – the French Paris, the Dutch Amsterdam, the Spaniards Tenerife, the Portuguese Cape St Vincent. For the British, since the foundation of the Royal Observatory in 1675, the standard meridian was that of Greenwich. If the local time at the position of a British ship at sea were 6.0 a.m., and if the time at Greenwich at the same moment were 8.0 a.m., the ship's longitude would be two hours or 30°, and its name (since the spin of the earth is eastward), would be west. The most obvious device of observing the difference was a mechanical one: if the ship carried an accurate time-piece – a clock, that is, whose error was small, consistent, and precisely known – and if the clock were set to record Greenwich time throughout the voyage, then the navigator could at suitable intervals find his local time, and by comparing the two times ascertain his longitude. This was all very well in theory, but in practice there were difficulties relating both to local and to Greenwich time. Local time had to be calculated exactly, from the altitude of a heavenly body, and the available instruments were not good enough to observe the altitude with the necessary precision. Greenwich time presented an even more formidable difficulty. The art of clock-making had advanced greatly in the second half of the seventeenth century. Accurate clocks existed; but they all depended for their accuracy on the isochronous swing of a pendulum. A pendulum clock, however carefully mounted in gimbals and otherwise protected, was unreliable at sea, because the irregular movement of the ship made the pendulum move irregularly. The gravity 'constant', moreover, upon which the swing of a pendulum depends, varies from pole to equator. As for spring-driven clocks without pendulums, the difficulties of regulating them, of lubricating them consistently, and of compensating for variations of temperature and humidity, seemed insuperable. Proposals by the French Academy, to investigate ways of improving the sand-glass and the water-clock, were counsels of despair. Most seagoing navigators and most astronomers in the early eighteenth century did indeed despair of mechanical methods of finding longitude, and rested their hope upon the discovery of an astronomical method.

Here, there were many possibilities. If the local time of an astronomical event – the eclipse, occultation or transit of a heavenly body – could be observed precisely; and if the time of the same event on a standard meridian could be predicted and set out in tabular form; then the observer's longitude could be calculated from the difference. For practical purposes, the event to be used must be readily observable and of frequent occurrence. In the late seventeenth and early eighteenth centuries, methods based on eclipses of the principal satellites of Jupiter (which Galileo had discovered) enjoyed a considerable vogue. Flamsteed, in particular, had high hopes of these methods.[5] On land, good results were achieved by their use. The eclipses occurred frequently. They could be observed accurately, however, only by using a big telescope; the difficulty of accommodating such a telescope on board ship, and providing a stable platform from which it could be used, proved an insuperable obstacle. The method was never effectively used by navigators.

By experiment and elimination, those who sought an astronomical solution of the longitude problem came to concentrate their attention on the moon. The idea was not new; the rapid nightly passage of the moon across the background of the fixed stars naturally suggested the movement of the hand of a giant clock. Gemma Frisius, in the sixteenth century, had suggested calculating longitude from the moon's movements, and had shown a clear understanding of the principles involved. Some 200 years later, the suggestion came within the range of practical possibility. Some of the methods explored in the late seventeenth and the early eighteenth centuries – observation of the local time of the moon's transit, or of the occultation of a fixed star by the moon – proved, for one reason or another, impracticable at sea. The method which finally found favour was that of lunar distance. Once the moon's movements were fully known and tabulated, the angle at the earth's centre between the moon's centre and that of another heavenly body at any moment, could be predicted. The measured angle between the moon and the other heavenly body – the lunar distance – could be reduced to what it would have been at the earth's centre at the time of the observation. The reduced measured distance, when compared with the predicted geocentric distance, should provide a measure of the longitude of the observer east or west of the meridian for which the predictions applied. The method, like most suggested methods of finding longitude, was relatively simple in principle and dauntingly complicated in application. Three main obstacles, in the early eighteenth century, stood in the way of its practical use. One was the familiar difficulty of making observations with the necessary degree of precision; a particularly serious difficulty when observing the moon, since an error of $5'$ in measuring lunar distance meant an error of $2\frac{1}{2}°$ in the longitude. Another arose from the elaborate calculations, far beyond the capacity of most seagoing officers, and the delicate corrections for refraction, parallax and semi-diameter, which the method required. The third was the most serious: the rudimentary state of lunar theory at that time. The movements of the moon were very far from being fully known and tabulated. They are, in fact, exceedingly complex; they follow a cycle more than eighteen years in duration. Over a short term, they appeared so irregular as to defy mathematical formulation. Newton said that the attempt to predict them was the only problem that ever made his head ache.[6] The available tables were based on empirical observations, and could not be relied on for accurate and systematic prediction. With so formidable a range of obstacles, the astronomical method of finding longitude might well appear as impracticable as the mechanical method; indeed the phrase 'discovery of the longitude' entered common speech at the time, to describe any practical impossibility. Yet all the difficulties were in considerable measure to be overcome in the course of the century.

The difficulty of making accurate observations affected all the processes of celestial navigation. An essential requisite for any improvement in navigational method was an accurate instrument for measuring angles; and among the various groups – astronomers, mathematicians, clock-makers, instrument-makers – working towards a solution of the longitude problem in the early eighteenth century, it was the instrument-makers who took the first decisive step. The secret lay in the use of mirrors. A fixed mirror, half silvered, half plain, could be aligned with the centre line on the horizon. A movable mirror, sliding on a graduated arm, could be used to reflect the heavenly body observed down to the silvered half of the fixed mirror, so that the lower limb of the reflection coincided with the horizon line. The measured angle could then be read on the graduated arm. A vernier scale and screw could be added, for greater precision. Correction for the semi-diameter of the heavenly body had, of course, to be made arithmetically. Like most ideas in this complicated story, the idea of a reflecting instrument was not new in the eighteenth century (Hooke had experimented with it in 1666, Newton in 1670), but it was not developed for practical use until the 1730s. Then a number of designs were invented within a few years: by Hadley in London, by Caleb Smith (using prisms instead of mirrors), by Fouchy in Paris, by Thomas Godfrey in Philadelphia. Astronomical research at that time was very much an international enterprise; but in the practical field of instrument-making, the English were generally acknowledged leaders.[7] Hadley's reflecting octant was the best and simplest of the new devices. It was communicated to the Royal Society (of which he was a Fellow) in 1731, and tested at sea by the Admiralty, in 1732. Its readings were found accurate to 2' or better. It was still a big instrument, made of oak, ivory and copper, twenty inches long (its descendant, the modern sextant, is less than half the size). It was light enough, however, to be held steady in one hand. By its means, most of the difficulties which had plagued the users of cross-staff and Davis quadrant, especially those due to the roll of the ship and the fatigue of the observer, were overcome. Its spread was rapid by eighteenth-century standards, considering the conservatism of seamen and the fact that each octant had to be made carefully by hand. Within twenty years it was in general use by up-to-date navigators, in France as well as in England. In Bouguer's *Traité de la navigation*, published in 1753, the author, after describing *arbalestrille* and *quartier anglais*, refers to the octant as 'un nouvel instrument incomparablement plus parfait'.[8] D'Après de Mannevillette, the distinguished hydrographer, used a London-made octant for his surveys from 1749, and expressed the hope that the instrument would make possible, at last, the fixing of longitude from observations of lunar distance.

So it did; but it was not the only factor. The astronomers and mathematicians had not been idle all this time. Throughout the first three-quarters of the eighteenth century many of the best mathematical minds in Europe applied themselves to the problem of compiling reliable tables of the moon's position. In England, Halley undertook the prodigious task of systematic observation over a complete eighteen-year cycle. When he succeeded Flamsteed as Astronomer Royal in 1720, he was already an elderly man, past his great creative period, but had lost nothing of his energy and assiduity, and had had considerable experience of observation at sea. He claimed in an announcement to the Royal Society in 1731 to have made 1,500 lunar observations. His work, and that of Lemonnier in France over the same period, made possible a progressive improvement in the tables. Tests carried out in ships of the French East India Company by the Abbé de la Caille in 1751 and by d'Après de Mannevillette gave encouraging results. But in so complex a matter, reliable prediction could not be attained by empirical observation alone, and it was not until the 1750s that mathematical theorems, upon which theoretically perfect tables of lunar movements could be based, were discovered. They were the work of the famous Swiss mathematician Euler, whose *Theoria Motus Lunae* was published in 1753; though Euler, in communicating his ideas to the Royal Society, paid handsome tribute to a predecessor, Newton, and to a contemporary, Clairaut. Euler's theories were skilfully developed in the form of tables by a Hanoverian professor of mathematics, Tobias Mayer, who submitted his tables to the Göttingen Royal Society in 1752 and to the English Board of Longitude in 1755. There followed the customary period of tests. Bradley, the Astronomer Royal, compared the predicted positions of the moon with observations made at Greenwich, and reported favourably. In 1757, 1758 and 1759 sea tests were made on board warships in precisely known positions within sight of land. All tests confirmed that with Mayer's tables a navigator could discover his longitude to the nearest degree or better. The basic problem had been solved.

Mayer's tables, in their original form, gave the moon's position at twelve-hourly intervals in terms of coordinates of the ecliptic system; in terms, that is, of celestial latitude and longitude. In this form they were published in 1761 in the Standard French almanac, *Connaissance des Temps ou des Mouvements Célestes* – a magisterial publication, originally founded by Jean Picard in 1679. The form was more convenient and intelligible to the astronomer than to the navigator, who had still to go through a great deal of laborious computation in order to obtain predicted lunar distances, with which he could compare his own observations. The final step needed to bring longitude-by-lunar-distance within reach of practical navigators was taken in England, by yet another Astronomer Royal, Nevil Maskelyne, a zealous exponent of the method. Under Maskelyne's auspices appeared the first British *Nautical Almanac and Astronomical Ephemeris* published in 1765 for the year 1767, and the companion publication *Tables requisite to be used with the Nautical Ephemeris for finding the Latitude and Longitude at Sea*. These official publications superseded, in England, the various privately printed almanacs, such as Tapp's popular *Seaman's Kalendar*, which had done duty up to that time. They included angular distances between the moon's centre and that of the sun and certain zodiacal stars, calculated at four-hourly intervals from a revised and extended version of Mayer's tables. This was what navigators wanted; from 1767, lunar distance became the standard method of observing longitude, and remained so throughout the rest of the eighteenth century and the first half of the nineteenth.[9]

It might be supposed that Euler and Mayer between them had earned the Board of Longitude's prize. They were indeed rewarded, but stingily. Euler got £300, Mayer – or rather his widow – £3,000. Technically they had not fulfilled all the conditions for the chief prize of £20,000, which called for a method fully explained for the use of seagoing officers, accurate to within $\frac{1}{2}°$

16 Canton in the early eighteenth century.

17 Acapulco, 1721; the Mexican home port of the Manila galleons

Empire builders: 18 (*above left*) James Cook, by J. Webber, who accompanied him on his last voyage. An interesting contrast with the formal portrait by Dance. 19 (*above right*) Clive, by N. Dance. 20 (*below left*) Cornwallis, by A. W. Davis. 21 (*below right*) Warren Hastings, by Sir Joshua Reynolds

22 The Palmer family, *c.*1786, by Zoffany. Major Palmer was a friend of Warren Hastings. He married a Muslim lady of distinguished family, the Bibi Faiz Baksh. After his retirement from the Company's military service, he remained in India as a private trader

23 Shah Alam conveying the grant of the *Diwani* to Clive, 1765, by Kent

24 The manufacture of clayed sugar: boiling house and curing house, 1764. The loaves are drying in pottery 'forms'. The man in the centre is boring a hole in the bottom of a loaf to improve drainage

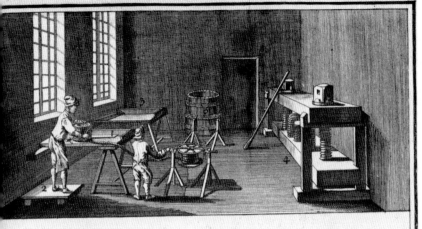

Plantes de Tabac.

25 The manufacture of tobacco, 1764. The men are rolling 'twist'

Slavery and the Slave trade in the West
Indies: 26 (*above*) The jolly view and
27 (*right*) The brutal view

The CRUEL MASSACRE

Of the PROTESTANTS, in

North America;

...wing how the French and Indians
...n together to fcalp the Englifh, and
...e manner of their Scalping, &c. &c.

...nted and Sold in Aldermary Church-Yard,
Bow Lane, **LONDON.**

Propaganda and cartoons: 28 (*above*)
The Red Indian as savage. English
atrocity propaganda, 1760. 29 (*below*)
The Red Indian as negotiator, during
Pontiac's War, 1764.

30 The beginning of the Seven Years War; an English view, 1755

31 Lord Macartney's embassy at Peking; an accurate forecast, 1792

tested over a voyage to the West Indies and back. These conditions might, indeed, have been met, given a little more time; but in the interval between Mayer's submission of his tables and the publication of the *Nautical Almanac*, competition had developed from another quarter: the clockmakers. A craftsman of genius succeeded in designing and making, contrary to expectation, an accurate spring-driven chronometer, compensated against the various conditions which could affect its mechanism at sea.[10] The man was the Yorkshire carpenter-turned-clockmaker, John Harrison. Harrison was already an old man. He had devoted the greater part of his adult life to designing accurate timepieces. The watch-type chronometer which he submitted to the Board of Longitude in 1761 was the fourth of a series of experimental timepieces, constructed with some financial help from the Board, and all, in their respective ways, mechanical masterpieces. His claims on behalf of no. 4 were received with some scepticism by the Board, especially by Maskelyne, who was deeply committed to the lunar distance method. No. 4 was subjected to a long series of tests, far more severe than those prescribed by the original act of 1714. It made two trial passages, to Jamaica in 1761 and to Barbados in 1764. Its error on the second trial, after allowing for its stated rate of going, was only 54 seconds, corresponding to 13·5 minutes of longitude – 13·5 nautical miles at the equator in 156 days; but the board demanded still further tests and explanations. The hard-earned reward was doled out in slow, reluctant instalments. 'Longitude Harrison' did not receive his full £20,000 until 1775. By that time other clockmakers, English, French and Swiss, were making chronometers on the principles, more or less modified, which he had introduced. The old man died in 1776; but not before his work received its final accolade, the approbation of Cook.

Cook, on his first exploring voyage, relied for his longitudes on the lunar distance method and took a prodigious number of lunar sights, which he worked (and made his midshipmen work) with unexampled accuracy. On his second and third voyages he took with him a replica, made by Larcum Kendall, of Harrison's no. 4. He continued to take 'Lunars', but the chief use which he made of the results was to check 'our trusty guide, the Watch'.[11] Longitude-by-chronometer was simpler and more accurate; it required fewer and easier observations and much less figuring; why, then, with such backing, did it not immediately supersede longitude-by-lunar-distance? Maskelyne's prejudice no doubt had its influence. So had nautical conservatism, a natural reluctance to entrust the safety of a ship to a piece of new-fangled machinery. In this same spirit, HM ships today carry standard magnetic compasses and annually perform the tedious ritual of 'swinging' them. A chronometer might stop; or the responsible officer might forget to wind it; better to have a method independent of clockwork. (Cook's chronometer did in fact stop on the third voyage, because of dirt in the mechanism. It was taken down, cleaned and re-started by an able seaman who had once been apprenticed to a clockmaker.)[12] The chief difficulty with chronometers, however, was their cost. Chronometers had to be made by hand, by expert craftsmen. They took time to make; Kendall had taken more than two years merely to copy Harrison's no. 4. Naturally they were expensive, and the demand for them long exceeded the supply. They did not become a regular issue to ships in the British navy until the 1820s; before that, officers wishing to use chronometers had had to buy their own.[13] Merchant shipowners – except for great corporations such as the East India Company – resisted even longer the pressure to supply their masters with chronometers. 'Lunars' remained, throughout the late eighteenth century and in the early nineteenth, the commonest means used by qualified navigators for finding longitude. Laborious though they were, they required no delicate and expensive piece of machinery; only a sextant and a set of tables. They remained part of the curriculum for midshipmen down to the end of the nineteenth century, to within a few years of the date when radio timesignals were to make precise timekeepers unnecessary at sea. Meanwhile chronometers grew cheaper, though never very cheap, and improved steadily in design, workmanship and accuracy; like sailing ships, like stagecoaches, like a hundred and one products of technological skill, they reached perfection on the eve of obsolescence.

With all its disappointments and false starts, the development of navigation in the eighteenth century represented an impressive sum of achievement. It is one of the few clear instances – at least until recent times – of a direct impact of pure science upon everyday technology. Besides the ingenuity and effort expended on the longitude problem, much attention was directed to more precise methods of finding latitude. Duillier in 1728, Richard Graham in 1734, the Dutch navigation instructor Cornelius Douwes in 1740, Samuel Dunn in 1776,[14] devised various methods using double altitudes; either two altitudes of the sun, with allowance made for the intervening run, or simultaneous altitudes of two stars. Another method, the 'ex-meridian' method, also associated with the name of Douwes, enabled the navigator to find his latitude on those occasions – not infrequent in northern waters – when a heavenly body was visible but the horizon was obscured. All these methods were clearly set out in the admirable textbook written by John Robertson for the mathematical scholars of Christ's Hospital.[15] Some are still used. One way or another, then, the late-eighteenth-century seaman could find his latitude within a few minutes, and his longitude within half a degree or better, several times in every twenty-four hours. (Latitude and longitude still required separate observations and calculations; the method of fixing a ship by the intersection of position lines, derived from the simultaneous, or nearly simultaneous observation of several heavenly bodies, was a nineteenth-century invention.) He could be sure of his position when out of sight of land and out of soundings, for the first time in the whole story of the use of the sea. He could know the bearing and distance of the nearest shoal, lee shore or other danger, with enough precision for safety, provided always that he had clear weather for taking sights; that he possessed the necessary skill and patience to work them out; and that the chart on which he plotted his observed positions was reliable.

At the beginning of the eighteenth century many old-fashioned navigators were still using hand-drawn charts based on a network of magnetic compass bearings, derived from the experience of coastal sailing and making no concession to spherical trigonometry. More up-to-date officers complained of the practice, and of the navigational errors to which it gave rise;[16] as late as 1753 Bouguer thought it necessary to explain the merits of a projected chart on which meridians, parallels, and a ship's thumb-line course could all be plotted as straight lines. There was little enough excuse for clinging to the old ways. Mercator had devised his famous projection in 1569; Edward Wright, in 1599, had explained, with tables, how to construct a map consistently on Mercator's principles; Robert Dudley's *Arcana del Mare* – a splendid atlas of Mercator charts – had appeared at Florence in 1646. The projection was well known and it use – the measurement of distances, for example, from the appropriate point on the latitude scale – well understood. The continued use of the 'plain chart', indeed, is one of the most striking instances of nautical conservatism. In the eighteenth century this beautiful and treacherous medieval survival finally disappeared from use. Throughout the century, virtually all printed charts intended for use at sea were Mercator charts. Throughout the century they improved steadily: in accuracy, as a result of better instruments and better methods of observation; in wealth of detail, ascertained by more assiduous surveys; in geographical extent, due to the extension of distant trade and exploration.

The history of the development of maps and charts follows a tidy secular pattern of national effort. In the fifteenth century nearly all the best cartographers were Italians. In the sixteenth century the Portuguese took the lead; in the seventeenth the Dutch, whose East India Company maintained a hydrographical service from an early date.[17] In the nineteenth century the British Admiralty chart attained an unrivalled excellence. The eighteenth century, cartographically speaking, as in many other respects also, was the French century. Cartography, and especially hydrography, were international in the sense that the major maritime nations kept close watch on one another's discoveries and inventions, and borrowed one another's ideas; in the eighteenth century – at least down to the Seven Years War – the charts to be copied were French. Much of the basic work for striking French improvements was done by members of Louis XIV's Académie Royale des Sciences, which had been founded in 1666. This body, unlike its counterpart the Royal Society, was a government-sponsored organisation which could be required to undertake royally directed research projects at royal expense. It was able to carry through, in 1669–70, Picard's precise measurement of a degree of the meridian (a task which Halley tried, and failed, to accomplish single-handed), and J. D. Cassini's impressive series of longitude determinations, using observations of the satellites of Jupiter. These investigations were mainly intended to facilitate the redrawing of the map of France itself, and the first-fruit was La Hire's *Carte de France corigée*,[18] a drastic rectification of the coastline; but the same methods were quickly applied to places outside France, and to the improvement of marine charts. In the last decade of the seventeenth century observers were sent to various countries in Europe, to French Guiana, the West Indies, West Africa and southern and eastern Asia. The values obtained, especially Richer's for Cayenne, set new standards of accuracy for this kind of work, and again the results were quickly made available in the fine collection of maritime charts on Mercator's projection, covering the western coasts of Europe from Spain to Norway, and known as *Le Neptune français*;[19] and by the stereographic-projection *Mappe-monde* of Guillaume Delisle.[20]

French pre-eminence in eighteenth-century cartography derived not only from thorough and accurate groundwork, but also from the critical judgment of compilers and designers, from the acumen of publishers and from the craftsmanship of engravers. Delisle was the first of the great names among eighteenth-century French map designers and publishers. In his *Mappe-monde* he set new standards in many ways: by the accuracy of his continental outlines; by his rigorous exclusion of guesswork and imaginative embellishment and his willingness, in default of reliable information, to leave the map blank; by his insistence on thorough revision in every new edition. He did much to free cartography from the tyranny of the engravers, who always preferred to re-use old plates or to draw new plates to the old designs. His maps, therefore, are valuable guides not only to what was known in his day, but to what was not known. The blanks on his maps supply the background against which the achievements of the eighteenth-century explorers must be judged. His successor, d'Anville, was more ruthless still in removing conventional and fictitious topography from the map, and in insisting on standards of perfection in engraving and lettering. He was an academic geographer, who never travelled beyond the outskirts of Paris; but an encyclopaedic and rigorous scholar who never embarked on a map without examining all the available evidence, ancient and modern.

D'Anville was the compiler of the first serious European maps of China, forty-six of them, based on Jesuit surveys and reports,[21] drawn to accompany du Haldé's *Description géographique* of the Chinese empire. Apart from China, and a series of European maps, d'Anville's most notable maps were those of the continents: North America, 1746; South America, 1748; Africa, 1749; Asia, 1751; Europe, in three sheets, 1754–60; and a general map of the world, in two hemispheres, 1761.

At the other extreme from the general cartographical work of d'Anville, and of much more interest to most sailors, were the detailed coastal surveys, also a characteristic innovation of eighteenth-century hydrography, made possible by the steady improvement of surveying instruments. Here the achievement was more widely spread, less predominantly French. In England, no less a personage than Halley devoted himself for several years to survey problems, and produced a survey of the Channel coast in 1693. The method used was that of resection; the position of offshore hazards was determined from an anchored vessel by taking compass bearings on three fixed points ashore. The same method was used initially for placing soundings on the chart. Individual 'spot' soundings had been marked on charts since the sixteenth century, and in the early eighteenth the number of recorded soundings increased rapidly. The first chart to indicate depths by lines of equal sounding was a Dutch one, of the Merwede estuary, made by N. S. Cruquius in 1729. (It is curious that the principle was not applied to land contours – lines of equal altitude – until twenty years later, by the French military engineer Milet de Mureau.) The first bathymetric chart of the English Channel was drawn in France by Philippe Buache, in about 1730; though not published until 1752.

The magnetic compass was a crude instrument for survey purposes, and the compasses in use in the early eighteenth century differed little from their predecessors 200 years earlier. An improved compass was devised in 1750, by a Dr Godwin Knight, FRS, which incorporated a fitting for reading azimuths; but for accurate charting, the marine surveyor needed to be freed from dependence on compasses. The usefulness of Hadley's octant for measuring horizontal angles as well as altitudes was recognised about the middle of the century; and about 1774 the first station pointers came into use, though they were not perfected for survey purposes until ten years later. Even with improved instruments, however, the development of accurate coastal charts was slow and unsystematic, even in frequented European waters. Surveying was expensive, and took much time. Governments rarely gave consistent encouragement or leadership; admiralties were only willing, and that only occasionally, to employ warships to chart coasts of major strategic interest. For the most part, hydrography was left to private enterprise. Chart-making firms sometimes paid for surveys; projectors of harbour works had surveys made of particular localities; naval officers, Trinity House pilots, and a large number of amateur marine surveyors – some, such as Murdoch Mackenzie,[22] very competent ones – made their own charts, either for their own use, or at the instance of learned societies, or for sale. In all these ways, a vast amount of hydrographical information was accumulated in the course of the century; but in spite of the growing demand for charts, there were endless difficulties in making it generally available. National governments hesitated to allow the publication of navigational details which might be of use to an enemy; the charters of Trinity House, for example, in 1685 and 1728, enjoined secrecy in such matters.[23] In other respects, too, corporations such as Trinity House made difficulties; the Elder Brethren in 1730 vigorously opposed a proposal by public-spirited private individuals to station a lightship – the first in the world – at the Nore, on the grounds that it would infringe the rights of Trinity House.[24] In this instance, they came to terms; but on many other occasions they objected to the private placing of navigational aids, and to the survey work associated with it, though they themselves were unable, with limited resources, to keep pace with the growing need.

Only at the end of the century, at least in England, did government itself recognise the urgent need both for good, readily available charts and for a more vigorous policy on navigational aids; only then did it endeavour to give a lead. The Hydrographical Office was established in the Admiralty in 1795. The first Hydrographer, the difficult Dalrymple, constantly badgered the Board to promote surveys, and warships were, when possible, made available. The capable Bligh, who had been master with Cook in the *Resolution*, was employed intermittently in this work between 1797 and 1803; but the Hydrographical Office was always short of funds. In other maritime countries the story was much the same; even for the familiar waters of Europe, the compilation and distribution of reliable charts lagged far behind the technical capacity for making them, and far behind the need.

Outside Europe, and especially in the East, the chief sponsors of hydrographical survey throughout the eighteenth century were the great chartered companies. Dalrymple, before he went to the Admiralty, had been cartographer to the East India Company. Some notorious places were surveyed quite early in the century. Philippe Buache, shortly after his pioneer work in the Channel, had been employed on a bathymetric survey of the island of Fernão de Noronha, off the coast of Brazil and on the route to the East. But even much later, such surveys were few and scattered. At first glance, it is true, the maps of the late eighteenth century show no startling degree of ignorance. The map of New Holland, for example, seems not much more misleading than that of Scotland before Mackenzie. Africa has much the shape to which we are now accustomed. Even the outline of Tasmania is not wildly wrong. But neither voyages of exploration, nor even regular trading visits, amount to hydrographical survey. Cook, the great perfectionist (who originally made his name as a navigator by his survey of the coast of Newfoundland for the Admiralty), insisted always that the careful sketch charts which he drew of the coasts he discovered, were not proper surveys. Many coasts, much longer visited by Europeans and much more familiar than those found by Cook, were unsurveyed. Policy, as well as ignorance, contributed to a conspiracy of concealment. Competing European monopolists regarded great stretches of coast as their own trading preserves. An English captain might trade in a rival preserve; but he could not easily buy a Portuguese chart of Timor or the China coast, a Dutch chart of the Moluccas, a Spanish chart of the coast of Chile. French slavers knew Madagascar and its neighbouring islands well, and would trade with anyone; but until the conquest of Mauritius they would not show English captains their charts. Men had been guillotined for less.

The cheerful confidence with which late-eighteenth-century seamen set out on distant voyages was, nevertheless, justified by experience. They had a good expectation of a safe return. The odds in their favour had increased enormously since Drake's day and very considerably since Anson's. Much of the improvement was due to striking advances in the techniques of navigation and cartography. It must be remembered, however, that the best navigating methods, the most accurate and up-to-date charts, were never the ones in general use. Fresh knowledge and better practice made slow headway; guesswork and rule-of-thumb maintained their stubborn rearguard actions, whatever the Fellows of the Royal Society might say. Moreover, there was always the weather to be considered. This brief sketch of eighteenth-century development, which began with one naval disaster in waters long familiar, may perhaps fittingly end with another.

During the French wars the British Admiralty usually provided heavy escorts for the ships which brought timber supplies from the Baltic, and kept a considerable fleet of warships in the area throughout the summer months. Since Great Britain had no Baltic base, this fleet had to be withdrawn in the winter. The ships returned to the Channel each year with the last convoy of the season. In 1811 the convoy, of 129 sail, was delayed by head winds, and did not leave the point of assembly (Hanö Bay on the Blekinge coast of Sweden) until 1 November. It was then dispersed by a severe storm, and driven back, with severe damage, to Vingö Sound near Gothenburg. The damage more or less repaired, it left Vingö finally on 17 December. It was again caught by heavy weather, again scattered, and a series of wrecks ensued. The *St George*, 98, and the *Defence*, 74, went ashore near the Holmen, on the west coast of Jutland, and broke up. Some days later the *Hero*, 74, and the gun-brig *Grasshopper* went on the Haak sands off the Texel. The *Hero* broke up; the *Grasshopper* got off, but was obliged to surrender to the Dutch. Two thousand men were lost. As in 1707, navigational error played its part in the disaster. The warships were well equipped; most of them had chronometers; but in continued thick weather they had no sights for days on end. The captains made insufficient allowance for leeway and for the current set up by strong nor'westerly winds; they believed themselves further west, nearer to the British coast than in fact they were; they recognised a lee shore too late to wear and claw out to sea. It is interesting that the merchant ships, though much less well equipped, having parted company from their escorts, mostly reached their home ports. A merchant skipper, after years on the same run, had a detailed familiarity with its hazards, difficult for a naval officer to acquire. In weather which precluded precise navigation, rule-of-thumb and experience could demonstrate their value.[25]

NOTES

1. E. G. R. Taylor, *The Haven-finding Art*, London, 1956, p. 255. C. H. Cotter, *A History of Nautical Astronomy*, London, 1968, pp. 70 ff.
2. Richard Norwood, *The Seaman's practice, containing a fundamental Problem in Navigation, experimentally verified, viz: touching the Compass of the Earth and Sea, and the Quantity of a Degree in our English Measure, also to keep a reckoning at Sea for all Sailing, etc.*, London, 1637. But there were many theories about knotting the log-line. The French used $47\frac{1}{2}$ feet, in accordance with Picard's measurement of the Earth in 1672. Taylor, *Haven-finding Art*, pp. 230–31.
3. The first world chart marked with isogonic lines (lines of equal magnetic variation) was prepared by Halley in 1699–1700. It was printed, reprinted and revised many times in the course of the eighteenth century. Taylor, *Haven-finding Art*, p. 253.
4. *A new method for discovering the longitude, both at sea and land, humbly proposed to the consideration of the Publick*, by William Whiston and Humphry Ditton, London, 1714.
5. His proposals were set out in the *Transactions of the Royal Society*, nos. 151, 154, 165, 177 and 178.
6. F. Hoyle, *Astronomy*, New York, 1962, p. 144.
7. This is clear from Nicholas Bion's *La Construction et l'Usage des Instruments de Mathématique*. Bion was instrument-maker to the king of France. His book was translated and enlarged in 1723: Edmund Stone, *Construction and Use of Mathematical Instruments*, London, 1758, especially Book VII.
8. P. Bouguer, *Nouveau Traité de Navigation*, Paris, 1753, p. 246.
9. *Man is not lost*. A record of 200 years of astronomical navigation with the Nautical Almanac, 1767–1967. Introd. D. H. Sadler, London, H.M.S.O., 1968.
10. For a succinct account of the functioning of Harrison's chronometers see *History of Technology*, IV, pp. 410 ff. The story is told in detail in R. T. Gould, *The marine Chronometer: its history and development*, London, 1923, pp. 40 ff., and more recently in H. Quill, *John Harrison, the man who found longitude*, London, 1966.

11. *Journals*, ed. Beaglehole, II, pp. 524–5, 653. Cook made many appreciative comments on 'Mr Kendalls watch'; especially *ibid.*, II, pp. 315, 692.

12. *Ibid.*, III, pp. 678 n., 1540, 1542.

13. Gould, *The Marine Chronometer*, pp. 131–2.

14. Samuel Dunn, *A New Epitome of Navigation*, London, 1777. This useful work was dedicated to the Honourable East India Company.

15. John Robertson, *The Elements of Navigation*, 2 vols, 5th edition rev. and ed. by W. Wales, London, 1786. For details of the methods see Cotter, *History of Nautical Astronomy*, pp. 145 ff., 165 ff.

16. e.g. Sir John Narborough, whose complaint is quoted by A. R. Crone, *Maps and their Makers*, London, 1953, p. 116.

17. Marcel Destombes, *Cartes Hollandaises. La Cartographie de la Compagnie des Indes Orientales*, Saigon, 1941.

18. La Hire, *Carte de France corigée par Ordre du Roi sur les Observāons de Mrs de l'Académie des Sciences*, Paris, 1693.

19. *Le Neptune français, ou Atlas nouveau des cartes marines . . . Revue et mis en ordre par les Sieurs Pene, Cassini et autres*, Paris, 1693.

20. Guillaume Delisle, *Mappe-monde Dressée sur les observations de Mrs de l'Académie Royal des Sciences*, Paris, 1700.

21. J. B. Bourguignon d'Anville, *Nouvel Atlas de la Chine*, Amsterdam, 1737.

22. A list of charts, mainly of the Scottish coasts, made by this remarkable man, is in A. H. W. Robinson, *Marine Cartography in Britain*, Leicester University Press, 1962, p. 165.

23. H. Mead, *Trinity House*, London, 1940, p. 140.

24. Robinson, *Marine Cartography*, p. 73.

25. A. N. Ryan, 'The melancholy fate of the Baltic ships in 1811', *Mariner's Mirror*, vol. 50, May 1964, p. 123.

13

The Voyages

Discovery, the charting by Europeans of the size, shape and disposition of the continents, was not a continuous process; it proceeded by fits and starts. The breathtaking Iberian voyages in the Atlantic, the Indian Ocean and the Asian archipelagos, in the late fifteenth and early sixteenth centuries; the first tentative crossings of the central Pacific, so costly in men and ships; the arduous penetration of the populous highland regions of the Americas; all these movements of reconnaissance had led to great rewards in trade and dominion. By the late sixteenth century the Iberian governments were too preoccupied with the problems of holding what they had, to spare resources or encouragement for further exploration.

The Iberian reconnaissance had been followed by a series of northern European exploring voyages in the north Atlantic, no less persistent, no less hazardous, no less brave, but yielding less obvious successes and fewer rewards. For the most part they had led into dead ends – the White Sea, Baffin Bay, Hudson's Bay – and to inhospitable shores. Fur trading, fishing, whaling had their attractions; so had plantations in North America as dumping grounds for surplus population and social misfits; but they were all ways of making the best of a bad job. The Spaniards and the Portuguese had found the sources of gold and silver, silks and spices. They had found also the best routes by which those sources could be reached.

Early in the seventeenth century, many prudent investors in England, France and the Netherlands reached the conclusion that the way to wealth lay in following the Iberians, imitating them, competing with them, occasionally robbing them, rather than in mounting further expensive exploring voyages. They followed this plan with great success in the first three or four decades of the century, establishing their own plantations, their own factories and trades, in both the East and West Indies. For most of Europe, the seventeenth century became increasingly an age of consolidation overseas, of trading and planting exploitation rather than of original discovery. Davis, Hudson, Baffin in the north, Mendaña, Quiros, Torres, Schouten and Le Maire, Tasman in the south, were the last great figures of the Age of Reconnaissance, and for many years no one followed up their discoveries. Mendaña's Solomon Islands, sighted and reported in 1568, wandered uncertainly about the map until 1793, when d'Entrecasteaux finally identified them.[1] The strait which bears Torres' name got no publicity; the last thing Spaniards wanted was a passage by which Dutch and English ships could pass from the Java Sea to the open Pacific and so to South America. To the Dutch East India Company, Schouten and Le Maire were mere commercial interlopers; their ships were confiscated. Tasman, it is true, had the company's backing; but what did he discover? 'No riches or things of profit, but only the said lands', according to his employers, who thus dismissed Tasmania and New Zealand from their calculations, along with the whole continent of Australia, as worthless;[2] worse than worthless, indeed. New Zealand was peopled by murderous savages. Australia, from what had been seen of its north and west coasts, was mainly arid rock and sand, the tepid waters of its gulfs and inlets alive, as they still are, with repellent poisonous creatures. Its great continental bulk was a barrier, lying inconveniently athwart the sea route between the East Indies and South America. Having found inhospitable shores on his first exploring voyage, Tasman found a dead end, or an apparent dead end, on his second. He was sent in 1644 in search of a possible strait on the east side of the Gulf of Carpentaria. The western mouth of Torres' Strait is shallow and masked by reefs and islands. Tasman, by inclination and training a deepwater navigator, failed to penetrate the maze. New Guinea remained, for Europeans, part of New Holland, until Cook sailed through the strait in 1770 (and, with characteristic generosity and precision, reported not a new discovery, but the confirmation of an old one).[3] On receiving reports of Tasman's voyage, the Heeren XVII told the governor general and council at Batavia to stick to their proper business, which was trade. The great commercial corporations which, by the middle of the seventeenth century, had come to control most European long-distance voyaging, all had shareholders to consider. They would not, as a rule, risk men, money and ships in a profitless pursuit of knowledge. Trade, which in the sixteenth century had been a prime stimulus to exploration, became its enemy in the seventeenth; geographical curiosity slackened, and the Reconnaissance petered out.

The second half of the seventeenth century, then, added greatly to European commercial familiarity with distant shores; but it was not a time of major new discovery, and the map of the world had not changed greatly in content (though it had changed in style) from Joan Blaeu to Guillaume Delisle. At the end of the century, the outline of South America, the Caribbean, the Atlantic coast of North America, the outline of Africa, the southern coasts of Asia, and the Asian archipelagos, were all known in varying degrees of detail to European navigators, and through atlases to the reading public. Here and there, knowledge went beyond the coastlines, chiefly in Spanish America, but also to some extent in Brazil, and in eastern North America, where French explorers travelled great distances in canoes and acquired some familiarity with the labyrinth of lakes and rivers used by Indian traders. In the Old World there had been little inland penetration. The interior of Asia was little better known to Europe in the late seventeenth century than it had been in the late thirteenth. The interior of Africa, the topography of its mountain ranges and the courses of its great rivers, was an almost total mystery. In general, the seas of the world were better mapped than were the land masses. The world outside Europe, as known to Europeans, was mainly a world of coastlines, roughly charted, of scattered harbours connected by a network of seaborne communication.

There were still immense gaps in the network, great blanks on the map, filled only by conjecture. Apart from the polar regions, where ships could not penetrate, the principal gaps were in the vast area of the Pacific. The only part of the Pacific known in any detail to Europeans was the coastline of the Spanish viceroyalties in America; a long coastline, to be sure, stretching from Lower California in the north to, approximately, Chiloé in the south. It was not continuously occupied, and certainly not surveyed or charted in any systematic fashion; but it had a series of small harbours strung at wide intervals along its 6,000 mile extent, and trickles of coasting trade crept slowly and uncertainly from harbour to harbour, converging on Panama. The coast had long been known only to Spaniards and occasional foreign raiders; but at the end of the seventeenth century French ships, presuming on the Bourbon succession in Spain, were beginning (as we have seen) to round Cape Horn and to visit the principal harbours.[4] Spaniards were the only Europeans who regularly crossed the Pacific: one or two big ships each year traversed, in thirsty scorbutic squalor, the immensity of open water between Acapulco and Manila. The route which these ships followed – the route forced upon them by the prevailing winds – took them clear of any land. They passed within a few hundred miles of the coast of Japan eastbound, but never called there; the policy of isolation, enforced by the Tokagawa Shoguns, had indeed for more than half a century closed Japanese harbours to most foreign shipping, and Europeans knew little of the geography of Japan. Formosa was still further off the galleons' track, and had in any event been virtually forbidden to most Europeans since the Ch'ing conquest.[5] As for the Hawaiian group, the galleons passed south of it westbound, north of it eastbound. So far as is known the islands had never been sighted by Europeans.

North of the route of the eastbound galleons was a vast area of ignorance. The Pacific coast of North America, north of Lower California, was almost unknown, and the longitudinal extent of the continent was the subject of wild and widely varying guesses. The Pacific coast of northern Asia similarly: Russian expeditions, coming overland, reached Kamchatka and began the conquest of the peninsula only at the very end of the seventeenth century. No one knew whether the Pacific, like the Indian Ocean, was landlocked in the north; or whether, like the Atlantic, it ran into a barrier of islands and pack ice; or whether there existed, between Asia and America, a stretch of open water, which might give access to a passage round or through North America – the strait whose Atlantic opening had been sought, so long and unsuccessfully, by English explorers.

Of the thousands of islands that dot the Pacific between the Equator and the Tropic of Capricorn, very few were known. At first sight, this is a little surprising; a number of exploring expeditions had crossed the ocean in tropical latitudes in the sixteenth and seventeenth centuries. But the islands were tiny crumbs of land in the great expanse of water which surrounded them; they were easily missed, even by ships on the right track for discovery. Once discovered, moreover, they tended to disappear, since their longitude could not be fixed, their latitude was not always fixed accurately, and subsequent navigators could not find them. The Solomon Islands were a famous example. Tasman, sailing north from New Zealand in 1643, had passed through the Tonga and Fiji groups; but his reports – which the Dutch company made no effort to conceal – were little help to his successors. East of Tonga, there had been no sightings of importance, only inconsiderable atolls. The reason for this was not simply ill-luck, but the inexorable pressure of the winds. Most exploring expeditions had entered the Pacific from the west, either round Cape Horn, or through Magellan's Strait, or sailing from the port of Callao. Finding difficulty in making headway against the prevailing westerlies, they had all reached far to the north, in some instances beyond the Equator, in search of a favourable wind for their westing. Except New Zealand and Hawaii, most of the important Polynesian groups lie between 10°S and the Tropic of Capricorn. The explorers, from Magellan onwards, had made their crossings too far north.

South of the Tropic of Capricorn was another, still vaster, area of ignorance. No one knew certainly, even, whether the space between New Zealand and Chile was mainly land or mainly sea. There were grounds for thinking that much of it might be land. The notion of a southern continent had a respectable antiquity. Ortelius had given it a conjectural shape on the map, various explorers in the southern oceans – not only in the Pacific – claimed to have sighted its capes and headlands; but in the Atlantic and Indian Oceans its northern coast, if it existed at all, must lie far to the south, whereas in the Pacific there was ample room in the area of ignorance for a great continental land mass, thrusting north to the southern Tropic. The Dutch, when they first became aware of the continent now called Australia, had often referred to that as the Great Southland. Tasman, however, by circumnavigating it, albeit far offshore, had proved that New Holland was not part of *Terra Australis*; or rather, it was *Terra Australis Cognita. Terra Australis Incognita* must be separate, further to the east; New Zealand, which Tasman discovered, might be part of it; so might the land which Juan Fernández claimed to have seen in 1563, west of the islands which bear his name; or the 'long Tract of pretty high Land' – probably Los Desventurados – sighted by the buccaneer Edward Davis in 1687 and reported by him to Dampier.[6] If a continuous coast connected all these places, it would run through 100° of longitude, truly a continental extent. For many years, however, no serious attempt was made to find this hypothetical coast, and the problem remained to intrigue the geographers and challenge the explorers of the eighteenth century.

In the late seventeenth and early eighteenth centuries interest in exploring began to revive, not on the part of the great trading corporations, but among private adventurers. First came the buccaneer-explorers, part of the *diaspora* of Caribbean cut-throats, the effect of whose presence on the Pacific coast of South America and in the Indian Ocean had already been noticed. They also visited the East Indies, Australia, and the western Pacific. Discovery was not, of course, their main motive. They prowled off distant shores 'to see what the country would afford us', in Cowley's phrase, and to prey on other people's shipping. Some of them were employed as captains of privateers, by syndicates of private investors. Some made notable voyages, including circumnavigations: Cowley (1683–6), Dampier (1679–91), Dampier, Funnell and Clipperton (1703–7), Woodes Rogers, with Dampier as pilot (1708–11), Shelvocke and Clipperton (1719–22). Dampier was the only one among their number who made any important additions to geographical knowledge. Despite his buccaneer background, he was by temperament a true explorer, curious, critical, persistent and brave. His qualities were recognised; in 1699 he was given a warship for a voyage of discovery upon the coasts of Australia. The poor old *Roebuck* was so rotten that she foundered 'thro' perfect age' on the way home – fortunately in harbour, at Ascension Island – but in her Dampier had sailed between New Guinea and New Britain and so lopped off a large island from the possible continental area of Australia. Of Australia itself he thought poorly: waterless, treeless, sparsely inhabited by 'the miserablest people in the world'. He had not seen its agreeable east coast; that was left for Cook.

The importance of these buccaneer-explorers lay in their articulateness. They wrote narratives and descriptions, some of which were published – heavily edited, with unctuous protestations of public spirit – by the aptly-named Captain Hack.[7] Dampier's book[8] became deservedly popular, and caused the learned and the official in England to take him to their hearts. His reputation, though it 'suffered extremely', as he lamented, by the loss of the *Roebuck*, had already been made by the book. Since the days of Hakluyt and Purchas very little travel literature had appeared in English. The buccaneer narratives initiated a whole new series of *Voyages: Churchill's Voyages*,[9] *Astley's Voyages*,[10] *Harris's Voyages*, the last-named especially influential in its second appearance in 1744–8, edited by the much admired economist, historian and political commentator, John Campbell.[11] In the middle decades of the eighteenth century these ponderous quartos and folios, in many editions, took their place with works of theology among the staples of any well-appointed private library. Both in England and in France, they helped to prepare the public mind for the second age of discovery.

The generation of the buccaneer-circumnavigators extended to the early 1720s; but the leader of the last important voyage of the period (and the last major Dutch voyage of discovery) was not a buccaneer, but a lawyer, retired rich from practice in Batavia. Roggeveen's expedition of 1721–2 was not particularly original either in planning or in execution. It followed more or less the same westbound track as many others; one might almost say that Roggeveen joined the procession. He did manage, however, to cross the Pacific in a slightly higher latitude, and to persist further west in it, than most of his predecessors. He was rewarded by the discovery – besides many minor atolls – of Easter Island and some of the Samoan group.[12] Here he was among substantial inhabited islands, not mere steep-to rocks or half-submerged reefs. Like Tasman earlier, but unlike Wallis later, and most unlike Cook (in the contrast one sees the difference in the qualities of the men) Roggeveen immediately fell foul of the Polynesians. Diffidence, to the point of murder, marked many of the earlier Pacific voyages; it was a difficult habit to break.

Roggeveen had been looking for *Terra Australis*, and although he failed to find it, his reports were to give much encouragement, later in the century, to those who wanted to believe in its existence. There was no immediate sequel, however. Rich men such as Roggeveen, willing to mount their own expeditions, were rare. Men of the stamp of Cowley, Dampier, Shelvocke – rootless searovers willing to take a ship anywhere – were also becoming rare. Most captains with buccaneer experience, by this time, had retired from the sea, or procured naval commissions, or died, or been hanged. The great companies remained either indifferent to exploration, or jealously hostile, according to who did the exploring, and where. (Roggeveen's voyage was vaguely sponsored by the Dutch West India Company, but his ships, like Le Maire's a hundred year earlier, were arrested by the officials of the East India Company when he came to Batavia, and were released only after prolonged litigation.) As for governments, the only other possible promoters, their interest was not yet engaged. After Roggeveen, therefore, came a pause, broken only by Bouvet's voyage of 1738–9. Bouvet discovered the abrupt, snow-capped South Atlantic island which bears his name, assumed it to be part of a mainland, and called it Cape Circumcision: another scrap of bogus evidence for the southern continent.

The next circumnavigation, Anson's in 1740–4, was a foray, not a voyage of discovery. Except that Anson was a respectable naval officer operating against the enemy in a time of declared war, his exploits had more in common with those of Drake than with those of Byron or Bougainville. Though the voyage added little to knowledge, however, it was of great indirect importance in the story of Pacific exploration. It was ably reported[18] and attracted much attention. It quickened Spanish fears, English hopes, French emulation. It reminded governments of commercial possibilities on the Pacific coasts, east and west. It demonstrated the feasibility, and the problems, of naval operations in the Pacific. It emphasised the importance of bases near the entrances to the Pacific, preferably island bases, where, without revealing their unwelcome presence to the Spanish authorities, fleets could refresh, and so avoid the appalling losses which Anson's people had suffered, from scurvy. These were arguments which any admiralty could appreciate. Upon them, the enthusiasts for the southern continent, the advocates of exploration in general, the geographers, naturalists and astronomers, succeeded in grafting their own far-reaching plans and theories.

Between Anson's return to England in 1744 and Cook's in 1775, there appeared a number of very able works summarising the evidence for southern continents and islands, and urging action. They were distinct from the popular collection of *Voyages* (being designed to persuade rather than amuse) but naturally not entirely unconnected. One, indeed, was Campbell's introduction to *Harris's Voyages*, in the 1744 edition.[14] Campbell wanted the east coast of New Holland–New Guinea explored. He believed, on Quiros' evidence, that it must produce spices and other precious commodities, and he advocated a settlement in Dampier's New Britain to exploit the trade. He also thought that the South Sea Company should justify its name by opening a new trade in slaves from New Guinea to Chile and Peru. For this, a base and port of call would be needed, at Juan Fernández. If, as Campbell thought likely, there was yet another southern continent, *incognita*, and if it proved inhabited and productive, then Juan Fernández would be handy for that trade too. He had a low opinion of Spanish imperial government,[15] and expected no serious opposition. Campbell was an orthodox mercantile economist, much respected in the City, certainly no visionary, and his words carried weight. His pamphlet, however (for so, in effect, it was) dealt only with one aspect of exploring purpose. Charles de Brosses, the French lawyer-geographer-*philosophe*, produced in his *Histoire des Navigations*[16] a work more widely representative of the age. De Brosses was concerned not only with trade (which, however, he did not despise) but with the extension of knowledge and with a French mission to promote civilised intercourse. He believed firmly in the existence of an inhabited southern continent, and set out arguments based not only on the evidence of voyages, but upon theoretical necessity. For men who saw the universe as an immense, beautifully designed, delicately balanced piece of machinery, who sought in geography a satisfaction both rational and aesthetic, a southern continent *was* a necessity. The preliminary steps which de Brosses recommended for the discovery of *Terra Australis* were similar to those suggested by Campbell: a settlement in New Britain, a base at Juan Fernández. (Like Campbell, he took no account of Spanish objections. In fact, the Spaniards, Family Compact notwithstanding, objected to French settlers almost as much as to English pirates, and decided at the end of the Austrian Succession War to fortify Juan Fernández themselves. When Carteret's *Swallow* struggled in there, desperate for refreshment, in 1767, he was warned off, and had to go on to Más Afuera, further west.)

De Brosses' book appeared in 1756, at the outset of the Seven Years War, so that its practical influence was delayed. It was taken very seriously; Cook had a copy with him in 1768. Its theories were spread widely in England by Callander,[17] who appropriated de Brosses' argument, without acknowledgment, and applied them to England instead of France. Callander's brazen piece of piracy (he plagiarised Campbell as well as de Brosses) was eloquent in the manner of the time, and proved popular, but it did not become the standard English statement of southern continent theory. It was superseded by the far more learned, more confident, and equally unrealistic exposition of Alexander Dalrymple. Dalrymple was an unlucky man; he had the misfortune to be overshadowed by genius, and he took it hardly. He may be convicted of self-conceit, of intellectual indiscipline; but he was neither a fool nor a charlatan. He was an assiduous collector and publisher of charts. He studied the record of Pacific exploration with a close attention almost unrivalled in his day. When he returned to England from the East in 1765 he had been five years in the service of the East India Company, and had made his own voyage of discovery, or of investigation and commercial diplomacy, to the Sulu Islands. He had served, for a short time, as governor of captured Manila. He was the initiator of the policy whereby the British sought to establish themselves in north Borneo and the southern

Philippines, to outflank the Dutch and the Spaniards, to create a chain of factories linking their establishments in India commercially with the south China coast.[18] These schemes of commercial imperialism produced little result in Dalrymple's own day, though some of them were successfully pursued later. Beyond all this, Dalrymple was passionately dedicated to the promotion of discovery. He was seriously considered by the Royal Society for the task of observing the 1769 transit of Venus in the South Seas, which was the first purpose of Cook's first voyage; but he wanted to command the ship, which the Admiralty, very properly, would not consider; so Cook was commissioned to make the observation, as well as commanding the ship. Dalrymple, in bitter disappointment, set to work to write and publish his views on the southern continent. He was convinced of its existence, partly on theoretical grounds similar to those of de Brosses, but even more by the numerous reports of land sighted by explorers, which he strung together, so to speak, to make a coastline. His assumption of a settled population, 50,000,000 or more, was pure speculation; but the coastline itself was not implausible. The dozens of islands which had been sighted did suggest a continental shelf. Dalrymple and his contemporaries were not to know that the south Pacific presented an unusual phenomenon: a deeply submerged sea-floor throwing up thousands of towering peaks, some of whose summits appeared above the water-line. It is a curious feature of a second age of discovery that the optimism, the confidence, emanated from the theorists, the scepticism from the practical explorers. Bougainville's celebrated dictum was the classic expression of that scepticism: 'Je tombe d'accord que l'on conçoit difficilement un si grand nombre d'îles basses et de terres presque noyées, sans supposer un continent qui en soit voisin. Mais la Géographie est une de faits. . . .'[19] Dalrymple's large work[20] appeared in complete form in 1771, the same year as Bougainville's. In the following year, Cook sailed on his second voyage of exploration, the great voyage which was to sink *Terra Australis* in the waters of the Pacific. Dalrymple's career, after this humiliation, was not undistinguished. He served again in India, as a member of the Madras council; and in 1795 he became the first Hydrographer to the Navy. In neither employment, however, was he much concerned with original discovery. In that field, facts had proved his undoing.

The second age of discovery – the systematic exploration of the Pacific by naval officers and scientists in concert – followed without pause on the end of the Seven Years War, and ran on through and beyond the War of American Independence. It was, indeed, the transference to a relatively peaceful field, of the rivalries of war; an affair of governments, with the collaboration of learned societies, not mainly of commercial companies or private adventurers. For the French, the Pacific offered hope of compensation for their great losses in America. For the British, too, though they had suffered no losses, the Pacific might compensate for disappointment in America. The West Indies were less profitable, relatively, than they had been; and in North America victory seemed to be producing nothing but trouble, resentment and expense. There was a tendency, among some influential people, to shift their interest and their hopes from an empire of plantations in the West to an empire of trade in the East;[21] how attractive, then – how doubly attractive – the proposal to establish contact with unknown lands in the Pacific, not, as Dalrymple was careful to insist, 'with a view to colonising; not with a view of conquest; but of an amicable intercourse for mutual benefit'.[22] To Spanish officials, of course, clinging still to a claim of navigational monopoly, talk of amicable intercourse was veiled menace, and professions of scientific curiosity mere excuse. French statesmen at times found Spanish obsession with the Pacific almost as irritating as English arrogance. Choiseul, for one, was clear that if the English were going to outrage Spanish susceptibilities in the matter, then the French should not be inhibited by their alliance from doing the same. Hence the preoccupation of all concerned, with the availability of bases.

The great series of Pacific voyages began with Bougainville's settlement in the Falkland Islands in 1764, Byron's formal 'taking possession' there a few months later, each unknown to the other, and the establishment of a British garrison at Port Egmont. The dangerous and slightly ridiculous game of Cox and Box played by English, French and Spanish in that windy, rain-swept archipelago, has already been noted.[23] Eventually, the islands were

327

abandoned; but meanwhile the process of discovery went on. Byron had been instructed to search for land in the south Atlantic (where the Falkland Islands were all he found) and then, entering the Pacific, to sail north and look for a passage through to the Atlantic in the region of Drake's New Albion. This instruction he ignored. He sailed across the Pacific as others had done, in the Tropics but too far north for any important discoveries, and so back to England, by way of Tinian in the Ladrones, and Batavia.[24] Byron made the fastest circumnavigation recorded up to that time: a year and eleven months; but this was not what he had been sent out to do. In other respects his voyage was undistinguished. His frigate, the *Dolphin*, was promptly sent out again, in the same year 1766, under Wallis. Wallis' instructions embodied a radical change of intention. He was to search for 'Lands or Islands of Great Extent . . . between Cape Horn and New Zealand'. He was to look for the great southern continent; and momentarily he seemed on the point of finding it. He made his crossing of the Pacific in a slightly higher latitude than Byron's, and having passed through the southern fringe of the Tuamotus – bird-haunted, steep-to, inaccessible – sighted against a June sunset the abrupt peaks of a large island. Much more than an island, it seemed; for in the far distance to the west and south there appeared range after range of high mountains. Banks of sunset clouds, no doubt – a common phenomenon in the Tropics; but they appeared real to the ship's company, so real that Wallis, for fear of being embayed, made for the 'northernmost land in sight', the island, Tahiti.[25] Perilously, the ship nosed through the surf into Matavai Bay, not the best anchorage, but good enough (it served Cook and Bligh after him) and for a month the *Dolphin* lay there, watering, recruiting the health of her men, establishing (after some initial skirmishes) amicable relations with the genial, if kleptomaniac, inhabitants. Wallis made no attempt, on leaving Tahiti, to investigate the supposed continent, to the intense disappointment of one, at least, of his officers.[26] He was prudent, no doubt, to leave the matter for others to investigate. It was customary, on voyages of this kind, to employ two ships; but Wallis was alone, having lost contact with his consort, the *Swallow*, in bad weather off the coast of Chile; he was ill; he wanted to get back to England. Tahiti in itself was a valuable discovery; Wallis had done enough. Back to England he went in Byron's track, to report his discoveries and to learn that yet another expedition was fitting out: that of Cook's *Endeavour*.[27]

The missing *Swallow* had not foundered, though she came near it; nor had she returned home, as she might justifiably have done. She was a leaky, unhandy tub of a ship, and should never have been employed in such service; but her captain, Carteret, was an outstanding officer, endowed with the explorer's quality which Byron and Wallis lacked, a tough pertinacity, a refusal to leave soluble problems unsolved. In a stormy and difficult Pacific crossing, constantly trying to make southing, constantly pressed north by the wind, he cast about systematically for all the lands alleged to have been sighted near his track: Davis' land he effectively removed from the map, he discovered Pitcairn, for what it was worth; passed several hundred miles south of Tahiti – no continent there; rediscovered Quiros' Santa Cruz; sailed through the Solomon Islands without recognising – since they were far to the west of Mendaña's reported position – what he had done; discovered and sailed through the strait which separates New Ireland from New Britain; sighted and named the Admiralty Islands; patched up his crazy ship, as best he could, at Bonthain in Celebes (despite the hostility of the Macassar Dutch), at Batavia and at the Cape; and anchored at Spithead in May 1769, a year after Wallis' return, nine months after Cook's departure. His voyage was a triumph of courage and professional ability, with very inadequate means.[28]

The *Swallow*, on her run home through the Atlantic, was overhauled and spoken by Bougainville's *Boudeuse*, also returning from a voyage of Pacific exploration: the French retort to British adventures and Spanish possessiveness in that region. Bougainville had gone out to the Falkland Islands for the third time in 1767 to hand over to the Spaniards, and had sailed on into the Pacific early in the following year, with a permission which the Spanish government, little as they liked it, could hardly in the circumstances refuse. His ships, a frigate and a storeship, were naval vessels and his instructions, similar to Wallis' but broader in scope, emanated from the Ministry of Marine. He himself, by training a soldier, whose only knowledge of navigation had been acquired by reading, and as a passenger on earlier voyages, held for this voyage the temporary rank of *capitaine de vaisseau*. His officers, who included several competent navigators, do not seem to have resented this arrangement; an interesting comment on the relatively non-professional character of the French navy at the time. Bougainville was the first of the explorer-commanders to take a team of scientists with him: Verron the astronomer and Commerson the botanist, both distinguished men, recommended respectively by de Brosses and Buffon. With him also went the prince of Nassau-Siegen, apparently for the adventure. The problem of fitting civilian specialists into the daily life of warships was a difficult one, requiring the experience of many voyages to work out the appropriate conventions and routine. The eccentricities of Bougainville's passengers – the prince's propensity for duelling, Commerson's crotchety humours and his transvestite 'valet' – provoked now quarrels, now episodes almost of farce; but Bougainville was a tactful man as well as a brave and intelligent one, and the voyage as a whole was very ably conducted.[29]

Bougainville's track from Cape Pillar followed closely that of Wallis. Like Wallis he found Tahiti, though he used a different anchorage; and like Wallis, he 'took possession', though the formal act had no immediate consequence (it was not until 1843 that a French naval force actually occupied the island). Bougainville's name is intimately associated with Tahiti. His bust, not Wallis', decorates the Qua Bir-Hackeim on the Papeete waterfront. More than any of his contemporaries he appreciated the symbolic significance of this beautiful, fragile island, the hold which it would exert on the imagination of Europeans for a hundred years and more. He was enchanted by the Tahitians, those not-so-simple children of nature, and they seem to have liked him. Perhaps his Canadian experience helped him in dealing with the 'Indians' of the Pacific islands. His appreciation was classically expressed in the name he gave the place. British explorers dutifully and decorously called the group, of which Tahiti forms a part, the Society Islands. For Bougainville, Tahiti was Nouvelle Cythère. Yet he was only there two weeks. He sailed on west, keeping approximately in 15°S, through the Samoan group, through the New

Hebrides, Quiros' Australia del Espíritu Santo, where he contrasted the disagreeable Melanesians with the idyllic people of Nouvelle Cythère, on west, further west than any predecessor had sailed in that latitude, till the breakers on the outliers of the Great Barrier warned him to alter course; then north-east, through the Solomons (which, like Carteret, he failed to recognise for what they were), through the Louisiades, covered then as now with a cloud of birds like swirling smoke, to New Britain (where he found traces of Carteret's landing, but no refreshment), round outside New Ireland, to Batavia and so home, in the spring of 1769.

These four voyages, plotted on the chart, reveal more similarities than differences. Each consisted, in essence, of a diagonal crossing of the Pacific, east to west, in latitudes where the prevailing winds favoured such a course. The great expanses further south in which a new continent might be found, in the latitudes of New Zealand and beyond, remained unknown. The barrier of the south-east wind, which had penned Bougainville and the rest within the tropical latitudes of the central Pacific, was penetrated (and not that barrier only) by the determination, skill and intelligence of Cook.[30] Cook was the central figure of the second age of discovery, the very type of maritime explorer in the Age of Reason, a man so singularly fitted by training and temperament for the tasks he was called on to perform, as to suggest a conspiracy of fate. Consider his early training: his time in the coal trade gave him a knowledge of coastal pilotage far more intimate than most naval officers had opportunity to acquire; the shoals between Thames and Humber were his preparation for the Barrier Reef. His five years of charting in the St Lawrence made him an expert and accurate navigator and marine surveyor; Newfoundland prepared him for New Zealand. All this, of course, was in addition to the routine professional skills of a man who served seven years as mate and master in ships of the Line engaged in naval operations.

Cook's varied experience and solid professional ability were well known at the Admiralty before his appointment to the *Endeavour*. Their lordships could not know, of course, of his superb power of command in crisis (he had never before commanded a ship of any size); his remarkable capacity for intellectual development; his sternly disciplined habits of thought and conduct. One may contrast him, in this last respect, with Byron and Wallis, both of whom had a short way with instructions, once beyond their lordships' reach; Cook took his instructions literally, and never departed from them, except to do more than was demanded of him. These qualities appeared on the *Endeavour* voyage. Palliser may have guessed at them before. Cook was fortunate in the senior officials with whom he had to deal; Palliser early recognised his ability and Sandwich became his firm friend. He was fortunate, as we have seen, in his ships, his stores, his equipment. He was fortunate, on all three voyages, in his officers; not all picked men by any means (at least not all picked by Cook) but enthusiastic, competent and loyal. Some of them had had previous exploring experience; most were capable of learning from Cook; some – Riou, Bligh, Vancouver – later became famous in their own right. He was fortunate in his scientist companions, at least on the first voyage. Banks, a spoilt child of fortune, could be ungracious and petulant on occasion, Solander irresponsible; but both were men of real distinction, and much easier to get on with than Commerson and the prince of Nassau-Siegen. Daily talk with them in the great cabin of the *Endeavour* formed part of Cook's own education. Finally, Cook was fortunate in the conjuncture of events at the time he sailed. Hopes were running high. Dalrymple had just completed his first, his shorter book on the southern continent,[31] and magnanimously gave Banks a pre-publication copy for the voyage. Wallis had just returned, with his report of Tahiti and of the supposed continental peaks to the south of it. Cook saw that in order to overcome the difficulties of exploring the south Pacific it was essential to have a base where a ship could refresh and wait, for months if need be, for the right wind and weather to make the necessary southing. Tahiti would serve this need. Tahiti, moreover, would be a suitable place from which to observe the transit of Venus in June 1769 – the first task and the ostensible purpose of the expedition.

So to Tahiti the *Endeavour* sailed, by an almost direct north-westerly course from Cape Horn (so, incidentally, pushing back by some hundreds of miles the possible continental coast). She lay

three months at Tahiti, her scientists observing, examining, specu-
lating, describing, her company emparadised. Venus observed, not
very successfully (through no fault of the observers), Cook then
embarked on the secret part of his instructions. He was to sail
south in search of Wallis' mountainous coast. If he found no land,
he was to turn west in latitude 40°S. In that latitude he should
encounter the east coast of New Zealand, perhaps a peninsula of
Terra Australis, whose west coast Tasman had roughly explored
more than a hundred years before. Cook spent six months in a
coastal survey of the two great islands and the strait separating
them, which bears his name; survey which, despite its rapidity and
the bad weather which hampered it, has amazed by its accuracy
all later hydrographers who have studied it. There were psychological difficulties: it is curious how tenaciously, passionately even,
Cook's companions, especially Banks – that cultivated representative of a supposedly sceptical age – clung to their belief in New
Zealand as a peninsula. The survey, however, settled the matter;
and with it, the assigned tasks of the voyage were completed. Cook
could choose his return route, either by Cape Horn, or by the East
Indies and the Cape of Good Hope. The dangers of a southern
winter at sea in a high latitude, and the state of his rigging, determined his choice; but characteristically he assigned himself an
immense additional task: to make a great detour to the west on his
way, to locate and examine the unknown eastern coast of New
Holland and to follow it north. Cook did not, of course, discover
Australia; he did discover that Australia was not mere desert, that
its coastal lands on the east were habitable, agreeable even, and
full of scientific interest. In regard of practical consequences, New
South Wales was perhaps the most important of all his discoveries.
His determination to 'keep the Main land on board in our rout to
the northward' led him to enter the terrifying labyrinth of the Barrier Reef, and later to confirm the existence, so long doubted or suspected, of Torres' Strait. So to Batavia, where dysentery and malaria devastated the health of a ship's company whom scurvy –
thanks to Cook's care in victualling – had failed to touch. And so
home, in July 1771, to national fame; though in the gossiping
world of amateur science much of the fame attached itself to
Banks rather than to Cook.[32]

333

The Admiralty knew better. They decided at once upon a second voyage, and considered nobody but Cook to command it. This voyage called for a new and larger strategy of exploration. It was now clear that in the Pacific, the southern continent nowhere projected north of 40°S. In the Atlantic the situation was less clear, and there Bouvet's 'Cape Circumcision', in 54°S, called for investigation. Cook therefore proposed a complete circumnavigation of the southern hemisphere in a high latitude. To take advantage of prevailing winds, the voyage would have to be east-about, from the Cape of Good Hope. The high-latitude crossing of the Indian Ocean and the Pacific should be made in summer weather, and would therefore have to be interrupted by hauls to the north each winter, so that the ships could wood, water and refresh in 'the more Hospitable latitudes'. For this, reliance could not be placed on casual supplies from islands in the track; even more than on the *Endeavour* voyage, known and reliable bases would be needed. The experience of the *Endeavour* voyage determined the choice: Queen Charlotte Sound in New Zealand, and Tahiti. There were to be two ships; the providential lump of coral that stuck in the *Endeavour's* side, like a bung, on the Barrier Reef, had lodged also in Cook's mind.

Cook's proposals became, in effect, his instructions. *Resolution* and *Adventure* left Plymouth for the Cape in July 1772; *Resolution* anchored at Spithead three years later. The whole voyage was a triumph, imaginative in planning, meticulous in preparation, brilliant in execution – except, indeed, in one particular, that failure to keep company, which plagued so many of these eighteenth-century voyages. Furneaux' *Adventure* twice lost contact, and returned to England a year ahead of Cook. *Resolution* carried out in full the intended circumnavigation between 50° and 60°S; and much more. Cook made five great sweeps away from his mean track. Three were to the south, one in the Atlantic and Indian Ocean, two in the Pacific, all three to the edge of the Antarctic ice, one to 70° 10'S, less than a hundred miles from the real Antarctic continent. The other two were winter cruises in the Tropics. The first, in 1773, from New Zealand to the Tuamotus, Tahiti, Tonga, and back to New Zealand, was in waters already roughly explored, though it yielded a great deal of new information. The second, in 1774, was in itself a distinguished voyage of discovery: due north from the Antarctic to Easter Island; then Marquesas, Tahiti, Niue, Tonga, the New Hebrides, New Caledonia, and finally to the agreeable Norfolk Island (whose subsequent history was to be far from agreeable); then to New Zealand, for a month's rest before the long haul east to Cape Horn and the final probe into the Atlantic–Antarctic, where Cook, in the vilest of weather, had to give Cape Circumcision–Bouvet Island the benefit of the doubt. It is sometimes said that this staggering voyage yielded chiefly negative results; but the results of the second tropical sweep were highly positive. Cook had Dalrymple's two-volume *Historical Collection* with him, and everywhere he went one can see the uncritically recorded discoveries of a dozen earlier voyages either dissolving into sea and air, or else solidifying into confirmed islands plotted upon the chart. West of Tonga, moreover, Cook left the slightly known world of Polynesia for the almost totally unknown world of Melanesia, and here he became once more discoverer rather than verifier. In the great island-studded area which he called New Hebrides, he found time for a running survey comparable with his earlier and more famous charting of New Zealand. Yet in regard to its main purpose, the achievement of the voyage *was* negative, triumphantly and conclusively so. There was no inhabited southern continent. A continent there might be – else how did millions upon millions of tons of fresh-water ice cave into the sea? – but if it existed, it lay inaccessible, uninhabitable, behind the ramparts of the ice.

During Cook's absence another major and perennial problem of geography had once more claimed the attention both of the Admiralty and of the Royal Society: the North-West Passage. English interest in the search for a passage, dormant for many years, had revived after the Treaty of Utrecht and become concentrated upon Hudson's Bay. The Hudson's Bay Company was required by its charter to prosecute the search. As a prospering commericial concern it was reluctant to spend money on exploration not directly concerned with its own trade; and as a monopolist it was inclined to discourage the explorations of others. Its captains, however, possessed the only first-hand knowledge of the intricacies of the bay; its factories were the only, the indispensable, winter bases; and its charter made it vulnerable to public accusations of obstruction, especially after 1745, when a £20,000 reward was offered by act of parliament for the discovery of a navigable passage. The company, therefore, allowed itself to be prodded into grudging collaboration with the Admiralty and with private groups, and even into some half-hearted investigations of its own. The seaborne expeditions[33] which, in the 1720s, '30s and '40s, searched the north-western shores of the bay found no outlet, because in that quarter none existed. Hopes of its existence were based, indeed, on very flimsy evidence: on casual observations of tidal flows in the bay, and on sundry reports of discoveries, by apocryphal Spanish expeditions, of 'straits' leading from the Pacific coast north of California, through to Hudson's Bay. One of Byron's tasks, which he neglected, was to investigate the basis of these yarns. They had no firm basis, and were discredited in 1767 by a company's servant, Samuel Hearne, who set out overland from Fort Churchill north-west to investigate Indian reports of copper mines, and who reached the shore of the Arctic Ocean at the mouth of the Coppermine River, in (so he estimated) 72°N. Hearne was not looking for a sea passage; but if there had been a passage from the Pacific to Hudson's Bay, he would have had to cross it. Hearne's experience, however, was not wholly discouraging: he reported the arm of the Arctic Ocean he saw to be partly open water, which seemed to confirm the opinion, widely held at the time, that salt water did not freeze. The Arctic Ocean was known – or, rather, was widely and correctly believed, as a result of Bering's voyage of 1728 – to be connected by a strait with the Pacific. If the Arctic Ocean was open water, bearing only fresh-water and therefore seasonal ice, it might be possible to sail through it, either into the North Atlantic, or else by way of a corresponding strait into Baffin Bay. This was insistently pressed upon the Admiralty by the geographical theorists, in particular by Daines Barrington, of the Council of the Royal Society, whom one might call a Dalrymple of the North. Barrington had no practical knowledge of the matter, but much enthusiasm and some political influence; and he was a friend of Sandwich. In 1773, accordingly, Phipps was sent with the *Racehorse* and the *Carcass*, both specially strengthened, to investigate the polar regions of the Atlantic. He was stopped by pack ice in 80°N: a setback, but not an end, for this was much further north than Hearne's Arctic coast – who was to know that a warm current melted the ice west of Spitzbergen? – and there remained the possibility of the Baffin Bay passage. Nothing much was known about the north-western part of Baffin Bay; it had not been visited since 1616; it was worth a gamble. In the following year, 1774, there appeared some encouraging information, or misinformation, in an English translation of von Stählin's account of Russian discoveries in the North Pacific.[34] According to this, the land on the east side of Bering's Strait, Alaska, was not part of the North American mainland, but a large island. There was thus another strait, well to the east of Bering's connecting the Pacific with the Arctic Ocean. Von Stählin was secretary to the St Petersburg Academy and also a Fellow of the Royal Society; he should have been, but was not, a reliable witness. Even Barrington was sceptical; but von Stählin's statements could not be disproved; his admirable, direct and open strait, if it existed, would be a great convenience, and the Admiralty, in its planning, had to take the possibility into account. Matters were in this state when Cook returned to England in 1775. What more natural than that the Admiralty should consult the most eminent explorer of his day about the planning of a proposed expedition? What more natural than that he should, without much difficulty, be lured from the prospect of dignified semi-retirement at Greenwich, to command it?

In the end there were two expeditions. Pickersgill, who had been twice round the world, with Wallis and with Cook, was sent in 1776 in a light warship to search Baffin Bay for the opening of a passage (and incidentally to chase away any American privateers who might threaten the English whaling fleet operating from Disko Island). Current sea-ice theory betrayed Pickersgill; he was stopped by ice in 68°N. (Whalers, in good seasons, often went beyond this, and Baffin, in 1616, had been to 78°N; but any whaling captain knew that the ice moved south in July.) Pickersgill took to the bottle in his frustration, and after his return to England was court-martialled and dismissed the service. So far, then, defeat. Meanwhile Cook, with *Resolution* and *Discovery*, had sailed for the Pacific, going by way of the Cape, New Zealand, Tonga and Tahiti.

During the period covered by Cook's two earlier voyages, a series of French explorers – Surville, Marion du Fresne, Kerguélen – had been at work in the Pacific and the southern oceans, and had made discoveries, reports of which had reached the Admiralty. Cook duly verified the position of the Prince Edward Islands, gave the Crozets the benefit of the doubt, inspected Kerguélen Island and pronounced it desolate and worthless. He touched briefly for water on the south coast of Van Dieman's Land (still 'the Southern Point of New Holland'; the geography of Tasmania owes nothing to Cook). At Queen Charlotte's Sound he lay for two weeks and landed European livestock. In the Tonga group he surveyed and charted, discovered several new islands, landed more livestock – his ships, on this voyage, were floating Arks – and inquired diligently into the local political structure and social customs. At Tahiti he made a discovery of a different kind: that a Spanish frigate dispatched by the viceroy of Peru, the energetic Amat, had made three visits there, in 1772, 1774 and 1775. Her captain had 'taken possession', warned the inhabitants against dealings with the English, and landed two Franciscan friars – the first Christian missionaries in Polynesia. The *Aguila*'s cruise was the last, ineffectual attempt of Spaniards to assert exclusive rights in the open Pacific (though on the Pacific coasts of the Americas they remained belligerently jealous, as the English were to find and resent at Nootka Sound). Nothing came of it. The Franciscans were a timorous pair, who asked to be taken off by the *Aguila* on her third visit. The only traces which Cook found, apart from Spanish pigs, which had crossed with the local breed and much improved it, were a mission house, prefabricated in Callao, and a wooden cross, on the reverse of which he carved a reminder of who the first discoverers had been. Then north and east to find the American coast; but on the way, Cook made a discovery of great importance, the widespread group which he called the Sandwich Islands, and which now bears the name of its biggest island unit, Hawaii. The people were Polynesians, obviously akin to the Tahitians, like them mercurial, genial and resentful by turns, always thievish. Cook, characteristically, wondered how they got there;

but at that moment, the importance of the islands lay in their value as a base, much handier than Tahiti for Arctic exploration. The American coast was nearer, further west, than most people expected. Cook encountered it in about 45°N in March 1778. He missed the real strait of Juan de Fuca, which leads to Puget Sound and separates Vancouver Island from the mainland; nobody approaching that towering coast for the first time would take Vancouver Island for an island. Cook spent a month in Nootka Sound for refreshment and repair, and then embarked on months of coasting, examining inlets and discarding them, making a running survey as best he could in recurrent gales and fog, north-west, west, south-west, until he found the Unimak Pass and could steer north for nine weeks through the Bering Sea and the Bering Strait, into the Arctic Ocean; and there he was stopped by the ice, not bergs, but an unbroken wall of salt-sea pack ice stretching across from Asia to America. Again defeat, then, and defeat by the same enemy that had beaten Pickersgill and a score of others. There was no navigable passage – no passage, that is, navigable by sailing ships. Cook did not deny that there might be a pasage of some sort. We now know that there is, and that a specially strengthened powerfully engined ship can force a way through;[35] but Cook's judgment, confirmed by Vancouver's detailed survey in 1792–5, still stands: if a passage existed, it must be far longer than anyone had supposed, and choked with ice.

The second age of discovery did not end with the return of Cook's ships in 1780. There was still maritime exploring to be done, within the limits of eighteenth-century techniques, and there were able men to do it: Malaspina and Vancouver on the Pacific coast of North America, Bass and Flinders on the Australian coasts, la Pérouse on both coasts of the Pacific, d'Entrecasteaux among the islands. Even those pillars of conservatism, the East India captains, followed the fashion and made their contributions.[36] Nevertheless, there was an air of finality about Cook's achievements, which his successors were aware of. La Pérouse remarked that, apart from the 'Tartary coast', Cook had left little for him to explore;[37] a generous exaggeration, but there was truth in it. Maritime exploration was fashionable, but it was yielding diminishing results, because there was less to discover. For seamen, no major areas of total ignorance remained, except in the inaccessible regions round the poles. The navigators of the last two decades of the century – able, meticulous, brave, as many of them were – were filling gaps in a general pattern drawn by Cook and his predecessors; one might almost say writing footnotes to Cook. Cook was the towering figure of the second age of discovery, as Magellan had been of the first, of the Reconnaissance. In the generation after Cook, as in the generation after Magellan, geographical curiosity began to turn to the land, to the interior of the great continents. Africa was to be the great preoccupation of the nineteenth-century explorers. Vancouver returned from his great survey of the north-east Pacific coast in 1795; in the same year Mungo Park left the Gambia in search of the Niger.

To set Cook beside Magellan is to suggest a whole series of comparisons between the two great ages of maritime discovery. Eighteenth-century ships were vastly more reliable and sophisticated in design than those of Magellan's day, and the ships used for discoveries were usually, though not always, carefully selected and fitted out for the purpose. In the sixteenth century, explorers were sent off in whatever ships happened to be available; one might almost suspect that in some instances, including Magellan's, ships were deliberately allocated to such hazardous service because they were old and expendable. Again, many sixteenth-century explorers were self-taught navigators; some were not even trained seamen. In the eighteenth century most voyages of discovery were commanded by professional naval officers. The second age of discovery, in fact, was marked by a very high level of professional competence. Its captains usually knew, within a degree or so, where they were. They confidently expected, having done their work, to bring their ships and men safely home, and most of them did; la Pérouse was a rare and tragic exception. Of Magellan's expedition, only one ship out of five, and eighteen men out of two or three hundred, completed the voyage, and this was not exceptional. Cook had the advantage of 250 years of steady technical and professional development.

The second age, considering its background of recurring European war, was surprisingly peaceful, much more so than the

Reconnaissance. On only two occasions did exploration bring nations near to war – over the Falkland Islands and over Nootka Sound – and on both occasions the dispute was over a threat to existing rights or alleged rights, not over new discoveries for their own sake. The commanders of exploring expeditions were rivals, of course, as were their respective governments, but they had some sense of common enterprise; they regarded one another with respect and treated one another, when their paths crossed, with guarded courtesy. Something of this attitude was reflected even in the behaviour of governments, despite their conflicting interests, in dealing with the problems of discovery. By Cook's day, discovery had quite lost its connection with buccaneering and privateering, and was even in some degree insulated against the effects of formal war. When Cook left on his third voyage in 1776, war was imminent, but nobody suggested cancelling the expedition. War actually broke out while he was at sea. To capture his ships would have been something of a *coup*; yet only the Spaniards contemplated it. The other belligerents, including the American rebels, instructed their sea commanders to leave Cook alone. His discoveries, they thought, were to the advantage of the whole world, and he, though a naval officer, should be exempted from the ordinary hazards of war. To the rulers of the age of Reconnaissance, such conduct would have been mere quixotry. Even in peacetime, the Portuguese authorities were strongly tempted to make away with Columbus, when they had him in their power, and they would probably have hanged del Cano if they could have caught him.

The navigators of the second age were humane men for the most part, solicitous of the welfare of their ships' companies, judicious and sparing in the award of punishment. Again the contrast: very few of the Reconnaissance captains got through their voyages without hanging somebody. The techniques of discipline, like those of shiphandling, had developed since Magellan's day, and insubordination was rare. Desertion was less rare; Cook flogged recaptured deserters; Cortés had cut off their feet. The same contrast is noticeable in relations with native peoples. Cook died, as did Magellan, in a shore-side affray; but Magellan's quarrel was of his own seeking, Cook's was not. The slave trade, in the eighteenth century, was a profitable enterprise, generally accepted as an economic necessity. Even the respectable East India Company traded in slaves. Yet one cannot imagine Cook or Bougainville blandly proposing, as Columbus and Vespucci both did, to make a profit on their voyages by kidnapping boat-loads of 'Indians' for sale as slaves. On the contrary, they consistently tried, as their instructions bade them, to avoid disputes and bloodshed. They respected, and made their men respect, native property and, so far as they understood them, native customs. They worried incessantly about the danger of carrying European diseases to Polynesian islands. Cook was at great pains to prevent his venereal cases going ashore. Bougainville was furious at the suggestion that his men had introduced venereal disease to Tahiti. Their pains were unavailing; but that pains should have been taken is significant.

Disinterested curiosity was a marked characteristic of the second age of discovery. It may have been characteristic of the Reconnaissance too, but if so, there is little evidence of it in the records. Vespucci and Pigafetta both show traces of it; but for the most part the explorers' talk was of immediate profit, of gold and spices, of free land and docile slaves to till it. Eighteenth-century governments hoped, of course, that discovery would lead to an expansion of trade; perhaps to an extension of dominion, though that was secondary, ancillary to trade. Yet even after Cook's second voyage had shown that the Pacific had relatively little to offer in the way of commercial advantage, there was no immediate slackening of interest. The learned societies still pressed the admiralties to mount expeditions, and the admiralties complied. As for the explorers themselves, they rarely showed much concern with trade or dominion. Some private trade, particularly in furs, was conducted by officers and men in Cook's and Vancouver's ships; but one cannot imagine either captain turning aside from the North West Passage, as Frobisher did, to pursue a dubious gold strike. They did indeed note the marketable products of the places they discovered, and they 'took posssession'; but this they evidently regarded as the merest formality. Their job was to explore, to describe, and to record what Cook called 'Remarkable Occurrences', by which he meant anything of interest, from longitudes and ocean currents to cannibals and kangaroos. They were content to let their charts and their journals be their memorials, with (in Cook's terse phrase) 'the pleasure which naturly [*sic*] results to a Man from being the first discoverer, even was it nothing more than sand and shoals'.[38]

NOTES

1. For the cartographical history of this elusive group, see Lawrence C. Wroth, *The Early Cartography of the Pacific*, New York, 1944, pp. 100–3.
2. Andrew Sharp, *The Voyages of Abel Janszoon Tasman*, Oxford, 1968, p. 311.
3. *Journals*, ed. Beaglehole, I, pp. 390, 410–11.
4. See p. 135 above.
5. See p. 115 above.
6. Lionel Wafer, *A New Voyage and Description of the Isthmus of America*, ed. L. E. Elliott Joyce, London, 1934, pp. 125–6. Wafer was Davis' surgeon. J. Masefield, *Dampier's voyages*, London, 1906, I, p. 357.
7. William Hack, *Collection of Original Voyages*, London, 1699.
8. William Dampier, *A New Voyage round the World*, 3 vols, London, 1697. 2nd edn., 3 vols, London, 1729.
9. Awnsham Churchill, *A Collection of Voyages and Travels*, 4 vols, London, 1704. 2nd edn., 6 vols, London, 1732. 3rd edn., 1744–6.
10. Thomas Astley, *A New General Collection of Travels ... in Europe, Asia, Africa and America*, 4 vols, London, 1745–47.
11. *Navigantium atque Itinerantium Bibliotheca; or, a Compleat Collection of Voyages and Travels*. By John Harris. Revised and enlarged by John Campbell. 2 vols, London, 1744–48. On the influence of eighteenth-century travel literature in general, see G. R. Crone and R. A. Skelton, 'English Collections of Voyages and Travels 1625–1846', in Edward Lynam, ed., *Richard Hakluyt and his Successors*, London, 1946, p. 65 ff.
12. There is no detailed account of Roggeveen's voyage in English. His journal is printed in F. E. Baron Mulert, ed., *De reis van Mr Jacob Roggeveen* The Hague, 1911. See Andrew Sharp, *The Discovery of the Pacific Islands*, Oxford, 1960, pp. 95 ff.
13. See p. 152 above.
14. See p. 322 above.
15. See p. 43 above.
16. Charles de Brosses, *Histoire des Navigations aux Terres Australes*, 2 vols, Paris, 1756.
17. John Callander, *Terra Australis Cognita*, 3 vols, London, 1766–9.
18. Harlow, *Founding of the Second British Empire*, I, pp. 70 ff. See also H. T. Fry, *Alexander Dalrymple and the Expansion of British Trade*, London, 1970.
19. L. A. de Bougainville, *Voyage autour du Monde*, Paris, 1771, pp. 183–4.

20. A. Dalrymple, *An historical collection of the several Voyages and Discoveries in the South Pacific Ocean*, 2 vols, London, 1770–1.
21. Harlow, *Founding of the Second British Empire*, I, pp. 62 ff.
22. Dalrymple, *Voyages and Discoveries*, I, pp. xxvi–xxix.
23. See p. 179 above.
24. R. E. Gallagher, ed., *Byron's Journal of his Circumnavigation 1764–1766*, Cambridge, 1964.
25. H. Carrington, ed., *The Discovery of Tahiti: A Journal of the Second Voyage of H.M.S. Dolphin round the World, under the command of Capt. Wallis, R.N. . . . by her Master, George Robertson*, London, 1968, p. 135.
26. Carrington, *Discovery of Tahiti*, pp. 234–5.
27. Wallis' own account of the voyage, in his journal, was published in a somewhat mangled form in Hawkesworth, *Voyages in the Southern Hemisphere*, 3 vols, London, 1773, I, pp. 362–522.
28. Helen Wallis, ed., *Carteret's voyage round the world*, 2 vols, Cambridge, 1965.
29. The most comprehensive account is in J.-E. Martin-Allanic, *Bougainville navigateur et les découvertes de son temps*, 2 vols, Paris, 1964. Bougainville published his own narrative: *Voyage autour du monde*, Paris, 1771.
30. Much excellent work on Cook has appeared in recent years, particularly the Hakluyt Society's splendid edition of the *Journals*, edited by J. C. Beaglehole, 4 vols, Cambridge, 1955. Professor Beaglehole is now preparing a biography. A good appreciation of Cook as a seaman is Alan Villiers, *Captain Cook, the seaman's seaman*, London, 1967.
31. A. Dalrymple, *An Account of the Discoveries made in the South Pacific Ocean, previous to 1764*, London, 1769.
32. Beaglehole, *Journals*, I, p. cxiii, II, p. xxviii.
33. See Glyndwr Williams, *The British Search for the Northwest Passage in the Eighteenth Century*, London, 1962.
34. J. von Stählin, *An account of the New Northern Archipelago Lately Discovered by the Russians in the Seas of Kamtschatka and Anadir*, London, 1774.
35. The first ship through the north-west passage from end to end was Amundsen's *Gjoa* in 1903–5. Since then there have been several expeditions by different routes. In 1970 the tanker-icebreaker *Manhattan*, with some difficulty, forced a way through. The possibility of commercial use has still to be demonstrated.
36. Parkinson, *Trade in Eastern Seas*, p. 118.
37. M. L. A. Milet-Mureau, ed., *Voyage de la Pérouse autour du Monde*, 4 vols, Paris, 1798, III, p. 14.
38. Beaglehole, *Journals*, I, p. 380.

14

Introductions and Dispersals

After the explorers, the exploiters. The explorers had opened for Europeans a second New World; what was to be done with it? Initially, not very much. The most obvious achievement of the second age of discovery had been the destruction of myths; the navigators had found open sea where there might have been continents, ice-fields where there might have been navigable passages; a series of disappointments. Of the land areas newly revealed to Europeans – eastern Australia, New Zealand, the many islands of the tropical Pacific, the northern Pacific coasts – none appeared to offer commodities immediately and profitably saleable in western Europe. Eastern Australia was habitable, agreeable even, according to its English discoverers, and offered opportunities for settlement. On general grounds of commercial strategy, a settlement there was desirable, to establish British possession; but planned and assisted settlement would be costly; and once settled, what would the place produce that anyone in England wanted? Why should valuable labour be exported, when agriculture at home was prosperous and industry increasing? England had no need of a 'vent' for surplus population; labour was in demand. Ministers, manufacturers, merchants looked abroad, rather, for populous markets and increasingly for supplies of raw material. Cook and his contemporaries had discovered no new populous markets; and of the new supplies of raw material they found, by far the most important was the product not of the land, but of the sea.

One of the most vital raw materials demanded by expanding industry was oil; oil for illuminating streets and factories, oil for lubricating machinery. In the late eighteenth century the chief sources of oil for these purposes, as distinct from cooking oil, were animal. Whale oil was the most commonly used; seal oil was clearer, more economical, less smelly, but was available only in relatively small quantities. In Cook's day the most active whaling centre in the world was Nantucket Island, off the coast of Massachusetts. The Quaker community of Nantucket drew their entire living directly or indirectly from the sea, perforce, since their island was little more than an extensive sandbank. They had long dominated the New England and Labrador whale fishery, and when the northern whale population began to show signs of depletion, had extended their operations to the Brazil Banks and other areas in the south Atlantic, where sperm whales, by far the most valuable species, were abundant. Longer voyages and continuous fishing made necessary the 'trying', the rendering, of blubber at sea, by methods which the Nantucketers were the first to develop. The oil which they produced found its principal market in England.

The War of American Independence was a calamity for the Nantucketers, and at the beginning they declared their intention of standing aloof from the conflict; but this did not preserve their market nor protect their ships from capture by British cruisers. Nor did the end of hostilities bring them much relief. The British market remained closed to them, by means of prohibitive duties on foreign oil imposed by Order in Council in 1783. A few families, with their ships and gear, removed to Dunkirk, and found in France an official welcome but a sluggish market. A few settled in Nova Scotia, where they were welcomed by the local government but were denied, on orders from London, the special assistance accorded to loyalists. A larger group tried to secure, by negotiation, a privileged position in England itself;[1] but neither the government nor the English whaling firms wished to encourage expert foreign competitors within the English tariff wall, and the negotiations failed.

The English attitude was understandable. English whalers had been the original pioneers of the Greenland fishery, but had been ousted from it by Dutch competition in the seventeenth century. Various chartered monopolies, including for a time the South Sea Company, had tried unsuccessfully to revive the industry. It was re-established eventually, in the middle of the eighteenth century, by means of an extravagant system of bounties; but even with this pampering its growth, in the face of Nantucket competition, had been modest. The outbreak of war, however, had eliminated the competition, created an acute shortage of oil in England, and presented the English whaling firms with an opportunity and a duty of very rapid expansion. They had seized the opportunity; and after the war some of the more enterprising among them, particularly the Samuel Enderbys, father and son, proposed to extend their activities to the southern oceans between the Cape of Good Hope and Cape Horn, where vast numbers of sperm whales had been reported by exploring expeditions. The government, though unwilling to extend the Greenland bounties to the new fishery, was prepared to offer premiums and other inducements, and to keep up the barriers against foreign – chiefly American – competition.

There were difficulties. Angry growls came from the dogs in the manger, the South Sea Company and the East India Company, holding the monopolies of trade and navigation west of Cape Horn and east of the Cape of Good Hope, respectively. The South Sea claims, as almost everyone privately admitted, were preposterous. The company was a mere 'money corporation'; it had not traded, nor done anything but husband its investments, for more than thirty years. Its charter, however, was still in force, and chartered rights were awkward things for politicians to meddle with. They could not be shrugged off; they had to be bought off, in this instance by requiring each whaler entering the Pacific from the East to secure (and of course pay for) a company licence. The East India Company was a more serious antagonist. Its directors pointed out, with reason, that whalers entering its preserves might engage in illicit trade; they were therefore highly suspicious of the whole project. Government pressure obliged them to concede the general principle of southern ocean whaling, but over its details they maintained a stubborn rearguard action. They insisted on collecting licence fees (down to 1802) and also upon a geographical limitation of the fishery. Their object was to keep whalers away from the Indian, Malay and Chinese coasts where the company did its business. They succeeded initially in reserving the Indian Ocean and most of the Pacific. Only reluctantly, step by step, were they induced to agree to the opening of the western and northern Pacific to English whalers.

Entrenched rights were not the only obstacles which the English whalers had to overcome; there were practical difficulties also, most serious among them the difficulty of manning. Whaling was disagreeable, dirty and dangerous; it involved long voyages in noisome conditions; and except on lucky voyages, it paid poorly. Even slaving, on all these grounds, was preferable. In a time of expanding shipping and high demand for men, experienced hands could usually choose their berths, in peacetime at least, and they avoided 'floating stinkpots'. On the other hand, whalers did not need many experienced seamen. Tubby, solidly built, under-canvassed and slow, they made relatively little demand upon handling skill, and though they needed large crews to man their boats, they could accept a high proportion of 'green hands'. The main difficulty lay not so much in getting men to work the ships, though that was a difficulty, as in getting men to kill whales; in recruiting skilled harpooneers and boat-steerers, the specialised experts of the trade. There were very few such men in England; whereas in distressed Nantucket there were many of them unem-ployed. Even before 1775 the Enderbys had employed Nantucket harpooneers in their ships. After the war they and their fellow owners, while anxious to have the Nantucketers excluded as rival 'venturers', were equally anxious to have them admitted as wel-come and valuable *employés*. Once again the government – Hawkesbury, in particular – was willing to oblige and able to find a formula, departing so far from the spirit of the Navigation Acts as to allow British ships in the southern whale fishery to be manned by 'Protestant aliens'. The first whaler to enter the Pacific was one of Enderby's, the *Amelia*, in 1789; but her captain, mates and harpooneers were from Nantucket.[2]

The British Act of Parliament of 1786 'for the Encouragement of the Southern Whale Fishery',[3] embodying all these con-cessions and safeguards, proved to be the foundation, for a time at least, of an important new industry, and incidentally a powerful stimulus to further exploration and maritime expansion. Whalers ranged the whole Pacific, calling regularly for refreshment at Tahiti, Hawaii and the Bay of Islands in New Zealand. They cruised off the Pacific coasts of the Americas and there found, in sealing, a valuable supplement to their main quarry. The whalers considered themselves entitled to land and kill seals on any coast unoccupied by Europeans, and they were soon followed by traders, buying skins from the local Indians. This quickly led to international dispute. The Spaniards had tacitly accepted, by then, that their monopoly of Pacific navigation was a formal pretence, but they were still grimly determined to defend their control of the coasts, at least from Cape Horn up to Cook Inlet in 60°N, where the Russians were already established. Matters came to a head with the seizure of British ships and the eviction of traders at Nootka Sound, by a Spanish warship in 1790. This act of force threatened British hopes of a valuable trans-Pacific trade, and brought inescapably into the open the old vexing question of the possession of 'desart' coasts; was it to depend on effective occupation or upon prescriptive right? Behind all this lay the unmentioned British hope of commercial penetration, by diplomatic agreement or extorted concession, in Spanish America; and the equally unmentioned possibility that the British government might, for commercial purposes, promote or encourage colonial rebellion. If Spain could have secured the support of another maritime power, the Nootka Sound crisis would almost certainly have ended in war; but the other powers had their own preoccupations, and the Spaniards gave way. The physical possessions which Vancouver formally repossessed on his visit to Nootka in 1792 were no great matter – a small tongue of land and some huts erected thereon by the fur traders; but in other respects the English made great gains: Spanish recognition of English whaling in the Pacific, and agreed right of access to the long coast between Spanish California and the Russian establishments in Alaska.[4]

While these exchanges were in progress, the newly discovered coasts and islands of the Pacific were being searched for anything marketable they had to offer, and other uses than the refreshment of whalers were being found for some of them. Eastern Australia, for example: though late-eighteenth-century England had no need of a 'vent' for surplus population, it did need a vent for surplus criminals, who were overflowing the prisons and filling verminous hulks in the Thames and Portsmouth harbours. The size of the prison population reflected not so much the prevalence of serious crime (though that was prevalent enough) as the severity of the criminal law, which provided prison sentences for many minor offences. The practice of transportation had, in the past, relieved the pressure on English prisons; but the West Indies had long ago made other arrangements for obtaining labour, and Virginia was no longer available. Here, then, was an obvious use for New South Wales. The establishment of a penal settlement at 'Botany Bay' (in fact at Port Jackson) no doubt owed something to criminological theory; to the hope that pioneering experience might turn convicted felons into hard-working, self-reliant citizens (as indeed it did, in some instances); but ministers, when they reached their decision in 1787, must also have considered New South Wales exceptionally suitable for the use they made of it, because it was exceptionally far away. There were other advantages: shipping was fairly readily available, partly because of interest in Pacific whaling prospects. Some of Enderby's ships earned outward freight by carrying convicts and stores. Whaling prospects also made it desirable to reinforce claims to the Australian coast by effective occupation, and no other method seemed likely to succeed. Probably no one would have settled there voluntarily.

Those who settled involuntarily, together with those sent out to guard them, came near to starvation on several occasions in the early years. A gaol cannot easily be made self-supporting; nor could a gaol 10,000 miles away be permanently maintained, without crippling expense, on government supplies sent from England. Port Jackson-Sydney must become a productive colony, or perish; but time was needed to clear heavy timber, to break rock-hard ground, to raise crops and breed cattle. The colony needed an exportable commodity, valuable enough to attract merchants, who would bring in supplies to pay for it. Sealing, along the coast and on the Bass Strait islands, was the quickest and most obvious way of meeting this need. Most of the capital for developing the new colonial seal fishery was supplied by country traders from Calcutta agency houses, whose ships carried from Bengal live cattle, textiles and tobacco, sugar, rice and rum for sale to the colonists, and returned with seal oil and skins. The return cargoes were mostly taken to Calcutta and there sold, in order to comply with the East India Company's rules; but most of the skins and oil were ultimately intended either for China or for Great Britain. Commericial ties with Bengal were not, for the Port Jackson settlers, an unmixed blessing. The cattle were of poor quality. Rum was the easiest and most profitable cargo; it served as currency in the early days of the colony, and its distribution was cornered by the officers of the New South Wales Corps, ill-disciplined soldier-gaolers, who used their monopoly to profit by the necessities of the convicts in their charge, and of the emancipist settlers. (Characteristically, the governor who tried to stop this abuse, and who provoked the resulting mutiny, was the ubiquitous Bligh.) Firms such as Campbell and Company, of Calcutta, brought to Port Jackson more rum than the colonists needed, far more than their early governors thought they should have. Nevertheless, it was to Robert Campbell, more than to any other single person, that the colony owed its survival.[5]

New Zealand, at first sight, was more attractive than Australia. Its climate was pleasant, its soil evidently fertile; and it offered a useful natural product, in its magnificent stands of tall, straight timber. From 1772 onwards, occasional ships put into the northern bays of North Island to cut spars for their own use, and sometimes a whole shipload was taken for sale to the East India Company's Indian yards.[6] The chief difficulty was labour. The Maoris were willing enough to trade with visiting Europeans, but they soon tired of the heavy work involved in cutting timber and delivering it to the ships. They were, moreover, truculent cannibals, unpredictably dangerous. They had killed Marion du Fresne and fourteen of his people. Sailors ashore on watering and wooding parties were often in danger of being ambushed, killed and eaten, either because they unwittingly violated some *tabu*, or because their ship had outstayed its welcome and the Maoris suspected that a protracted visit might turn into a settlement. From a European point of view, only systematic settlement could make New Zealand economically productive; but the place was even more remote than New South Wales, and for more than half a century after Marion's death hardly anyone seriously advocated such a course.

The islands of the tropical Pacific, Hawaii and Tahiti especially, had been so ecstatically described by some of their early European visitors that they had taken on, for many people, a symbolic rather than a practical significance. They were among the properties of an incipient romantic movement. They produced some marketable products, however: tortoise shell, mother-of-pearl, sandalwood, and *bêche-de-mer* (trepang), repulsive but edible sea-slugs which proliferated on reefs and beaches. In the early 1790s the possibilities of trade in these improbable commodities became known to Europeans, and a small but growing number of English and North American ships entered the business. As in New Zealand, labour presented a problem. *Bêche-de-mer*, in particular, required a good deal of hard work. It was obtained by diving, first boiled and then dried on racks in enclosed 'batters' heated by continuous slow fires. The Polynesians of Hawaii and the Society Islands were more biddable than the Maoris, however, and island chiefs eager for firearms and iron tools, were able to drive their people to work cutting and hauling sandalwood, collecting and curing *bêche-de-mer*, and delivering them to visiting ships. New England ships were prominent in these trades from the beginning, and when supplies began to dry up in Tahiti and Hawaii, the New Englanders were the first to exploit the still more plentiful product of Fiji.[7]

The principal market for the island products was in China, and the cargoes were usually sold at Canton, the only Chinese port lawfully open to European traders. The same was true of furs from the Pacific coast of North America, especially the most valuable of them, the skins of sea otters. These beautiful animals, never plentiful and now exceedingly rare, were peculiar to the north Pacific coast, where their pelts could be procured by barter from kayak hunters. At Canton they fetched extravagant prices. English traders in these precious furs, however, faced the difficulty that they were buying in the preserve of one monopolist the goods which they sold in the preserve of another. Worse still, from the monopolists' point of view, traders who sold furs or island products in Canton would wish to return in ballast to the North American coast or the islands; they would load Chinese goods, for sale in the East Indies, in India, or in Europe, so completing (in many instances) a commercial circumnavigation with a profit on each stretch of the voyage. The British government was disposed to facilitate these arrangements, in order to make the most profitable use of the 1790 convention with Spain. Here, indeed, was something for the dogs in the manger to bark about. The East India Company, ever since the end of the American war, had been under pressure to make larger and larger concessions to the whaling interest. Reluctantly, they had complied, on the understanding that whalers would not trade in the East. Now they were being pressed to make much greater concessions to avowed traders. Naturally the directors balked. They were prepared – so they told the Board of Control in 1791 – to agree to the sale of furs at Canton, only provided that the traders returned directly whence they came. They refused any suggestion that the traders might be regarded as 'country traders'; and in the matter of the 'Europe' trade they were adamant. The utmost concession they would consider, was that the trans-Pacific traders might carry a limited quantity of Chinese goods to Europe on account of the company, acting as its agents.[8] The matter was taken no further. The company's charter was due for renewal in 1793, and the future shape of the China trade was uncertain. Pitt and his colleagues hoped, by means of direct negotiation with the Chinese imperial government, to gain access to some port or ports in north China, and so break the Canton monopoly. Lord Macartney's pompous and slightly ridiculous embassy visited Peking for this purpose in 1793. Nothing came of it all. Macartney's mission was a failure; its only notable result, one might almost say, was Gillray's celebrated cartoon.[9] The arrangements at Canton – slow, confining, corrupt – continued as before. The Charter Act of 1793 made no material concessions to trans-Pacific trade. The maritime fur trade, for a time highly profitable, had a short life. By the end of the century it had passed from English to American hands;[10] the New Englanders in their turn gave way to the traders of the North-West Company coming overland, and dealing chiefly in the skins of land animals. By the 1830s the maritime fur trade had disappeared, and so had most of the sea otters.[11]

Throughout the Pacific the restrictions imposed by the chartered monopolists placed English traders at a serious disadvantage against their New England competitors. Probably, also, the New Englanders, with their small, cheaply built ships, showed greater flexibility and greater enterprise; for them, the Pacific trades were relatively more important than they were to the English; and during the crucial decades they were not involved, as the English were, in a major war. By the early nineteenth century their ships predominated in the island trades, as they did in the maritime fur trade. In the whaling business, in which English firms had shown great enterprise and had won notable victories over the chartered companies, the outcome was much the same, but for somewhat different reasons. The English industry, though it made big profits for about forty years, never outgrew its dependence on alien skill. The British market for whale oil began to decline fairly early in the nineteenth century because of the increasing use of coal gas and paraffin, which were cheaper; whereas the New England whalers enjoyed an expanding, chiefly rural, home market. By 1820 the New Englanders had reasserted their old predominance; by the middle of the nineteenth century more than three-quarters of the world's whaling fleet was American,[12] and English whalers had almost disappeared from the Pacific and southern oceans.

While the British, then, began to settle eastern Australia and north-western North America, each in a limited and specialised way, the Europeanising of the Pacific islands in the late eighteenth and early nineteenth centuries was chiefly the work of American whalers and traders. These men were the nautical counterparts of the pioneers who opened up the American west, like them representative of, probably, the most efficiently destructive society the world has ever known. Their impact upon the islands was one of unregulated private enterprise; there was no responsible imperial government to temper or control it. They did not immediately send the whales the way of the sea otters; that was left for later, more highly mechanised hunters. Nor did the Polynesians immediately go the way of the Mohawks; for neither whalers nor traders settled permanently in their territory. Nevertheless, the loosing of these wild undisciplined crews upon the islands created havoc in the fragile societies which inhabited them. In Tahiti the disintegration of Polynesian life had begun almost with the first European visits. Cook and Bougainville both predicted it, and both correctly identified the principal factors: disease, the familiar battery of contagious diseases, including of course venereal disease, spreading among isolated peoples who lacked acquired immunities; a dangerous dependence on European tools and artefacts and a consequent neglect and loss of native skills; a growing disregard of traditional discipline and contempt for the sanctions by which it was enforced, encouraged by the presence of powerful strangers against whom those sanctions were powerless. Bligh, after his second visit to Tahiti in 1792, reported that whalers were already calling there; the manufacture of stone axes and of *tapa* – bark cloth (the beauty of which Cook had remarked) had almost ceased; many natives had discarded their own graceful dress in favour of cast-off clothes obtained from seamen, and their very speech was mixed with 'a jargon of English'. They had become dirty; many were infected with venereal disease, and the disease was spreading.

Rum and firearms completed the pattern of dissolution. Many Tahitians, said Bligh, were already addicted to spirits. As for firearms, Cook's old friend Tu (Pomare I) had acquired a number of muskets from the *Bounty* mutineers and was on the way to becoming what Cook had mistakenly assumed him to be, paramount chief of much of the island. Both rum and muskets became valuable articles of trade, with which whalers paid for the supplies they needed. A chief's power was measured by the number of European weapons he possessed. Muskets introduced a new destructiveness to the frequent tribal wars, a new and ruthless despotism in the conduct of rulers; and their possession placed a premium on the services of men who knew how to use them and (more important) repair them. Hence the importance of beachcombers – mutineers, maroons, deserters from whalers, escaped convicts from New South Wales; men who entered Polynesian society, who accepted Polynesian ways, who disarmed Polynesian resentment by their initial helplessness, and who often became the protégés of Polynesian chiefs. Many had no other ambition than to lie about in the sun in an alcoholic haze; but there were also beachcomber traders, beachcomber mercenaries, beachcomber politicians, even in some small places beachcomber rulers, all helping indirectly to sap the society which tolerated them.[18]

At the opposite end of the range of European intruders stood the missionaries. The eighteenth century was not a conspicuously religious age anywhere in Europe. Evangelising zeal found little support in official or aristocratic circles, or even in the officially recognised Churches. Neither the Propaganda in Rome, nor any of the Catholic Orders, nor the comfortably established missionary societies of the Church of England, moved promptly to spread the Gospel in the South Sea. The London Missionary Society represented English middle-class dissent; a social group which – apart from some half-hearted attempts in seventeenth-century New England – had never before concerned itself with evangelising in the world outside Europe. The party of thirty-nine who arrived at Tahiti in the *Duff* in 1797 included four nonconformist ministers; the rest were artisans, some with their wives and children. They stood in the sharpest contrast with every other group in the story: with the Polynesians, obviously; with the transient whalers and the raffish beachcombers; with the detached but curious naval officers of the school of Cook; with the fashionable scientific circle of Banks and his friends. They were a brave and lonely group, and their success in evangelising is all the more remarkable. It was due in part, no doubt, to their stern dedication and to their certitude – something solid and predictable in a disintegrating world; but also it was due to their prescience and persistence in securing the support of leading chiefs. Pomare I befriended them fitfully, though he died, in 1803, an unrepentant pagan. Pomare II saw the advantages of a state religion with himself as its patron and protector. He became a Christian in 1812, and had his subjects driven to church by warriors armed with bamboo sticks. The missionaries put a stop to human sacrifice and cannibalism in the islands where their influence was strong, and in this they appear to have had considerable native support. They did their best to prevent the landing of rum and firearms, though they could not deport the beachcombers or keep the whalers away. They tried to diversify the economic bases of island life: they imported English looms, in the hope of starting a weaving industry; they began an export trade in coconut oil; they played a prominent part in organising the preparation and sale of salt pork for shipment to New South Wales, a trade which in the first three decades of the nineteenth century brought in acceptable profits and helped to keep the wretched inmates of Port Jackson from starving.[14] As always, labour was the difficulty. It was more difficult to persuade Polynesians to persevere in monotonous work than to get them to go to church. Church-going was accepted without much demur; though the demands of the strait Christianity which the missionaries introduced – the rigid sexual morality, the modest clothing, the teetotalism, the strict Sabbath observance, the prohibition of 'wanton' dances – placed a heavy strain upon the converts. In many islands the missionaries had their way in this respect, and have it still. They had little appreciation of Polynesian culture, no interest in preserving ancient art and custom. In cleansing Polynesian life of its barbarities, they robbed it of its gaiety. In their way, they too helped to sap the spirit of the people they intended to save.

The overall effect of European intrusion in the Pacific appears most starkly in demographic estimates, rough guesses though most of them are.[15] Cook's companions reckoned the population of Tahiti at about 40,000. The London Missionary Society's people at the end of the century put it at 16,000, and blamed war, infanticide and disease. At its nadir the figure was to drop to 6,000. The decline was general in the area, wherever Europeans traded or settled in any number. In Melanesia it was accelerated, later in the nineteenth century, by black-birding. In Australia, the Tasmanoids are extinct, the mainland aborigines a pitiful remnant. In its effects upon native populations the second age of discovery resembled the first. Both produced demographic catastrophe.

In other respects – in consequences seen from the point of view of the discoverers – the analogy between the two great ages of discovery breaks down. The establishment of maritime contact between Europe and Asia, the discovery and subsequent settlement of the Americas, were among the most significant events in the history of the world. To mention only one set of consequences, the New World made immense contributions to the sources of wealth available to the Old. Mention has been made of the vital part which New World silver played in Old World trade. Tobacco, similarly, was a commercial stimulant of great importance. More important still, in the long run, was the addition of

New World cultivated plants to the Old World food supply.[16] In the later eighteenth century these contributions were developed on an immense and increasing scale; without potatoes, without maize, without cassava, rapidly growing populations in Europe, in China, in West Africa, could not have been supported, or could only have been supported at a near-starvation level. The Pacific area made no contributions of comparable value. There is, indeed, an ironic contrast between the cost, the publicity, the careful preparation, the sheer competence, of the eighteenth-century voyages of discovery, and their relatively small economic results. The newly discovered lands had little to offer. Some of their natural resources were commercially valuable, but soon became depleted by careless exploitation. The Polynesians were cultivators, but their range of crop plants was limited; many of their staples – particularly the various species of *colocasia*, taros or eddos – had spread, at some unknown time, from south-east Asia.[17] Of their native plants only one, the breadfruit, was laid under extensive cultivation, and achieved celebrity because of the manner of its introduction to the West Indies.

The domestic agriculture of the West Indian islands had long depended on introduced staples.[18] Various species of yam (of southern Asian origin, but widespread in West Africa) had been brought in by slavers in the course of the sixteenth and seventeenth centuries, and had largely displaced the native cassava (which, however, had travelled in the opposite direction). The eighteenth century had added eddos, akees and mangoes; the last two intimately associated with the overland slave trade in Africa. Much additional food, however, had always to be imported from North America. American independence produced a food crisis in the islands, and intensified the demand for high-yielding starchy food crops. The Pacific breadfruit had attracted the attention, successively, of Dampier, Anson and Cook; and Banks – become president of the Royal Society, with a finger in every pie – hit on the idea of introducing breadfruit to feed West Indian slaves. In 1787 Bligh – his name recurs at every turn – was sent off in HMS *Bounty* to Tahiti to effect the transfer. He was prevented by the mutiny of part of his ship's company, who had come in the course of a long stay to like Tahiti all too well; but in 1793 he tried again, in the *Providence* brig, and this time reached Jamaica with several hundred rooted cuttings and seedlings of breadfruit and other plants.[19] It was a notable feat, and notably recognised: the Jamaica Assembly gave Bligh a thousand guineas; the Royal Society admitted him to its fellowship; and George Keate, in an ecstatic ode, likened his achievement to that of Jason in securing the Golden Fleece.[20] But what came of it all? Not much. Slaves refused to eat a plant which bore no resemblance to anything they had known in Africa or the West Indies. Breadfruit was fed to pigs for fifty years.

New Zealand and coastal areas in Australia, Australia more quickly than New Zealand, became in time the sites of highly prosperous colonies of settlement. The first merino sheep reached New South Wales in 1797. The immense grasslands west of the Blue Mountains, which were to make Australia the biggest fine-wool producer in the world, were discovered in 1813. Eventually the discovery of gold and other minerals lured prospectors even into the interior deserts. Pastoral and agricultural prosperity depended on cultivated plants and domestic animals introduced from Europe or Asia. Except for New Zealand kauri, neither Australia nor New Zealand had contributed to the world's stock any plant or animal of significant economic importance. Even their wild fauna and flora – peculiar to the region and of immense interest to scientists – were invaded and greatly modified by European species. Many native species became extinct or nearly so; some introduced species, in the absence of their natural predators, became extremely troublesome pests.[21] Both areas suffered an acute ecological revolution. Each became in effect a transplanted Britain, an Antipodean Europe beyond Asia. These developments could hardly have been predicted at the beginning of the nineteenth century. At that time the most obvious characteristics of both countries were their remoteness and their relative lack of marketable natural resources. The magnificent timber of New Zealand (though it was to be extensively, too extensively, cut in the later nineteenth century), was difficult of access and expensive to transport. Much of Australia, as exploration proceeded, turned out to be not only unproductive but uninhabitable. Neither country offered a reliable source of labour; that too had to be imported. Development, therefore, was initially very slow. For fifty years after Cook's discoveries, neither Australia nor New Zealand attracted much attention in Europe.[22] They were poor substitutes for the imaginary riches of *Terra Australis*. In general, the second age of discovery produced more disappointment than promise. It did not divert the dominant groups of western Europe from their long-standing extra-European aims: trade and dominion, mixed in varying proportions, in the Americas and in the East.

NOTES

1. Harlow, *Founding of the Second British Empire*, II, pp. 295 ff.
2. Ernest S. Dodge, *New England and the South Seas*, Cambridge, Mass., 1965, p. 35.
3. 26 Geo. III, cap. 50.
4. For a summary of this episode see Harlow, *Founding of the Second British Empire*, II, pp. 419 ff.
5. M. Steven, *Merchant Campbell, 1769–1846, a study of Colonial Trade*, Melbourne, 1965, pp. 105 ff.
6. C. W. Hawkins, 'To New Zealand for Kauri', *Mariner's Mirror*, LII, 1966, p. 315.
7. Dodge, *New England and the South Seas*, pp. 86 ff.
8. Harlow, *Founding of the Second British Empire*, II, pp. 322–25.
9. Draper Hill, *Fashionable Contrasts*, London, 1966, p. 138.
10. The figures are these:

Years	British Ships	American Ships
1785–1794	35	15
1795–1804	9	50
1805–1814	3	40

F. W. Howay, 'An outline sketch of the Maritime Fur Trade', *Canadian Historical Association Report*, 1932, p. 7.
11. *Ibid,*, p. 14. H. A. Innis, *The Fur Trade in Canada*, Toronto, 1956, pp. 204–6, 262.
12. Seven hundred and thirty-six ships out of a total of about 900. See W. S. Tower, *A History of the American Whale Fishery*, Philadelphia, 1907, pp. 50–3.
13. On beachcomber society, see H. E. Maude, *Of Islands and Men*, Melbourne, 1968, pp. 134 ff.
14. *Ibid.*, pp. 178 ff.
15. On the demographic history of the islands since the European intrusion, see D. L. Oliver, *The Pacific Islands*, Cambridge, Mass., 1951, chapter XIX; and S. M. Lambert, *The Depopulation of Pacific Races*, Honolulu, 1934, pp. 41 ff.
16. The literature on this subject is extensive. See especially C. O. Sauer,

Agricultural origins and dispersals, New York, 1952, and R. N. Salaman, *The History and social influence of the potato*, Cambridge, 1949.

17. On the cultivated plants of Polynesia see W. E. Safford, *Useful plants of Guam*, Washington, 1905.

18. J. H. Parry, 'The Indies richly planted', *Terrae Incognitae*, I, 1969, pp. 11–22.

19. *Journals of the Assembly of Jamaica*, IX, p. 210.

20. George Keate, *To Captain Bligh, On his return to England in 1793 . . .*, London, 1793.

21. T. G. B. Osborn, 'The effect of introduction of exotic plants and animals into Australia', *Pan Pacific Conference*, Canada, 1933, VI, 8. A. Grenfell Price, *The Western Invasions of the Pacific and its Continents*, Oxford, 1963, pp. 195 ff.

22. The French explorer de Freycinet, who visited eastern Australia in 1800, advised his government to seize the place; but apparently no serious attention was paid. See E. Scott, *Terre Napoléon*, London, 1910.

PART IV

Alterations of Course

15

Merchants and Manufacturers

'We prefer trade to dominion'; so Shelburne in 1782, putting a brave face on what most contemporaries considered a grave imperial disaster. This celebrated slogan was not, in itself, particularly original; it was, indeed, almost commonplace. In theory, nearly everyone preferred trade to dominion. The ideal of commercial profit without political responsibility had a long history. The great Francisco de Vitoria, the founder of modern international law, writing at a time when most Spaniards thought of oversea enterprise in crude terms of conquest, plunder, tribute, compulsory conversion and the mining of precious metals by forced labour, had asserted, as a basic principle, that every nation had a right to trade peacefully with every other nation. He urged his countrymen to avoid wars of conquest wherever possible, and pursue peaceful trade, as the Portuguese did in the East.[1] Such a policy would not only accord better with the law of God and the law of nations; it would be more effective in promoting willing conversion, and in the long run it would be more profitable. Vitoria's doctrine was accorded its place among the orthodox European conventions of international behaviour; European governments, while constantly departing from it in practice, usually respected it in theory, or at least paid it lip service.

Vitoria was misinformed about what the Portuguese were actually doing in the East; they were pursuing trade by force. Some three generations later, the directors of the Dutch East India Company had repeatedly to warn their servants there to avoid the mistakes which the Portuguese had made, to refrain from acquiring territory, to confine themselves to trade. Later still, the English company similarly told its people not to emulate the

Dutch, but to stick to trade. None of these injunctions, of themselves, had had much effect; the outcome usually depended not on doctrinaire policy, but on local circumstances. In some places, trade was carried on for many years without benefit of dominion. In China, for example, with the trifling exception of Portuguese Macao, Europeans traded on Chinese soil, on Chinese terms, under Chinese supervision. Dealing with Chinese officialdom was an irritating experience, often enough; the amount and type of business allowed was narrowly restricted; captains and supercargoes had to put up with indignities, close surveillance of their movements, and perpetual 'squeeze'. Eighteenth-century China, however, was far too big, too powerful, too well organised, for Europeans to contemplate armed reprisal, much less the acquisition of territory. The Chinese authorities did at least keep order, and afford protection against open robbery and assault; and the profits, even upon a small volume of regulated trade, were enough to induce European merchants to accept an unsatisfactory situation for more than a hundred years. In West Africa also, in very different circumstances, Europeans traded as strangers, on terms laid down by their hosts. The diffuse and chaotic fragmentation of power on the Guinea coast would have made territorial dominion extremely difficult, as well as unattractive; but in any event it was unnecessary. On several thousand miles of coast, there was room for everyone to trade, without much conflict. The coastal rulers wanted European goods – textiles, firearms, pots and pans – and had slaves to sell. They welcomed traders and facilitated trade, so long as they could, each in his own chiefdom, monopolise it. Ironic circumstance, that this most degrading and brutal of trades should have formed the basis for mutually profitable, even genial intercourse between white traders and black rulers, but so it did, for many years. Most European groups – the Portuguese in Angola were the exception – did not trouble themselves to acquire or govern any territory outside the immediate neighbourhood of their barracoons.[2] Similarly, at first, in India: English, Dutch and French companies for many years traded successfully without any significant attempt to acquire territory. In the greater states such acquisition was unnecessary, and the greater rulers would not have tolerated it. Even among the smaller, less stable principalities in the centre and south, lightly fortified factories with modest grants of adjoining land were considered adequate protection against pillage and local disorder. Not until the 1740s did the decline of Mughal power, and mutual suspicion and uneasiness among European groups, set off a competitive scramble for political influence and territorial dominion. Even then, the directors at home did their best to keep acquisitiveness within narrow bounds.

There were many parts of the world, however, where peaceful trade without some dominion appeared impossible or unprofitable from the start. It was impossible in 'desart' regions, where desired commodities could be produced and trade initiated only by colonising, often by importing slaves. It was impossible in places where local rulers refused to admit traders; or could not, or would not protect them against piracy, brigandage, or extortion by local officials; or, in time of European war, against European attack. It was unprofitable in places which produced only small quantities of high-priced commodities – spices, for example – the market for which was limited. In these circumstances, a very little competition could spoil the market, and only monopoly, the exclusion of other Europeans, could ensure satisfactory profits. So European groups acquired territorial footholds where they could, by settlement, grant or conquest, and used territorial dominion to support, protect and extend their trade.

European statesmen and directors of European trading corporations, in trying to formulate imperial policy in Asia and Africa in the later eighteenth century, were not simply making a choice between trade and dominion, for the two were inextricably connected. The question was rather, how much dominion was needed to support and protect any particular trade. A number of factors, not directly connected with the protection of trade, complicated the calculation. In some circumstances, dominion itself could be a source of profit. The Dutch company used its political power in Java and the Moluccas to obtain goods for shipment to Europe, either without payment, or at artificially low prices. The revenue of Bengal, in good years, yielded the English company a surplus over the costs of administration; the company treated this surplus as trading capital, and used it to buy goods for shipment to

Europe, so entangling trade and dominion still further. Against these more or less disguised tributes in kind, of course, was to be set the cost of war. The maintenance and extension of dominion often involved war, whether against other Europeans or against native rulers. Wars interrupted trade, and could turn surplus into deficit very quickly. The balance of advantage and disadvantage in any particular acquisition was far beyond the capacity of contemporary accounting systems to determine. Another complicating factor was the recurrent difference of opinion between the directors of trading companies in Europe and their servants abroad. The men on the spot were more acutely conscious of weak points in their defences, than were their employers, and usually more willing to pursue an aggressive policy. For the soldiers, hope of plunder was always a consideration; 'loot' was one of the first Hindustani words to be adopted into the English language. In general, company servants, though their basic business was trade, acquired a vested interest in dominion, and nowhere more than in India. It was the political power of the company that enabled at least some of its servants to make fortunes by private trade on privileged terms, by money lending, by manipulating and diverting public revenue or public contracts to private ends. The directors of the company disapproved of these activities, and eventually, under governmental pressure, were to take effective measures to put a stop to them. Neither the company, however, nor the British government, nor any European government with Eastern interests, can be said to have maintained, in practice, a marked reluctance to exercise dominion. They all clung to their territories, and acquired more when they could; but with discrimination, when they thought that considerations of trade or strategy demanded it. The motto, 'Trade with informal control if possible; trade with rule when necessary'[3] could be applied as aptly to late-eighteenth-century mercantilists as to the free-trade expansionists of a hundred years later.

In the Americas similar problems posed themselves, so to speak, in reverse. Nearly all European colonies in the New World had originated in acts of dominion, either by the subjugation of native peoples, or by settlement in 'desart' places. The settlements and conquests had been supported, naturally, in the hope that trade would follow; but the dominion came first, and metropolitan governments had asserted their authority from the beginning. The question for statesmen in Europe had been, not how best to protect existing trades by judicious acquisitions of dominion, but how best to exploit existing dominion to encourage desirable trades. Again there was the complicating consideration, that dominion in itself could be a source of profit. The Spanish and Portuguese governments from the beginning had drawn from their American possessions – often to the detriment of trade – a direct tax revenue which they spent in Europe. Neither English, French nor Dutch governments ever succeeded in doing this, nor did they seriously try; but they did use their political authority, exerted through fiscal pressure or by direct command, in endeavours to confine colonial trade to channels profitable to themselves or to their metropolitan subjects. The various systems which they devised for this purpose worked tolerably well; many individuals on both sides of the Atlantic grew rich by colonial trade; and governments derived a substantial indirect revenue from customs duties. Until the last quarter of the eighteenth century, the right of metropolitan governments to regulate colonial trade was never seriously questioned, and only a few *avant-garde* economists doubted the economic advantages to be secured by regulation.

When, therefore, thirteen of the British colonies in North America succeeded, by their own (though not unaided) efforts, in shaking free of metropolitan control, British statesmen faced a new and dismaying situation, without experience or precedent to guide them. There was no question, in practice, of a choice between trade and dominion. Dominion was lost, and with it a degree of dignity, of 'face'. Lost, too, was an important element of maritime strength. The efficient mercantile marine of the United States was no longer British; might even, in some future war, contribute to the strength of an enemy. Hence the renewed anxious concern of the British government with 'nurseries of seamen': the southern whale fishery, the Pacific fur trade, and (much more important) the Banks fishery. Hence its determination – despite Shelburne – to exclude American shipping (though not, perforce, American supplies) from Newfoundland.[4] But did all this imply, as many believed, that British trade with the United

States must be lost or seriously diminished? Shelburne, in his eccentric but far-sighted way, insisted that it did not; that the Americans, formidable trading competitors in many areas, were perforce also trading partners. Events were to prove him right. The United States, after much argument, acquired a federal government which, despite its cumbrousness and pedantic rigidity, was effective; it maintained order. It was commercially minded and protected legitimate business; its main revenue, indeed, came from import duties. The country depended heavily on trade with Great Britain; no other European country could supply, at competitive prices, the manufactured goods which the Americans needed; nor purchase in adequate quantity the raw materials which they produced. This dependence was to increase, as population increased and moved west, and as pioneer settlement in the north, cotton planting in the south, absorbed energies which might otherwise have been used in building up industries on the eastern seaboard. The United States, in short, offered an example, for some years the only example, of a country outside Europe in which European merchants – specifically British merchants – could trade freely, extensively and profitably, without a European government, or a corporation chartered by one, assuming any responsibility for administration or defence.

What was true of North America was not necessarily true of the rest of the world. Shelburne's dictum could not be accepted as a universal principle. Some Englishmen, it is true, already hoped that some parts of Latin America might go the way of the thirteen colonies, and provide further opportunities for trade without dominion; but more at that time thought that trade under British dominion would be better. Few responsible people shared Shelburne's easy confidence over the future of American trade in general. Fewer still followed him to the conclusion that settlement colonies must, by their nature, demand independence sooner or later, and that no further money or effort should be wasted in establishing new ones. Hardly anyone suggested that existing colonies should be voluntarily abandoned. On the contrary: British colonial administrators, reflecting on the lessons of American independence, concluded that similar movements in other British colonies could and should be prevented, by making colonial government stronger, more efficient, less corrupt and more acceptable to respectable elements among the governed. French, Dutch and Spanish administrators, their natural *schadenfreude* mixed with some misgiving, remained resolute in determination to suppress rebellion in their own colonial preserves.

There was no general 'revulsion from colonisation'.[5] British plans for settling Nova Scotia and Upper Canada went ahead. The delays and hesitations over New South Wales arose more from lack of willing settlers, and from dismay at the cost of settlement, than from doubt of its desirability. Sierra Leone was intended to be a colony as well as an asylum. The Spaniards pushed on their attempts to establish towns and settle people in California, and on the Gulf coast of Texas, Louisiana and Florida. As for the West Indies, their reputation as money-makers stood higher than ever, as cotton came more and more to rival sugar as their most sought-after product. The West Indies, moreover, were likely to gain in commercial and strategic importance, if there should be a rebellion in Spanish America. In the late eighteenth century nearly every statesman interested in colonies still desired, in George III's phrase, 'to have as much possession in the West Indies as possible'.

There was no general policy of withdrawing from the contentious Americas, in favour of more promising, and perhaps less troublesome, commercial developments in the East. Such a shift might, in the circumstances, have been expected. Much had been written about a 'swing to the East' in British imperial policy, in the last three decades of the eighteenth century and the first two decades of the nineteenth.[6] It is true that throughout that period British statesmen, company servants, and independent traders engaged in a persistent search for convenient trading posts in the shallow seas between India and China; that India itself, where great fortunes had recently been made, commanded anxious public attention, especially in 1784–5; that government entertained high hopes of more extensive trade in China. But if there was indeed a 'swing to the East' in those decades, it was not particularly effective, and certainly was not at the expense of interest in the Americas. The official values of British export trade reveal this. Exports to Asia doubled between 1772 and 1798; but so did

371

exports to North America, while those to the West Indies multiplied nearly four times.[7] As late as 1812 the export trade to India was less than half the trade to Jamaica alone. Perhaps four-fifths of British overseas investment was in the West Indies. The Americas, after 1783 as before, were vastly more important in British overseas trade than the whole of Asia. It was not until well into the nineteenth century, when dominion in India was virtually complete, that the proportionate share of Asia significantly increased.

There was no general tendency, in any of the colonial empires, to abandon metropolitan control of colonial trade. There were changes, it is true, in the patterns of control. The Spanish government, after the American war, went still further in the direction indicated by the 'Free Trade' decree of 1778.[8] Restrictions on intercolonial trade were largely removed, except for such commodities as cotton, which Spain needed, wine, which Spain supplied, and bar silver. Duties on all colonial trade were further simplified, even reduced. In 1789 the New Spain *flotas* were discontinued; New Spain and Venezuela were added to the territories covered by the 'Free Trade' decree, so that the trade of all the Indies lay open to the shipping of all of Spain, and the privileges of Seville and Cadiz disappeared. In 1790, the *Casa de la Contratación*, so long an old man of the sea on the back of Spanish trade, closed its doors. Between 1778 and 1790, Spanish colonial trade had multiplied at least four-fold. It continued to increase, and customs revenue to mount, down to 1796. Contemporaries attributed this growth to the influence of the new legislation, to the 'freeing' of trade. There was no thought, however, of going further, of making open concessions to foreign shipping. 'Free Trade' still meant merely permitted trade, and only Spanish trade was permitted.

In England, mercantilism remained the rule; negotiations with the United States and subsequent Acts and Orders in Council slightly modified the working of the navigation system and made some concessions to the special position of the Americans. American shipping was fully admitted after 1783 to the trade between Great Britain and the United States. American goods, but not American ships, were admitted to the British West Indian Islands. There were ways round this, of course; the British authorities were no better able than the Spanish to keep smugglers away from their colonial preserves, when the smugglers had goods which the colonists wished to buy; but the general object was clear: to remove American shipping from the colonial carrying trade. In particular, the 1786 Navigation Act sought to encourage British shipbuilding, to confine British colonial trade more closely to British ships, and to apply more rigorous definitions of 'British build' and 'British registration'. Mention has been made of the use, by both British and French, of colonial free ports as channels of trade with other peoples' colonies; of the special concessions made to favoured industries, such as whaling; and of the progressive reduction of the privileges of chartered companies in the East, down to the abolition of the East India Company's monopoly of the India trade in 1813. These developments, also, no doubt contributed in some degree to a 'freeing' of trade; but they were intended as improvements and refinements within an existing system, not as steps towards the abolition of the system itself. None of the legislative changes in the patterns of colonial trade in this period contradicted the basic assumption, that overseas empires were major sources of profit; that the profit from them was best secured by a system of planned national monopoly; and that in most circumstances effective monopoly required the maintenance of political dominion.

This is not to say that imperial governments in the late eighteenth century had learned nothing and forgotten nothing; far from it. Beneath the general appearance of continuity in the pattern of trade and dominion could be discerned a number of alterations of course, or perhaps, rather, alterations of emphasis, social, administrative, economic, in the general conduct of the major European colonial empires. Three of these changes, very broadly defined, may be selected as particularly significant for the future: the first, a tendency, within the general framework of imperial trade, to concentrate more attention on the export of metropolitan goods, to regard the metropolis less as an entrepôt and more as a specialised workshop; the second, a growing concern with administrative standards, an increasing interest in rational and orderly administration, on generally recognised principles, as an end in

373

itself; the third, a growing sense of social responsibility, an increasing tendency to assess colonial policy in terms of its probable impact upon the inhabitants of colonies, whether settler or native. All three tendencies were affected by the experience of North American independence, but none originated with it. All three were present, in some degree, in all the colonial empires; but all three – and especially the first – showed themselves most clearly in the biggest and most aggressive, the British.

European colonies and oversea trading stations, from their beginnings, had traditionally been valued more for what they produced than for what they consumed. The whole object of establishing plantation colonies had been, for investors, to secure supplies of commodities which Europe could not produce; for governments, to secure safe reserves of strategic materials, 'naval stores'. Thus, British plantations in the Americas produced sugar, tobacco, dyestuffs, all exotic to northern Europe; and timber, tar and hemp, not exotic, and usually in peacetime not economic to bring across the Atlantic, but vital to England in war, when Baltic tar and timber might be difficult of access and fine Flemish hemp unobtainable.[9] Trading stations and growing territorial enclaves in India, similarly, supplied exotic plant products, such as pepper and indigo, and a strategic material, saltpetre; but also, and much more important, cotton textiles. The factory at Canton – not indeed a colony, but a tolerated toehold – supplied tea and porcelain. All these goods, except the strategic materials, were doubly valued as imports into England, because a considerable proportion of them (some after a further process of manufacture, such as sugar refining) could be re-exported to continental Europe. Other Europeans, the Spanish, French, Dutch, who had access to colonial territories, operated in much the same way, though on a somewhat smaller scale and with a slightly different range of commodities, including cocoa, cochineal, spices and coffee.

A striking feature of the trade in colonial imports to Europe in the first three-quarters of the eighteenth century, was the relatively high proportion of manufactured goods involved. Indian cottons and Chinese porcelain were of course, finished goods, better and cheaper than anything Europe could produce of their kind. Sugar, indigo, coffee, tobacco, all had to go through some

374

processes of manufacture in their places of origin; in the case of sugar, quite elaborate manufacture, with important byproducts. France and Portugal (but not England) even imported refined sugar from their respective colonies. The cost and difficulty of importing timber into England from North America has been noted; but English shipowners could and did buy American-built ships.[10] As sources of raw material for European export industry during this period, colonial territories were relatively unimportant: dyestuff, a little raw cotton,[11] a little pig-iron,[12] a little timber, beaver fur for making hats – an 'inconsiderable trade'[13] – these were the characteristic contributions. By far the most important English export industry was the manufacture of woollen textiles. Iron and hardware probably came second, a long way behind. England produced most of its own pig-iron; high quality bar iron, for use in making cutlery, was imported, mostly from Sweden. The English woollen industry was remarkable for its independence of imported raw materials. It imported some of its dyes, but nearly everything else, including nearly all the raw wool it used, was home produced. It was almost the mercantilist ideal: it exported about a third of its product at the beginning of the century, about half by 1740.[14]

In general, the value of oversea possessions as markets for European exports was less obvious, in the first half of the eighteenth century, than their value as sources of exotic supply. In the East, few European goods were saleable. The East India Company dutifully exported woollens, but only in Persia could they find a reluctant market. Apart from silver money and bullion, itself largely the product of Spanish America, the English had nothing to offer India but their administrative and commercial services, such as these were. Similarly with the Dutch in Java. In China neither goods nor services were wanted. As late as 1793 the Emperor Ch'ien Lung and his entourage remained wholly unimpressed by the elaborate trade exhibition which Lord Macartney carried to them. Chinese tea had to be purchased, if not with silver, with cotton and opium from India. It was by participating in inter-Asian trades, not by selling European goods, that European merchants made their profits and paid for their imports to Europe. In the Americas the situation was very different; no sophisticated manufacturing tradition stood in the way of the spread of European goods. English economists often expressed the confident hope that the North American Indians would in time be brought to 'civilitie' and taught to wear broadcloth. This particular hope was disappointed; even the more settled and much larger Indian population of Spanish America had little purchasing power. The European population in all the settled parts of the Americas, on the other hand, grew steadily and rapidly throughout the eighteenth century, and so did its demand for imported goods. Spaniards, Frenchmen and Englishmen sold a great variety of such goods, textiles predominating, in Spanish America, the French through Spanish agents, the English through the South Sea Company or by smuggling. The West Indian islands, with their highly specialised monocultures, imported nearly everything: their slaves, much of their food, their tools – mostly of a primitive kind, cutlasses and digging-hoes – their mill machinery, the casks, or rather bundled hoops and staves, which they needed in great numbers for shipping their sugars, and all their clothing; this last in great variety, light woollens, calicoes, muslins for planters' ladies, and great quantities of coarse cottons and of osnaburg, the linen-and-cotton fustian commonly used for clothing slaves. British merchants provided nearly all the manufactured items for the British islands, the French for the French; though many of the textiles were the product not of Britain or of France, but of India. As for the British colonies in North America, they were the most vigorously growing market of all, a market for straight-forward ironmongery, tools and weapons; for plain durable textiles; and for sundry luxury items, including oriental products such as tea.

All these were goods which Britain was well able to supply; but the market, though extensive, was not an easy one. The Americans, chronically short of coin and with the terms of trade against them, had difficulty in paying for their purchases. They were enabled to do so only by developing their trade to the West Indies in food and timber products, a trade in which they competed successfully with English shipping. Alternatively, they could, to some extent and in crude fashion, produce manufactured articles themselves. In England, cloth was manufactured mostly by a putting-out system, in which clothier capitalists provided the materials, and handloom weavers and their wives worked them up, with their own equipment in their own homes. Many branches even of the metal-working industry were also on a very small scale, domestic or semi-domestic in character. The processes were simple, and could be imitated overseas. The metropolitan government sometimes tried by legislation to discourage this tendency. The Iron Act of 1750 was an attempt to stop the working of wrought iron in the colonies and to encourage, by bounties, the production and export to England of pig and bar. The Act achieved only modest success.[15] As for textiles, government could hardly hope by regulation to control the activities of domestic spinners and weavers in the colonies, whether in wool or in cotton. British manufacturers had some cause for uneasiness, for caution. British exports, predominantly manufactures, showed a distinct levelling off in the third quarter of the eighteenth century; the volume of woollen shipments fell from the late 1750s; cottons faltered and iron goods dropped sharply in the late 1760s;[16] in part at least, the figures reflect the unreliability of the American market. The variability of overseas markets in general had, it is true, a positive aspect; erratic bursts of overseas demand, by placing abrupt and severe burdens on the productive system, enhanced the incentive for technological advance.[17] At the time of the War of Independence, however, this process had not gone very far. Few British manufacturers at the end of the war shared the loud confidence of politicians such as Shelburne and Pitt, in the general competitive superiority of British exports. Merchants – still as a class richer, more influential, more highly regarded than manufacturers[18] – were confident and aggressive in their search for markets overseas; manufacturers in general were more defensive, still more interested in maintaining an adequately protected home market. Great Britain, with its widespread overseas possessions and its big merchant fleet, was already a major commercial agency; an agency of interchange between widely separated parts of the world, between producers of manufactured goods and growers of primary products. In lesser degree the same was true of Holland, France, Portugal and Spain. No European country could yet claim to be a centralised industrial agency, drawing in raw materials from all parts, sending out to all parts its own manufactured goods. In the next two or three decades, Great Britain, and only Great Britain was to become such an agency. Its network of distribution, its machinery for capital formation, its instinct for profit, already existed; technological change, albeit in a limited range of industries, was to ensure the necessary productivity.

The British industrial revolution of the late eighteenth century was mainly a revolution in two industries, iron and cotton. Of the two, cotton, certainly in its implications for overseas trade, was the more important. Throughout its history in Europe, cotton has been intimately associated with colonial empire. All the commercial cottons (there are four cultivated species of *gossypium*, two Old World and two New World in origin) are tropical or subtropical in their range; none grow in Europe; and cotton fabrics made in Europe have often, and in England nearly always, found their best markets overseas. Europeans first encountered woven cotton in Asia and in Central America. Appreciation of its virtues for lightweight clothing, and as a substitute for linen as underwear, spread in the later seventeenth century, when the companies trading to the East began to bring it to Europe in appreciable quantity. In some countries, particularly in France, Spain and England, cotton imports provoked complaints from the established textile industries. In England in particular, wool was part of the national folklore; clothing interests were geographically widespread and politically influential; and at the time when the question came to a head, the East India Company was in trouble with parliament. Hence the 'Calicoe Acts': the first, in 1700, prohibited the import, the second, in 1721, the use, of Indian printed cottons. These Acts were less drastic than they appeared, however: the finer fabrics such as muslins were exempt from their restrictions, and apart from widespread smuggling the term muslin could be stretched; nothing in the Acts prevented the manufacture of cottons in England, or the import of unprinted white piece goods. The company was not seriously incommoded, and the unintended effect of the Acts was to protect a small but growing cotton industry in England. Initially the processes undertaken were limited: the printing of white calico brought from India; the weaving of fustian, using linen thread for the warp, since English spinners could not make a fine thread strong enough for this purpose, from the inferior raw cotton then available to them. Many of the prints and most of the fustians were exported, and much of the Indian material brought in by the company re-exported, to slaving stations in West Africa, and to the West Indies. It was not only through an accident of climate that cotton manufacture was first established near the main slaving and colonial trading ports of Bristol, Glasgow and Liverpool, and that it became concentrated in the hinterland of the last and biggest of these; in Lancashire.

The industry grew slowly, by fits and starts, and only gradually extended the skill, the range and the variety of its operations. In 1775 the import of raw cotton into England was still less than 5,000,000 lb.[19] Some of this still came from the Levant, the rest from the West Indies; not so much from the British islands as from the French, via the free ports. Some of it was even re-exported to France, where the manufacturers had just persuaded Turgot to allow them to buy it. During the American war there was a spurt: 12,000,000 lb. of raw cotton came in in 1782. This was due partly to interruptions in the supply of Indian piece goods, but more to technical innovation. The industry had always suffered from an imbalance between its spinning and weaving branches; handwheel spinning was much slower work than handloom weaving, especially after the introduction of the flying shuttle, which had been invented in the 1730s but became widespread only in the 1760s. There was always a shortage of yarn, and this impeded the growth of the industry as a whole, despite the steady growth in the demand for its product. The East India Company might have helped, by importing Indian yarn; but the same difficulty existed in India – handloom weavers demanded all the yarn they could get. The company, in any event, was a conservative body, set in its ways; it found piece goods easier and more profitable to handle. The balance was tipped, in England, by technical ingenuity; by the invention of spinning machinery, the jenny of the 1760s, the water frame of 1768, which first used rollers and spindles, and the mule of the 1780s, a combination of frame and jenny to which power, whether water or steam, could be applied. Cotton, because of its straight fibre, its tensile strength, and its relative homogeneity, lent itself well to handling by rough and simple machines: much better than wool, which, even apart from the conservatism

379

of a long-established industry, presented greater variety and difficulty, and defied mechanisation much longer. With the introduction of the mule, cotton spinning began to move from the cottage to the factory; the first factories in the modern sense were spinning mills. Weaving kept pace initially not by widespread mechanisation – though a powerloom was invented in the 1780s – but by a multiplication of handlooms. In the agricultural conditions of the time, rural labourers were easily attracted to domestic weaving. Until the French wars were over, clothiers with plentiful yarn available preferred to put it out, rather than to sink their capital in weaving mills.

The processes of the early industrial revolution in cotton were relatively simple. They were British inventions, but they could easily be imitated. Other countries had cotton industries; why was the revolution confined, for two generations at least, to Britain? Why, indeed, did it start there? The internal factors which, in each country, favoured or hampered industrialisation are beyond the scope of this book; they have been much discussed;[20] but it may not be out of place to emphasise again the colonial aspect of the matter, the guaranteed access to necessary raw material and appropriate markets, the authority to decide by administrative action, that this or that crop should be introduced here, encouraged there, prohibited somewhere else. Trade and dominion both contributed to industrial revolution. Cotton was an exotic; its extended use in Europe called for a change in personal habits. Despite growing taste for light clothes in summer and for easily washable underwear at any time, probably no single European country could have offered a market big enough to support an industrial revolution in cotton. The big markets were overseas. The example of Spain is instructive. The progressive opening of the Indies market, especially in the 'Free Trade' decree of 1778, encouraged the growth of a cotton industry in Catalonia, importing its raw cotton and dyestuffs initially from the Caribbean, but after 1789 also from Mexico, shipping its product, the gay prints known as *indianas*, from Barcelona to all parts of Spanish America. The industry was protected by a decree of 1771, which prohibited the import of cotton prints into Spain and admitted colonial raw cotton duty-free. In the 1780s the spinning process was widely mechanised, using imported English machines, including water-driven mules. In 1795 there were over 3,000 small factories in Catalonia, employing about 100,000 people, mostly women.[21] Under protection, the industry throve, but the opening of the Indies ports to neutrals in 1797 dealt it a heavy blow. Thereafter, the French War, British competition, and the loss of control in the Indies, combined to kill it – not stone dead, for it had a home market; but for a hundred years it limped along with little further development. Europe as a whole (with the significant exception of Sweden) suffered a similar setback as a result of the continental blockade. Despite the many leaks in the system, it was turned back upon itself, upon its internal markets and its own raw materials. Britain, conversely, was driven outwards, obliged to seek compensation for its European losses by extending its markets overseas, especially in its own and other people's colonies. For this purpose, at that time, factory-made cotton goods were the best possible commodity.

In the last two decades of the eighteenth century the main obstacle to the rapid growth of the British cotton industry lay not in production, nor in marketing, nor in the availability of labour or of capital, but in the supply of raw material. After 1783 a vigorous search for new sources of cotton began; Brazil, for example, produced considerable quantities; though Portugal, with its own heavily protected cotton manufacture and its own imperial monopoly, made difficulties over exports of raw cotton, and adamantly refused to lower its duties on English cotton goods. More significant, and more traditional, were the attempts sponsored by government, with the enthusiastic help of Sir Joseph Banks, to introduce better strains of cotton from India and Persia into the British West Indies.[22] These efforts achieved considerable success; the West Indies became producers of fine cotton, in welcome quantity; in 1790, of a total import of about 33,000,000 lb., some seventy per cent came from the West Indies as a whole, including Guiana.[23] Probably less than half of this, it is true, was British-grown; as cotton was then admitted duty free, customs officials did not distinguish precisely. So far as it went, this was satisfactory; but demand continued to grow, and the production of a limited land area in the West Indies clearly could not be increased indefinitely, even if – as in fact happened – war was to give Great Britain an opportunity to seize some of the best cotton-producing territories from the Dutch and the French. Serious shortage in the 1790s was prevented by the entry of the United States into the raw cotton trade. In 1792 Whitney invented his saw gin, which cleaned short-staple cotton efficiently and cheaply, and made the cultivation of such cotton by slave labour on a very large scale a profitable undertaking. Regular quotations of Georgia cotton on the English markets began in 1793. In 1800 the United States supplied 16,000,000 lb. out of a total British consumption of about 55,000,000 lb. The West Indian proportion of this greatly increased quantity had declined, relatively, to thirty-five per cent, conquered colonies notwithstanding. The rest was made up from the Levant, Brazil, and, a significant innovation, India and the East Indies. India supplied only inferior varieties, however; its own handloom manufacture still absorbed the best; and the East India Company showed no great zeal in importing raw cotton, grumbling that it was unprofitable. After the turn of the century, the same trends continued, accelerated, because planters along the Carolina coast turned from coarse short-staple cottons to fine 'sea island', so competing with the West Indies in quality as well as in quantity and price; while West Indian production, which was now mostly of long-staple, hand-cleaned and expensive, began to decline absolutely as well as relatively. Neither the 1808–9 embargo nor the 1812 war checked the flow of North American cotton. After the end of the French War, the United States supplied nearly half of British requirements, India and the East Indies a little over a quarter, the West Indies only seven per cent. The total import in 1820 was over 140,000,000 lb. With the spread of powerloom, factory-centred weaving in Britain, it grew at accelerated speed, and so, absolutely and relatively, did the American share, which by 1830 had reached three-quarters of the total need.

In the first few decades of the nineteenth century the United States more than answered Shelburne's far-sighted hopes, not only as a source of raw material, but as a market. They had a cotton industry, but they still bought prodigious quantities of British cotton goods. They had an iron industry too, of long standing, but

382

they bought British-made tools, hardware, machinery, even wrought iron and steel. The pattern in iron was less reciprocal, it is true, than in cotton – the Americans no longer shipped pig-iron to England, because their own industry absorbed all they produced; but from a British point of view this no longer mattered. Britain had its own sources of pig-iron; and its iron industry, quickened by technical innovation, by the demands of war, by the demands of cotton, was growing almost as dramatically as the cotton industry itself. Whole districts in Britain had become smithies, clanging with iron. With such power of cheap, mill-organised production, iron-masters no longer needed to worry about North American nail-making and slit-mills.

Curious irony, that after more than a generation of independence, the Americans should come to fit so neatly into the mercantile pattern, which for so many years they had evaded or openly defied; that slavery and the slave trade, which Lancashire manufacturers were among the first to denounce, should be given a new lease of life by Lancashire's insatiable demand for cotton; that the West Indians, who had served the needs of Lancashire well and adjusted their economy to do so, should be faced with a prospect of ruin. After the war, in 1819, the British government, having in the war years laid a revenue duty on cotton, gave the West Indians a small preference; but no amount of preference could then have drawn from the West Indies the quantity – nor indeed from the East Indies the quality – of raw cotton which Lancashire was demanding; and in price they could not hope to compete. Their share of the British market in 1830 was down to $2\frac{1}{2}$ per cent and dwindling fast. They were forced back to their old dependence upon sugar, and this had become precarious. The long-expected attacks were developing, upon the slavery by means of which West Indian sugar was produced and the tariff preferences which alone allowed it to be profitably sold. How long would government be willing to continue the special privileges of colonies whose economic system was being denounced as inefficient, whose social structure was an anachronism, but whose leading landowners had long been conspicuous for ostentatious wealth? Manufacturers, the mill-owners and iron-masters as well as clothiers, had become a powerful interest, well able on occasion to shout down the colonial and mercantile interests in parliament. They wanted not only cheap raw materials, but cheap labour. This meant cheap food, and West Indian sugar was not particularly cheap, not as cheap as the sugars produced in many other parts of the world. The West Indians settled down to a long and bitter rearguard action against the forces of change, and in time change overcame them. Once the pampered favourites of empire, they became its neglected and importunate poor relations.

The industrial revolution in British textiles, then, had profound and diverse consequences all over the Americas. Its repercussions in the East, particularly in India, came later, but when they came were still more striking. The whole pattern of trade between Britain and India was reversed within a few decades. India, which for more than 200 years had been the chief source of high-quality cotton fabrics for the whole of Europe, became an importer, and eventually the principal market for the factory-made cottons of Lancashire. The most widespread, most characteristic of Indian industries was virtually extinguished. The East India Company, in its commercial capacity, played no significant part in this reversal. Its Indian trade, down to the last days of its monopoly, still consisted chiefly in the import of piece goods to England. The volume of goods handled had increased only slightly over a hundred years. It was limited by the Calicoe Acts, and after the repeal of the Acts in 1774, by the heavy duties substituted for them; but also by the commercial conservatism of the company itself. Apart from the Chinese tea business, the company became less and less interested in its trading functions as time went on. The renewed charter of 1813 abolished the Indian trade monopoly, and drew, for the first time, a much-needed distinction between the company's commercial and administrative activities.[24] Thereafter it must find the money for paying dividends only from its trading profits, in effect from the profits of the China trade; the surplus revenue of Bengal might no longer be regarded as profit, nor used as working capital in the India trade. The company continued to send a few cargoes of general goods (including, even, small shipments of Lancashire cottons) to India, and to import piece goods and raw cotton in diminishing quantities, down to 1825. From that year it ceased entirely to trade in India; its ships took nothing there but passengers, and stores for its army and civil establishment.

The company had to fight hard in 1813 to retain its China monopoly. The abolition of the India monopoly was almost a foregone conclusion; it was easy to demonstrate that for many years the company had done much less to develop the trade than competitive private businesses might be expected to do. The questions remained, what businesses? and what kind of trade? The attacks on the company had been based on diverse, and to some extent contradictory, arguments. Private merchants, especially the big Calcutta trading houses, wanted to enter the import trade in piece goods to England. Manufacturers in England wanted increased imports of raw cotton, and were thinking of India as a market for their own products. Questions put to witnesses, at the inquiry preceding the renewal of the charter, indicate that ministers were thinking along the same lines as the manufacturers: what demand existed, or could be stimulated, for British goods in India?[25] Many witnesses with experience of the country gave discouraging answers. Sir Thomas Munro, who knew India better than most, said that Lancashire fabrics were inferior to Indian, and that Indians would not buy them; further, that in any event most Indians were too poor to buy imported goods.[26]

Events were soon to prove these witnesses wrong. Imports of piece goods to England increased in the two or three years after the opening of the trade, the fashion for genuine Indian goods still persisting – '... but five shillings a yard ... and a true Indian muslin', says Henry Tilney, in *Northanger Abbey*, of the gown he bought for his sister; but only the finest Indian fabrics could now compete in England. The day was approaching when the true would be hard to distinguish from the millmade counterfeit. Imports fell off sharply after 1815. Imports of Indian raw cotton increased, and maintained their increase, though the quantities did not approach those coming from the United States. Exports of Lancashire piece goods to India and other parts of the East began to increase, and continued to increase at an ever-accelerating rate in the 1820s, '30s and '40s, as powerloom weaving increasingly dominated the British industry and multiplied its productive capacity. It was a matter of price; handloom weaving could not compete, beyond a certain point, with machinery. The Indian peasant got his cloth cheaper and bought eagerly; but the Indian handloom weaver, like his English counterpart, was gradually starved out of his employment. Only heavy protection could have preserved the traditional Indian industry; perhaps not even that, for if the industry had been protected, either British or Indian capitalists might well have established cotton mills in India itself, forty or fifty years before they actually did. But in any event, in nineteenth-century India, with a government responsible, however remotely and indirectly, to parliament, and with a parliament increasingly attentive to the interests of British manufacturing industry, protection was out of the question. Any attempt on the part of the government of India to place duties, other than purely revenue duties, on cotton goods, produced an immediate outcry from Manchester. Birmingham and Sheffield were similarly vigilant to preserve their unhindered access to the Indian market. Political dominion, which in the eighteenth century had been used to regulate trade in the interests of commercial and strategic predominance, served in the nineteenth to maintain industrial predominance by insisting on Free Trade.

NOTES

1. Francisco de Vitoria, *De Indis*, Lectio III, § 18.
2. They took no chances, however. Many of the barracoons were formidable strongholds as well as prisons. Some survive intact today. See A. W. Lawrence, *Trade castles and forts of West Africa*, London, 1963.
3. J. Gallagher and R. E. Robinson, 'The Imperialism of Free Trade', *Economic History Review*, 2nd series, VI, 1953, p. 13. See also Bernard Semmel, *The Rise of Free Trade Imperialism, 1750–1850*, Cambridge, 1970.
4. Harlow, *Founding of the Second British Empire*, II, pp. 274 ff.
5. Harlow's phrase: *ibid.*, I, p. 4. Shelburne himself used a similar phrase, referring in 1790 to the Pacific North-West: 'a madness to think of colonies, after what had passed in North America'. *Parliamentary History*, XXVIII, p. 946. But compare Henry Brougham, *An Inquiry into the Colonial Policy of European Powers*, Edinburgh, 1803. Brougham was a rising Whig who later became a prominent anti-slavery man and expressed sceptical views on the value of colonies (or some colonies); but his *Inquiry* is pure mercantilism.
6. Notably by Harlow, *Founding of the Second British Empire*, I, pp. 62 ff. See Ronald Hyam, 'British imperial expansion in the late eighteenth century', *Historical Journal*, XI, 1967, pp. 116 ff.

7. The figures are summarised in W. Schlote, *British Overseas Trade*, London, 1952, pp. 79–80, as follows:

Exports to	1772/73 (£m)	1797/98 (£m)
Europe	5	5·5
North America	2·6	5·7
West Indies	1·2	4·6
Asia	0·8	1·6
Africa	0·5	0·6

8. J. Vicens Vives, *Historia económica de España*, Barcelona, 1959, p. 520.

9. Until 1765 only mast timber qualified for bounty on import from North America to England. In that year the bounty was extended to 'good deals and other squared timber', both for ship and house building, hemp and flax. After 1776, of course, the bounties applied only to British North America.

   They had little effect in the eighteenth century, either before or after 1776. As late as 1802, Great Britain imported only 7,500 loads of timber of all kinds from North America, as against 247,000 from Europe. Napoleon's war, however, sent Baltic prices soaring and permanently reversed the trend of the trade. In 1821 the British import figures were 318,000 loads colonial, 99,000 loads European. *Cambridge History of the British Empire*, vol. 11, 1940, pp. 218–20.

10. See p. 276 above.

11. Between 1770 and 1775 England imported between 4,000,000 and 5,000,000 lb a year, most of it from the Levant, the rest from the West Indies. *Cambridge History of the British Empire*, vol. II, 1940, p. 224.

12. Between 1770 and 1775, about 4,800 tons a year from North America, mostly pig, against 44,300 tons from European sources, all bar. These amounts in addition, of course, to home production of pig and bar. *Ibid.*, p. 222.

13. Hardwicke's phrase. Throughout the period 1700–75, fur of all sorts accounted for less than $1\frac{1}{2}$ per cent of all imports into England, by value. Fur hats were under $1\frac{1}{4}$ per cent of exports. M. G. Lawson, *Fur: a study in English Mercantilism, 1700–1775*, Toronto, 1943, p. 70.

14. Phyllis Deane, 'The output of the British woollen industry in the eighteenth century', *Journal of Economic History*, XVII, 1957, pp. 209–10, 211–13, 215–16, 220.

15. T. S. Ashton, *Iron and Steel in the Industrial Revolution*, London, 1924, chapter V.

16. Phyllis Deane and W. A. Cole, *British Economic Growth, 1688–1959*, Cambridge, 1967, pp. 46, 59.

17. See Professor Lande's admirable discussion of this point in *Cambridge Economic History of Europe*, VI, Cambridge, 1965, p. 288.

18. According to Joseph Massie's estimates in 1760, 13,000 merchants, 7,500 retail tradesmen and 2,500 master manufacturers had annual incomes of £200 or over; 1,000 merchants, but no tradesman or manufacturer, had £600. One hundred and fifty noble landed families had each an income

of £6,000 or more. See E. J. Hobsbawm, *Industry and Empire*, London, 1968, p. 17.

19. *Cambridge History of the British Empire*, II, p. 224.
20. Recently and most cogently by Professor Landes, *loc. cit.*
21. Vicens, *Historia Económica de España*, pp. 482–3.
22. Harlow, *Founding of the Second British Empire*, II, pp. 283 ff.
23. T. Ellison, *The Cotton Trade of Great Britain*, London, 1886, p. 86. *Cambridge History of the British Empire*, II, pp. 224–5.
24. C. H. Philips, *East India Company*, pp. 190 ff.
25. R. C. Dutt, *The Economic History of India*, London, 1901, pp. 257 ff.
26. *Parliamentary Papers*. Session 1812–13, X, Minutes of Evidence, etc., on the Affairs of the East India Company, pp. 123 and 172.

16

Agents of Government

The period ... cannot be far distant, when by the natural expiration of
... existing interests, the country will reap the full benefit (either by the
acquisition of effective services, or by pecuniary saving) of those successive
efforts which, from 1782 onwards, have operated in gradually disencumbering
the finances of the Country from the justly obnoxious pressure of sinecure
emoluments.[1]

So, complacently, a Select Committee on Sinecures reviewed in
1834 the efforts of the previous fifty years to rationalise the appointment of administrative officials in Great Britain and the colonies. In the colonies, since eighteenth-century colonial officials
did not usually receive salaries, the gain was mostly in the form of
'effective services' rather than 'pecuniary saving'. In this respect
the committee had ground for complacency. By the 1830s an established, if not yet quite a professional, colonial administrative
service had come into existence. A major, if largely silent, revolution had taken place in both the principle and the practice of
colonial government. The concept of office-as-post-of-duty had
replaced the older notion of office-as-place-of-profit, or, one
might almost say, office-as-rent-yielding-property, throughout the
empire.

The administrative revolution was not confined to the British
empire, nor did it originate there. The hankering after order and
rationality, characteristic of later-eighteenth-century thought; the
optimistic belief in the possibilities of improvement by means of
intelligent administration; the growing tendency to judge political
institutions and practices by their effectiveness in promoting prosperity and power, rather than by their conformity with precedent
– these mental habits and attitudes affected all the European

empires in greater or less degree. In each empire, rationalising governments had to wage a long war of attrition against 'existing interests'. In each, at some time in the later eighteenth century, a sharp shock – political overturn, military defeat, or natural calamity – gave an impulse to administrative reform. The first to feel the impact were the most conservative, the most inert: the Portuguese under José, or rather under Pombal his minister, whose dictatorship began in the aftermath of the Lisbon earthquake in 1755; the Spanish under Charles III, whose reign began with the defeats of the Seven Years War.

Charles III himself was no reforming bureaucrat (Goya's portrait of a hunting squire does not suggest an innovating mind) but he was an appropriate master for able and innovating ministers. Among themselves, indeed, they called him the Master – *El Amo*. He had an exalted view of the nature of royal authority. It never occurred to him to desist from a course of action which his ministers recommended and he approved, merely because his subjects hated it. He could be savage in dealing with opposition; there was a military brutality about many of the proceedings of his reign. On the other hand, he was not so naïve as to assume that his wishes would be obeyed in the distant Indies, merely because they emanated from a king. Decrees reorganising the defences, the revenues and the commercial structure of a whole empire, required skilled enforcement. The 'enlightened despots' in general, and Charles might be called a somewhat enlightened despot, appreciated the importance of a reliable administrative service. He was the only Spanish monarch in the eighteenth century who actively encouraged his ministers to create one.[2]

A civil service, to be effective, must conform to certain basic principles of staffing. Officials must be selected and promoted for their competence; they must be responsible to clearly recognised superiors; they must be removable upon misconduct; they must be adequately paid. In the Spanish Indies most officials – viceroys and higher judges were the only general exceptions and they not always – obtained their posts by methods unconcerned with merit: by purchase, lease, inheritance or personal patronage.[3] Office was generally regarded as a form of property; if a purchase price were paid, it was an investment. Proprietary officers could not easily be removed, even by a viceroy; if, occasionally, they were, they expected compensation. The viceroys enjoyed an unchallenged pre-eminence; no formally constituted councils advised them. They were supposed, in matters of importance, to consult the judges of the central appeal courts, the viceregal *audiencias* (who were by training lawyers, not administrators); but this check on viceregal power was falling into disuse. On the other hand, the captains-general or governors of some outlying provinces, Guatemala, Chile, Venezuela, Philippines, corresponded directly with the crown, and were in effect independent of the viceroys. Within the viceroyalties proper, no clear chain of command connected the viceregal secretariats with the subordinate organs of government. The judicial service, at least in the higher courts, had always been independent. The revenue service was fragmented; each major tax had its own collecting staff, or else was privately farmed. In the treasuries, most of the offices were proprietary, in fact if not in law, and the viceroys had little control over them. In the provinces, the district officers and local magistrates, *corregidores*, operated almost unsupervised, except occasionally by *audiencia* judges on circuit. There were about 200 of them in New Spain, mostly local gentry, small men; real power in the localities was in the hands of the big men, the land-owning, mine-owning and ranching magnates. Few officials were paid. Viceroys and higher judges had stipends generous enough to raise them above petty venality, and the viceroys kept considerable state. Senior treasury officials received salaries, though inadequate ones; here the implication was obvious. Most revenue officers were remunerated on a commision basis. The numerous officials who staffed the secretariats, the law courts and the municipal governments were mostly unpaid; they lived on the fees they collected from people who had public business to transact. As for the corregidores, the humble workhorses of administration, they received only token salaries, charged on the Indian tributes. Most of their income came from perquisites, in particular from the profits of the *repartimiento de comercio*. This arrangement, not to be confused with the labour-*repartimiento*, the *corvée*, had been intended for the improvement of agriculture, by distributing stock, seed and tools to Indian farmers. Corregidores used it for their own profit, by compelling Indians to buy miscellaneous imported goods which they did not want and could not afford to pay for. The debts were collected, of course, in labour.

A vast, invertebrate organism, then; an enlightened despot's nightmare. The process of inserting an administrative backbone began in 1765 with the work of Gálvez as *visitador* in New Spain. Gálvez' report, which he submitted in 1771 and implemented, as minister for the Indies, between 1772 and 1788, covered every aspect of colonial government; but the heart of it was the abolition of the office of corregidor and the division of each viceroyalty, between 1782 and 1786, into intendancies; twelve in New Spain, six in Peru, eight in Río de la Plata. Each intendant (the word, like the office, was French in origin)[4] governed an extensive province. He was first a financial supervisor – Gálvez grasped that an efficient treasury is the first essential of good administration – but he had also the supervision of the three other principal heads of governmental activity: defence, justice and *policia*. *Policia* meant much more than police; it included both public order and public works, and is best translated as 'general administration'.[5] The intendants were not great noblemen as most viceroys were – socially, they represented a degree of *embourgeoisement* – nor needy place-seekers as the corregidores had been; they were career governors, armed with clear instructions[6] and entrusted with wide powers. They received generous salaries. They were provided with a staff of subordinate officers, *subdelegados*, nominated by them and appointed by the viceroys, to represent them in individual districts. Here, then, were the essential elements of an imperial civil service: a body of professional administrators, recruited for efficiency, responsible, removable and paid. The Gálvez reforms, on paper at least, were a drastic break with the past, the longest step in the direction of effective government to be taken by any European colonial empire in the course of the eighteenth century.

There were difficulties, of course; in particular, the difficulty of finding men suitably qualified to serve as intendants. The legal profession had its own well-established career structure, and yielded few recruits. Ecclesiastics, who in the past had played a prominent part in the government of the Indies, were unacceptable. Charles III himself was an orthodox Catholic – his confessor sometimes attended meetings of ministers – but he was always suspicious of the Church in politics; and some of his ministers, notably Aranda, were anti-clerical freemasons. Another limiting factor was the government's suspicion of Creole magnates, and its preference for peninsular Spaniards who could more easily be held to account. The preference was natural in the circumstances, and justified by events. Some, at least, of the few Creoles who were appointed – Torre Tagle in Peru was a notorious example – were to prove unreliable when the time for testing loyalties arrived. The principal source of recruitment was the army. Some very able military officers became intendants. While Gálvez lived these men were selected with considerable care; but he and Charles III both died in 1788. Under Charles IV less care was taken, and the practice grew of appointing retired officers as intendants, in reward for past services rather than in expectation of services to come. Towards the end of the century it was even rumoured that intendancies were being offered for sale. The recruitment of *subdelegados* presented even greater difficulty. Many corregidores, deprived of their jobs, became *subdelegados* instead. The government, moreover, decided on financial grounds not to pay fixed salaries to *subdelegados*, but to allow them a percentage commission on the tributes they were supposed to collect. In many districts, this arrangement yielded an insufficient amount, and everywhere it invited abuse. Naturally the old rackets soon reappeared under new names, despite all the intendants could do.

However able and upright an intendant might be, he could not avoid one difficulty inherent in a powerful newly created office: that of conflict with older jurisdictions. Military commanders disliked the intendants' financial supervision in matters of pay and supply. Ecclesiastics disliked their interference in matters of *patronato*. Even the viceroys found that some intendants had ideas above their station. The precise boundaries of authority were difficult to define beforehand. The Gálvez plan had provided initially for *surintendentes*, stationed in the capitals, to oversee all the finances of each viceroyalty. The viceroys soon persuaded the government to rid them of these unwelcome competitors; but conflicts persisted. Viceregal opinions on the system differed widely. Bucareli in New Spain, Teodoro de Croix in Peru, disliked the intendancies and wanted them abolished. The second Revillagigedo, though critical in detail, thought that they gave added strength to his own authority as well as to the administration in general. No doubt personalities had something to do with these differences. Croix was a prickly martinet; Bucareli, with all his energy and ability, something of a racketeer. Revillagigedo was one of the most upright and able viceroys who ever went to the Indies, and had the gift of inspiring loyalty in his subordinates. The conflicts, however, were genuine. The new offices and the old could have been fitted together in a smooth-running administrative machine, only by a process of accommodation, by trial and error, by a long series of rulings in particular cases; and for this there was insufficient time. When sea communication with Spain was cut, when Spanish government itself collapsed under invasion, the task of governing the Indies fell to an administration at odds within itself.

Gálvez' reform of Spanish colonial administration was only the most obvious instance of a general trend. Daendel's prefects in Java were intendants in all but name. What Gálvez and Floridablanca did for the Spanish Indies, Pombal, in his ferocious, unsystematic fashion, endeavoured to do for Brazil; though even his ablest and most conscientious viceroy, Lavradio, was no Revillagigedo.[7] In each instance the inspiration, directly or indirectly, was French. The course of events in British colonies offered striking contrasts, but also striking analogies. Great Britain, as a metropolitan power, had two great advantages over its imperial competitors: maritime communications with the colonies could be relied on, always in peace and usually in war; and growing industrial productivity made it worth almost everybody's while to maintain at least commercial contact. On the other hand, the British administrative structure in the 1760s sprawled more spinelessly than the Spanish. The discipline and uniformity prescribed in governors' instructions was an unconvincing façade. There were no viceroyalties; Carleton was later to become the prescient advocate of a viceroyalty of British North America, presumably with himself as viceroy;[8] but none of the local legislatures would have tolerated such a scheme. Each of thirty or so colonies – some very small – was administered by a governor who corresponded directly with the centre. The scale of government was modest, and so was the governors' style and dignity, as may be seen from the surviving buildings of the period. The governor's house, for example, lovingly preserved at Williamsburg, Virginia, is an elegant but unassuming country gentleman's residence. Most governors shared their political authority with councils nominated from among local notables, and relied precariously for revenue upon elected assemblies; arrangements originating in the political circumstances of seventeenth-century England, and notoriously productive of friction. More serious, from an administrative point of view, governors had no civil service upon which they could rely. The reason for the deficiency was the same as in the Spanish empire: proprietary offices. The governors themselves were appointed by royal commission, were paid, and were removable; their terms of office were usually relatively short. Most other senior colonial officials were appointed by Letters Patent for life.

The British crown did not sell offices; at least, not officially. Long-standing tradition, embodied in statutes from the middle of the sixteenth century, discouraged the use of such extra-parliamentary sources of revenue; but offices, though not offered for money, were given for money's worth. Patents might be granted by ministers to political supporters, election managers, clients, friends, relatives, protégés, or people thought on any ground to be entitled to pension or gratuity. The principal patent officers in most colonies were the colonial secretary; the treasurer and receiver general; the provost marshal, responsible for public order, police and prisons; sometimes the attorney general; the clerk to the naval office, who enforced regulations concerning trade, immigration and the movements of shipping; and the clerks of courts and markets. These officers received no salaries, or only token salaries; they were remunerated by fees and commissions. Nothing in their patents required them to perform their duties in person, or even to reside in the colonies, and few of them did; they leased their offices to deputies for terms of years, and charged a rent, usually about half the expected yield of the fees. The deputies were almost always colonial residents, often local politicians, sometimes men who distinguished themselves in opposition to the government they were supposed to serve. They were irresponsible and virtually irremovable, except by the intervention of the patentees, who held absolute property in their places, and cared little so long as the rents arrived regularly. They were not even personally acquainted with their deputies, as a rule; the business was handled through agents, usually commerical firms active in colonial trade. Governors whose subordinates were appointed in this fashion were in a dangerously isolated position, powerless to enforce unpopular instructions except, occasionally, by the use of regular troops, if any were available; but this was a last and desperate resort. Governors complained repeatedly, both about individual officials and about the system in general; ministers as repeatedly ignored their complaints; the patronage was too valuable to be given up, the patentees too influential to be dislodged.[9]

A single but not unusual example will illustrate the difficulties of a conscientious governor. In 1776 Lord George Germain as secretary of state caused the office of treasurer and receiver general of Jamaica – a major post of trust, obviously – to be patented in the name of his son, then a boy of six. An agent was appointed to arrange for deputies, and in 1782 this agent leased the deputation to one Fitch, a New Englander resident in the island, who throughout the war had made no secret of his rebel sympathies, and who was known to have engaged in the clandestine sale of ships and naval stores to the enemy. The governor protested vigorously against the appointment; the secretary of state (Sydney), after a six months' interval, professed himself unable to intervene – it was the patentee's affair, he said; the patentee, aged twelve, had no views, and nothing could be got out of his agent but bland unhelpful letters. Fitch kept the job and outstayed several governors.[10] An interesting feature of this unedifying story is the support given to Fitch by the Jamaica assembly. The colonists and their representatives rarely complained about the patent system; on the contrary, it suited them well. They had no wish to see their affairs administered by efficient and zealous officers sent from England; still less did they want valuable and persuasive patronage placed in the governors' hands.

Many people with wide colonial experience saw in the patent system one of the main causes of the inability of governors in

North America to hold their colonies in obedience. Carleton (Lord Dorchester) was one of these. Writing from British North America, ten years after the War of Independence, he described the system as

> coeval with His Majesty's governments in North America and the cause of their destruction. As its object was not public but private advantage, so this principle was pursued with diligence ... and the governors reduced almost to mere corresponding agents, unable to resist the pecuniary speculations of gentlemen in office, their connections and associates, or any enormity whatever. It was not therefore surprising that this phantom of an executive power should be swept away at the first onset of a political storm.[11]

These views had been widely expressed during the war itself; and defeat had shocked government into a shortlived attempt at reform. In 1782 Shelburne, as secretary of state, had got through an act[12] requiring all officers appointed by Letters Patent to reside and perform their duties in person, unless granted leave of absence by a governor. The act, in the eighteenth-century manner, respected existing interests; it applied only to future patents. It roused a storm of protest, however, and ways were soon found of evading it. A minister need not use the ponderous machinery of Letters Patent to appoint colonial officials; he could, by simple warrant, order a colonial governor to make the desired appointment under the seal of the individual colony, and by the same instrument could instruct the governor to grant indefinite leave of absence. Shelburne's successors undid his work. The act was a dead letter.

During the interwar period and the ensuing war with Republican France the number of colonial sinecures increased, and as the work of the colonial department increased also, a considerable share of the spoils came to be regarded as a perquisite of the under-secretary. Sydney's under-secretary, Evan Nepean, an able official who did much to improve the routine efficiency of the department, was also clerk to the naval offices of Grenada, St Vincent and Dominica, and secured several offices in Jamaica by reversion. He visited Jamaica to take possession, secured formal leave of absence, and consulted the governor – a rare act of courtesy – over the appointment of deputies. When he left the colonial department and became secretary to the Admiralty, he retained all his colonial sinecures. The acquisition of conquered colonies in the 1790s added to the list of offices available for distribution. The Duke of Portland, at the turn of the century, excelled all previous secretaries of state in generosity to his friends and dependants. By his day well over a hundred colonial offices were formally patented and served by deputy, in addition to offices in the gift of the Admiralty and the commissioners of customs.[13] The list now included such picturesque titles as exploiteur in Demerara and vendue master in Berbice.

Progress down the slippery slope, in a purely administrative sense, did not imply indifference to colonial questions; much careful attention was paid, in the same period, to colonial constitution-making. Canada presented, in this respect, a specially intractable problem. The Québec Act of 1774 had made the governor, with his nominated council of *seigneurs* and officials, virtually the whole government. This was well enough, while the inhabitants were mostly peasants accustomed to a conveniently feudal order of society, and anxious only to be left alone. After the American War, the influx of loyalists, especially into Upper Canada, and the growth of an English merchant community at Montreal, brought demands for a government nearer to the traditional English model, with English law, an English ecclesiastical establishment, and representative institutions. Many arguments inclined government to accede to these demands: the loyalists' just deserts; the inherent superiority of English institutions; the expectation that the 'New Subjects' – the French – would become anglicised; the high cost of Québec Act paternalism, and the necessity of creating some sort of representative assembly in order to raise taxes. There was also a widespread feeling, after 1783, of resigned inevitability. Yet security must not be endangered; Canada must be protected both against possible French plots, and against the contagion of American republicanism and democratic excess. The anglicising of illiterate peasants would take time; meanwhile, promises concerning the free exercise of their customs and religion had to be honoured. On the other hand, the discipline of seigneurial authority must be maintained, and the *habitans* must not be allowed, by the number of their votes, to overwhelm the loyalist immigrants.

The Canada Act of 1791,[14] accordingly, separated the two populations, by creating two separate provinces: Québec French, Upper Canada English, in language, religion and law. They were tenuously united by the executive authority of the governor general – initially Carleton – but had separate legislatures. Each was provided with an elected assembly of the traditional type, but in addition each was to have an upper house, a legislative council, composed of substantial land-owners nominated for life – a miniature House of Lords, in intention, to serve as guardian of property and order and as a protection against rash innovation or democratic excess. The merchants of Montreal were left to come to terms with their French neighbours as best they could. Neither Carleton in Canada nor Sydney in England cared much for the Act; it was chiefly the work of Sydney's successor, Grenville. It contained all the seeds of dissension which produced rebellions in both Canadas in the 1830s, and which plagues the federal government of Canada today.

The Canada Act was the last exercise for many years in the design of representative institutions for British colonies. The French Revolution and the slave mutiny in St Domingue, even more than the American rebellion, impressed on the English mind the dangers of democratic excess. A warning of a different kind had been provided by the island of Grenada; the assembly there, established after the acquisition in 1763, had been the scene of repeated bitter quarrels between French and British factions.[15] This warning also had its effect. No assemblies were created in the territories conquered from the French, the Dutch and the Spaniards during the French wars. The arrangements adopted were nearer to the Québec Act than to the Canada Act. Existing revenues continued to be collected and existing systems of law were retained – in territories taken from the French, the system of the *ancien régime*. Executive authority was concentrated in the hands of the governors, ruling with the help of advisory councils in which officials predominated. Crown-colony government was to have a long run in many places. The arrangements hastily applied to conquered West Indian islands in the 1790s became the model for larger and more distant territories such as Cape Colony, Mauritius and Ceylon, where large non-British populations had to be both governed and conciliated. Governors such as 'King Tom' – General Sir Thomas Maitland, who ruled successively in Ceylon, Malta and the Ionian Islands – were benevolent despots, often forthright defenders of the interests of the local populace, but under no obligation to consult the views of local notables.

No administration could be more efficient than the officials who ran it. The spread of crown-colony government threw the abuses of the patent offices into sharp relief. From about 1806 a new and sustained attack on them began; or, rather, two attacks, one oblique, the other direct. The oblique attack was part of a general drive to reduce expenditure by abolishing sinecure offices in Britain; offices, that is, which involved salaries without duties. Colonial sinecures, since they cost the treasury nothing, were only a minor and incidental target of this attack; but the reports of a series of select committees dealt briefly with them. They called attention to the many evasions of the act of 1782, and prepared the way for the direct attack; the passage, in 1814, of a new and sterner act.[16] This provided that colonial officials, by whatever instrument appointed, might hold office only while they performed their duties in person, and that leaves of absence must be confirmed by the secretary of state. Like its predecessors, the act respected existing interests; Sir Evan Nepean, now governor of Bombay, was safe in possession of his West Indian sinecures; but changes in the central administration for the colonies now made it likely that the law requiring colonial officials to work for their living would, for the first time, be enforced.

In 1794, a third secretary of state had been appointed, to deal with matters of war. In 1801, colonial affairs had been transferred from the Home Department to the department of the third secretary. In 1817, the war well over, it was decided to retain the third secretary, to deal only with colonial affairs. The secretary of the time, Bathurst, was committed to reform; and the whole debate on the subject bore witness to the growth, since the early years of the century, of a new and more serious attitude towards the colonial empire. In the twenty years after the act, the patent system died of attrition. No fresh patents of the old type were issued. By 1835 only two colonial sinecure-holders survived, both ripened products of the old régime. One was Charles Greville, clerk to the Privy Council, a grandson of the Duke of Portland; the other, the Honourable George Germain. As the patentees died off, they were replaced by men appointed to serve in person and removable if they served badly. Gradually, as local finances allowed, payment by salary began to replace emolument by fees. Colonial administration was becoming, for some Englishmen (and Scots and Irishmen) a recognised career. The first issue of the Colonial Regulations, put out by Lord Glenelg in 1837, contained the first official use of the term Her Majesty's Colonial Service.

All these changes, more revolutionary in fact than in form, reflected analogous but separate developments in the government of India. The 'King Tom' of the conquered colonies reproduced, on a small scale, the authority of autocratic governors general in Calcutta. Cornwallis' insistence, in 1785, on a free hand in India, had set this precedent. Unfettered authority and ministerial support, together with his own strong will and transparent honesty of purpose, had enabled him to do in India what Bathurst, a little later, was to do in the territories administered by the Colonial Office. He collected and organised, for the first time, a disciplined and effective civil service.

The East India Company already possessed a civil service of sorts. Ever since the company 'stood forth as Diwan' in Bengal, young men appointed as junior clerks had found themselves involved in collecting revenue, maintaining local order, presiding over local courts, even though their duties, often enough, were no more than the cursory supervision of work done by Indians. The service offered a career; many of its recruits were mere boys who (if they survived) grew up in the company. It had its own *esprit de corps*; though the *corps* resembled a medieval Free Company more nearly than a modern bureaucracy. The trouble lay partly in the manner of appointment, by patronage in the hands of individual directors, who naturally obliged their friends; but much more in the circumstances of life in India, where enormous temptations beset men earning token salaries. Since the company did not pay them properly, its servants helped themselves. Regulations under Pitt's act forbade them to engage in private trade and threatened them – to their intense indignation – with prosecution for disobedience; but by leaving the bulk of the patronage with the company, the act left discipline in the hands of a body notoriously incapable of enforcing it. Company servants had long been accustomed to evade and sometimes to defy the orders of their employers. In 1784–5 the orders of government brought them near to open revolt.

Cornwallis faced a long and uphill task. Venality was common enough in England; India notoriously was a place for plunder and a quick getaway. His policy in the matter was straighforward, like himself, and he pursued it with dogged persistence: to abolish sinecures; to insist on the payment of generous salaries; to require those who received them to devote their whole energies to the duties for which they were paid; to make examples of such offenders as could be caught; to send the more obvious scalliwags and adventurers back to England; to return polite but unhelpful answers to prominent people who wanted jobs found for their protégés. Only a bold and confident governor general would have ventured to remind Hawkesbury that his task was to seek 'the man for the place, and not the place for the man'.[17] Dundas cannot have relished, either, the demand for higher salaries, at a time when he was trying desperately to economise on Indian expenses; but Cornwallis by steady persistence got his way, and achieved considerable economies as well. Most remarkable of all, he actually succeeded, in many instances, in finding 'the man for the place'. The 'temper of the times' was changing, as Cornwallis himself said. There were men of ability, experience and integrity in the company's service, who only needed firm leadership and support. Cornwallis trusted his senior officials, some of them distinguished experts, such as James Anderson, Charles Warre Malet, John Shore, Jonathan Duncan, though he did not always take their advice. He was less trustful of the collectors – the workhorses of administration, corregidores or *subdelegados* of the British system; his separation of the duties of revenue collection from those of district jurisdiction arose partly from this distrust. He was wholly distrustful of Indians as officials, and thought them all incorrigibly corrupt.[18] His civil service – in those ranks, at least, where final decisions might be made – was to be staffed by Englishmen.

In 1793 the company's charter was renewed without much argument or any major change; and Cornwallis retired. For twenty years after his retirement the administration of British India remained much as he had left it. This conservatism was due partly to the immense prestige of his work and to the piety of officers who had worked under him; partly to the pressure of war and political circumstance. In large measure also, however, it was deliberate policy, due to the desire for permanence, to the preference for 'steady adherence to almost any one system', characteristic of Cornwallis himself and of his successors. The settlement of the Bengal land revenue is an example of this obsession with stability. To Englishmen with Whiggish ideas of property, rent and land tax, the obvious first step was to look for the owners of the land, and the zemindars were the people who most nearly fitted the description. In fact, they were a very heterogeneous class, whose functions and standing bore little real resemblance to those of landlords in the English sense; but they seemed to be the most convenient parties to negotiate with, and the settlement was made with them. In Bengal it could not easily have been made in any other way. The compilation of an adequate Domesday Book, recording in detail the rights and obligations of millions of ryots, was probably beyond the capacity of the administration of the time; at best it would have required many years' work, during which the prevailing uncertainty would have been prolonged. The wisdom of making the zemindari settlement a permanent one was questioned, even by some civil servants.[19] Permanent settlement robbed the revenue of elasticity and entrenched the interests of a class of landlord-taxgatherers; but it introduced an element of certainty into a complex and uncertain situation, and for the sake of stability it was adopted. In Madras, on the other hand, there were no zemindars. Munro had to seek stability by other means, and actually succeeded in getting the revenue settled with individual cultivators.[20] Attempts to introduce the Bengal system in Madras were successfully reversed. Whatever the relative merits of the two systems – and controversy has gone on to this day – each, once adopted in a particular province, became permanently established there. Similarly with the code of regulations which Barlow drafted and Cornwallis promulgated; it had many imperfections and imprecisions; Cornwallis' successors tinkered with it, but made no radical change. Similarly with the separation of judicial from revenue duties: this was highly inconvenient, and often involved a denial of justice because of the congestion of the courts and their inaccessibility to many peasants; yet not until after 1813 did the collectors begin to recover the judicial powers which Cornwallis had taken from them. In the 1820s they were once more to become magistrates and the state's men-of-all-work.

The prospect of another charter renewal in 1813 caused a flurry of investigation and talk of reform in the years immediately preceding it. Grenville, in the most thoughtful and most radical of the many parliamentary speeches on the subject,[21] proposed a clear avowal of the sovereignty of the crown in India, the separation of government there 'from all intermixture with mercantile interests and transactions', and the abolition of patronage. Recruits for the civil service in India, he thought, might best be selected by 'free competition and public examination'. Revolutionary notions: too revolutionary for a government preoccupied with the final stages of a major European war. In the event, the company kept the government of India; though its administrative functions there were clearly separated, for the first time, from its attenuated commercial activities – in itself a major reform. As for patronage, investigation had not revealed any scandalous misuse of it by the directors; so they kept their privileges, and the threat of competitive examination was staved off for another forty years. In most other respects, the general outlines of the Cornwallis structure remained. In particular, officials in India resisted all moves by the home government to employ Indians in posts of major responsibility. This exclusiveness was to remain characteristic of the government of India, in principle until 1833, and in practice much longer. The Englishmen who went to India in the eighteenth century were not more alien, or not much more alien, than the Mughals had been when they first conquered Hindustan; but the Mughals, in ruling India, were absorbed, the British were not. Many individual Englishmen learned to love India, and to know and understand the people among whom they worked; but in general the nineteenth-century Indian civil service – intelligent, tireless, puritanically devoted – remained what Cornwallis intended it to be, a body of alien administrators.

A disciplined, professional civil service is, in most circumstances, a more efficient instrument of government than a haphazard collection of placemen. To most serious statesmen in the late eighteenth century this seemed so obvious as to need no argument; and the rulers of all the European colonial empires worked, some more strenuously than others, to create such a service. The results, whether from the point of view of metropolitan governments, or from that of colonial subjects, did not always entirely answer expectations. There were limits to what even the most devoted civil service could achieve, and in some quarters increased efficiency produced resentment. In Spanish America, the creation of intendancies did not immediately remove the obstacles to good government represented by the sale of offices, though it reduced them; nor did it end – though it mitigated – the extortions and oppressions connected with Indian tributes and the forced labour system. These ancient invitations to abuse were not abolished, even in law, until 1812. Of the value of the new system in straightening the finances and increasing the revenue, on the other hand, there is little doubt. Some intendants were active and successful, also, in promoting local industrial enterprise and in prodding the municipal councils into some show of useful activity.[22] As might be expected, the civil service was unpopular. The leaders of Creole society were prepared to respect viceroys, who were the king's representatives, and usually magnates themselves; they had no such feelings towards intendants, who were newly arrived and had more modest social pretensions; who represented efficient tax collection, unwelcome interference and centralised control. As it had often done in the past, Spanish administration attempted too much. The Creole magnates were too powerful locally to be browbeaten. They controlled large sections of the Indian population and most of the sources of taxable wealth; and they officered the colonial militia. The Indies could not be governed smoothly without their co-operation, or at least their acquiescence. If Spain had not been invaded, if communications had not been interrupted by war, a *modus vivendi* might have been found. As it was, for the purpose of maintaining obedience and loyalty to the crown, the intendancies were more of a liability than an asset. Wherever a *junta* of local notables 'pronounced' for Ferdinand, the intendant was usually the first official to be shipped home.

Charles III's colonial service operated in troubled times and lasted only as long as the empire itself, less than fifty years. The Indian civil service was to have a much longer run. Once discipline had been established within its own ranks, it faced less obvious obstacles. It had no entrenched community of European landowners to contend with. Its communications with England were never seriously interrupted. In the event of overt rebellion or defiance, it could call on substantial military force; behind the shopfront of a trading corporation, the East India Company represented the sword. The tasks confronting it were immense in scale and diversity; yet the administrative objects it was set were limited, defined, practical, attainable. In considerable measure, they were attained. Bengal in the late eighteenth and early nineteenth centuries enjoyed a notable return of prosperity (though probably in the long run the zemindars were the principal beneficiaries). The revenue increased (though much of it was absorbed by local wars). Oppression and extortion by Europeans, whether officials, soldiers, or private individuals, became the exception rather than the rule (though government was less successful in preventing the oppression of Indians by other Indians). The police system became steadily more effective, especially against the more obvious forms of crime, such as dacoity. The authority of government was never seriously challenged.

To attribute these successes solely to the operations of a wise and powerful government would, of course, be unrealistic. The development of a colonial society, or any society, is not to be explained simply in terms of administrative intention. The relative success of the government of British India owed much to the fact that – powerful though it was in a military sense – it accepted the constraints which local forms of society exercised upon the shaping of administration. It is significant, for example, that the advocates of the two rival forms of land revenue settlement, zemindari and ryotwari, equally disclaimed any intention of innovating. Each claimed to be supporting the system most conformable to native custom, the only system which, in a particular area, would work. The land revenue systems of British India were not based upon theories imported from England; they were not designed wantonly to shatter the frame of Indian society; on the contrary, they were designed to operate in broad conformity with the existing tenurial structure.[23] This was true not only in the formulation of policy, but much more in its application. At the district level, under the surveillance, necessarily the somewhat cursory surveillance, of European officials, Indians gathered the revenue, and gathered it in time-honoured ways. Obviously the zemindars did so in Bengal; but so also did the sub-bureaucracy, mostly of Maratha Brahmins, which carried out the day-to-day work in south India.[24] Similarly with the administration of justice; the provision of courts under the Cornwallis dispensation was relatively generous, but still quite inadequate to deal with the volume of litigation.[25] Increasingly the hearing of civil cases had to be left to Indian *munsiffs*, whose powers were defined in 1814 and extended in 1821. Even in the higher courts the European judges, administering a vague and unfamiliar amalgam of law and custom, depended on the advice of Indian interpreters of the law who were attached to every court.

Every colonial government, if it is to maintain itself without a ruthless and ruinously lavish use of force, needs the collaboration of an influential group within the society to be governed. The Indian civil service secured such collaboration, and the collaborators exacted their price: influence, support, privileged opportunities for peculation, a large share of the initiative in local matters, a power of blackmail, implicit in the possibility of recourse to the courts or of complaint against one official to another and higher official. The administration of British India was directed by a small body of Englishmen; it was run in detail by a much larger body of Indian subordinates, upon whom the officials were heavily dependent. The government, in theory unchallenged, was in practice narrowly limited in its range of effective action by this dependence. Any initiative from above might be checked or reversed by passive resistance or unobtrusive modification from below. The 'corruption' of which officials complained was not an eradicable ailment of the society they ruled; it was a network of mutual agreements which held the society together and made it impermeable to change. Most officials must have felt the frustration of being surrounded by this flexible, invisible net. Masters of India, they were also, by that very fact, its captives.

NOTES

1. House of Commons, *Report of Select Committee on Sinecure Offices*, 1834, vi, 519.
2. For an assessment of his achievement see G. Céspedes del Castillo, *Lima y Buenos Aires*, Seville, 1947.
3. For the history of these practices, see J. H. Parry, *The Sale of Public Office in the Spanish Indies under the Hapsburgs*, Berkeley, 1953.
4. A. Vieillard-Baron, 'L'intendant américain et l'intendant français', *Revista de Indias*, nos. 43–4, 1951, p. 235.
5. A. Vieillard-Baron, 'L'établissement des intendants aux Indes par Charles III', *Revista de Indias*, 49, 1952, p. 524. See also J. Lynch, *Spanish Colonial Administration; the Indendant System in the Río de la Plata*, London, 1958, pp. 46 ff., 62 ff.
6. *Real ordenanza para el establecimiento y instrucción de intendentes de ejército y provincia en el reino de Nueva España*, Madrid, 1786. Though issued for New Spain, the ordinance was generally applied. It runs to 400 closely printed pages. An extensive English summary is included in L. E. Fisher, *The Intendant System in Spanish America*, Berkeley, 1929 – a work which in other respects has little to recommend it.
7. See D. Alden, *Royal Government in Brazil*, Berkeley, 1969.
8. Harlow, *Founding of the Second British Empire*, II, pp. 707, 746.
9. J. H. Parry, 'The Patent Offices in the British West Indies', *English Historical Review*, April 1954, p. 200.
10. Parry, 'Eliphalet Fitch'.
11. A. G. Doughty and D. A. McArthur, *Documents relating to the Constitutional History of Canada, 1791–1818*, Ottowa, 1914, p. 169.
12. 22 Geo. III, *c*. 75.
13. House of Commons Select Committee on Sinecure Offices, 1810–11, *Second Report* (246) iii, 961, appendix 4, and 1812, *Third Report* (181) ii, 191.
14. Harlow, *Founding of the Second British Empire*, II, pp. 770 ff.
15. *Ibid.*, p. 773.
16. 54 Geo. III, *c*. 61.
17. In 1789. Harlow, *Founding of the Second British Empire*, II, p. 219
18. He was not alone in this, of course; the point has been laboured in many books, recently in G. D. Bearce, *British attitudes towards India, 1784–1858*, Oxford, 1961.
19. *Cambridge History of the British Empire*, IV, pp. 449 ff.
20. T. H. Beaglehole, *Thomas Munro and the Development of Administrative Policy in Madras*, Cambridge, 1966, pp. 129–30. See also Nilmani Mukherjee, *The Ryotwari System in Madras*, Calcutta, 1962.

21. *Parliamentary History*, XXV, 709.

22. J. Fisher, 'The intendant system and the cabildos of Peru', *Hispanic American Historical Review*, XLIX, 1969, p. 430.

23. B. H. Baden-Powell, *Land Systems of British India*, 3 vols, London, 1892, I, pp. 281 ff., 291 ff.

24. On this point see in particular R. E. Frykenberg, *Guntur District 1788–1848. A History of Local Influence and Central Authority in South India*, Oxford, 1965.

25. *Cambridge History of the British Empire*, IV, pp. 456 ff.

17

Wards and Guardians

In the colonial fighting which accompanied recurrent European war in the first three-quarters of the eighteenth century, the belligerents were moved by a relatively uncomplicated acquisitiveness. Each endeavoured to capture its rivals' oversea territories, either to be retained permanently as sources of commercial or strategic strength, or to be exchanged at a peace for other advantages, within Europe or outside. After 1763, however, the matter became more complex; belligerent imperial governments discovered another purpose in overseas fighting: to encourage and support the colonial subjects of enemy empires in rebellion against their metropolitan rulers. This was a dangerous game, as those who played it were aware. Imperial governments obviously had no interest in promoting colonial independence for its own sake. In exploiting particular colonial rebellions, in order to weaken and embarrass particular imperial rivals, they invited retaliation. More, they gave implicit support, however inadvertently, to the libertarian ideas and slogans of rebellion, and promoted the spread of those ideas among their own subjects at home and oversea. However unwillingly, they opened up the theory of empire – the value of colonies, the prerogatives and obligations of metropolitan governments in dealing with them, the rights and duties of colonial subjects – to eager (if sometimes clandestine) debate.

In most colonies the metropolitan government, apart from its own interests and those of its metropolitan subjects, had two sets of local interests to consider: the interests of European residents and the interests of the people among whom they were settled. These interests frequently conflicted; and each might present internal complexities. In some places – Canada, for example, or Nova Scotia, or Grenada – where sovereignty had been transferred by conquest, there were two separate groups of Europeans, whose interests also conflicted; in others, such as Jamaica or Guadeloupe, the non-European group was not native, but imported, and in so far as it consisted of slaves, its interests might be thought to be no concern of the metropolitan government. With all these variations, however, a rough general pattern can be seen. In most colonies, a problem of settler–'native' relations existed, which complicated the increasingly difficult problem of relations between metropolis and dependencies.

Most major colonial rebellions in the late eighteenth and early nineteenth centuries (nearly all the successful ones) originated among European or European-descended residents. (The rising of Tupac Amaru in Peru was a conspicuous exception; though Tupac Amaru himself was a Europeanised *mestizo*, a man of property and a local magistrate.) In nearly every major rebellion, settler–'native' relations were among the causes of dispute. English colonists in North America after the Seven Years War thought the British government excessively tender of 'Red' Indian interests; Indians to them were idle and unreliable savages. British statesmen and their official agents in America also regarded Indians as savages; but savages who might, in time and in favourable circumstances, become useful trading partners, savages who had, surely, some rights in their own homeland, some claims to justice and protection, savages who might, if provoked to desperation, be seriously dangerous. They tried – hopeless task – to keep Indians and colonists apart. Their attempts in the proclamation of 1763 and in the Québec Act, to declare a great area of Indian hunting grounds out of bounds to settlers, were fiercely resented. The quarrel between the French West Indian planters and the French National Assembly in 1790–1 developed over the status and treatment of free persons of colour. When this parochial dispute was swallowed up in the desperate crisis of servile revolt, the Jacobin government of France, for reasons both political and doctrinaire, took the side of the slaves. The metropolitan rulers of the Spanish empire could hardly be accused, in the later eighteenth century, of excessive solicitude for Indian interests; but some of their legislation – the suppression of the office of corregidor and of the *re-partimiento de comercio*, later the abolition of the *mita* and the *tributo* – sharply curtailed, in law at least, Creole opportunities for exploiting Indian labour, and contributed to Creole resentment against metropolitan officialdom. In India the very vocal, though ineffectual, protests of the European residents of Calcutta and Madras against Pitt's India Act arose partly from resentment at seeing their privileged opportunities for profit at the expense of the Indian population taken away or greatly reduced. In general, the metropolitan governments in the later eighteenth century showed themselves less and less willing to leave 'native' affairs in the hands of 'settler' groups; everywhere they tended increasingly to interfere, to regulate such matters by legislation; and everywhere they ran the risk of trouble, of one kind or another, with their European subjects oversea.

These recurrent conflicts naturally affected general European attitudes towards the world outside Europe. In the last quarter of the eighteenth century, as more and more Europeans came to know something of non-European societies, it became harder for them to look at those societies objectively. More and more, Indians, Malays, American Indians, Polynesians, appeared in European eyes not as peoples with cultures of their own, interesting in their own right, deserving (or undeserving) of respect; but as peoples standing in this or that relation to Europeans – peoples who had something to offer to Europeans, or who stood in the way of European interests, or who needed protection against exploitation. To say that familiarity bred contempt, is to oversimplify; but certainly involvement made calm appraisal and sympathetic understanding far more difficult. The rise and fall of the 'noble savage' – that characteristic conceit of the mid-eighteenth century imagination – illustrates the process admirably. He was invented, or at least first brought into literary and philosophical fashion, by Rousseau, in the *Discours sur les Arts et Sciences* in 1749. The vogue he enjoyed was chiefly French, though he had his English admirers too. He was vaguely associated at first with the North American Indian. During the Seven Years War, and immediately after, the nobility of this particular kind of 'savage' was called in question, especially in England, where the story of

Lieutenant Lismahago in *Humphry Clinker* probably represented the current view of the subject among the reading public. This did not much matter; the 'noble savage', as a symbol of unsophisticated freedom and virtue, did not perhaps need precise embodiment. But then came the discovery of Tahiti, and the ecstatic description of Polynesian life by Bougainville and others; the 'noble savage', it seemed, really existed. Disillusion followed in due course; the death of Cook caused a general revulsion of feeling, and descriptions of some of the less attractive Polynesian customs – Webber's grisly drawing, for example, of the human sacrifice witnessed by Cook – got wide publicity. Later explorers, even French ones, wrote of the Pacific islanders with angry contempt; to La Pérouse, in general an intelligent and tolerant man, they were 'more malignant than the wildest beasts'. The Polynesians who killed Cook, one might almost say, killed the 'noble savage' too. But that was not the end of the matter. It became clear in the last two decades of the eighteenth century that even such virtues as the island societies admittedly possessed were being damaged, and in some instances the societies themselves destroyed, by contact with Europeans. The factors of destruction were the same as afflicted the North American Indians: rum, firearms, contagious disease and, in general, increasing dependence on imported European artefacts for the ordinary purposes of living. To some Europeans the inference was obvious: that their duty required them to do what they could to save primitive man both from himself and from other Europeans. There was a pattern in late-eighteenth-century attitudes towards the 'savage', a progression from curious, even admiring interest, to disillusion; from disillusion to anxious, even guilty, concern. And not the 'savage' only; with some exceptions and many modifications, the same general pattern can be traced, in the later eighteenth century, in the development of European attitudes towards non-Europeans almost everywhere in the word.

Many of the people with whom Europeans came into increasing contact in the later eighteenth century could by no stretch be called 'savages'; some were representatives of ancient civilisations, beside which the nations of western Europe might appear as uncouth upstarts. Thoughtful Europeans were aware of this. Like the 'noble savage', though on a different plane of attainment, the noble Brahmin and the noble Chinese sage each became a symbolic figure; each had, for a time, his vogue in Europe, and each went through a similar progression in European thought and literature. As usual, the progression began in France and was initated in a modified fashion in England. The *philosophes*, priding themselves upon an outlook detached, humane, and worldwide, were very ready to acknowledge and to learn from the attainments of civilisations outside Europe; and China especially caught their imagination. Their actual knowledge of China was slight; it was derived mainly from the reports of Jesuits at Peking, who had their own reasons for liking China and for representing it to their fellow-Europeans almost at its own valuation. Here, it seemed, was a cultivated, industrious people, a vast yet tranquil and orderly state, governed on rational principles by learned and benevolent scholar-magistrates.[1] The commodities which came from China – silk, porcelain, tea – reflected the bland and sophisticated attractions of country and people. Tea-drinking, as a substitute for gin-drinking, did much to soften the brutalities of urban life in Europe, especially in England, and encouraged admiration for the country which produced the tea. The merchants who actually went to China to fetch it, however, and who paid for it partly by selling Indian opium, naturally saw different aspects of Chinese life from those described by the Jesuits and idealised by the *philosophes*. Disillusion with China began with commercial and diplomatic frustrations; especially in England, with the failure of the Macartney mission, which encountered an impenetrable barrier of xenophobia and courteously veiled contempt, but which also revealed Chinese military weakness and vulnerability. Gillray's cartoon of the episode indicated that the fashion for uncritical admiration of China, in England at least, was reaching its end. Respect for China, however, never dropped to the point where Europeans felt impelled to take on the responsibility of directing Chinese affairs. China was a vast, remote, independent state; and whatever Europeans thought of it, they were unlikely to be able to influence it, except by the crude, straightforward method of exerting military pressure to extort commercial concessions from its government. This – despite Macartney's own warning

– was the method which trading Europeans eventually adopted.

India, like China but in lesser degree, had its vogue among the *philosophes*. Voltaire greatly admired the 'sublime ideas' of Brahmanic religion, which he interpreted in deistic terms; though he admitted that these ideas were the preserve of a select few, existing beside gross superstition and repugnant ritual among the many.[2] A number of English writers on India – Scrafton,[3] Dow, Holwell, all roughly contemporary with Voltaire – expressed somewhat similar views. Holwell maintained that Hinduism was one of the three religions (Judaism and Christianity being the other two) which 'manifestly carry the divine stamp of God'.[4] The admiration of all these philosophical and historical writers was for Hindu India; they all showed traces of the old medieval dislike of Islam, both as a religion and as a political system. 'The faith of Mahommed,' says Dow, 'is peculiarly calculated for despotism; and it is one of the greatest causes which fix for ever the duration of that species of government in the East'.[5] He admits that the Mughal princes were benevolent despots, 'humane' and 'engaging', but wonders all the same why gifted Hindus accepted their despotism so easily. The climate, he thinks, made the Indian people 'phlegmatic', 'slothful', and so submissive.[6] All this, though respectful, is a long way from the adulation accorded to China in the same period. India was too familiar. Europeans had traded there regularly since the early sixteenth century. Since the 1770s considerable areas of the country had fallen under British political control, and British social and political life was being seriously affected by the contact. The French, formally confined after 1763 to a few minor stations in India, hoped by negotiation with princes whom the British antagonised, to prepare the way for return. Europe could not ignore India; but the relation was too close for uncritical admiration.

This is not to say, of course, that all Europeans who served in India despised Indian civilisation. On the contrary, some made it the subject of admiring, fascinated study. The conquistadores, the Dupleix, the Clives, the Cootes, it is true had been interested chiefly in power and plunder. They had become assimilated to India only in the sense that they behaved like Indian military adventurers and accepted Indian feudal titles. For the most part – Bussy was a rare exception – they did not feel intellectually drawn to Indian law and traditions of government, to Indian philosophy, literature or art; but some of their successors did. It was the generation of Warren Hastings which initiated the tradition of serious scholarly study of India by British officials. Hastings himself was a competent Persian scholar and a well-informed collector of Indian paintings and manuscripts. As governor general, he encouraged the pioneer Indologists in their work, fought for them in the Supreme Council, and held long discussions with them on their subjects of study. He gave the full weight of his support to Sir William Jones, the Bengal judge, poet, philologist, Sanskrit scholar and student of Eastern philosophy, whose many ambitious projects included a magisterial digest of Hindu and Muslim law, and whose *Works*, edited by John Shore, Cornwallis' successor as governor-general, fill thirteen heavy volumes.[7] Jones was the founder (in 1784) and first president of the Asiatick Society, in which all these varied scholarly interests found organised expression. The late eighteenth century was a great age of amateur learned societies, and this was not the only organisation of its kind – the Batavian Society had been founded in Java in 1778 – but it became the most fruitful and widely known. Hastings was the Asiatick Society's patron; an office held also by most of his successors as governor general.

There was a practical side to all this, naturally. Jones and Hastings believed that an India better understood would be an India better, more easily, governed. 'The best intended legislative provisions,' wrote Jones, 'would have no beneficial effect ... unless they were congenial to the disposition and habits, to the religious prejudices, and approved immemorial usages' of the people for whom they were enacted.[8] Hastings thought of the 'British empire in India' as an Indian state, governed ultimately by Englishmen, to be sure, but governed in Indian ways, according to Indian law and custom, with Indians intimately concerned at every level of the process. The British India which actually emerged in the nineteenth century was governed, at least at its upper levels, by Englishmen (or Scots), in western ways, according to western-based law with Indians concerned in the process, until late in the century, only in a subordinate or advisory capacity; and, perhaps most significant, eventually with a western system of education using English as the language of instruction. Here indeed was an alteration of course, whose explanation is to be sought both in Indian circumstances and in British attitude.

One is tempted, in reading about Hastings, Jones, Halsted, Wilkins and their like, to assume that the 1770s and 1780s were a golden age in which Englishmen and Indians could meet as friends and equals, in which Major Palmer could marry his Bibi Faiz Baksh and no one would raise an eyebrow; and that extended political power later brought racial arrogance and contempt.[9] So it did; but we must not exaggerate the extent of social change. To judge from contemporary memoirs and correspondence, most Europeans in India, in the eighteenth as in the nineteenth century, kept to themselves, perhaps more from laziness than anything else. The behaviour of the gently-mannered, the *sharif* in Indian phrase, was aloof, though not usually discourteous or contemptuous. Europeans who were not *sharif* – Hastings' 'Europeans of the Lower Sort' – then as later were often extremely ill-mannered towards Indians, and so, often, were the young and thoughtless. Europeans with a serious intellectual interest in Indian culture – the Joneses – were relatively few. The Asiatick Society had thirty members in 1784 and 110 in 1792; attendance at ordinary meetings, roughly once a month, was rarely more than a dozen or so; Jones himself wrote many of the papers; and until 1829 there were no Indian members. The influence of the society was considerable, but not pervasive. The 'golden age' of understanding and sympathy is largely a nostalgic myth. Nevertheless, there *was* a change of attitude, and the ordeal of Warren Hastings was a symptom of it. The impeachment, of course, had an element of political manoeuvre; but the fact that such a trial could be mounted and taken seriously was significant in itself, and in two distinct ways. Explicitly, the prosecution expressed a widespread indignation against the sort of crimes Hastings was (wrongly) accused of; but implicitly, perhaps unconsciously, it also indicated growing impatience with the things Hastings really stood for. Men concerned with Indian affairs in England were becoming less tolerant, not only of the predatory activities of Englishmen in India, but also of what they considered the defects of Indian society itself, and the willingness of company officials to accept those defects. Englishmen were becoming less willing to learn from India. They were not unwilling to learn *about* India, which was the obvious duty of any conscientious official; but learning about India did not necessarily increase admiration. On the contrary, increased knowledge revealed to a wider European public the anarchy which prevailed in many parts of India, the grinding poverty of many of its inhabitants, their vulnerability to flood, famine or local war. It gave publicity to customs such as *sati*, infant marriage, female infanticide, repugnant to European feeling (and repugnant also to the feeling of some sensitive Indians). It called attention to the capricious nature of government, the uncertainty of law, in many Indian states and provinces. It produced disillusion. Disillusion, however, found effective expression not in contemptuous indifference, but in an acute and didactic sense of responsibility. Burke was not alone in thinking of India as a 'trust'. It was not enough to protect Indians from plunder by unscrupulous Europeans. Gradually the conviction gained ground in England that Indian society must itself be guided and reorganised by British officials and in British ways. By 1818 this conviction was almost universal among Englishmen who thought about India. The final defeat of the Maratha confederacy left the British masters, directly or indirectly, of most of the peninsula. No sham suzerainty, no subterfuge, remained, whereby they could shuffle off responsibility for governing it.

A sense of responsibility implies, on the part of the guardian, confidence in his own judgment and competence, lack of confidence in the judgment and competence of the ward. However conscientious, however benevolent, it implies an assumption of superiority. Cornwallis – certainly no lover of innovation for its own sake – had excluded Indians from his administrative service not because he disliked or feared them, but because he thought their habitual dishonesty made them unfit for responsible office. A generation later, administrators imbued with modish Utilitarian ideas were to apply their rigid, tidy formulae to the solution of Indian problems, and again, since calculated happiness, not liberty, was the object of government, and happiness required protection, there was to be little room for Indian participation in the process.[10] Nor was there much respect for Indian custom and tradition. The Utilitarians had no more use for the sensitive antiquarianism of a man like Jones, than for the subjects of his study.

There was something faintly absurd about

'Harmonious Jones who in his splendid strains
Sings Camden's sports on Agra's flow'ry plains.'

To Bentham, Jones was 'an industrious man with no sort of genius'. His digest of Indian law, completed by others after his death, had in fact little practical value, for all its erudition. At the time of its compilation, Indian law was already changing rapidly under the impact of British conquest; the pundits who helped Jones were more conscious of the changes than he was himself. When at last it was completed, the time for it had passed. Mill called it 'a disorderly compilation of loose, vague, stupid and unintelligible quotations and maxims'.[11] Under the influence of Mill and his successors, the legal traditions which Jones had studied were to be replaced by a more consistent, if not necessarily more appropriate system of British-made law. Similarly with education; though here it must be added that education of European type spread in India, and was encouraged by government, partly because prominent Indians, Ram Mohun Roy most notably, wanted it so.

English attitudes towards India in the early nineteenth century represented a great range of opinion and experience. If the Utilitarian-minded officials who came to run India House had known more of India at first hand, they might have had less confidence in formulae, in the cult of administrative expertise, in the ability of government to mould society. The men most influential in the government of India itself in the 1820s, Munro, Malcolm, Metcalfe and Elphinstone, all distrusted Utilitarian dogmatics and complained constantly of 'innovation'. By 'innovation' they usually meant legislation by the central government. They were not hostile to reform; on the contrary, they prided themselves on their liberal outlook; but there was more Burke than Bentham in their intellectual ancestry. They thought – the words are Malcolm's – that 'great and beneficial alterations in society, to be complete, must be produced within the society itself; they cannot be the mere fabrications of its superior'. They did not distrust Indians, as Cornwallis had done; their attitude, rather, was one of affectionate, paternal guardianship. The guardianship, they thought, would be long, but not perpetual. They wanted unofficial Englishmen kept out; if settlement were allowed – this was Elphinstone – 'the people of India would sink to a debased and servile condition ... resembling that of the Indians in Spanish America'. They could even contemplate a future, a distant future, to be sure, in which an enlightened India would be governed entirely by Indians:

> We should look upon India [wrote Munro in 1824] not as a temporary possession, but as one which is to be maintained permanently, until the natives shall in some future age have abandoned most of their superstitions and prejudices, and become sufficiently enlightened to frame a regular government for themselves, and to conduct and preserve it. Whenever such a time shall arrive, it will probably be best for both countries that the British control over India should be gradually withdrawn. That the desirable change here contemplated may in some after age be effected in India, there is no cause to despair.[12]

The 'paternalists', Munro and his younger contemporaries, had learned their business in a period of mounting imperial ambition and rapid military expansion, first under Wellesley, whom they all admired, and then Lord Hastings, down to 1818. They had been soldiers and diplomats before they became administrators, and they had enjoyed it. They all had a streak of the romantic, a nostalgia for chivalry, a love of the wild and natural scene. They knew that they represented a passing era; that they could not stave off 'innovation' indefinitely, that the father-figure in district or province must defer to the planning bureaucrat in the central secretariat, that uniformity (or superficial attempts at it) would replace diversity as a pattern of imperial policy. They hated the prospect, but they accepted its inevitability. The paternal guardian at one extreme, moreover, and the Utilitarian legislator at the other, had more in common than appeared at first sight. Both attitudes were far removed from the straightforward acquisitive opportunism of a Clive, or the supple, cautious tolerance of a Warren Hastings.

No official responsible for Indian affairs could have maintained flatly in 1818, as Hasting had done in 1773, that 'the people of the country do not require our aid to furnish them with a rule for their conduct, or a standard for their property'. Both schools, in their notions of the scope and function of government, went far beyond the conventional Whiggishness of Cornwallis – the reliance, within an administrative frame designed chiefly to control the activities of Europeans, upon *vis inertiae*. They both – and this was the essential point – accepted the duty of tutelage. That supremely arrogant phrase, *mission civilisatrice*, had not then been coined; but the feeling of didactic responsibility was already strong. India was not merely to be policed and regulated; by one method or another, whether gradually or abruptly, whether by slow evolution supervised by Europeans or by reforming legislation imposed by them, it was to be guided, enlightened and transformed.

Guided whither? Transformed into what? Inevitably, 'enlightened' came to mean 'anglicised': assimilated not necessarily to England as it then was, but to England as this or that reforming group would have liked it to be. The attraction of India for the Utilitarians lay not only in its evident need of administrative reform, but in the belief that it presented fewer obstacles to authoritarian reformers than England did. They could see it, or imagine they saw it, as a lump of clay awaiting a moulding hand. Other strong motives, more pervasive and more deeply rooted in English thought of the time, also urged an anglicising policy. One of the most powerful of these motives was religious. In the last decades of the eighteenth century the widespread religious revival, which had originally taken the form of Methodism, was spreading beyond the ranks of the labourers and artisans to whom Wesley and Whitefield had preached, and finding adherents among upper-middle-class people, mostly people engaged in commerce or industry. Some of the men so affected, notably John Shore and Charles Grant, were prominent in the East India Company. Both Shore and Grant, upon their return from India, settled in Clapham, where they were Wilberforce's neighbours. A new enthusiasm for missionary enterprise was inherent in the nature of Evangelical Christianity, and circumstances naturally directed the attention of these men to India. The leaders of the

Evangelical movement in England interested themselves in the remoulding of Indian society, not merely because they thought that society was malleable and in need of rational reorganisation, but because they thought it was evil. For Wilberforce the Hindu divinities were 'absolute monsters of lust, injustice, wickedness and cruelty'. Wilberforce knew nothing of India at first hand; but Charles Grant, a senior company official who had served there devotedly for years on the commercial side, said much the same:

> ... we cannot avoid recognising in the people of Indostan, a race of men lamentably degenerate and base; retaining but a feeble sense of moral obligation; yet obstinate in their disregard of what they know to be right, governed by malevolent and licentious passions, strongly exemplifying the effects produced on society by a great and general corruption of manners, and sunk in misery by their vices. ... [13]

For this state of affairs, Grant blamed oriental despotism, Hindu law, and above all Hindu religion, with its 'crafty and imperious priesthood'. Hindu law was admittedly being modified by British legislation, but legislation – *pace* the Utilitarians – could not change human nature. The plain duty of government was to support a vigorous Evangelical mission, and a campaign of education designed, at least, to enable people to read the Bible. The first and most obvious obstacles to such a programme, and to the ultimate transformation of Indian society, lay in the entrenched power and long-established policy of the East India Company.

The company from its first beginning had carefully avoided, had indeed sternly discouraged, any kind of missionary zeal, from obvious motives of prudence if nothing else. It had maintained a scrupulous respect for Indian religions, as well as for Indian customs, institutions and laws. Cornwallis had broken with this traditional policy to the extent of modifying the forms and method of government, but he had no use for missionaries and considered attempts at Christian proselytising to be visionary as well as unwise. In this, he represented the opinion of most of the company's directors and senior officials. To overcome their opposition, or to persuade government to over-ride it, the Evangelical leaders needed allies. They had to argue, through years of public controversy, from grounds of economic expediency as well as of Christian duty. This presented no great spiritual or intellectual difficulty. The Evangelicals were characteristically willing to accept material success, the fruit of hard work, as a sign of divine favour. Grant argued, and Wilberforce echoed him in parliament, that a proselytising, anglicising policy would help the export trade:

> Those distant territories ... providentially put into our hands ... were given to us, not merely that we might draw an annual profit from them, but that we might diffuse among their inhabitants ... the light and benign influence of the truth, the blessing of well-regulated society, the improvements and comforts of active industry. .... In every progressive step of this work, we shall also serve the original design with which we visited India, that design still so important to this country – the extension of our commerce.[14]

No doubt; but who was to conduct the commerce? The company was a conservative body, and whatever its apologists might say, in fact its commercial monopoly was as much an obstacle to expanding exports, as its restriction on missionaries was to expanding Christianity. To attack one was to attack both; the logical outcome of Evangelical agitation was free trade, free European settlement, and the abolition of the company as a commercial organisation. The Clapham leaders, conservative in politics and with close company connections, could not or would not see this. Grant, as a director, was committed to the monopoly, and took the lead in defending it in the debates on the charter renewal. In 1813, therefore, the attacks on the company were delivered separately. The Evangelicals got their way, to the extent of an Indian Church establishment, with a bishop, freedom for missionary work, and the appropriation of an annual sum for education; but the free trade merchants got *their* way, in the abolition of the company's monopoly of trade to India. It was a Pyrrhic victory for Grant. Eventually, in the 1820s, the overt alliance was formed. The younger Charles Grant, the son, became a Whig, a free trader, and president of the Board of Control.

The Evangelicals had little in common with the Utilitarians except the didactic urge – call it sense of responsibility, call it the itch to set the affairs of others to rights – characteristic of European, above all of British imperialism in the early nineteenth century. India, however, had an enormous capacity either to resist outside influences, or to absorb and transmute them. The Evangelicals could not succeed in making India a Christian country, any more than the Utilitarians could succeed in making it a uniform, tidily-administered one. They created an Indian Protestant Church, which in time developed a vigorous life of its own. They took a lead in insisting on the abolition of certain cruel practices. They also provoked a stubborn resistant suspicion. In every Indian insurrection, in every sepoy mutiny from Vellore in 1806 to the great upheaval of 1858, one of the major motives of the insurgents was determination to preserve their religious usages against Christian attack.

Wilberforce described the Christian mission in India as 'the greatest of all causes'; but he and his Clapham associates are chiefly remembered today for their espousal of another cause, the abolition of the British slave trade. Their attitude in this matter was unequivocal. They were not merely trying to change the policy of a respectable corporation, in whose affairs some of them were actively involved; they were seeking the total prohibition, by statute, of a trade in which none of them was directly concerned and which they all considered an unmitigated evil. They took their stand on moral grounds. They did not try to argue that abolition would be commercially advantageous; on the contrary, they knew that, in the short term at least, it would entail serious loss for many people. Slaving firms, obviously, would lose their employment – a serious matter nationally as well as privately; manufacturers and suppliers of the trade goods which slavers exported would lose their markets, or part of them; West Indian planters would be inconvenienced, to say the least, by restriction of their labour supply. 'The subordination, which the vulgar call slavery, is the source of good government, peace, sugar and coffee, national prosperity, ships, and fine colonies.' So the *Edinburgh Review* in 1805, in a sarcastic but not wildly exaggerated summary of the arguments used to support the continuance of the trade.

The European slave trade as a whole, during four centuries of operation, probably carried some 10,000,000 people from Africa.[15] Of this total, about sixty per cent were transported in the century between 1721 and 1820. Nearly all went to the Americas; other directions of the trade were negligible; the East India

Company, for example, carried small numbers of slaves and employed them on some of its Eastern stations, but it dropped the business entirely in 1764. The transatlantic trade ran at its highest volume between 1741 and 1810. During this period the average annual delivery of slaves was about 60,000, naturally with wide fluctuations due either to maritime wars between European powers, or to wars in Africa itself which affected the rate of supply. Nearly ninety per cent of the trade was in the hands of three national groups of carriers, English, French and Portuguese; of these, the English share in most years was roughly equal to the French and Portuguese combined. English slavers were always able to supply the needs of the British West Indies, and usually also to provide a large surplus for sale in Spanish, French, above all Portuguese America. The total volume of the trade declined in the 1790s, as the result of general war, and after 1792 the French almost dropped out; but even in this difficult decade the English trade remained fairly constant, and 1798 was a record year. A hundred and sixty slave ships cleared from English ports in that year, the majority from Liverpool; a town of some 60,000 inhabitants, which regularly dispatched between seventy and a hundred slavers each year in the last two decades of the century. It was reckoned at the time that some 18,000 people were employed in England in the manufacture of goods for export to Africa, chiefly to pay for slaves; and that this export trade alone amounted to 4·4 per cent of total British exports.[16] The 'Saints', in short, were proposing the abolition of a business of major national importance in its own right, apart from its even greater indirect importance as supplier of essential labour for the manufacture of sugar, cotton and tobacco; a business which, at the time the attack upon it was launched, was at the height of its prosperity.

It is often said, or implied, that public opinion in Europe, down to the last quarter of the eighteenth century, accepted slavery and the slave trade as part of the immutable order of things, and that no one seriously questioned their propriety. This was never quite true; there was always an undercurrent of moral uneasiness; in every century there were voices raised in protest and denunciation. Yet it is true that the denunciation was never, or very rarely, absolute. Slavery – so ancient, so widespread, so intimately associated

425

with the economic activity of Europeans in the Tropics – as a subject of moral inquiry characteristically lent itself to equivocation.[17] Some of the fiercest denunciations of slavery ever written were the work of sixteenth-century Spaniards. These men were not all missionaries; and some of them attacked slavery in general, not only the enslavement of the submissive Indians. A careful analysis of their writings, however, suggests that in almost every instance the object of attack was not slavery itself, but the physical brutality and spiritual neglect associated with it, indeed inseparable from it. The line was hard to draw; but most of the Spanish and Portuguese anti-slavery writers shrank from the full implications of declaring that *no* enslavement was permissible. The same was true of the seventeenth- and early- eighteenth-century philosophers. Locke's theories of social contract and of inalienable rights might seem, at first sight, to exclude any justification of slavery, and certainly Locke wrote of slavery with deep and evident dislike. Yet he invested in the Royal African Company, and his theories admitted exceptions. Prisoners taken in just war or convicted of capital crimes might legitimately be killed; equally legitimately they might be enslaved. It was commonly assumed in eighteenth-century Europe that slaves became slaves in one or the other of these ways, or else by self-sale. The state of slavery, so originated, was accepted by public opinion. It was nowhere illegal, until 1772, when Mansfield's judgment in the Somersett case made it so in England; or at least deprived it, in England, of the support of law. The Scriptures did not condemn it; conversion to Christianity – a Christian duty, admittedly – did not, in most thoughtful people's opinion, affect it. The Society for the Propagation of the Gospel owned slaves in Barbados. Enslavement, to be sure, was no longer a reputable practice within Europe; it was unthinkable that Europeans should deliberately enslave other Europeans, Christians other Christians. It would be wrong, moreover, as well as impolitic and dangerous, for Europeans to invade other continents in order to enslave their inhabitants; but since in many countries in other parts of the world, in Africa, in particular, enslavement was the accepted custom, there was no moral reason why Europeans should not visit those countries to buy captives in the way of peaceful trade. People who were genuinely affected by the suffering of Mrs Behn's Oroonoko could draw comfort from the reflection that African slaves were the subjects of independent rulers over whom Europeans had no jurisdiction; that they were captured in wars in which Europeans played no part; and that they were already slaves when the European traders bought them. Between such purchases, and crude kidnapping, there seemed to be a satisfactory moral distinction.

Obviously slavers, especially private traders, could not afford in practice to investigate the origins of every slave they bought; but the distinctions were not mere sophistries; they were taken seriously by conscientious people, and the Royal African Company, at least, endeavoured to observe them. The story of Job ben Solomon is a striking example, and not the only one, of how the rules might be applied. Job was the son of a Muslim religious leader in Bondou, a Fula principality in the interior of Senegal. The father owned slaves, and occasionally sold small numbers to the company. In 1731 he sent Job with two boys for sale, to the company's factory, Fort James, which stood – its ruins still stand – on an island in the Lower Gambia. Job foolishly strayed into Mandingo country, and there was kidnapped, and sold along with his own slaves. Arrived in Barbados, he wrote a letter in Arabic to his father, describing his misfortune and asking for ransom. His planter owner agreed to forward the letter by a returning company ship, and it went to England, where it was shown as a curiosity to General Oglethorpe, who had it translated at Oxford. Oglethorpe was deputy governor of the company, and despite his determination to exclude slaves from his own colony of Georgia, had no quarrel with slavery in general; but he was an upright and compassionate man, who observed the rules. Job clearly had been unlawfully enslaved; indeed, a person of his standing should not be enslaved in any event. Oglethorpe arranged for him to be redeemed and brought to England. In London he was hospitably entertained, and attracted considerable attention, including that of Sir Hans Sloane. Eventually he was sent home to the Gambia, where for some years he continued to provide the company with valuable commercial contacts.[18]

Distinctions between legitimate and illegitimate enslavement

427

enabled men of conscience to participate in the slave trade, provided that the rules were observed, and so long as these distinctions were accepted, no abolition movement could succeed. The leading abolitionists in America, in England and in France in the later eighteenth century rejected all distinctions; they insisted that all enslavement and all dealing in slaves was by its nature immoral, and that no argument and no circumstance could justify it. In this root-and-branch rejection lay the originality and strength of their propaganda and the secret of their eventual success. Their abhorrence sprang partly from rationalising philosophy of the egalitarian rights-of-man variety; partly from humane indignation and compassion; largely (especially in the English-speaking world) from religious conviction. The Quakers were the first religious group to speak out effectively; slavery was made illegal in Pennsylvania in 1780. Evangelical Christianity, which was to become so pervasive an influence in English life, was also essentially opposed to slavery. It was intensely individualistic: a man must come to terms individually with his God, by prayer; it was also intensely practical, a gospel of action and mission in the external world. Industry, frugality and perseverance were the outward daily disciplines of the soul against sloth, and also provided the material means for furthering the Kingdom upon Earth. A man could throw off the load of sin which burdened his soul, only if he was physically as well as spiritually free to pursue these ends, by his individual determination and choice.

The Saints had their blind spots, as the spokesmen of the West India interest were quick to point out; but their leaders were socially influential and politically shrewd. They detested slavery, not merely the trade in slaves; but sound tactical instinct made the trade the initial object of attack. They could not hope to move parliament to action, merely by appeal to religious convictions which many did not share; they had to mobilise in their support a great wave of humanitarian sentiment; and in this respect the trade was more vulnerable to attack than the institution. Observers of the West Indian scene – Lady Nugent, for example, or the author of *Tom Cringle's Log* – superficial, though not callous, often described life on the sugar plantations as quite a merry affair; slaves, to be sure, were flogged if they misbehaved; but so

428

were soldiers, sailors and schoolboys, and few people thought that unreasonable. No one who knew anything about the slave trade could write of it in such terms. The long, laden march to the coast, the roundup at the barracoons, the close-packed misery of the middle passage, the humiliation and indignity of the actual marketing – these were its ordinary, daily horrors; to say nothing of atrocious incidents such as that of the *Zong* in 1783, which even cold-hearted Mansfield described as 'a very shocking case'.[19] On economic grounds also, it was possible, for propaganda purposes, to drive a wedge between the slaving interest and the West Indian interest. The arguments for maintaining slavery were strong. To abolish it would be to cripple West Indian production, essential to British prosperity. It was all very well for Adam Smith to proclaim that free labour was more economical than slave; West Indian planters were familiar with the inefficiencies of slave labour, but they had no alternative. There was no free labour available. The existing slave labour could be made free by general emancipation; but only on condition, as Sheffield pointed out, of a ruinously expensive compensation. Who was to pay for it? And in the event of sudden emancipation, what would happen to the white population? An ominous answer to this question came, in 1791, from St Domingue. The arguments for maintaining the slave trade were less strong, and could more easily be countered. Abolition would certainly inconvenience the West Indian planters; but would it not also encourage them to take better care of the slaves they already possessed, and to do something to rectify the dangerous imbalance, in many colonies, between black and white population? Abolition would damage the export trade to Africa; but West Africa produced other commodities – could not the exports be paid for in gum and ivory? Abolition would destroy a 'nursery of seamen', but was it so valuable a nursery? Statistics of mortality among slavers' crews suggested that the trade was rather a seamen's grave. Finally, there was the political fact of the West Indian 'lobby'. It was too powerful and too well-organised to be easily defeated in a head-on attack; if possible, it must be placated. Every consideration of sound tactics impelled the Abolitionist leaders to attack the trade, and to hold off, or at least postpone, any appearance of an assault on slavery itself.

For twenty years the Abolitionists ran a propaganda campaign unprecedented in English history for perseverance, intensity and scale. They created a formidable wave of public indignation against the trade, and eventually, after many disappointments, they got it prohibited. That clever, practical politicians such as Pitt and Fox, far from being dragged behind public opinion, gave their support at a relatively early stage, is perhaps surprising. Pitt's support, it is true was neither as firm nor as persistent as Wilberforce would have liked. It has even been argued that he was merely pursuing national economic advantage under a 'cloak of humanitarianism';[20] that he favoured abolition in order to deny slaves to the French West Indies; that he proposed to sacrifice British West Indian interests by admitting East Indian sugar at lowered rates, in order to recapture from France the export trade in sugar to continental Europe. This is to push cynicism to the point of naïveté. The proposal about East Indian sugar was made in 1792, when the principal source of French sugar, St Domingue, was already convulsed by civil war; it was a natural enough suggestion in the circumstances. As for the sale of slaves to the French, it could be prevented, as Pitt himself pointed out, by a more limited measure; this was in fact done later, in 1806, in an act prohibiting British subjects from selling slaves to foreign colonies, or to recently conquered colonies, which might be restored at a peace.[21] The 'cloak of humanitarianism' argument will not do. Pitt disliked the slave trade, as an affront to civilised conduct; there is no good evidence that his opinion changed after 1792. On the other hand, he had good reason to shrink from a head-on attack. Abolitionism was politically dangerous, because it could be confused, in muddled minds, with domestic Jacobinism. Its opponents were powerful, stubborn and vituperative. Pitt's own cabinet was divided on the issue: Hawkesbury (Liverpool), for one, opposed abolition; so did members of the royal family. With England once more in a major war, divisive issues were best avoided or postponed. These difficulties amply explain why Pitt hesitated from year to year; why it was not his cabinet, but a stronger group, the 'Ministry of all the Talents', which finally secured the passage of the Abolition Act in 1807; why it was not Pitt himself, but the more radical and impetuous

Fox, after Pitt's death, who introduced the successful Bill.

The abolition of the British slave trade was a victory of principle (or sentimentality, or squeamishness) over national economic self-interest; or over self-interest as it appeared to most people at the time. The French commercial community certainly regarded it in this light, and were astonished and delighted at the prospect of taking up what their rivals had abandoned.[22] The British trade, it is true, did not at once collapse, because of the difficulties of enforcement. British slavers continued to carry slaves, for some years, mostly to Cuba and Brazil, usually under other flags. But the government was serious and determined in its intention; warships were sent to cruise against slavers, and penalties were stiffened progressively, down to 1824, when slaving was declared piracy, punishable by death. By the time this ferocious penalty was enacted, however, the need for it had passed; the British slave trade was virtually extinct. The Evangelicals and their allies had turned their attention to the plight of slaves already in the West Indies. Despairing of colonial Amelioration Acts, they were in the process of launching their final assault on slavery, as it survived in a group of sugar colonies increasingly impoverished and less and less able to resist. The Anti-slavery Society was formed in 1823. Ten years later slavery was declared illegal in all British territories. Meanwhile, however, the total volume of the international slave trade remained relatively little affected by British abolition;[23] and here, from the British point of view, principle and self-interest coincided. The effort and loss of abolition would obviously be wasted, if others took up the trade which the British had dropped, or any considerable part of it. In West Africa, moreover, the sale of British goods could be maintained only by substituting some legitimate trade for British slaving; the missionary activity so much desired by Evangelical Christians could be initiated only by peaceful travel in the interior; but this was impossible, or very difficult, while international slaving continued. Hence the attempts to get anti-slaving clauses inserted into the 1815 peace treaties; hence, failing that, the series of bilateral treaties on the subject; and hence the widening of the duties of the British anti-slaving patrols, with all the risks of unpleasant international incidents when warships stopped and searched suspected slavers, of unknown nationality, upon the high seas. The patrols were not very effective; there were not enough warships, they were not nimble enough to catch fast-sailing slavers, and the seas were wide; but their very existence was evidence of a new stage of European imperialism, the imperialism of conscious well-doing. In this development Great Britain, victorious in a major war, led the way. Great Britain, for a time, had far outstripped its European rivals in imperial possession and in industrial strength. Great Britain alone, in the 1820s, possessed the self-confidence, the righteous arrogance and the naval force to police the seas of the world and to send armed ships in pursuit of sinners. The British, first, in their dealings overseas, effectively combined commercial aggressiveness with a sense of didactic responsibility towards less-favoured peoples. In all this, they were early; but they were not alone; they were anticipating sentiments and policies which were to become common property among all the major nations of western Europe in the course of the nineteenth century. Europeans were coming to think of themselves as guardians; of the teeming peoples of the world beyond Europe, as their wards.

NOTES

1. G. F. Hudson, *Europe and China*, London, 1931, p. 317.
2. Voltaire, *Fragments sur l'Inde*, Paris, 1763, pp. 42–3.
3. L. Scrafton, *Reflections on the Government of Indostan, with a Short Sketch of the History of Bengal*, London, 1770.
4. J. Z. Holwell, *Original Principles of the Ancient Brahmins*, London, 1779, p. 5.
5. A. Dow, *The History of Hindostan*, 3 vols, London, 1768–72, III, xiii.
6. *Ibid.*, vii–ix.
7. Sir William Jones, *Works*, edited by John Shore, Baron Teignmouth, 13 vols, London, 1807. See S. N. Mukherjee, *Sir William Jones: a study in eighteenth century British Attitudes to India*, Cambridge, 1968.
8. Jones, *Institutes of Hindu Law*, London, 1796, iii.
9. See, for example, T. G. P. Spear, *The Nabobs*, Oxford, 1932.
10. Eric Stokes, *The English Utilitarians and India*, Oxford, 1963, pp. 64 ff.
11. James Mill, *History of British India*, 2nd edn., 6 vols, London, 1820, V, p. 513.
12. Sir Thomas Munro, *Selection from his Minutes*, ed. Arbuthnot, London, 1881, II, p. 327.
13. Charles Grant, *Observations on the State of Society among the Asiatic Subjects of Great Britain*, London, 1797, p. 71.
14. *Ibid.*, p. 220.

15. These and succeeding figures are taken from Philip D. Curtin, *The Atlantic Slave Trade, a Census*, Madison, 1969, especially, pp. 265 ff.

16. G. R. Mellor, *British Imperial Trusteeship, 1783–1850*, London, 1951, pp. 429–31.

17. On the whole question of moral attitudes to slavery, see David Brion Davis, *The Problem of Slavery in Western Culture*, Ithaca, 1966.

18. The story of Job is told in Douglas Grant, *The Fortunate Slave*, Oxford, 1968.

19. Mellor, *British Imperial Trusteeeship*, p. 39.

20. Eric Williams, *Capitalism and Slavery*, Chapel Hill, 1944, pp. 146–50. The general thesis of this book, that abolition and emancipation reflected economic rather than humanitarian concern, has been adequately refuted by Mellor, *British Imperial Trusteeship*, pp. 51–9, 443–7; and by Roger T. Anstey, 'Capitalism and Slavery', *Economic History Review*, August 1968, pp. 307 ff.

21. 46 Geo. III, *c.* 52. See Mellor, *British Imperial Trusteeship*, p. 66.

22. *Ibid.*, pp. 54, 56.

23. Curtin, *Atlantic Slave Trade*, p. 267.

CONCLUSION

The Dominion of the Sea

GOVERNORSHIP OF COVENTRY ISLAND. – H.M.S. *Yellowjack*, Commander Jaunders, has brought letters and papers from Coventry Island. H.E. Sir Thomas Liveseege had fallen a victim to the prevailing fever at Swamptown. His loss is deeply felt in the flourishing colony. We hear that the Governorship has been offered to Colonel Rawdon Crawley, C.B., a distinguished Waterloo officer. We need not only men of acknowledged bravery, but men of administrative talents to superintend the affairs of our colonies; and we have no doubt that the gentleman selected by the Colonial Office to fill the lamented vacancy which has occurred at Coventry Island is admirably calculated for the post which he is about to occupy.

Thackeray exaggerated, perhaps, the unpleasantness of the tropical outpost ('three thousand a year, delightful climate, excellent government house, all your own way in the colony, and a certain promotion') to which he consigned the non-hero of *Vanity Fair*; but his attitude towards such places was fairly representative. In the convalescent decades after Waterloo, British public opinion displayed little imperial enthusiasm; surprisingly little, in view of the many territorial acquisitions which had been made as a result of the French war, and which continued to be made, in India particularly, after the war was over. There was no revulsion, it is true, against empire as such, and no general disposition to throw away gains made in war and duly confirmed by treaty. Minor claims might be given up: that to the French stations in Madagascar, for example, fever-stricken holes which had been assumed, absent-mindedly, to be dependencies of Mauritius until the French government asserted the contrary; but no one proposed to abandon places of actual or potential commercial value, still less places of strategic importance. The Cape of Good Hope was a profitless possession, a source of constant trouble and expense; but prudence dictated that it should be held and modestly fortified. Similarly Ceylon, though the great harbour at Trincomalee with its resounding nautical names – Silver Island and Sober Island, Yard Cove and China Bay – was to remain empty of shipping for many years. The dominant concerns of empire persisted. Colonial mercantilism, though its assumptions were being questioned, was by no means extinct, and the Colonial Office was constantly pressed to protect British mercantile interests overseas, to ensure supplies of essential commodities, to insist that the fiscal arrangements in the colonies should not hamper British exports. In the Colonial Office and India House permanent civil servants increased in numbers and in influence, and pursued the search for tidy, consistent administrative devices overseas. There was still scope for freelance adventurers; but in the established colonies the screws continued to tighten on sinecure-holders and political agitators, and the crown colony remained the favoured form of government. The Colonial Office and India House searched diligently for men of 'acknowledged bravery and administrative talents' to govern the territories under their respective control, chiefly among civil servants or naval or military officers; but 'interest' persisted, and they were frequently reduced to employing the likes of Rawdon Crawley. The sense of didactic and humanitarian responsibility remained strong: the anti-slavery 'lobby', having secured the abolition of the British slave trade, pressed in the 1820s for the emancipation of slaves. They had to face not merely the opposition of a West Indian interest, whose wealth and influence were declining and who could be bought off by compensation, but the ridicule of radicals who thought compassion would be better directed towards the victims of agrarian reorganisation and industrial revolution at home. In 1833 the anti-slavery lobby had their way; slaves were emancipated throughout the British possessions. The French followed in 1848. In both empires, a substitute had to be provided for colonies short of labour, and eventually one was found in the import of labourers from crowded places, India and China chiefly, under an indenture system which, though legally acceptable, produced its own problems and despite attempts at regulation, its own miseries. As for

438

the victims of economic upheaval in the British Isles, a way out for them was also found eventually, not so much in the Poor Law and the Factory Acts, as in opportunities for emigration, both to the United States and to temperate empty spaces within the empire.

The economic advantages of possessing oversea territory, as distinct from merely having access to it, were less obvious in the early nineteenth century than they had been in the eighteenth. American commercial success in China and the South Sea, without benefit of colonies or naval bases, supplied an object lesson. So did the expansion of textile exports; English manufacturers and merchants pushed their cottons as vigorously in the independent or soon-to-be-independent Americas as they did in conquered India. Similarly with the humanitarians: many of the causes they had at heart were international rather than imperial in range. They wanted not only slave emancipation in British colonies, but vigorous action to suppress the slave trade everywhere. This was a matter of foreign policy. The Foreign Office could and did bring pressure on some governments, the Portuguese, for example, whose subjects engaged in slaving; but others, notably that of the United States, refused to be bullied, and the Foreign Office was reluctant, in the absence of firm treaties, to support interference with American shipping. The American flag covered not only the activities of American slavers, whose own government had not the means to suppress them, but those of any slavers who could contrive to look American when they met an English cruiser. The trade could be suppressed, and was eventually suppressed, only by international co-operation, supplemented on occasion by flagrant departures from the normal conventions of international behaviour and, ironically, by British annexation of sundry unwanted territories around the coasts of Africa. The interior of Africa, whence many of the slaves came, was still almost wholly unknown. It was beginning to attract the attention of explorers, missionaries, scientists and trading adventurers, but their expeditions were privately, not nationally supported. Neither government nor general public in any European country took more than a passing intellectual interest in them, in the decades after Waterloo. There was, as yet, no thought of a competitive rush to annex the territories they traversed.

439

It was not, in general, an 'imperialist' generation. This indifference can be attributed in part to war-weariness, in part to anxiety over distress and discontent at home, but still more perhaps to a sense of confidence and security at sea and overseas, itself the consequence of successful, if wasting war. The British empire, after Waterloo, was no longer one of a group of similar competing empires; its pre-eminence in the colonial and maritime fields seemed obvious, and soon came to be taken for granted. Lack of imperial enthusiasm followed from lack of imperial competition. The French colonial empire had almost disappeared. There remained of it two West Indian islands; Senegal; Bourbon in the Indian Ocean, restored because it had no harbour; three minor trading posts in India – little more. France itself was a rich and powerful country with a marvellous capacity for recuperation: but it was burdened by an immense war indemnity; its navy and merchant fleet were almost destroyed and would take decades to rebuild. French adventures in the Mediterranean – Charles x's Algerian expedition, for example – could still produce automatic reactions of alarm in English statesmen concerned about the route to India; French diplomats, traders and adventurers busily pushed French interests in the Levant; and while Napoleon lived there was always the nightmare possibility of a second escape; but in general, for a generation after Waterloo, France was not a dangerous competitor in the world outside Europe.

The Spanish Indies in 1815, or large parts of them, were semi-independent. In most provinces, the resumption of royal government provoked mutiny or civil war. They could not be reduced to obedience by Spain's unaided efforts, and within ten years the empire broke up. Only Cuba, Puerto Rico and the Philippines remained. These, it is true, were more than mere fragments; Moreau de Jonnès could still, in 1825, seriously compare the Spanish empire with the colonial possessions of France, England and the Netherlands, while pointing out that both Manila and Havana did considerably more business with Great Britain and the United States than with Spain. Puerto Rico, however, had little economic activity; it had been valued chiefly as the outer defence of Mexico. Even relatively prosperous Cuba required initiative and capital for the development of its potential wealth, and

Spaniards, their home economy shattered by war, were neither able nor even willing to provide them. Ferdinand VII, from his restoration to his death, clung stubbornly to his imperial prerogatives; but few of his subjects shared his concern. During the constitutional interlude of 1820 to 1823, America was hardly ever mentioned in debates in the Cortes. After 1825, humiliation over the loss of the greater part of the Indies was quickly succeeded by disillusion with empire in general, and by a tendency to belittle the value of what remained. The officers who returned defeated from Ayacucho, some of them brave, capable and devoted soldiers, were received with cold indifference. Plans for the reconquest of Mexico attracted neither interest nor support. Disillusion was reinforced by the current fashion of liberal economic theory. Canga Argüelles, the most distinguished Spanish economist of his day, who had been a minister from 1820 to 1823, argued that Spaniards for more than 300 years had poured men, goods, ideas and experience into America, to the great advantage of the kingdoms of the Indies and to the impoverishment of Spain. Measures for the development of Cuba and Puerto Rico would benefit those islands more than Spain itself. Colonial investment would be throwing good money after bad. The Indies were well lost.

The Dutch, surprisingly, recovered most of their colonial empire; nearly all the most productive parts of it. Ceylon and the Cape had been objects of expense rather than sources of profit, and far-sighted Dutchmen did not much regret their loss. In the East Indies, the unwelcome, booming activity of Singapore (which, regarded legally as an Indian port, was open to private trade) had to be accepted. The British government, after some initial hesitation, was adamant on this. Otherwise, Dutch power in the central and eastern archipelago was fully restored, and the Dutch doggedly set about re-establishing a close national monopoly of its trade. The situation produced a great deal of friction; but the British government had good political reasons for avoiding quarrels with the Dutch, the Dutch lacked the naval force to back an aggressive policy outside their recognised preserves, and the East India Company was more interested in Chinese tea than in Indonesian spices. The Dutch were left to themselves in the islands, on the understanding that they would not interfere in the Malay peninsula nor impede British shipping in the Strait of Malacca or along the route to China.

The Portuguese empire, in a decayed and attenuated form, survived. Brazil, by far its biggest and most productive possession, separated itself from Portugal in 1822, with relatively little fighting. The Portuguese government, because of British diplomatic pressure, royal family feeling, and conviction of the impossibility of reconquest, recognised Brazilian independence in 1825. There remained Timor, Macao, and the settlements in India, none of them places of much account; and Angola and Mozambique, whose only significant commercial activity was the slave trade. By a treaty with Great Britain in 1815, Portugal agreed to restrict the sale of slaves for export from these areas, to Portuguese vessels sailing to other Portuguese possessions; Great Britain undertook not to molest *bona fide* Portuguese slavers operating within these rules, south of the Equator. A supplementary convention in 1817 provided for the mutual right of visit and search. As might be expected in the circumstances, especially after the loss of Brazil, the Portuguese government could never compel its colonial governors to enforce these rules. In view of the right of visit and search, the Portuguese flag was never as reliable a flag of convenience as the American; but the trade went on. Slaves were sold to any visiting purchaser, however surreptitious. Despite patrols, predominantly British, but also occasionally French or American, they were shipped to any country – Brazil, Cuba, the French West Indies, the United States – where a market offered. Despite steadily mounting British pressure, Portugal did not agree even to formal abolition until 1842. In practice, the transatlantic trade was not stopped until well after the middle of the century. Not until then were Portuguese administrators forced to face the problem of finding other means by which their African colonies could pay their way.

Neither France nor Spain nor Portugal nor the Netherlands presented, for the time being, any serious threat to British power, trade and influence outside Europe. The Americans were formidable commercial competitors in some areas, but not imperial rivals. India, it is true, was vulnerable on its landward frontier; and there the possible threat came not from one of the ancient

442

maritime rivals, but from the Russians, slowly extending their power and influence across the expanses of Central Asia. It took the government of India some years to identify Russia as a potentially dangerous enemy; when they did, they took the menace seriously, and allowed themselves to be drawn into rash and ultimately disastrous interventions in Afghanistan. But India was not endangered. Probably the threat was exaggerated. British power in Asia was expanding more rapidly and more effectively, in the first half of the nineteenth century, than Russian.

British pre-eminence in those decades has often been explained in naval terms; the British navy commanded the sea. So it did, in a somewhat negative sense. It was not that British warships were everywhere, but that there were no other warships in significant concentration anywhere. No other power operated naval bases of any strength, anywhere from Cape St Vincent to the Sydney Heads, or anywhere in the Americas outside the United States. Gibraltar, over which so much powder had been burned, was more important as a symbol than as a base; but within the Mediterranean, the great rock fortress of Malta, athwart an alternative route to India, could shelter a British fleet in the great harbour enclosed by its limestone cliffs. These widely scattered bases, it is true, after the end of the war were parsimoniously maintained and relatively little used. Most of the ships stationed overseas were small: sloops, gun-brigs, rarely anything larger than a frigate. The Line ships, most of them, were laid up in reserve, as they had been after every eighteenth-century war, and rotted quietly at their moorings. There was very little for them to do. No large-scale action was fought between major battle-fleets for more than a hundred years, from Trafalgar to Jutland. The nearest approach to one, the battle fought at anchor in Navarino Bay in 1827, arose from a misunderstanding; no more than a demonstration had been intended. Naval officers, like ships, were underemployed. Sea service and promotion alike were determined by influence or by seniority; in this respect the navy lagged behind the civil services. Senior and senile admirals crowded the head of the Navy List, without sea employment but blocking the promotion of others. The overseas stations were mostly commodores' or at most rear admirals' commands. Career-minded officers jostled and intrigued for service on such stations, for the sake of prize-money and sea experience; but most post-1815 officers lived out their service lives without hearing a shot fired in anger.

The small ships stationed overseas were deployed chiefly around the coasts of Africa and the Indian Ocean. India had replaced the West Indies as the main focus of imperial attention; the West Indies – apart from acrimonious disputes about specific issues, amelioration, emancipation, and the preferential duties – were increasingly neglected. So was British North America, except when, as in the 1830s, it gave serious trouble. There was not much for warships to do in the north Atlantic, rather more in the south Atlantic, more still in the Indian Ocean. Particular attention was paid to the Mozambique Channel, not only because of the slavers which frequented its mangrove-lined inlets, but because of the possibility that the French, active in Madagascar, might establish themselves on the African coast. To Frenchmen, the English mixture of righteous indignation, commercial pushfulness and naval bullying was a source both of irritation and of sardonic amusement. The ships were employed mainly in chasing illicit slavers and in putting down piracy. There were not enough of them to achieve anything like complete success in either task: economising governments at home set limits on their numbers; but they recaptured and released some 150,000 slaves between 1810 and 1864, in addition to another 10,000 or so released by French and American cruisers, and the seas were safer, probably, than they had ever been before. The work was arduous and could be dangerous; by the 1830s not only European slavers, but many Arabs also, mounted carronades, and boat-work in tropical estuaries was not to everyone's taste. Inevitably, there were long periods of boredom and inaction. In quiet intervals, ships 'showed the flag' in the coastal sheikhdoms; or engaged in the exacting but sedative routine of survey – work of great and permanent value, though unproductive of glory or prize-money; or obligingly provided transport for the 'wandering tribes', as Malcolm called them: the many explorers, natural scientists and archaeologists who travelled to remote places in search of adventure, knowledge or the spoils of ancient tombs. The British, of course, had no monopoly of this kind of activity; scientific curiosity was international. Many of the most eminent explorers were French, and the conduct of scientific expeditions was a principal employment of an attenuated French navy. But the British had many more ships, and ranged more widely. It was not particularly difficult to arrange for sixty-five Chinese cannon to be carried to India 'for the purpose of being cast into a column'; or for stones from the walls of Halicarnassus, weighing many tons, to be brought to the British Museum.

British command of the sea was command in a vacuum; it was maintained in large measure by bluff. If other major states – France, say, or Russia – had found an interest in challenging it, in starting a naval arms race, the distribution of power overseas and the pattern of imperial development might have been very different. But they did not; the bluff was effective. It was enough, for example, to deter any European state from helping Ferdinand VII to repossess his Indies. Great Britain in the decades after Waterloo possessed greater freedom of action in the maritime and colonial fields than any European power had enjoyed since sixteenth-century Spain.

It was not an 'imperialist' age; but it was, for the British at least, an age of expanding empire. There were annexations, treaties of protectorate, armed interventions, minor wars, undertaken for many different purposes – to safeguard frontiers, to stop the slave trade, to protect explorers and missionaries, above all to support merchants in the pursuit of trade. Englishmen tended to assume that they had a 'right' to trade anywhere, to sell their goods to anyone who would buy them, irrespective of the wishes of their customers' governments. The British government was prepared to support this claim by diplomatic means, and on occasion to use force, to expand its subjects' area of trade, and where necessary or appropriate to extend its own dominion. On the other hand, empire, whether territorial or commercial, formal or informal, was not much discussed in public. The relative absence of serious opposition, competition and danger made the process unexciting except to those directly involved in it. It was the chosen preserve of a comparatively small, predominantly upper-middle-class section of society. The political grandees, with a few notable exceptions, stood benevolently aloof. Parliament was ill-informed and usually indifferent, except in so far as it insisted on limiting expense. In this, it reflected the views of the relatively narrow section of society by which the Commons were elected. The great mass of the unrepresented cared even less. Mobs did not clamour for victories, as they had often done in the eighteenth century; they clamoured, sensibly, for bread, for employment, for the vote. They did not clamour for peace, because they hardly noticed the wars. There was no need to 'sell' the idea of empire to a broad electorate, no occasion for the strident vulgarity and mass emotion which, in a later generation, was to be associated with 'imperialism'. No one now supposes that the British empire was acquired in a fit of absence of mind; but considerable portions of it were acquired, in this period, in the absence of effective parliamentary and public scrutiny.

The men who ran the Colonial Office, India House, the Foreign Office and the Admiralty (which at that time, more than at any other, was an arm of the Foreign Office) had thus a remarkably free hand. They used it, on the whole, with restraint. They were not fanatics of empire. They usually supported their agents overseas, but they were capable of curbing rashness or excess of zeal, especially when it seemed likely either to cause serious trouble with another European power, or to lead to the acquisition of expensive and unwanted dominion. They showed increasing skill, as time went on, in selecting their senior servants, especially in India. They were usually (not always – there were some disastrous exceptions) reasonably adept at calculating risks. The most remarkable feature of the 'gunboat diplomacy' associated with Palmerston's name was not that it used force or threats of force to achieve diplomatic or commercial ends – there was nothing new about that – but that it so often achieved its ends with so economical a use of force. In the exercise of dominion, where it already existed, the same quality of restraint was also usually evident, dictated partly by parsimony and a desire to avoid trouble, but also by a sense of responsibility, and by anxious thought among a small circle of informed people. Those responsible, again, were not fanatics (though some of them were doctrinaires); they did not, for the most part, feel passionately about empire; but they took it seriously and conducted its affairs, in so far as their knowledge and resources allowed, with conscience and with care.

For France, then, irritated frustration, tempered by realistic assessment of adverse circumstances. For Spain, sour and disillusioned indifference, which undermined royal determination to reduce the Indies to obedience. For Portugal, a feeble but pertinacious clinging to the relics of empire, a tardy, querulous acquiescence in the views of other people on the slave trade which was one of the empire's chief supports. For Holland, a stubborn and resourceful concentration upon a limited but potentially very productive colonial estate. These were the legacies, in the field of colonial activity, of the years of war. For England, in the decades after Waterloo, maritime strength, a tradition of naval invincibility, an extraordinary – if temporary – lead in industrial development, combined to favour a very rapid expansion of overseas trade and a more hesitant, more tentative expansion of dominion. The situation was transient, of course. Other countries were to develop mechanised industry and to scour the world for markets and raw materials. Navies were to be rebuilt. Competition in territorial acquisitiveness outside Europe was to be resumed, and new competitors were to enter the field. The word 'imperialism' was to be brought into use, both as a focus of enthusiasm and as a target of resentment and dislike. The 'imperialists' of the later nineteenth century, it might be supposed from some of their pronouncements, and from some of the abuse later hurled at them, had learned nothing and forgotten nothing. Nevertheless the alterations of course, the changes of attitude, which occurred in the late eighteenth century and the early nineteenth, had left their mark on European imperialism. A morality, however imperfect, however honoured in the breach, had entered the conduct of empire – or perhaps one should say, remembering sixteenth-century Spain, re-entered it – and never afterwards wholly disappeared. Europeans, moreover, had been given a lesson in the contingent, the transitory nature of empire, which they never again wholly forgot. Partly, perhaps, for these reasons, when Europeans found, in the twentieth century, that their imperial stance had become unprofitable, or untenable, or – in the opinion of many, rulers as well as ruled – unjustifiable, they were able, most of them, to abandon it with realism and with a measure of grace.

LIST OF WORKS CITED

List of Works Cited

Abdul Majed Khan, *The Transition in Bengal 1756–1776*, Cambridge, 1969.

Adams, J. T., *Provincial Society 1690–1763*, New York, 1927.

Albion, R. G., *Forests and Sea Power*, Cambridge, Mass., 1926.

Alden, D., *Royal Government in Brazil*, Berkeley, 1969.

Alvord, C. W., *The Mississippi Valley in British Politics*, Cleveland, 1917.

Anderson, A., *An Historical and Chronological Deduction of the Origin of Commerce 1764*, rev. edn. 4 vols, London, 1787–9.

Anderson, R. C., *The Rigging of Ships in the Days of the Spritsail Topmast, 1600–1720*, Salem, 1927.

Andrews, C. M., *The Colonial Period of American History*, 4 vols, New Haven, 1938.

Anon., *La Commerce de l'Amérique par Marseille*, 2 vols, Avignon, 1764.

Anstey, Roger T., 'Capitalism and Slavery', *Economic History Review* (August 1968), 307.

Antonil (João Antonio Andreoni, S.J.), *Cultura e Opulencia de Brasil por suas Drogas e Minas* (1711), Bahia, 1950.

Armytage, Frances, *The Free Port System in the British West Indies. A study in Commercial Policy 1786–1822*, London, 1953.

Arnade, Charles W., 'Cattle Raising in Spanish Florida 1513–1763', *Agricultural History*, XXXV, 1961, pp. 116–24.

—, 'The Failure of Spanish Florida', *The Americas*, XVI, 1959–60, pp. 271–81.

Artiñano y de Galdácano, G. de, *La Arquitectura Naval Española en Madera*, Madrid, 1920.

Ashton, T. S., *Iron and Steel in the Industrial Revolution*, London, 1924.

Astley, Thomas, *A New General Collection of Travels in Europe, Asia, Africa and America*, 4 vols, London, 1745–7.

Baddeley, J. F., *Russia, Mongolia, China*, London, 1919; New York, 1964.

Bailyn, Bernard, *The Ideological Origins of the American Revolution*, Cambridge, Mass., 1967.

Bal Krishna, *Commercial Relations Between India and England 1601–1757*, London, 1924.

Bamford, P. W., *Forests and French Sea Power, 1660–1784*, Toronto, 1956.

Baron Mulert, F. E., ed., *De Reis Van Mr Jacob Roggeveen*, The Hague, 1911.

Bassetts, D. K., 'The Trade of the English East India Company in the Far East, 1623–1684', *Journal of the Royal Asiatic Society*, 1960, pp. 154–6.

Bastin, J., *The British in West Sumatra 1685–1825*, Kuala Lumpur, 1965.

Beaglehole, T. H., *Thomas Munro and the Development of Administrative Policy in Madras*, Cambridge, 1966.

Bearce, G. D., *British Attitudes towards India 1784–1858*, Oxford, 1961.

Beaston, R., *Naval and Military Memoirs of Great Britain from 1727 to 1783*, London, 1804.

Beer, G. L., *The Old Colonial System*, New York, 1933.

Biddulph, J., *The Pirates of Malabar*, London, 1907.

Bion, Nicholas, *La Construction et l'Usage des Instruments de Mathematique*, trans. Edmund Stone, *Construction and Use of Mathematical Instruments*, London, 1758.

Birmingham, David, *Trade and Conflict in Angola: The Mbundu and their Neighbours Under the Influence of the Portuguese 1483–1790*, Oxford, 1966.

Bolton, Herbert Eugene, *Rim of Christendom: A Biography of Eusebio Francisco Kino, Pacific Coast Pioneer*, New York, 1936.

Boog Watson, W. N., 'Alexander Brodie and his Five Hearths', *Mariner's Mirror*, LIV, no. 4 (November, 1968).

Borah, Woodrow W., *New Spain's Century of Depression*, Berkeley, 1951.

Bougainville, L. A. de, *Voyage Autour du Monde*, Paris, 1771.

Bouguer, P., *Nouveau Traité de Navigation*, Paris, 1753.

Bourguignon d'Anville, J. B., *Nouvel Atlas de la Chine*, Amsterdam, 1737.

Bourne, Ruth, *Queen Anne's Navy in the West Indies*, New Haven, 1939.

Boxer, C. R., *Salvador de Sà and the Struggle for Brazil and Angola*, London, 1952.

—, *The Golden Age of Brazil*, Berkeley, 1962.

Broglie, Duc de, *The King's Secret: Being the Secret Correspondence of Louis XV with his Diplomatic Agents*, 2 vols, London, 1879.

Brosses, Charles de, *Histoires des Navigations aux Terres Australes*, 2 vols, Paris, 1756.

Brougham, Henry Peter, *An Inquiry in the Colonial Policy of the European Powers*, Edinburgh, 1803; New York, 1969.

Brown, Gerald Saxon, *The American Secretary*, Ann Arbor, 1963.

Bruce, J., *Annals of the East India Company*, London, 1810.

Burke, Edmund, *Works*, 12 vols, London, 1808–13.

Callander, John, *Terra Australis Cognita*, 3 vols, London, 1766–9.

Campbell, John, *The Spanish Empire in America*, by an English Merchant, London, 1747.

Campbell, W., *Formosa under the Dutch*, London, 1903; New York, 1970.

Campillo y Cosío, José, *Nuevo Sistema de Gobierno Económico para la América*, Madrid, 1789.

Carrera Pujal, Jaime, *Historia de la Economía Española*, 5 vols, Barcelona, 1943–7.

Carrington, H., ed., *The Discovery of Tahiti: A Journal of the Second Voyage of H.M.S. Dolphin Round the World, under the Command of Capt. Wallis, R.N. ... by her Master, George Robertson*, London, 1968.

Céspedes del Castillo, G., *Lima y Buenos Aires*, Seville, 1947.

Champion, Richard, *Considerations on the Present Situation of Great Britain and the United States*, London, 1784.

Charlevoix, P. F. X., *Histoire de l'Isle Espagnole ou de S. Domingue*, 4 vols, Amsterdam, 1733.

Charnock, John, *History of Marine Architecture*, 3 vols, London, 1802–3.

Charteris, E., *William Augustus, Duke of Cumberland*, London, 1925.

Chevalier, François, *La Formation des Grands Domaines au Mexique: Terre et Société aux XVI–XVII Siècles*, Paris, 1952.

Churchill, Awnsham, *A Collection of Voyages and Travels*, 4 vols, London, 1704.

Cobbett, W., and Wright, J., *Parliamentary History of England*, XVIII.

Colenbrander, H. T., *Gedenkstucken der Algemeene Geschiednis van Nederland*, The Hague, 1813.

Cook, James, *Journals*, ed. J. C. Beaglehole, 3 vols, Cambridge, 1966.

Cook, Warren L., *Flood Tide of Empire*, New Haven, 1973.

Corbett, J. S., *England in the Seven Years' War*, 2 vols, London, 1907.

Cotter, C. H., *A History of Nautical Astronomy*, London and New York, 1968.

Coupland, R., *East Africa and its Invaders*, Oxford, 1936; New York, 1965.

Coxe, W., ed., *Memoirs of John Duke of Marlborough*, London, 1818–19.

—, ed., *Memoirs of Sir Robert Walpole*.

Crone, G. R., *Maps and their Makers*, London, 1953; New York, 1966.

Crone, G. R., and Skelton, R. A., 'English Collections of Voyages and Travels 1625–1846', in Edward Lynam, ed., *Richard Hakluyt and his Successors*, London, 1946.

Crouzet, François, *L'Economie Britannique et le Blocus Continental*, 2 vols, Paris, 1958.

Curtin, Philip D., *The Atlantic Slave Trade*, Madison, 1969.

Dahlgren, E. W., *Les Relations Commerciales et Maritimes entre la France et les Côtes de l'Océan Pacifique*, vol. I, *Le Commerce de la Mer du Sud*, Paris, 1909.

Dallas, R. C., *History of the Maroons*, 2 vols, London, 1803; New York, 1969.

Dalrymple, A., *An Historical Collection of the Several Voyages and Discoveries in the South Pacific Ocean*, 2 vols, London, 1770–1; New York, 1967.

—, *An Account of the Discoveries Made in the South Pacific Ocean, Previous to 1764*, London, 1769.

Dampier, William, *A New Voyage Round the World*, 3 vols, London, 1697; New York, 1968.

—, *A Voyage to New Holland in the Year 1699*, J. A. Williamson, ed., London, 1939.

Dasi, T., *Estudio de los Reales de a Ocho*, 2 vols, Valencia, 1950.

Davies, K. G., *The Royal African Company*, London, 1957; New York, 1970.

—, 'The origin of the commission system in the West India trade', Royal Historical Society, *Transactions*, fifth series, vol. II.

Davis, David Brion, *The Problem of Slavery in Western Culture*, Ithaca, 1966.

Davis, Ralph, *The Rise of the English Shipping Industry in the Seventeenth and Eighteenth Centuries*, London, 1962; New York, 1963.

Day, Clive, *The Policy and Administration of the Dutch in Java*, Oxford, 1967.

Deane, Phyllis, 'The Output of the British Woollen Industry in the Eighteenth Century', *Journal of Economic History*, XVII, 1957, p. 209.

Deane, Phyllis, and Cole, W. A., *British Economic Growth 1688–1959*, Cambridge, 1967.

Debien, G., *La Société Coloniale au XVIIème et XVIIIème Siècles* Paris, 1953.

—, *Esprit Colon et Esprit d'Autonomie à Saint-Domingue au XVIIIème Siècle* (*Notes d'Histoire Coloniale, XXV*), Larose, 1954.

Deerr, N., *The History of Sugar*, 2 vols, London, 1950.

Defoe, Daniel, *Two Great Questions Considered*, London, 1700.

—, *The True-born Englishman*, London, 1701.

Delgado, Ralph, *Historia de Angola*, 4 vols, Lobito, 1948–55.

Delisle, Guillaume, *Mappe-monde Dressée sur les Observations de Mrs de l'Académie Royale des Sciences*, Paris, 1700.

Dermigny, L., *La Chine et l'Occident, 1719–1833*, 3 vols, Paris, 1964.

Destombes, Marcel, *Cartes Hollandaises. La Cartographie de la Compagnie des Indes Orientales*, Saigon, 1941.

Deventer, M. L. van, *Het Nederlandsch Gezag over Java en Onderhoorigheden Sedert 1811*, The Hague, 1891.

Dodge, Ernest S., *New England and the South Seas*, Cambridge, Mass., 1965.

Dodwell, H. H., *Dupleix and Clive, the Beginning of Empire*, London, 1920; Cambridge, Mass.

Doughty, A. G., and McArthur, D. A., *Documents Relating to the Constitutional History of Canada, 1791–1818*, Ottawa, 1914.

Dow, A., *The History of Hindostan*, 3 vols, London, 1768–72.

Drummond, J. C., and Wilbraham, Anne, *The Englishman's Food*, London, 1939.

Dunn, Samuel, *A New Epitome of Navigation*, London, 1777.

Dunn, William Edward, *Spanish and French Rivalry in the Gulf Region of the United States, 1678–1702*, Austin, Texas, 1917.

Dusenberry, William H., *The Mexican Mesta: The Administration of Ranching in Colonial Mexico*, Urbana, Ill., 1963.

Dutt, R. C., *The Economic History of India*, London, 1901.

Edwards, Bryan, *History of the West Indies*, 3 vols, London, 1794.

Ellison, T., *The Cotton Trade of Great Britain*, London, 1886.

Entick, John, *General History of the Late War*, London, 1765.

Feiling, Keith, *Warren Hastings*, London, 1954; Cambridge, Mass., 1967.

Fernández Duro, C., *Armada Española desde la Unión de las Reinas de Castilla y de Aragón*, Madrid, 9 vols, 1895–1903.

Fisher, J., 'The Intendant System and the Cabildos of Peru', *Hispanic American Historical Review*, XLIX, 1969, p. 430.

Fisher, L. E., *The Intendant System in Spanish America*, Berkeley, 1929.

Fitzmaurice, E. G. P., *Life of William Earl of Shelburne*, 2 vols, London, 1912.

Fortescue, J. W., *History of the British Army*, 13 vols, London, 1899–1930; New York, 1970.

Franklin, Benjamin, *Writings*, ed. A. M. Smyth, 10 vols, New York, 1907.

Frémy, E., *Histoire de la Manufacture Royale des Glaces de France au XVIIème et au XVIIIème Siècle*, Paris, 1909.

Freyre, Gilberto, *The Portuguese and the Tropics*, Lisbon, 1961.

Fry, H. T., *Alexander Dalrymple and the Expansion of British Trade*, London, 1970.

Frykenberg, R. E., *Guntur District 1788–1848. A History of Local Influence and Central Authority in South India*, Oxford, 1965.

Furber, Holden, *Bombay Presidency in the Early Eighteenth Century*, New York, 1965.

Furnivall, J. S., *Netherlands India, a Study of Plural Economy*, Cambridge, 1944.

—, *An Introduction to the History of Netherlands India*, London, 1934.

Gallagher, J., and Robinson, R. E., 'The Imperialism of Free Trade', *Economic History Review*, 2nd series, VI, 1953, p. 13.

Gallagher, R. E., ed., *Byron's Journal of his Circumnavigation 1764–1766*, Cambridge, 1964.

Gandía, Enrique de, *Buenos Aires Colonial*, Buenos Aires, 1957.

Gaston-Martin, *L'Ere des Négriers*, Paris, 1931.

Gillespie, Leonard, *Observations on the Diseases which Prevailed on Board a part of His Majesty's Squadron on the Leeward Island Station between November 1794 and April 1796*, London, 1800.

Gipson, L. H., *The British Empire before the American Revolution*, vol. X, *The Triumphant Empire; Thunder-clouds Gather in the West, 1763–1768*, New York, 1961.

—, vol. VII, *The Great War for the Empire; the Victorious Years, 1758–1780*, New York, 1949.

—, *The Coming of the Revolution, 1763–1775*, New York, 1954.

Glamann, K., *Dutch Asiatic Trade 1620–1740*, Copenhagen, 1958.

Godinho, V. Magalhaes, 'Le Portugal, les Flottes du Sucre et les Flottes de l'Or, 1670–1770', *Annales*, 1951.

Goebel, J., *The Struggle for the Falkland Islands*, New Haven, 1927.

Gosse, P., *St. Helena 1502–1938*, London, 1938.

Gould, R. T., *The Marine Chronometer: its History and Development*, London, 1923.

Grant, Charles, *Observations on the State of Society among the Asiatic Subjects of Great Britain . . .*, London, 1797.

Grant, D., *The Fortunate Slave*, London, 1968.

Grant, W. L., 'Canada v. Guadeloupe' *American Historical Review*, XVII, July 1912, pp. 735–43.

Greenberg, M., *British Trade and the Opening of China*, Cambridge, 1951.

Greene, L., *The Negro in Colonial New England 1620–1776*, New York, 1942.

Grenard, F., *Grandeur et Décadence de l'Asie*, Paris, 1947.

Haan, F. de, *Oud Batavia*, Bandung, 1935.

Hack, William, *Collection of Original Voyages*, London, 1699.

Hackett, Charles W., and Shelby, Charmion C., *Revolt of the Pueblo Indians, of New Mexico and Otermín's Attempted Reconquest 1680–1682*, 2 vols, Albuquerque, 1942.

Hagedorn, B., *Die Entwicklung der wichtigsten Schiffstypen bis ins 19 Jahrhundert*, Berlin, 1914.

Hall, D. G. E., *History of South East Asia*, London, 1964.

Hall, J., 'Notes on the Early Ch'ing Copper Trade with China', *Journal of the Royal Asiatic Society*, 1949, p. 452.

Hamilton, E. J., 'The Decline of Spain', *Economic History Review*, VIII, 1937–8, pp. 168–78.

Harlow, V. T., *The Founding of the Second British Empire*, 2 vols, London and New York, 1952 and 1964.

Harper, L. A., *The English Navigation Laws*, New York, 1939.

Harris, John, *Naviganim atque Itinerantium Bibliotheca; or, a Compleat Collection of Voyages and Travels*, revised by John Campbell, 2 vols, London, 1744–8.

Harris, R. C., *The Seigneurial System in Early Canada*, Madison, 1966.

Hawkesworth, J., *Voyages in the Southern Hemisphere*, 3 vols, London, 1773.

Hawkins, C. W., 'To New Zealand for Kauri', *Mariner's Mirror*, LXII, 1966, p. 315.

Hecksher, Eli, *The Continental System, an Economic Interpretation*, ed. H. Westergaard, Oxford, 1922.

Helleiner, K. F., 'European population', *The Cambridge Economic History of Europe*, vol. IV, Cambridge, 1967.

Higonnet, P. L.-R., 'The Origins of the Seven Years War', *Journal of Modern History*, vol. 40, no. 1, March 1968.

Hill, Draper, *Fashionable Contrasts*, London and New York, 1966.

Hobsbawm, E. J., *Industry and Empire*, London and New York, 1968.

Holroyd, John Baker, 1st Earl of Sheffield, *Observations on the Commerce of the American States*, London, 1783.

Holwell, J. Z., *A Review of the Original Principles, Religious and Moral, of the Ancient Brahmins*, London, 1779.

Howay, F. W., 'An Outline sketch of the Maritime Fur Trade', *Canadian Historical Association Report*, 1932, p. 7.

Hoyle, F., *Astronomy*, New York, 1962.

Hudson, G. F., *Europe and China*, London, 1931.

Hyam, Ronald, 'British Imperial Expansion in the Late Eighteenth Century', *Historical Journal*, XI, 1967.

Imbault-Huart, C., *L'île Formose, Histoire et Description*, Paris, 1893.

Jackson, Melvin H., *Salt, Sugar and Slaves: The Dutch in the Caribbean*, James Ford Bell Lectures, no. 2, 1965.

James, W., *Naval History of Great Britain*, London, 1902.

Johnson, Charles, *The General History of the Pirates*, London, 1724.

Jones, Sir William, *Works*, ed. John Shore, Baron Teignmouth, 13 vols, London, 1807.

Juan, Jorge, and Ulloa, Antonio de, *Noticias Secretas de América*, Madrid, 1749.
—, *Relación Historica del Viaje a la América Meridional*, Madrid, 1768.

Keate, George, *To Captain Bligh, On his Return to England in 1793*, London, 1793.

Kent, H. S. K., *War and Trade in Northern Seas*, Cambridge, 1973.

Klerck, E. S. de, *History of the Netherlands East Indies*, 2 vols, Rotterdam, 1938.

Klerk de Reus, G. C., *Geschlichtlicher Ueberblick der Administrativen, Rechtlichen und Finanziellen Entwicklung der Niederländisch Oostindischer Compagnie*, Batavia, 1894.

Knollenberg, B., *Origins of the American Revolution 1759–1766*, New York, 1961.

Koebner, Richard, *Empire*, Cambridge, 1961.

Labaree, L. W., *Royal Government in America: A Study of the British Colonial System Before 1783*, New Haven, 1930.

Labat, J. B., *Nouveau Voyage aux Isles de l'Amérique*, 6 vols, The Hague, 1724.

La Hire, *Carte de France Corrigée par Ordre du Roi sur les Observãons de Mrs. de l'Académie des Sciences*, Paris, 1693.

Lambert, S. M., *The Depopulation of the Pacific Races*, Honolulu, 1934.

Landes, D. S., *Bankers and Pashas*, London, 1958.

Laude, N., *La Compagnie d'Ostende et son Activité Coloniale au Bengale*, Brussels, 1944.

Law, Jean, ed. A. Martineau, *Mémoire sur Quelques Affaires de l'Empire Mogul*, Paris, 1913.

Lawrence, A. W., *Trade Castles and Forts of West Africa*, London, 1963.

Lawson, M. G., *Fur: a Study in English Mercantilism, 1700–1775*, Toronto, 1943.

Lee, J., *Colonial Government and Good Government, a Study of the Ideas Expressed by the British Official classes in Planning Decolonisation, 1939–1964*, Oxford, 1967.

Legrelle, A., *La Diplomatie Française et la Succession d'Espagne*, Ghent, 1892.

Leur, J. C. van, *Indonesian Trade and Society*, The Hague, 1955.

Lewis, Michael, *The Navy of Britain*, London, 1968.

Ligon, R., *A True and Exact History of the Island of Barbados*, London, 1657; New York, 1970.

Lloyd, C., and Coulter, J. S. L., *Medicine and the Navy*, 4 vols, London, 1961.

Lohmann Villena, H., *Las Minas de Huancavélica en los Siglos XVI y XVII*, Seville, 1952.

Low, C. R., *History of the Indian Navy*, 2 vols, London, 1877.

Lynch, John, 'British Policy and Spanish America 1783–1808', *Journal of Latin American Studies*, I, 1969.

Lynch, J., *Spanish Colonial Administration; the Intendant System in the Río de la Plata*, London, 1958.

Macanaz, M. de, *Testamento de España*, Mexico, 1821.

Mackesy, Piers, *The War for America, 1775–1783*, London and Cambridge, Mass., 1964.

MacNutt, W. S., *The Atlantic Provinces, the Emergence of Colonial Society*, Oxford, 1965.

Malcolm, John, *Life of Robert, Lord Clive*, 3 vols, London, 1836.

Malone, J. J., *Pine Trees and Politics*, Seattle, 1964.

Manning, H. T., *British Colonial Government after the American Revolution*, Oxford, 1933.

Mansvelt, W. M. F., *Rechtsvorm en Geldelijk beheer bij de Oost-Indische Compagnie*, Amsterdam, 1922.

Mark, J. D., *Matthew Flinders 1774–1814*, London, 1967.

Martin-Allanic, J. E., *Bougainville Navigateur et les Découvertes de son Temps*, 2 vols, Paris, 1964.

Martínez de Mata, Francisco, *Discursos*, 1650–60.

Masefield, John, ed., *Dampier's Voyages*, London, 1906.

Maude, H. E., *Of Islands and Men*, Melbourne, 1968.

Mauro, Frédéric, *Le Portugal et l'Atlantique au XVIIème siècle*, Paris, 1960.

Mead, H., *Trinity House*, London, 1940.

Mellor, G. R., *British Imperial Trusteeship, 1783–1850*, London, 1951.

Milburn, W., *Oriental Commerce; containing a geographical description of the principal places in the East Indies ... with their Produce, Manufactures and Trade ...*, 2 vols, London, 1813.

Milet-Mureau, M. L. A., ed., *Voyage de la Pérouse autour du Monde*, 4 vols, Paris, 1798.

Mill, James, *The History of British India*, 10 vols, London, 1858.

Miller, John C., *Sam Adams, pioneer in propaganda*, Boston, 1936.

Mims, S. L., *Colbert's West Indian Policy*, New Haven, 1912.

Morgan, E. S., and H. M., *The Stamp Act Crisis*, New York, 1963.

Morse, H. B., *The Chronicles of the East India Company trading to China, 1635–1834*, Oxford, 1926; New York, 1965.

Mukherjee, Nilmani, *The Ryotwari System in Madras*, Calcutta, 1962.

Mukherjee, S. N., *Sir William Jones: A Study in Eighteenth-Century Attitudes to India*, Cambridge, 1968.

Muro, Sir Thomas, *Selection from His Minutes*, ed. A. Arbuthnot, 2 vols, London, 1881.

Namier, Sir Lewis, *Crossroads of Power*, London, 1962.

Nightingale, Pamela, *Trade and Empire in Western India 1784–1806*, Cambridge, 1970.

Norwood, Richard, *The Seaman's practice, containing a fundamental Problem in Navigation, experimentally verified, viz: touching the Compass of the Earth and Sea, and the Quantity of a Degree in our English Measure, also to keep a reckoning at Sea for all Sailing, etc., etc.*, London, 1637.

Ogelsby, J. C. M., 'Spain's Havana Squadron and the Preservation of the Balance of Power in the Caribbean, 1740–1748', *Hispanic American Historical Review*, XLIX, 1969, p. 473.

Oliver, D. L., *The Pacific Islands*, Cambridge, Mass., 1951.

Osborn, T. G. B., 'The Effect of Introduction of Exotic Plants and Animals into Australia', *Pan Pacific Conference*, Canada, 1933, VI, p. 8.

Pares, R., 'Merchants and Planters', *Economic History Review*, Supplement 4, Cambridge, 1960.

—, *War and Trade in the West Indies*, Oxford, 1936.

—, *A West India Fortune*, London, 1950; Cambridge, Mass., 1968.

—, *Yankees and Creoles*, London, 1956; Cambridge, Mass., 1968.

—, *Colonial Blockade and Neutral Rights 1739–1763*, Oxford, 1938.

Parkinson, C. N., *Trade in the Eastern Seas 1793–1813*, Cambridge, 1937.

Parry, J. H., *The Age of Reconnaissance*, London, 1963.

—, 'Eliphalet Fitch', *History*, June 1955.

—, 'The Indies Richly Planted', *Terrae Incognitae*, I, 1969.

—, *The sale of public office in the Spanish Indies under the Hapsburgs*, Berkeley, 1953.

—, 'The Patent Offices in the British West Indies', *English Historical Review*, April 1945, p. 200.

Pebrer, Pablo, *Taxation, Revenue, Expenditure, Power, Statistics and Debt of the Whole British Empire*, London, 1833.

Pelliot, R., 'L'origine des relations de la France avec la Chine. Le premier voyage de l'Amphitrite en Chine', *Journal des Savants*, Paris, 1930.

Pene, Cassini et autres, *Le Neptune Français, ou Atlas Nouveau des Cartes Marines. . . . Revue et mis en ordre*, Paris, 1693.

Petty, Sir William, *The Petty–Southwell Correspondence, 1676–1687*, London, 1928.

Philips, C. H., *The East India Company 1784–1834*, Manchester, 1940.

Pinot, V., *La Chine et la Formation de l'Esprit Philosophique en France*, Paris, 1932.

Pitt, William, Earl of Chatham, ed. W. S. Taylor and J. H. Pringle, *Correspondence of the Earl of Chatham*, 4 vols, London, 1838–40.

Postlethwayt, Malachy, *The Universal Dictionary of Trade*, London, 1751.

Price, A. Grenfell, *The Western Invasion of the Pacific and its Continents*, Oxford, 1963.

Quill, H., *John Harrison, the Man who found Longitude*, London and New York, 1966.

Quinn, D. B., *The Roanoke Voyages*, 2 vols, London, 1952–5.

Raffles, Thomas Stamford, *Substance of a Minute Recorded on 11 February 1811*, London, 1814.

Ragatz, L. J., *The Fall of the Planter Class in the British Caribbean*, Washington, 1928.

Rashed, Z. E., *The Peace of Paris 1763*, Liverpool, 1951.

Reussner, A., 'L'hygiène navale à la fin du XVIIIème siècle', *Revue d'Histoire des Colonies Françaises*, XIX, 1931.

Richmond, H. W., *The Navy in the War of 1739–48*, 3 vols, Cambridge, 1920.

—, *The Navy in India 1763–1783*, London, 1931.

Robertson, C. G., *England under the Hanoverians*, London, 1962.

Robertson, John, *The Elements of Navigation*, 2 vols, 5th edition rev. and ed. by W. Wales, London, 1786.

Robinson, A. H. W., *Marine Cartography in Britain*, Leicester University Press, 1962.

Rodríguez, P., Conde de Campomanes, *Epítome de los discursos*, in *Apéndice a la Educación Popular*, 4 vols, Madrid, 1775–7.

Rogers, Woodes, ed. G. E. Manwaring, *A Cruising Voyage around the World*, London, 1928.

Roover, R. de, 'L'organisation administrative et commerciale de la Compagnie d'Ostende', *Bulletin d'Etudes et d'Informations de l'Institut Superieur de Commerce St. Ignace*, XI, pp. 659–81, Antwerp, 1934.

Ryan, A. N., 'The melancholy fate of the Baltic ships in 1811', *Mariner's Mirror*, vol. 50, May 1964.

Sadler, D. H., Introd. *Man is not Lost:* a record of 200 years of astronomical navigation with the Nautical Almanac, 1767–1967, London, H.M.S.O., 1968.

Safford, W. E., *Useful Plants of Guam*, Washington, 1905.

St Paul, H., ed. G. C. Butler, *Correspondence*, 2 vols, London, 1911.

Salaman, R. N., *The History and Social Influence of the Potato*, Cambridge, 1949.

Sauer, C. O., *Agricultural Origins and Dispersals*, New York, 1952.

Scelle, Georges, *La Traite Négrière aux Indes de Castille*, 2 vols, Paris, 1906.

Scholte, W., *British Overseas Trade*, London, 1952.

Schuyler, R. L., *Parliament and the British Empire*, London, 1929.

Scott, E., *Terre Napoléon*, London, 1910.

Scott, W. R., *The Constitution and Finance of English, Scottish and Irish Joint Stock Companies to 1720*, 3 vols, Cambridge, 1910–12.

Scrafton, L., *Reflections on the Government of Indostan with a Short Sketch of the History of Bengal*, London, 1770.

Semmel, Bernard, *The Rise of Free Trade Imperialism; Classical Political Economy, the Empire of Free Trade and Imperialism, 1750–1850*, Cambridge, 1970.

Sharp, Andrew, *The Voyages of Abel Janszoon Tasman*, Oxford, 1968.

—, *The Discovery of the Pacific Islands*, Oxford, 1960.

Sherwig, John M., *Guineas and Gunpowder, British Foreign Aid in the Wars with France*, Cambridge, Mass., 1969.

Shirley, William, (Lincoln, ed.,) *Correspondence of William Shirley, Governor of Massachusetts and Military Commander in America, 1730–1760*, 2 vols, New York, 1912.

Singer, C., Holmyard, E. J. and others, eds., *A History of Technology*, 5 vols, Oxford, 1958.

Smith, Adam, ed. E. Cannan, *Wealth of Nations*, London, 1904.

Smith, Robert Sidney, *The Spanish Guild Merchant, a History of the Consulado, 1250–1700*, Durham, N.C., 1940.

—, 'The Institution of the *Consulado* in New Spain', *Hispanic American Historical Review*, XXIV, 1944, pp. 61–83.

Spear, T. G. P., *The Nabobs*, Oxford, 1932.

Stählin, J. von, *An Account of the New Northern Archipelago, Lately Discovered by the Russians in the Seas of Kamtschatka and Anadir*, London, 1774.

Steel, David, *Elements and Practice of Rigging and Seamanship*, 2 vols, London, 1794.

—, *Elements and Practice of Naval Architecture*, 2 vols, London, 1805.

Steven, M., *Merchant Campbell 1769–1846, a Study of Colonial Trade*, Melbourne, 1965.

Stokes, Eric, *The English Utilitarians and India*, Oxford, 1963.

Sutherland, Lucy C., *The East India Company in Eighteenth-century Politics*, Oxford, 1952.

Swift, Jonathan, *Prose Works*, ed. Temple Scott, 12 vols, London, 1897–1908, V. 'The Conduct of the Allies'.

Taylor, E. G. R., *The Haven-finding Art*, London, 1956.

Temperley, H. W. V., 'The causes of the War of Jenkins' Ear, 1739', *Royal Historical Society, Transactions*, 3rd series, III, 1909, pp. 197–236.

—, 'The Peace of Paris', *Cambridge History of the British Empire*, I, Cambridge, 1929.

Te Paske, John Jay, *The Governorship of Spanish Florida, 1700–1763*, Durham, N.C., 1964.

Tertre, Jean Baptiste du, *Histoire Générale des Antilles habitées par les Français*, 4 vols, Paris, 1667–71.

Thornton, A. P., *Doctrines of Imperialism*, New York, 1965.

—, *West India Policy under the Restoration*, Oxford, 1956.

Toussaint, A., *Histoire de l'Océan Indien*, Paris, 1961.

Tower, W. S., *A History of the American Whale Fishery*, Philadelphia, 1907.

Tucker, Josiah, *The Case of Going to War for the Sake of Procuring, Enlarging or Securing of Trade*, London, 1763.

—, *The True Interest of Britain, set forth in regard to the Colonies: and the only means of living in peace and harmony with them*, London, 1774.

Tunstall, W. C. B., *Admiral Byng and the Loss of Minorca*, London, 1928.

Ulloa, Bernardo de, *Restablecimiento de las Fábricas y Comercio Español*, Madrid, 1740.

Uztáriz, Geronimo de, *Teoría y Práctica de Comercio y de la Marina*, Madrid, 1724; trans. J. Kippax, *The Theory and Practice of Commerce and Maritime Affairs*, 2 vols, London, 1751.

Verger, Pierre, *Flux et Reflux de la Traite des Nègres entre le Golfe de Bénin et Bahia de Todos os Santos*, Paris, 1968.

Vicens Vives, J., *Historia Económica de España*, Barcelona, 1959.

Vieillard-Baron, A., 'L'intendant américain et l'intendant français', *Revista de Indias*, nos. 43–4, 1951, p. 235.

—, 'L'établissement des intendants aux Indes par Charles III', *Revista de Indias*, no. 49, 1952, p. 524.

Vieira, Antonio, S.J., João Lucio d'Azevedo, ed., *Cartas*, 3 vols, Coimbra, 1925–8.

Villiers, Alan, *Captain Cook, the Seaman's Seaman*, London, 1967; New York, 1970.

Vitoria, Francisco de, *Relectiones de Indis*; facsimile of 1969 (Frankfurt) edition, edited with Spanish translation by J. Malagón, Washington, 1963.

Voltaire, François Marie Arouet de, *Fragments sur l'Inde, sur le Général Lalli, et sur le Comte de Morangies*, Paris, 1763.

Waddington, R. P., *La Guerre de Sept Ans*, 3 vols, Paris, 1899–1904.

Wadia, R. A., *The Bombay Dockyard and the Wadia Master-builders*, Bombay, 1957.

Wafer, Lionel, *A New Voyage and Description of the Isthmus of America*, ed. L. E. Elliott Joyce, London, 1934; New York, 1970.

Wallis, Helen, ed., *Carteret's Voyage round the World*, 2 vols, Cambridge, 1965.

Walpole, Horace, *Memoirs of the Reign of King George the Third*, London, 1845.

Walter, R., *A Voyage round the World*, London, 1748.

Walton, G. W., 'Sources of Productivity Change in American Colonial Shipping, 1675–1775', *Economic History Review*, 2nd series, vol. XX, 1967.

Washington, George, *Writings of*, ed. John C. Fitzpatrick, 39 vols, Washington, 1931–44.

Weber, H., *La Compagnie Française des Indes*, Paris, 1904.

Whiston, William, and Ditton, Humphry, *A New Method for Discovering the Longitude, both at Sea and Land, Humbly Proposed to the Consideration of the Publick*, London, 1714.

Wilks, M., *Historical Sketches of the South of India*, London, 1817.

Williams, Eric, *Capitalism and Slavery*, Chapel Hill, 1944.

Williams, Glyndwr, *The British Search for the Northwest Passage in the Eighteenth Century*, London, 1962; New York, 1967.

Williamson, J. A., *The Caribbee Islands, under the Proprietary Patents*, Oxford, 1925.

Wilson, C. R., ed., *Early Annals of the English in Bengal*, 3 vols, Calcutta, 1895–1917.

—, *Old Fort William*, 2 vols, London, 1906.

Wood, G., 'A note on Mobs in the American Revolution', *William and Mary Quarterly*, no. 23, 1966.

Woodman, Dorothy, *Himalayan Frontiers*, London and New York, 1970.

Wroth, Lawrence C., *The Early Cartography of the Pacific*, New York, 1944.

Zook, G. F., *The Company of Royal Adventurers Trading to Africa*, Lancaster, 1919; Westport, Conn., 1970.

MAPS

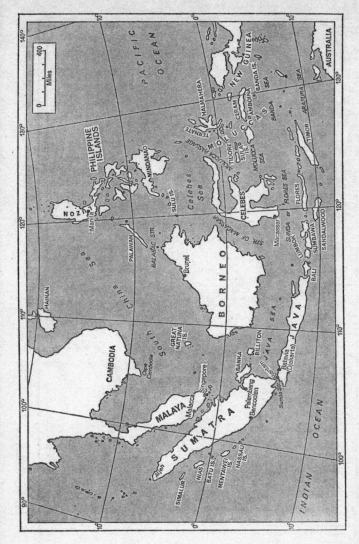

The East Indies

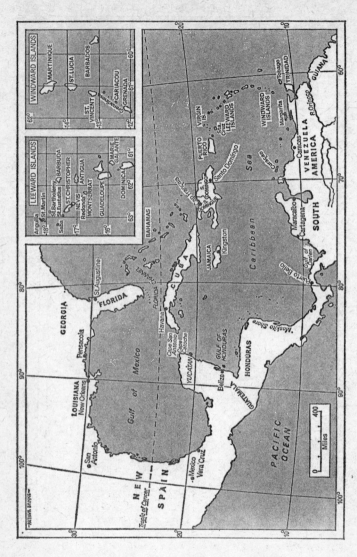

The Caribbean Sea

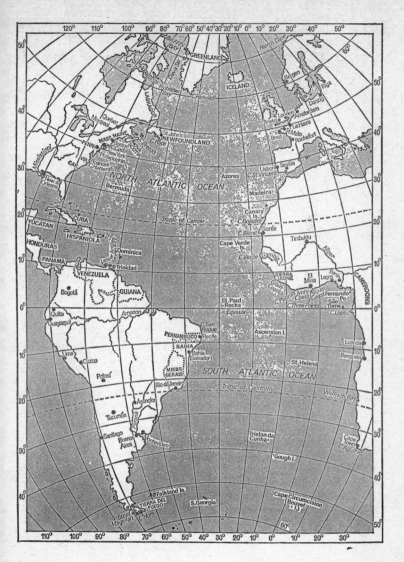

The Atlantic Ocean

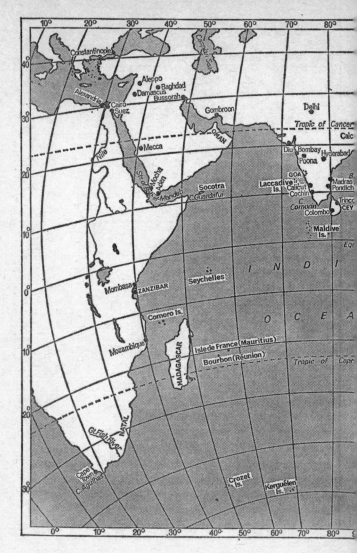

The Indian Ocean

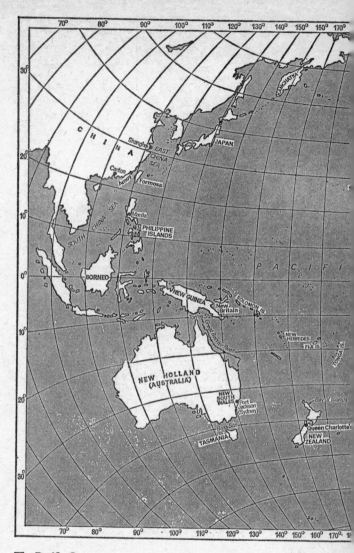

The Pacific Ocean

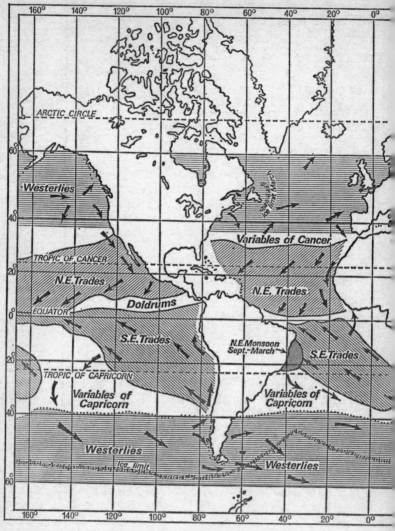

Wind Chart of the World in the first quarter of the year

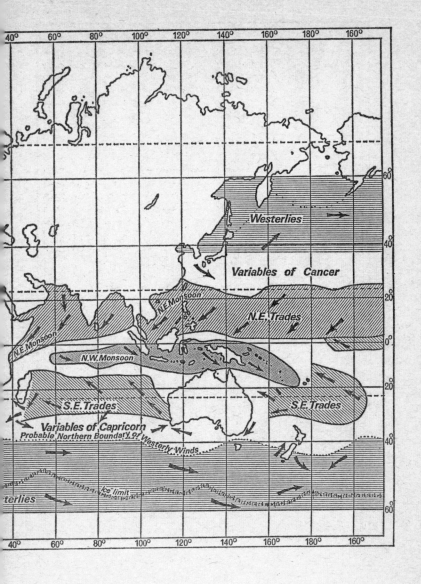

The Arctic Regions

INDEX

HISTORY OF CIVILISATION

THE AGE OF RECONNAISSANCE

Discovery, Exploration and Settlement 1450 to 1650

J. H. PARRY

The Age of Reconnaissance was the period during which Europe discovered the rest of the world. It began with Henry the Navigator and the Portuguese voyages in the mid-fifteenth century and ended 250 years later when the 'Reconnaissance' was all but complete.

Dr Parry is concerned with an analysis of the factors which made the voyages possible. These factors include the rapidly developing technical devices used by seamen – the ships, the charts, the instruments and the weapons – but they also include new pressures and inducements, political, economic and psychological, which favoured overseas enterprise. The first part of the book is devoted to analysis and description, the second part to a narrative of events. The third part summarises the geographical knowledge which the discoverers accumulated; describes the various types of commercial and colonial settlement established by different European nations in the lands which the discoverers revealed; and comments on the legal and moral problems with which the European governments of the time were confronted in dealing with wars of conquest, competitive claims to colonial territory, the government of weaker peoples, slavery and the trade in slaves.

'A major work of historical synthesis and an important contribution to our knowledge of the society, economy, and historical geography of the sixteenth and seventeenth centuries'
The Guardian

£1·00 *Illustrated*

HISTORY OF CIVILISATION

EUROPE IN THE EIGHTEENTH CENTURY
Aristocracy and the Bourgeois Challenge

GEORGE RUDÉ

A description of Europe during the three quarters of a century between the death of Louis XIV and the industrial revolution in England and the social and political revolution in France. George Rudé has organised his material into three main parts: population, land and peasants, industry, urban growth and society; government, administration, religion, the arts, ideas; tensions and conflict within nations and in their external relations. Particular attention is paid to why these factors contributed to the overthrow of the established order in some countries – notably in France in 1789 – but not in others, and how the growth of social classes and their subsequent conflicts acted as agents of historical change.

'This is a book that really can be recommended to beginners, not because it over-simplifies but because it provides them with all the basic information'.
Times Literary Supplement

£1·40 Illustrated

HUMBOLDT AND THE COSMOS

Douglas Botting

Alexander von Humboldt was born in 1769 into a Prussia where science was considered an unworthy subject for a person of his social standing. In 1799, after a short but brilliant career as a Prussian mining official, he set out to explore the little-known world of South America. The formidable mass of scientific data he collected during his five-year expedition laid the foundations for modern physical geography, and his investigations as a naturalist established the concept of plant geography.

The world of Humboldt, the last truly Universal Man, is vividly recalled in this biography by Douglas Botting. He describes Humboldt's expeditions all over the world, his investigations as a naturalist, his political activities which made him the idol of the German revolution of 1848, and, in the last years of his life, the completion of his greatest work – *The Cosmos* – his vision of the nature of the world.

For this book, Douglas Botting followed Humboldt's route on the Orinoco and Casiquiare. The book contains many of the engravings which illustrated Humboldt's own work, together with other contemporary prints and paintings of the places he visited and the people he met.

£1·75 Illustrated